activeBook included

Paper 3:

The making of modern Russia, 1855-1991

Rob Owen
Series editor: Rosemary Rees

ALWAYS LEARNING
PEARSON

Published by Pearson Education Limited, 80 Strand, London, WC2R 0RL

www.pearsonschoolsandfecolleges.co.uk

Copies of official specifications for all Edexcel qualifications may be found on the website: www.edexcel.com

Designed by Elizabeth Arnoux for Pearson

Typeset and illustrated by Phoenix Photosetting, Chatham, Kent

Produced by Out of House Publishing

Cover design by Malena Wilson-Max for Pearson

First published 2016

19

10 9 8 7 6 5

British Library Cataloguing in Publication Data

A catalogue record for this book is available from the British Library

ISBN 978 1 447 985488

Printed in the UK by Ashford Colour Press Ltd, Gosport, Hampshire

Websites

Pearson Education Limited is not responsible for the content of any external internet sites. It is essential for tutors to preview each website before using it in class so as to ensure that the URL is still accurate, relevant and appropriate. We suggest that tutors bookmark useful websites and consider enabling students to access them through the school/college intranet.

A note from the publisher

In order to ensure that this resource offers high-quality support for the associated Pearson qualification, it has been through a review process by the awarding body. This process confirms that this resource fully covers the teaching and learning content of the specification or part of a specification at which it is aimed. It also confirms that it demonstrates an appropriate balance between the development of subject skills, knowledge and understanding, in addition to preparation for assessment.

Endorsement does not cover any guidance on assessment activities or processes (e.g. practice questions or advice on how to answer assessment questions) included in the resource, nor does it prescribe any particular approach to the teaching or delivery of a related course.

While the publishers have made every attempt to ensure that advice on the qualification and its assessment is accurate, the official specification and associated assessment guidance materials are the only authoritative source of information and should always be referred to for definitive guidance.

Pearson examiners have not contributed to any sections in this resource relevant to examination papers for which they have responsibility.

Examiners will not use endorsed resources as a source of material for any assessment set by Pearson.

Endorsement of a resource does not mean that the resource is required to achieve this Pearson qualification, nor does it mean that it is the only suitable material available to support the qualification, and any resource lists produced by the awarding body shall include this and other appropriate resources.

Contents

How to use this book 4
Introduction: A Level History 6
Introduction: The making of modern Russia, 1855–1991 8

Aspects in breadth: the land and the peasantry, 1855–1991

1 The changing status and condition of the peasantry 10
2 Agriculture and productivity: meeting the country's needs? 38

Aspects in depth: reform and revolution

3 The political reforms of Alexander II, 1855–70 64
4 Revolution and reform, 1904–06 86
5 The end of the Romanovs and the triumph of the Bolsheviks, 1916–18 108
6 Khrushchev and attempts to reform the Soviet system, 1956–61 130
7 Gorbachev and the downfall of Soviet communism, 1985–91 152

Preparing for your A Level Paper 3 exam 175
Index 188
Acknowledgements 191

How to use this book

STRUCTURE

This book covers Paper 3, Option 38.1: The making of modern Russia, 1855–1991 of the Edexcel A Level qualification.

You will also need to study a Paper 1 and a Paper 2 option and produce coursework in order to complete your qualification. All Paper 1/2 options are covered by other textbooks in this series.

EXAM SUPPORT

The examined assessment for Paper 3 requires you to answer questions from three sections. Throughout this book there are exam-style questions in all three section styles for you to practise your examination skills.

Section A contains a compulsory question that will assess your source analysis and evaluation skills.

A Level Exam-Style Question Section A

Study Source 3 before you answer this question.

Assess the value of the source for revealing the reasons for discontent in Russia, and the attitudes of the opposition against the tsar.

Explain your answer using the source, the information given about it and your own knowledge of the historical period. (20 marks)

Tip

A good answer will interrogate the evidence of the source in relation to both enquiries with confidence and discrimination. This might involve showing a range of ways the source could be used, such as by distinguishing between information and claim or opinion.

Section B contains a choice of essay questions that will look at your understanding of the studied period in depth.

A Level Exam-Style Question Section B

To what extent did the legal and local government reforms of Alexander II allow greater participation in politics by the Russian people in the years 1855–70? (20 marks)

Tip

Make sure you cover both legal and government reforms, and that you give a clear judgement on their extent (the amount of change the reforms actually caused, not just what they were).

Section C will again give you a choice of essay questions but these will assess your understanding of the period in breadth.

A Level Exam-Style Question Section C

How far do you agree that the government's need for political control over the peasants was mainly responsible for limiting changes to the peasants' living standards between 1855 and 1991? (20 marks)

Tip

Your answer should be dominated by a discussion of the stated factor, in this case the need for political control by the state. You should also examine other factors, such as the economic infrastructure of agriculture, the incompetence of management, the relationship between urban and rural areas. Weight should be given for each factor and the links between them should be explored.

The Preparing for your exams sections at the end of this book contains sample answers of different standards, with comments on how they could be improved.

FEATURES

Extend your knowledge

These features contain additional information that will help you gain a deeper understanding of the topic. This could be a short biography of an important person, extra background information about an event, an alternative interpretation, or even a research idea that you could follow up. Information in these boxes is not essential to your exam success, but still provides insights of value.

EXTEND YOUR KNOWLEDGE

The most successful peasant farmers

The Cossacks, who numbered over three million by 1900, were a unique case in Russia. They were soldier-farmers, who would offer 20 years' military service to the tsar in exchange for nearly 81 acres of land. This was over four times the average state peasants' allotment and eight times the average allotment of former landlords' peasants. However the farms, though large, used many of the same techniques as other peasant holdings, and each Cossack had to provide his own horse in the army.

There were 11 Cossack forces spread out on the fringes of the empire. In peacetime, they devoted themselves to their land and even their villages were often outside the general structure of provincial administration. The tsars required their special services right up to the last days of the empire.

Knowledge check activities

These activities are designed to check that you have understood the material that you have just studied. They might also ask you questions about the sources and extracts in the section to check that you have studied and analysed them thoroughly.

ACTIVITY
KNOWLEDGE CHECK

The Land Decree

1 How does Extract 3 suggest the peasants will react to the Land Decree?

2 What potential difficulties might be created by the Land Decree? Explain your answer.

3 Do you think the Land Decree was a genuine attempt by the Bolsheviks to fulfil their promise of 'land' or a more cynical attempt to gather as much support as possible?

Summary activities

At the end of each chapter, you will find summary activities. These are tasks designed to help you think about the key topic you have just studied as a whole. They may involve selecting and organising key information or analysing how things changed over time. You might want to keep your answers to these questions safe – they are handy for revision.

ACTIVITY
SUMMARY

The changing status and condition of the peasantry

1 Construct two timelines, one to show how each period of reform and change brought positive outcomes for the peasants, the other one showing negative outcomes.

2 Try to extend this by weighing up the true impact and extent of each point.

3 How far do you agree with the opinion that there was a steady improvement in the lives of Russian peasants over the years 1855-1991?

Thinking Historically activities

These activities are found throughout the book, and are designed to develop your understanding of history, especially around the key concepts of evidence, interpretations, causation and change. Each activity is designed to challenge a conceptual barrier that might be holding you back. This is linked to a map of conceptual barriers developed by experts. You can look up the map and find out which barrier each activity challenges by downloading the progression map from this website: www.pearsonschools.co.uk/historyprogressionsapproach.

progression map reference

THINKING HISTORICALLY Evidence (6b)

The strength of argument

1 Read Extract 3.

a) What is weak about this claim?

b) What could be added to it to make it stronger?

2 Read Extract 4.

a) Is this an argument? If yes, what makes it one?

b) How might this argument be strengthened?

3 Now read Extracts 2 and 4 together, both from the same book by Orlando Figes.

a) How does the addition of Extract 2 give a more rounded view of Kerensky and therefore strengthen Orlando Figes' interpretation of Kerensky's abilities?

b) Reading Extracts 2-4 together, how could you sum up Kerensky's abilities?

c) What elements make a historian's claims strong?

Getting the most from your online ActiveBook

This book comes with three years' access to ActiveBook* – an online, digital version of your textbook. Follow the instructions printed on the inside front cover to start using your ActiveBook.

Your ActiveBook is the perfect way to personalise your learning as you progress through your A Level History course. You can:

- access your content online, anytime, anywhere
- use the inbuilt highlighting and annotation tools to personalise the content and make it really relevant to you.

Highlight tool – use this to pick out key terms or topics so you are ready and prepared for revision.

Annotations tool – use this to add your own notes, for example links to your wider reading, such as websites or other files. Or, make a note to remind yourself about work that you need to do.

*For new purchases only. If the access code has already been revealed, it may no longer be valid. If you have bought this textbook secondhand, the code may already have been used by the first owner of the book.

Note on the text

On 14 February 1918, the date system changed in Russia from the old Julian calendar to the Gregorian calendar, with the removal of 13 days. Therefore, the Bolshevik takeover of power is known as the October Revolution as it happened on 25 October 1917 in the Julian calendar, but in the Gregorian calendar it was actually on 7 November. In this book the dates used are the Julian calendar before 14 February 1918, and the Gregorian calendar thereafter.

Introduction A Level History

WHY HISTORY MATTERS

History is about people and people are complex, fascinating, frustrating and a whole lot of other things besides. This is why history is probably the most comprehensive and certainly one of the most intriguing subjects there is. History can also be inspiring and alarming, heartening and disturbing, a story of progress and civilisation and of catastrophe and inhumanity.

History's importance goes beyond the subject's intrinsic interest and appeal. Our beliefs and actions, our cultures, institutions and ways of living, our languages and means of making sense of ourselves are all shaped by the past. If we want to fully understand ourselves now, and to understand our possible futures, we have no alternative but to think about history.

History is a discipline as well as a subject matter. Making sense of the past develops qualities of mind that are valuable to anyone who wants to seek the truth and think clearly and intelligently about the most interesting and challenging intellectual problem of all: other people. Learning history is learning a powerful way of knowing.

WHAT IS HISTORY?

Figure 1 Fragment of a black granite statue possibly portraying the Roman politician Mark Antony.

History is a way of constructing knowledge about the world through research, interpretation, argument and debate.

Building historical knowledge involves identifying the traces of the past that exist in the present – in people's memories, in old documents, photographs and other remains, and in objects and artefacts ranging from bullets and lipsticks, to field systems and cities. Historians interrogate these traces and *ask questions* that transform traces into *sources of evidence* for knowledge claims about the past.

Historians aim to understand what happened in the past by *explaining why* things happened as they did. Explaining why involves trying to understand past people and their beliefs, intentions and actions. It also involves explaining the causes and evaluating the effects of large-scale changes in the past and exploring relationships between what people aimed to do, the contexts that shaped what was possible and the outcomes and consequences of actions.

Historians also aim to *understand change* in the past. People, states of affairs, ideas, movements and civilisations come into being in time, grow, develop, and ultimately decline and disappear. Historians aim to identify and compare change and continuity in the past, to measure the rate at which things change and to identify the types of change that take place. Change can be slow or sudden. It can also be understood as progressive or regressive – leading to the improvement or worsening of a situation or state of affairs. How things change and whether changes are changes for the better are two key issues that historians frequently debate.

Debate is the essence of history. Historians write arguments to support their knowledge claims and historians argue with each other to test and evaluate interpretations of the past. Historical knowledge itself changes and develops. On the one hand, new sources of knowledge and new methods of research cause *historical interpretations* to change. On the other hand, the questions that historians ask change with time and new questions produce new answers. Although the past is dead and gone, the interpretation of the past has a past, present and future.

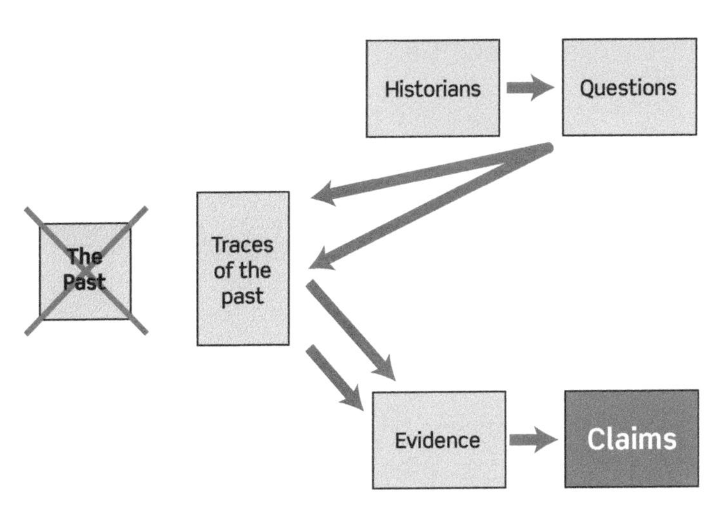

Figure 2 Constructing knowledge about the past.

THE CHALLENGES OF LEARNING HISTORY

Like all other Advanced Level subjects, A Level history is difficult – that is why it is called 'advanced'. Your Advanced Level studies will build on knowledge and understanding of history that you developed at GCSE and at Key Stage 3 – ideas like 'historical sources', 'historical evidence' and 'cause', for example. You will need to do a lot of reading and writing to progress in history. Most importantly, you will need to do a lot of thinking, and thinking about your thinking. This book aims to support you in developing both your knowledge and your understanding.

History is challenging in many ways. On the one hand, it is challenging to build up the range and depth of knowledge that you need to understand the past at an advanced level. Learning about the past involves mastering new and unfamiliar concepts arising from the past itself (such as the Inquisition, Laudianism, *Volksgemeinschaft*) and building up levels of knowledge that are both detailed and well organised. This book covers the key content of the topics that you are studying for your examination and provides a number of features to help you build and organise what you know – for example, diagrams, timelines and definitions of key terms. You will need to help yourself too, of course, adding to your knowledge through further reading, building on the foundations provided by this book.

Another challenge is to develop understandings of the discipline of history. You will have to learn to think historically about evidence, cause, change and interpretations and also to write historically, in a way that develops clear and supported argument.

Historians think with evidence in ways that differ from how we often think in everyday life. In history, as Figure 2 shows, we cannot go and 'see for ourselves' because the past no longer exists. Neither can we normally rely on 'credible witnesses' to tell us 'the truth' about 'what happened'. People in the past did not write down 'the truth' for our benefit. They often had clear agendas when creating the traces that remain and, as often as not, did not themselves know 'the truth' about complex historical events.

A root of the word 'history' is the Latin word ***historia***, one of whose meanings is 'enquiry' or 'finding out'. Learning history means learning to ask questions and interrogate traces, and then to reason about what the new knowledge you have gained means. This book draws on historical scholarship for its narrative and contents. It also draws on research on the nature of historical thinking and on the challenges that learning history can present for students. Throughout the book you will find 'Thinking Historically' activities designed to support the development of your thinking.

You will also find – as you would expect given the nature of history – that the book is full of questions. This book aims to help you build your understandings of the content, contexts and concepts that you will need to advance both your historical knowledge and your historical understanding, and to lay strong foundations for the future development of both.

Dr Arthur Chapman
Institute of Education
University College London

QUOTES ABOUT HISTORY

'Historians are dangerous people. They are capable of upsetting everything. They must be directed.'

Nikita Khrushchev

'To be ignorant of what occurred before you were born is to remain forever a child. For what is the worth of human life, unless it is woven into the life of our ancestors by the records of history.'

Marcus Tullius Cicero

The making of modern Russia, 1855–1991

The story of modern Russia is often told through its industrial workers. It is a story of the tsars holding back industry to preserve their way of life. Then the communist cities of steel and smoke rose almost overnight, a brief flowering before a long decline. However, if told through the eyes of the peasants, a deeper story can be revealed. Russia was always a land of peasants and their families huddled together in small communities. In spite of harsh masters and harsher weather, they scratched a living from the soil. The peasants hungered for ownership of the land, even though for centuries the majority of them were tied to working as serfs for their landlord masters. In 1861, Tsar Alexander II liberated the peasants from this bond. The story of what replaced it is also the story of modern Russia.

The land and the peasantry, 1855–1991

The first two chapters of this book trace the experience of the peasants as successive authorities imposed new bonds on their lives. The tsar abolished serfdom, but he made the peasants pay for the privilege with heavy taxation. Then his ministers tried to mould them into deferential, loyal subjects. After the 1917 revolutions, the centralised authority of the USSR preferred to use confrontation to smash the rural communities and compel them to form collective farms, where the individual peasant was little more than a tool to work the land. Despite famine, migrations and terror on an unheralded scale, the peasants continued to work and to grow the country's food. The most efficient agriculture among the giant fields of the collective farms was always to be found in the small private plots that the state had reluctantly allowed each peasant household to control and work. It was these plots, reminiscent of their traditional strips of earth, which the peasants farmed with the most passion and energy. Not surprisingly, these plots produced the highest yields and the widest variety of produce.

The governments of this period refused to accept this simple observation. To them, the farms were there to grow grain, which could be sold abroad for foreign capital, could feed the army to keep it marching, or could nourish the workers to keep them operating the factories. To the government, be it imperial or communist, food was a resource to be exploited and the conditions for the peasants mattered little, since they too were to be exploited. The rulers of Russia believed that only they had the expertise to increase production and modernise the farms. With each failed drive to introduce new technology and new crops, usually applied in a blanket of enforced reforms, the peasants suffered and went hungry. Yet they persisted and worked their plots in the moments they could escape from the grain fields. Even when the grain fields failed under the weight of communist incompetence and inertia, and grain had to be imported, the peasants and their plots managed to keep the country fed. Through 150 years of oppression, the peasants retained their stubbornness, their capacity for hard work, and their constant hunger for land. They built, or rather grew, the foundations of the country. A modern proverb notes that if you scratch a Russian, you will find a peasant.

1855 – Defeat in Crimean War; Alexander II begins series of political reforms

1892 – Famine in Russia

1905 – Bloody Sunday and Year of Revolution

1917 – February: fall of tsarist regime

October: fall of Provisional Government; Bolsheviks seize power

1921 – Lenin launches NEP

1928 – Stalin becomes leader; launches Five-Year Plans, including collectivisation

1941 – Nazi Germany invades USSR; Great Patriotic War begins

1946 – Famine in USSR

1956 – Khrushchev becomes leader and gives 'Secret Speech'

1964 – Khrushchev removed; Brezhnev becomes leader

1982 – Death of Brezhnev

1986 – Chernobyl nuclear reactor disaster

1855 1892 1905 1917 1921 1928 1941 1946 1956 1964 1982 1986

1861	**1861** - Emancipation of serfs
1904-05	**1904-05** - Defeat in Russo-Japanese War
1906-11	**1906-11** - Stolypin's reform in agriculture
1918-21	**1918-21** - Russian Civil War
1922	**1922** - Famine in Russia
1932-34	**1932-34** - Famine in USSR
1945	**1945** - USSR victorious; start of Cold War with USA
1953	**1953** - Death of Stalin
1956-60	**1956-60** - Period of de-Stalinisation
1972	**1972** - Annual import of foreign grain begins
1985	**1985** - Gorbachev becomes leader
1991	**1991** - August: attempted conservative coup December: Gorbachev resigns; USSR dissolved

Reform and revolution

Chapters 3–7 explore in depth five periods that highlight intense times of crisis in Russian society that triggered a wave of reforms and sometimes escalated into revolution. War was often the catalyst for change; its impact, whether through the loss of morale in defeat or the devastation of the land in conflict, could force a ruler into action or spur the masses into revolt. It was the defeat in the Crimean War that prompted Tsar Alexander II to implement a myriad political reforms, and the humiliation of the defeat by Japan helped to ignite the masses in bloody unrest against Tsar Nicholas II in 1905. His reforms, though limited, saved him in the short term, but the destruction wrought by the First World War proved too great to save either his rule or his dynasty. With memories of the unprecedented desolation of the Second World War fresh in the people's minds, Khrushchev tried vainly to steer the USSR away from the monolithic approach of Stalin. Even Gorbachev's doomed reforms of the Soviet system in the late 1980s were begun because of a failing economy drained by decades of Cold War tension with the West.

SOURCE

A set of *matryoshki* (Russian nesting dolls) showing Russian leaders of the 20th century. From the smallest: Tsar Nicholas III, Lenin, Stalin, Khrushchev, Brezhnev, Gorbachev and Yeltsin.

While the shadow of war is a common factor in all these periods, so are issues of leadership. Despite their varied experiences, backgrounds and personalities, the leaders share many similarities. The tsars ruled openly as autocrats, firmly believing that only they knew what was right for Russia. The communist leaders had delusions of a Party-based collective rule, but each individual, be it Lenin, Khrushchev or Gorbachev, believed that they personally had the answer to the ills of the USSR. Khrushchev may have criticised Stalin, his predecessor, for his cult of personality, but he too enjoyed the trappings of power and the singular attention of the media. The tsars and the communists, likewise, could not let go of their fundamental ideology. They could not allow the reforms to run their natural course and change the system. To them, any reform was ultimately a method to shore up power rather than a genuine desire for something new. Even Gorbachev, who oversaw the downfall of the USSR, only ever wanted to create a modern communist USSR. In the end, the revolutions that ended both systems came from the people, and both were relatively free of bloodshed. It was a young parliament, enjoying new freedoms, which removed the tsar. It was the masses, likewise enjoying new freedoms that quickly gained momentum, who removed the Communist Party. These five short episodes share many common traits as key moments in the epic history of Russia, and are therefore valuable lessons in comprehending the past, as well as a prerequisite for understanding Russia today.

The changing status and condition of the peasantry

KEY QUESTIONS

- What was the impact of government policies on the status and condition of the peasantry in imperial Russia, 1855–1917?
- What was the impact of government policies on the status and condition of the peasantry under communist rule, 1918–91?

INTRODUCTION

The Russian peasants experienced a range of reforms designed to improve both the conditions and circumstances of agriculture. They were usually applied either without the consultation of the peasants or in open contrast to their wishes. The aim of the state, whether tsarist or communist, was to increase grain production in order to make the state wealthier and feed the growing cities. There was little thought to the welfare of the peasants themselves. Even when this was desired or accidentally encouraged, such as by Stolypin's brief attempts to create wealthier peasants, or Lenin's even briefer acceptance of the peasants taking ownership of the land, it was more for the political gain in harnessing peasant support than any genuine concern for the well-being of the rural masses.

In around 1890, the minister of finance, Vyshnegradskii, reported his prediction for agricultural production as, 'We will starve, but we will export.' By 'we', he meant the peasants, of course. There were three famines over the next decade, but only in the countryside. His sentiments were echoed as the infant Bolshevik government stole the seeds from the peasants to feed the army and workers in order to survive the Civil War, and as Stalin forced collectivised workers to hand over grain to sell for foreign capital, while millions died of a mix of hunger, murder and despair, either in their homes or in exile in distant Siberia. It would seem that whenever the state announced any reform to agriculture, famine and suffering quickly followed. The peasants starved, but the state always managed to export.

While still yoked by serfdom, the Russian peasants would say to their aristocratic landlords, 'We are yours, the land is ours.' This land hunger was constant over a century of turmoil, though they came

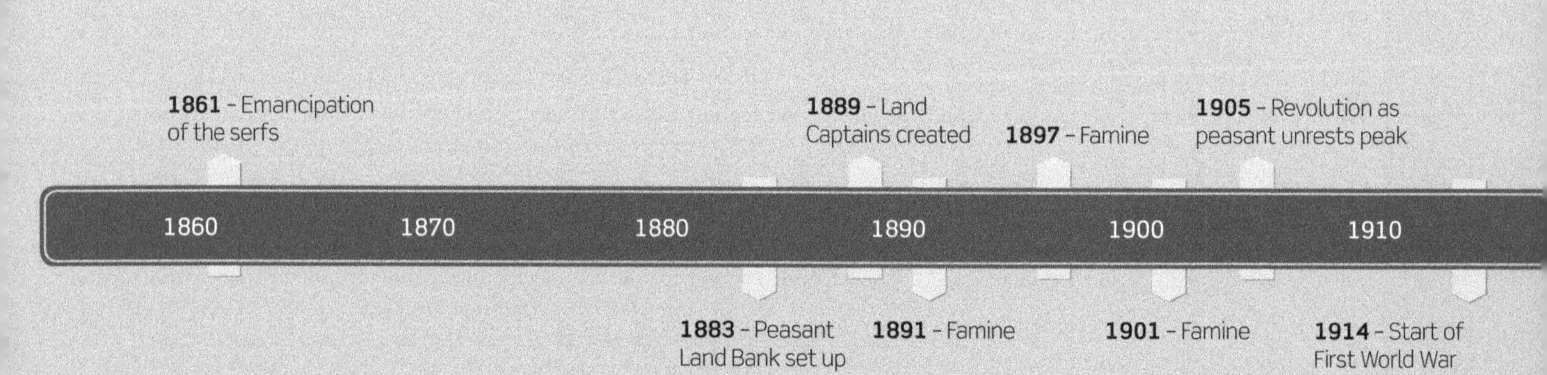

tantalisingly close to true land ownership for a few months in 1917. The peasants, once 'freed' of serfdom, remained in heavy debt to the tsarist government and then in almost slave-like employment to the communist state. Even after Stalin was replaced by Khrushchev, who actually had some empathy with the peasantry, they still failed to gain as reforms fizzled into a slow but steady decline.

The peasants, whether Russian or Soviet, are an example of what happens when a centralised authority continually imposes its ideas on a population without acknowledging their desires or expertise. It is a tale of grand ideas and future visions that falls tragically short, and of individual stories lost in the scale of social manipulation and immense suffering in the fertile fields of the Russian plains.

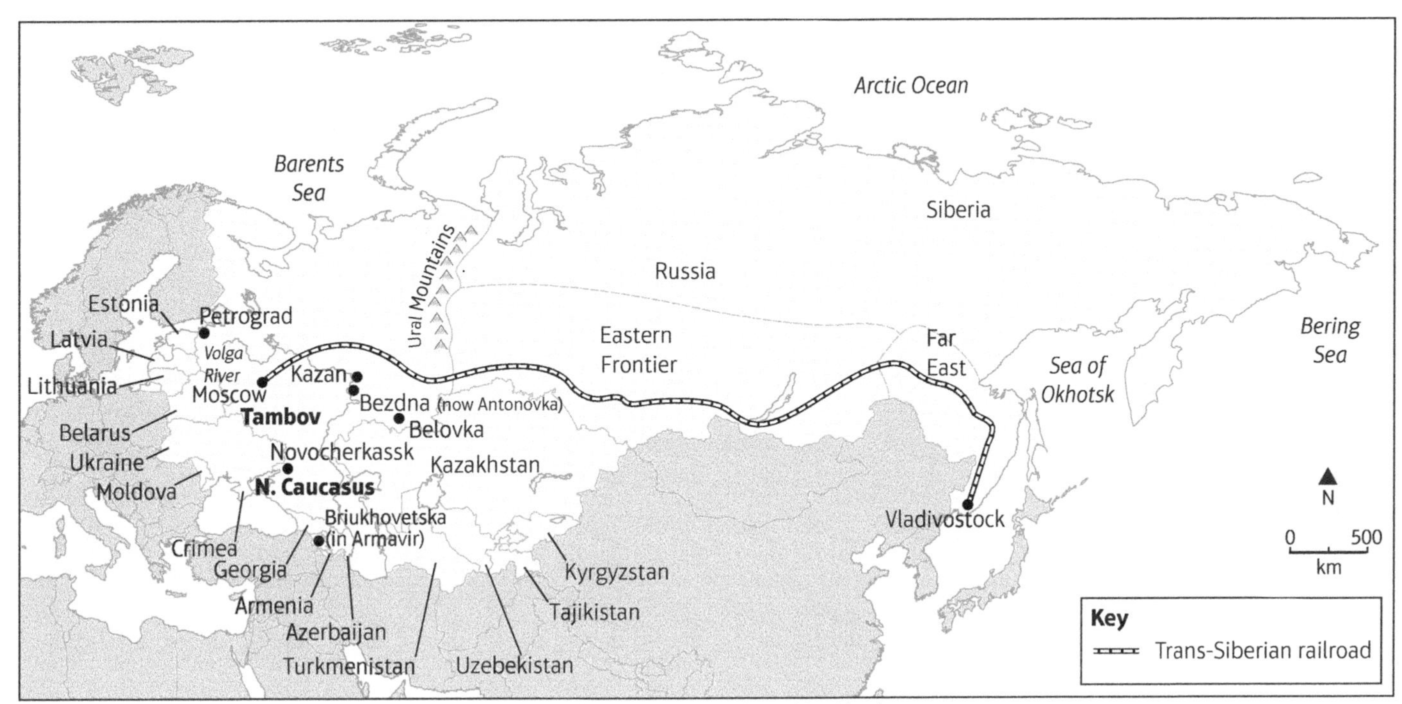

Figure 1.1 Russia, showing key provinces and cities, as well as places mentioned in this chapter.

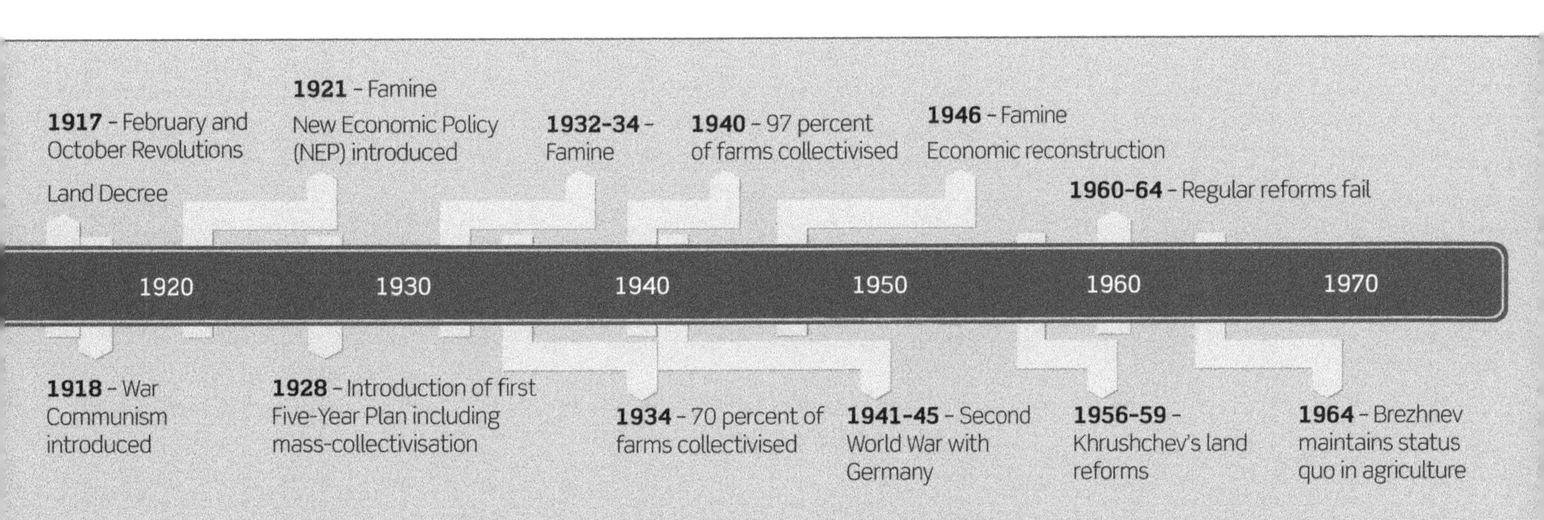

WHAT WAS THE IMPACT OF GOVERNMENT POLICIES ON THE STATUS AND CONDITION OF THE PEASANTRY IN IMPERIAL RUSSIA, 1855-1917?

Why was serfdom a problem in 19th-century Russia?

A common misconception equates the Russian serf with slavery. Another is that all Russian peasants were serfs. Neither of these was the case. Firstly, a Russian serf had his own house and usually worked under the supervision of his own family. The land the serfs worked on was the property of the landowner. Serfs were required to set aside part of their working time (about three days a week) and part of their produce as tribute to the landowner, an arrangement that had carried on for many generations. The landowner also had some control over marriages, so as to encourage the next generation of serfs by arranging peasants to marry young.

Secondly, the 1859 census showed that out of a population of 60 million, around 40 percent were serfs, while another 40 percent were peasants owned by the state who, although bound to the land, were not bonded to any landowner. They generally had a higher standard of living. The central provinces around Moscow and the western provinces on the Polish border had the most serfs.

Even this is misleading in that many serfs, especially in areas less suited to agriculture, performed non-farming tasks in rural factories or mines. They undertook extra work to supplement their income, working as carpenters and other artisan jobs. Many paid rent in lieu of work and produce. In 1857, over a million serfs were granted internal passports allowing them to work far outside their villages. The Russian writer, Pushkin (1799–1837), noted the hard-working entrepreneurial spirit of the serfs and compared their standard of living favourably with that of English factory workers. Finally, some seven percent of serfs worked as domestic servants for the wealthiest landowners. These had no land at all by which to support themselves, and were totally reliant on their owner for all welfare.

While the average lot of a serf in 1850 may have been better than that of an Irish peasant or an African-American slave, there were still many problems. Serfdom had arisen over the centuries to enable the **autocracy** to control scattered populations in an expanding empire. The landowners policed the rural areas for the state, which gave them almost unlimited authority over the serfs. There are many examples of excessive cruelty, though this was by no means universal. Indeed, it was the lack of overall state control that led to the varied and complex nature of Russian agriculture.

By 1855, as the industrial revolution gained momentum in Europe, it was becoming clear that Russia was falling behind other countries, and the continuation of serfdom was increasingly seen as a key cause of Russia's inertia. This was for a number of reasons.

- Defeat in the **Crimean War** highlighted the inefficiencies of an army recruited, often reluctantly, from the serfs. Russia was beaten by the 'free' French and British soldiers.
- Grain yields on serf-farmed lands were lower than in the rest of Europe, which increasingly used modern techniques and machinery to farm the land intensively. Russia still favoured the system of communal strip-farming that had been used in medieval England.
- Restrictions on the movement of serfs were believed to hinder the growth of Russian industry, as labour was needed in urban areas.
- Serfdom was seen as the cause of an increasing number of peasant uprisings. There were around 70 spontaneous uprisings each year between 1855 and 1861.

Nicholas I, tsar between 1825–55, had recognised the problem and set up committees to formulate a plan to replace the system, but the complex structure of Russian agriculture meant nothing was achieved. His son, Alexander, had served on one of those committees and Nicholas, on his deathbed, had apologised to his son for the poor state of the Empire. As the new tsar, Alexander II could see that Russia's backwardness caused it to be looked down on by western Europe. If Russia was to be a Great Power, especially after the defeat in the Crimean War, the serfs had to be emancipated. The question was whether they should be given land with their freedom, or just become landless labourers. Serfdom had been the foundation of Russian society for generations, so any reform would have far-reaching effects.

KEY TERMS

Autocracy
A system of government in which an individual or a small group has unlimited authority, for example the Romanov dynasty in Russia, who ruled as the tsars from 1613 to 1917.

Crimean War, 1853-56
A war fought by Russia against an alliance of France, Britain, the Ottoman Empire and Sardinia. The main cause was the question of who would gain from the declining Ottoman Empire, and the war was fought over control of the Black Sea. It was one of the first wars to use modern technologies and to be documented with modern techniques. Despite British disasters such as the 'Charge of the Light Brigade', the war ended in defeat for Russia after the fall of Sevastopol. It is also known as the Eastern War.

EXPAND YOUR KNOWLEDGE

Alexander II (1818–81)
The son of Nicholas I, Alexander was tsar of Russia from 1855 until 1881. He was responsible for a series of reforms across a broad range of issues, of which serf emancipation was the most important. He was in the process of instituting an elected representative assembly when he was assassinated in 1881 by the revolutionary organisation, People's Will. His death brought the period of reforms to a swift close.

He was succeeded as tsar by his son, the reactionary Alexander III.

Famously, Alexander II announced in March 1856 that it was 'better to begin abolishing serfdom from above than to wait for it to begin to abolish itself from below'. The threat of uprising may have encouraged reform, but Alexander II wanted the nobility on board with any reform. The Secret Committee on Peasant Affairs was created in 1857 to formulate plans with the nobility, which it did in over 400 meetings. Despite opposition from some landowners who would clearly lose influence in any emancipation, as well as resistance from the Orthodox Church and even his own family, Alexander II personally steered the Great Emancipation Statute into law during February 1861. The result was a series of compromises that diluted many of the intentions and failed to satisfy anyone.

What was the impact on the peasants of the 1861 Edict of Emancipation which abolished serfdom?

SOURCE 1 *Lunch at the Village*, a painting by Pyotr Alexandrovich Suchodolski (1864), showing an idyllic and comfortable lifestyle that was not necessarily an accurate reflection of reality.

The immediate impact was that the serfs were now free, meaning they could own property, set up businesses and have no legal restrictions on their marriage. After a brief transition period, each peasant household would be granted an allotment from the landowner's estate. The state would generously and immediately compensate the nobility for the land. To finance the reform, the peasants would repay the state in the form of a **redemption tax** over the next 49 years at an interest rate of six percent per year. The ***mir***, or peasant commune, was in charge of the peasants at a local level and quickly became the central organisation in peasant life.

KEY TERMS

Redemption tax
Money paid by the freed serf to the state for 49 years, with six percent annual interest. Alternatively, they could work for 30–40 days a year on the lord's land. Only when the tax was paid in full would the peasant have legal title to the land. Unsurprisingly, the taxes were unpopular with the freed serfs.

***Mir* (plural *mirs*)**
A Russian peasant organisation, also known as *obshchina*, which served as a village government after emancipation. It held power over every aspect of village life, and organised the redemption payments through an elected village elder and tax collector.

Alexander II, in his Emancipation Edict, stated that he expected the freed serfs would 'appreciate and recognise the considerable sacrifices which the nobility had made on their behalf'. However, the nobility often kept the best quality land for themselves, and the allotments granted were often too small for a peasant family to survive on. On average, peasant families worked 20 percent less land than before 1861, while household serfs received no land at all. The result was a sharp increase in peasant unrest in all but one province affected by the changes. The army was used to control nearly 450 riots, with the most serious occurring in Bezdna, in the Kazan province of central Russia. Disappointed by the limited reform and inspired by a literate peasant, Anton Petrov, 5,000 peasants gathered to protest against the nobility, though they remained loyal to the tsar. The army killed between 57 and 91 peasants and arrested Petrov, who was executed on the direct orders of the tsar.

SOURCE

From Prince Kropotkin's *Memoirs of a Revolutionist*, (1898). He was a serf-owner and is describing the reaction to the Emancipation Edict. Born into nobility and a page to Alexander II, Kropotkin believed in a society based on voluntary communes with no central government.

The same enthusiasm was in the streets. Crowds of peasants and educated men stood in front of the palace, shouting hurrahs, and the Tsar could not appear without being followed by demonstrative crowds running after his carriage... When I saw peasants, fifteen months after the liberation, I could not but admire them. Their inborn good nature and softness remained with them, but all traces of servility had disappeared. They talked to their masters as equals talk to equals.

SOURCE

From *A History of the USSR* (1948), used as a textbook in Soviet schools and universities. According to the USSR's official biography of Stalin, he was the author.

The abolition of serfdom was a turning point in Russia's history. The country's economy was becoming capitalistic. Industrial capitalism in Russia developed faster than it had before 1861, in spite of the existing vestiges of serfdom which retarded its progress. The state system of feudal tsarist Russia underwent a slow and steady progress of bourgeois reformation. Herein lay the progressive significance of the reform of 1861. 'This was,' wrote Lenin, 'a step towards the transformation of Russia into a bourgeois monarchy.' But since the reform was carried out by the serf-owners, they tried to retain as many of their privileges as possible. Robbed by the landlords, the peasants found themselves entangled in a new form of enslavement, that of economic thrall to the landlords.

The two-year transitional period before the land was redistributed caused confusion among the peasants, as did the concept that they would have to pay for the land that they felt was inherently theirs. Emancipation had legally changed the serf's status to that of a free peasant, but authority was wary about freeing the peasants completely from their attachment to the land. Continuity was achieved through the *mir*.

Though the *mir* had to manage the link between the landowner and the state with the peasants, it would be wrong to portray it as working against the peasants' interests, as at a basic level its function was to provide stability and assistance in hard times. However, this was achieved by organising their lives as a group, not as individuals. The heads of households formed an assembly with an elected village elder at the top. The assembly was responsible for a range of activities in the village, such as repairing roads, maintaining public order and the imposition of small-scale punishments, providing aid for the sick, the elderly and orphans, organising schools and church. The *mir* regulated farming practices along traditional lines, making it fundamental in maintaining a sense of community. Peasant sayings of the time neatly summarised the relationship between peasant and commune, as in, 'What one man can't bear, the *mir* can' and 'No one is greater than the *mir*'.

The 140,000 *mirs* across European Russia held more than 80 percent of peasant land (95 percent in the central provinces) and their decisions on how to farm could not be refused by any individual. The dominating influence of the hated landowners and nobility may have been reduced, but the *mir* was a cohesive bond that controlled almost every aspect of peasant life and directly affected the extent of any change in the peasants' living standards in the late 19th century.

The burden of redemption payments and over-population

For the privilege of the change in legal status, the peasants had the constant burden of the redemption tax, which often outweighed the value of the land. The perceived unfairness of this direct tax was one of the most common forms of grievance, next to the lack of land ownership. Some tried to escape the redemption taxes by accepting only a quarter of the normal allocation of land, known as 'beggar's holdings'. The *mir* was responsible for the organisation and payment of the redemption taxes, and was the main contact between the peasant and the imperial world outside the village. Therefore, it wanted to retain its members in order to pay the tax and could withhold passports to keep peasants from leaving, especially if they were in arrears. The *mir* allowed some peasants to go to the cities, but only in controlled circumstances. Employment in the cities would maximise the commune's incomes; as long as the link to the *mir* was maintained, it made sense to increase earnings in the cities if the redemption taxes were to be met. In 1890, over two-thirds of St Petersburg's population was born outside the city, and nearly all sent money to support relatives on farms. Only when a redemption debt was fully paid would the *mir* officially hand over a peasant's allotment. Redemption payments acted as a factor to resist change as well as being an additional burden on the peasants.

The tax demands caused peasants to sell all their grain, often leaving themselves short of food, while general poverty meant that they slipped further into arrears. The government extended the loan period and reduced the payments in the 1880s and 1890s, but by 1900 the debt arrears were greater than the annual payments. In 1906, facing a hopeless situation, the government finally wrote off any outstanding debts, but the payments had already had half a century to thwart peasant development.

While emancipation itself had little social impact, population growth (from 75 million in 1860 to 175 million in 1914) and the continual expansion of the empire (particularly in Central Asia as well as the Caucasus) both affected the peasants. The increase in peasant numbers was encouraged further as the *mir* put pressure on peasants to marry early and have large families, just as the pre-emancipation landowners had done, in order to provide new labour for the fields. The consequences of over-population led to an occasional need to repartition land within the commune. This peaked in the 1870s and 1880s and threatened the stability of the peasant communities enough to cause the government to implement measures to restrict the process, such as setting time-limits of 12 years between repartitions. Rural overcrowding led to a period of migration, as the high populations strained the farmland of European Russia. The government also helped to finance new farms in the harsh conditions of Siberia and Central Asia, to encourage peasants to move to the new lands. Between 1894 and 1903, 115,000 peasants each year moved eastwards, though the inhospitable conditions did force some to return. This rural migration was far outweighed by the movement to the cities, which grew from six to 18 million between 1860 and 1914 as peasants sought work in the new industries.

Long-term impacts of the abolition of serfdom

The post-emancipation peasant lived a life of self-imposed conformity within the umbrella of the village commune and life could be harsh. A lack of health care and medical advancement meant that child mortality rates remained high, with around half the children in peasant areas dying before the age of five. Peasant life was often portrayed in contemporary literature as drenched in alcohol, violence and unrelenting misery, with writers often blaming these misfortunes on the peasants themselves. This can paint a misleading picture, as these accounts are selective and often written from an anti-tsarist view. It seems that, socially, there is little to differentiate peasant life before and after the 1861 emancipation.

On the other hand, some peasants did enjoy increased prosperity. They were able, through the *mir*, to buy, sell and rent extra land. This was given extra impetus by two factors. First, many nobles wanted to sell land (almost half their holdings went on the market in the 50 years after emancipation). Secondly, a Peasant Land Bank was set up in 1883 to aid purchases of land. Though initially many peasants preferred to avoid using it, perhaps mistrustful of its government origins, the bank assisted in around 20 percent of deals. Only around a third of peasants and communes had the resources for such expansion, but nevertheless emancipation did create, to a limited extent, the personal freedom to integrate some peasants into the imperial economy, despite the more traditional influence of the *mir*.

EXTRACT

From Orlando Figes' *A People's Tragedy: The Russian Revolution 1891–1924* (1996), in which he describes peasant village life at the end of the 19th century.

Peasant life in Russia really was nasty, brutish and short. It was also cramped by strict conformity to the social mores of the village. Dissident behaviour brought upon its perpetrators various punishments... A favourite punishment was to raise the victim on a pulley with his feet and hands tied together and to drop him so that the vertebrae in his back were broken; this was repeated several times until he was reduced to a spineless sack...

It is difficult to say where this barbarism came from... Many people explained the violence of the peasant world by the weakness of the legal order and the general lawlessness of the state. The Emancipation had liberated the serfs from the judicial tyranny of their landlords but it had not incorporated them in the world ruled by law, which included the rest of society. Excluded from the written law administered through the civil courts, the newly liberated peasants were kept in a sort of legal apartheid after 1861. The tsarist regime looked upon them as a cross between savages and children.

Emancipation initiated a more subtle change in the peasants' lives. The freedom gained from the landowners developed into a desire for liberty and greater participation in the political process. The election of the village elder every three years sparked a sense of democracy. This was more prevalent among younger peasants, who would sometimes break free of the household elder in order to set up their own farms, especially if they had earned extra money by working elsewhere. Aspirations were reinforced by growing literacy rates, which allowed access to more abstract political and technological concepts. The higher literacy rates resulted from the increase in primary schools attended by half of all peasant children in the early 19th century. With the population increase, younger peasants became a majority and 65 percent of all peasants in 1897 were under the age of 30.

This new social group became the focus of revolutionary organisations, such as the People's Will, and there were concerted attempts to tap into the evolving political conscience of the peasantry. In the 1870s, around 2,000 urban and student radicals went into the countryside to promote revolution among the more literate and outward-looking peasants. Though these groups were historically influential, as in the 1881 assassination of Alexander II by the People's Will, it would be wrong to suggest that the peasants flocked to the cause. Indeed, many idealistic radicals met with suspicion and violence in the villages. Though the peasantry failed to embrace the revolutionary message, it is still possible to trace the beginnings of the rural political awakening to the emancipation of 1861.

An indication of the imperial authorities' concern over the growing power of the peasants was the creation in 1889 of 2,000 Land Captains, or 'little tsars', as the peasants called them. These were officials chosen from the gentry who had considerable powers to overturn the commune's decisions and could even order the public flogging of peasants. Unsurprisingly, they were resented and hated in equal measure by the peasants who saw them as a return to the restrictions of serfdom.

ACTIVITY
KNOWLEDGE CHECK

The impact of emancipation on the peasants

1. How do Sources 2 and 3 differ in their interpretations of the consequences of emancipation?
2. To what extent was the failure of the Crimean War the key factor in Alexander II's decision to emancipate the serfs?
3. From your own knowledge, what information could support and/or challenge the views of Extract 1?
4. Make a list of the aims that Alexander II wanted to achieve with the emancipation of the serfs.
5. To what extent were these aims achieved? Try to find examples of both success and failure.
6. What do you consider to be the key success and the key failure in the decades after 1861?
7. To what extent was the imposition of heavy redemption payments the reason the peasantry failed to develop into a modern agricultural system?

Stolypin's reforms, 1906–11

After the 3,000-strong peasant uprising that accompanied the 1905 revolution (see pages 91–102), the politician Stolypin pushed through the new wave of reforms to tackle the *mir*. Stolypin's land reforms had two basic functions. First, there was the desire to economically modernise agriculture, which the *mir* hindered, and second to calm the rural unrest that spread after 1905, that the *mir* had failed to police. Stolypin believed that a prosperous and above all stable peasantry would create a loyal powerbase for the tsar. This new class of contented peasantry would reject the ideas of the revolutionaries and would provide food and investment for the industrialisation of Russia, through the sale of surplus grain. He called this potentially regime-saving class his 'wager on the sober and strong', and their success depended on removing the peasants' attachment to the *mir*. Therefore the reforms had a political function as well as a purely economic one.

EXTEND YOUR KNOWLEDGE

Pyotr Stolypin (1862–1911)

Stolypin was a minister for Tsar Nicholas II and rose to prominence after the attempted 1905 Revolution. He worked on a range of reforms in industry and agriculture and through working with the newly elected **duma**. He used severe repression against radicals and political opponents, and was assassinated in 1911. Some see his death as ending the tsarist regime's last chance to evolve into a constitutional monarchy.

KEY TERM

Duma
The elected legislative for the major Russian cities, such as St Petersburg and Moscow. It was first created by Catherine I in 1785, but was expanded to all Russian cities by the 1870 statute.

As prime minister, Stolypin introduced land reforms in November 1906 with a range of linked terms to encourage a more independent peasant. His ideas had been rejected by the newly elected *duma*, so he forced them through by decree, a process designed for emergencies. This indicates not only the opposition Stolypin faced, but also the desperate situation he felt agriculture was in.

- Peasants were allowed to leave the *mir* without its consent.
- Once free, the peasant's farm could be in one large consolidated package rather than the scattered strips of the *mir*.
- Peasants were to be awarded financial aid through the state's Land Bank in order to purchase consolidated farms.
- All state and crown lands were made available for the peasants to buy.
- Extra assistance was offered to peasants willing to set up farms in eastern provinces like Siberia.
- Redemption payments were removed, increasing purchasing power by about 15 percent, as peasant deposits in post-office savings banks indicate.

However, once again despite the clear intentions, the reform had a mixed impact on rural Russia.

The impact of the 1906 land reforms on the peasants

The immediate impact was to encourage peasants to leave the *mir*. In both 1908 and 1909, over half a million households left the *mir*, though this had dropped to a more stable 130,000 each year by

1911. About 20 percent of peasants received the title deeds to their land, while half of those, about 1.3 million of the over 12 million peasant households, had set up fully independent and consolidated farms. These richer peasants, or ***kulaks***, proved less rebellious, with the 3,000 episodes of peasant rioting in 1905 falling to just 128 in 1913. However, there is evidence that the peasants' anger was targeted more at those individuals encouraging people to leave the *mir* than at the state itself.

It also sparked a second period of migration, with more than 750,000 peasants moving east in 1908 alone. (Conditions were still harsh, however, and 75,000 made the return journey in 1910.) This migration helped to integrate the empire. Others moved to urban areas. By 1914, Russia had 13 cities with over 100,000 people. The rate of urban population growth was double that of the countryside, but was largely made up of rural immigrants; in 1910, some 15 percent of Moscow's nearly 1.75 million population had lived there less than a year. Meanwhile, grain production rose from 45.9 million tonnes in 1906 to 61.7 million in 1913. While these figures show a positive impact and a period of relative prosperity, they disguise other issues that held back Stolypin's success.

Though an individual peasant could legally and quickly leave the commune, the process of extracting their land from the commune was complicated and needed time-consuming surveys of the land and its soil quality to ensure that the new consolidated farm was as good as the strips of land that had been given up. Even when this was achieved, only 25 percent of the peasants who had consolidated farms actually moved out of the village, and then many returned in the winter. The sense of community fostered by the *mir* remained too strong for Stolypin to break. This dependence on mutual assistance increased further during the terrible hardships of the First World War, and the creation of new farms ground to a halt. In 1916, *mirs* held 61 percent of all peasant land (down from 77 percent in 1905), while half the land purchased through the Land Bank was actually bought by *mirs* and collectives. The most over-populated areas saw the least change: only around five percent left the protection of the commune in Tambov, while the figure was closer to 50 percent in the Ukraine.

The peasants were still wary of reform and greatly mistrusted the government agents and surveyors sent to measure, calculate and remove parts of the land that they felt was naturally part of the *mir*. Stolypin also used the Land Captains to facilitate the process. The peasants hated these even more than the surveyors, as they had been largely responsible for putting down the 1905 unrest, and the Captains despised Stolypin, whom they felt was undermining the power of the nobility in the countryside.

KEY TERM

Kulak
Originally richer peasants, Stolypin's 'sober and strong' who would modernise the countryside, they were seen by the Bolsheviks as the cause of all rural problems and as enemies of the revolution. The definition was broadened to include any peasant who opposed any aspect of communist agricultural policy, and millions were killed, exiled and imprisoned during Stalin's collectivisation policy of the 1930s.

SOURCE 4 Rural police terrorising the farmers of Trubetschino village in the area of Lebedyansk in 1906.

ACTIVITY
KNOWLEDGE CHECK

Stolypin's Russia

What does Source 4 suggest about the relationship between the authorities and the peasants? Explain how it would hinder the reforming aspects of Stolypin's agricultural policy.

The typical peasants who left the commune were the two extremes. They were either the wealthiest ones, destined to be the *kulaks*, looking to expand further, or the poorest ones, who just wanted to leave the countryside altogether. Most peasants were largely unaffected by the reforms. Those who successfully left the commune were now legal citizens with all the same rights as any individual in the new cities, but for the majority little changed in the period 1905–14. In fact, the situation actually caused an increase in tension, not just between the commune and the state, but also within the village, as land was dissected to provide for the *kulaks*, whom many peasants resented.

For the true consolidated farms with their enclosed large fields and more modern tools, the standard of living rose noticeably. They might own a few horses and a dozen cows, hire labour and sell fruit and vegetables to the city. However, these pioneers of a new European-style agriculture were few, and the separation from the *mir*'s social services, such as schools and the church, made the transition difficult and risky. The government was perhaps more successful in encouraging migration to Siberia, which by 1913 had become an important region for peasant co-operative dairy farming. Between 1900 and 1913, some five million peasants voluntarily moved to Siberia, though about 15 percent returned.

Like the 1861 Emancipation Edict, Stolypin's land reforms were legal acts which did not fundamentally address the economic reality of low-level production failing to meet the demands of expanding cities and a rapidly rising population. Stolypin had wanted 20 years of peace in order for his ambitious reforms to work, but Russia had just eight years before war blocked any further reforms. The reforms had slowed considerably before 1914, due to obstacles from all sides. The *mir* may have resisted the changes, but the nobility, including the tsar, also reacted against any move to alter the status quo. The tsar, having witnessed the assassination of his grandfather in 1881, felt he had to learn what a reform-minded leader would lead to. Now he wanted to preserve his autocracy in a country toying with the notion of an elected *duma*. With such half-hearted support, Stolypin could make little headway.

Alexander had used the *mir* to ease the transformation from serf to peasant, in which the village commune acted as a continuity to keep the peasants attached to the land. Stolypin felt that his attempt to create a new loyal class of farmer was disrupted by the *mir*, as its structure kept the peasants, and therefore Russia, poor. This was a basic misreading of the situation. In fact, the *mir* existed to allow the peasants to cope with their poverty. It is not a surprise, therefore, that this bond continued to strengthen as Russia began to feel the consequences of the First World War.

EXTEND YOUR KNOWLEDGE

Stolypin's assassination - a most symbolic death

Stolypin's murder, while attending the Kiev opera in September 1911, highlights the difficult political world that he tried to reform. He had survived previous attempts by revolutionary groups to kill him and as he sat in the front stalls, with Tsar Nicholas II present in the royal box, he had ignored a police warning of a plot. During the interval, a young student-revolutionary, who was also a police informer, shot Stolypin at close range. Stolypin calmly took off his gloves and unbuttoned his jacket to reveal a blood-soaked waistcoat. He sat down, announced to all that, 'I am happy to die for the tsar', looked up at the royal box and blessed the tsar with the sign of a cross. Stolypin died four days later, and the tsar prayed over his corpse, repeating the phrase, 'forgive me' over and over.

No one is certain who was involved in the plot and rumours abound that the tsar was at least aware of it. Stolypin's death certainly met with enthusiasm from both the revolutionaries and the nobility, and this explains why his land reforms failed to have the desired impact. Every section of society actively slowed down his work, including the tsar for whom he was content to lay down his life. The reality is that Stolypin was politically dead before he felt the assassin's bullet, as he tried to modernise a most reluctant country.

EXTRACT

Orlando Figes in *A People's Tragedy: The Russian Revolution 1891–1924* (1996) discusses the overall impact of Stolypin's reforms and how they have been misinterpreted by many historians.

The majority of western historians had tended to assume - often more on the basis of their own ideological prejudices than empirical evidence - that Stolypin's land reform 'must have been' a success. It is argued that were it not for the First World War, which brought the separations to a halt, the reform might have averted the agrarian revolution by converting the peasant into a class of yeoman landowners. This fits with the view of those historians who stress that tsarist Russia after 1905 *was* becoming stabilized and strengthened as a result of its evolution towards a modern society and that, if it had not been for the war, the revolution would never have happened... In fact, long before 1914, Stolypin's land reforms had ground to a halt. Stolypin had claimed that they would need at least twenty years to transform rural Russia. But even if they had continued at the same rate as they had been progressing before the First World War, it would have taken the best part of a century for the regime to create the strong bourgeoisie on which it had evidently decided to stake its future. The land enclosure movement, like every other reform of the tsarist regime, came too late.

ACTIVITY
KNOWLEDGE CHECK

Agriculture under the tsarist regime

1 Why does Extract 2 suggest that western historians assume that Stolypin's reforms were successful?

2 Using Extract 2 and your own knowledge, to what extent can the reforms of Alexander II and Stolypin be seen as too little, too late to have a significant impact on the agricultural problems of Russia?

3 Using all of the information so far, collect examples to show how the period 1855-1917 saw the peasants undergo periods of famine, migration and prosperity.

4 For each example examined in question 3, explore the various factors that caused it. To what extent were they caused by government policy?

WHAT WAS THE IMPACT OF GOVERNMENT POLICIES ON THE STATUS AND CONDITION OF THE PEASANTRY UNDER COMMUNIST RULE, 1918–91?

The Land Decree, 1917

The First World War was a heavy burden on the Russian peasant as well as the country as a whole. The conscription of vast numbers of peasants into the imperial army led to severe labour shortages in the fields. The disrupted food supplies and diverted agricultural resources hurt the peasant farms, as did the enormous casualty rates. Yet the tsar's eventual abdication in February 1917 was due more to pressure from the cities, such as Petrograd, and political groups than the mass will of the peasantry.

The tsar's replacement, the **Provisional Government**, failed to address the fundamental problem of the war and struggled to rule in conjunction with the growing influence of the Petrograd Soviet, a **Bolshevik**-dominated organisation.

KEY TERMS

Provisional Government
The ruling authority, which replaced the autocratic tsar after the February Revolution of 1917. Despite its democratic leanings, it failed to call for national elections while it continued the war with Germany. Despite being led by the charismatic politician Kerensky in July 1917, it failed to retain the authority and support of the Russian people, resulting in its overthrow in October 1917.

Bolshevik
A member of the Russian Communist Party, led by Lenin. The Party believed in the immediate revolutionary overthrow of the government. It achieved this in October 1917, and proceeded to rule Russia as a single-party state. In 1923, it created the Union of Soviet Socialist Republics (USSR) and renamed itself the Communist Party.

The attritional nature of the war continued to drain both Russia's resources and any public willingness for the government to continue. By October, the Bolsheviks had manoeuvred themselves into a position to take power from the imploding government. The Bolshevik slogan of 'Peace, Bread and Land' was a rallying cry to the masses, which for the first time clearly targeted the peasantry as part of a collective group with the workers to overthrow the government.

EXTEND YOUR KNOWLEDGE

The February Revolution and the October Revolution (1917)
The February Revolution of 1917 was when Tsar Nicholas II was forced to resign after protests in St Petersburg. He was replaced by the Provisional Government, largely made up of members of the fourth *duma*, or national government.

However, within eight months, the situation in Russia had deteriorated further and in October 1917 the government was overthrown by a highly organised, but small communist group, known as the Bolsheviks, led by Lenin.

While the largely peasant-based army desired peace, the Bolshevik leader, Lenin, hoped the promise of land would bring the peasantry flocking to the Bolshevik cause. The new authority needed their support to achieve any hope of survival, as they were a party of only around 300,000 in a nation of over 160 million. The new government's first acts were the October Decrees, a series of legislations designed to gather immediate support for the new regime. These included the Decree on Peace to end the war, and the Worker's Control Decree to allow the workers to gain control over the industrial workplace. However the key decree for the peasants was the Decree 'Concerning Land' of October 1917, which abolished all private ownership of land without granting any compensation to the former owners.

EXTEND YOUR KNOWLEDGE

Vladimir Ilich Lenin (1870–1924)
Lenin was the leader of the Bolshevik Party and then of the Soviet Union from 1917 until 1924. A skilled politician, he adapted Marxist communism to fit the Russian model. While seen as a champion of workers' rights by some, others see him as a dictator responsible for setting up the apparatus of repression and terror that Stalin later used. Ill-health limited his impact after 1922 and he died in 1924.

The Bolsheviks' desire to grab as much support as possible can be seen clearly in the Land Decree, as it demonstrated the need for support overruling the implementation of communist ideology. The original programme was to nationalise all land and turn it into large government-owned consolidated farms, but Lenin realised that peasant support was crucial, so he was prepared to allow the peasants to gain direct control of the land. The situation could be addressed at a later stage.

As with all policies applying to the peasantry, it was not as simple as it appeared. The Land Decree, like much early Bolshevik legislation, was a paper decree, in that it merely stated what was already happening, rather than initiating the change. The army had almost disintegrated as soldiers deserted from the front in their thousands; the workers had wrested control of the factories from the managers, while many peasants already had the land in their possession. The Land Decree gave 'official approval' to what was already done. Making the process legal earned the new Bolshevik government the support, as least passively, of the peasantry. Indeed, it was popularly known as Lenin's Decree.

This dramatic process was started and controlled by the *mir* rather than the new government. The majority of the peasants who had followed Stolypin's push for consolidated farms had willingly returned to the commune during the war. Indeed by 1921, 98 percent of peasants were farming within the *mir*. The February Revolution had given the peasants hope, and this was seen in the more radical outlook of the *mir*, which particularly favoured the **Social Revolutionary (SR) Party,** whose socialist

KEY TERM

Social Revolutionary (SR) Party
A revolutionary group. Their socialist values were based on the peasantry rather than urban workers. This gave them, in 1917, a much larger base of support than other revolutionary groups, like the Bolsheviks or Mensheviks.

manifesto gave the peasants a historical and moral right to the land they worked.

During the spring and summer of 1917, the *mirs*, in large numbers and armed with farming tools, marched on their local manor houses. Demands were made on the gentry, starting with the lowering of rents, but escalating by the summer to full confiscation of the land. This more militant approach was partly encouraged by deserting soldiers returning home full of the revolutionary propaganda that the groups such as the Bolsheviks had targeted at them as they awaited their turn at the front line. The timing was also due to the rhythm of the farming year, as the peasants needed the land by early May if it was to be sown and planted in time for harvest. The gentry had no choice but to concede, though they badgered the Provisional Government for military assistance to return their land to them.

The Provisional Government could do nothing, indeed any military brigades sent out to enforce discipline in the countryside quickly deserted to return home to claim land for themselves. In May 1917, the First All-Russian Peasant Assembly endorsed the peasants' land grab, undermining any attempt by the Provisional Government to maintain rural control. The assembly was dominated by SR activists, though the peasants moved even faster than the SR wanted, as they saw any resolution passed by the assembly as legitimising the acquisition of land. The peasant revolution was enacted by the *mir*, and land was distributed through the traditional method of pacing out the plots and allocating them by the number of people in a household. It seemed the peasants' dream of owning land and controlling their lives was being fulfilled. They believed they were creating a nation of smallholding family farmers. The Bolsheviks, through their belated Land Decree, were keen to take some of the credit.

It is a testament to the organisational skills of the *mir* that this ultimate repartition of land was generally peaceful. Many of the gentry had fled, but those who remained usually had enough resources and land to set up a sizeable farm themselves, as they adapted to their new lives as peasants. As late as 1925, some 10,000 former landowners (about ten percent of the 1917 landowners) were living on their manors side-by-side with the peasants. Subsequent Bolshevik publications and propaganda emphasised conflicts between peasants and richer *kulaks* over land. This is untrue, though there were inter-village wars as *mirs* argued over the right to an estate. The returning demobbed soldiers, spurred on by Bolshevik slogans to 'loot the looters', tended to instigate violence.

In the elections for the Constituent Assembly, called by the Provisional Government but permitted by the Bolsheviks in November 1917, the peasants expressed their gratitude by voting overwhelmingly for the SRs because they most closely associated that peasant-based party with the issue of land. The Bolsheviks, though disappointed to lose the election, were insightful enough to realise that the peasants were voting on the single issue of land, in which the SR's stance was similar in tone to their own. It just happened that the SRs were better known in rural areas. The Bolsheviks ignored the result and dissolved the Constituent Assembly, hoping that the peasants' allegiance would switch to them.

For over 50 years the Russian government had tried to juggle the impossible. They wanted a modern agricultural economy, but one that still functioned in a traditional, almost feudal, countryside dominated by the nobility. The peasant *mir* was then seen as a brake to progress. In the chaos of a year of international war and internal revolution, the peasants themselves had grabbed the opportunity to gain control. The Land Decree just confirmed what had already happened and seemed to stamp the new communist approval on their actions. The 56-year journey from serf to citizen to landowner had seen the peasants' status, if not their living conditions, transformed. They were now free to sow, plant and harvest – free to work the land and enjoy the fruits of their labour. It would have been a snapshot of hope and unbridled optimism, if only time had stood still.

EXTRACT 3

From Robert Service, *A History of Modern Russia From Nicholas II to Putin* (2003).

The Decree on Land had a large impact on opinion amidst the peasantry, and became known as Lenin's Decree. But Bolsheviks were extremely small in number; and most of the very few village 'soviets' were really communes under a different name...

Many a household divided itself into several households so as to increase its members' claim to land. The unintended consequence was that sons had a say in communal affairs whereas previously the father would have spoken on their behalf. As young men were conscripted, furthermore, women began to thrust themselves forward when decisions were taken; gradually the revolutions in the villages were affecting rural relationships. But the main feature was the peasantry's wish to arrange its life without outside interference. Liberated from indebtedness to the landlord and from oppression by the land captains, peasants savoured their chance to realize their ancient aspirations.

ACTIVITY
KNOWLEDGE CHECK

The Land Decree

1. How does Extract 3 suggest the peasants will react to the Land Decree?
2. What potential difficulties might be created by the Land Decree? Explain your answer.
3. Do you think the Land Decree was a genuine attempt by the Bolsheviks to fulfil their promise of 'land' or a more cynical attempt to gather as much support as possible?

The New Economic Policy (NEP), 1921

What were the circumstances that would force the introduction of the NEP?

The new government under Lenin might have had the support of the majority of the peasantry, but the one-sided 1918 peace treaty with Germany, the Treaty of Brest-Litovsk (see page 125), focused all opposition against the Bolsheviks and, with no Constituent Assembly, the only way for the opposition to express themselves was through civil war.

The resulting conflict of 1918–21 saw unprecedented terror and destruction in Russia. Trotsky, the leader and organiser of the newly formed **Red Army**, acknowledged that any price would be paid for victory, even if it meant ruining the entire country. The fighting and resulting disease killed over five million, while the massive conscripted Red Army, as well the factory workers manufacturing military supplies, needed food. Through the policy of **War Communism**, this was provided by the peasants fulfilling state procurements at a low cost to the Bolshevik government. Despite the ideological origins of its name, it was a practical policy which for the peasants simply meant that special military units were sent to requisition grain from the farms, forcibly if required. Any resistance was met with terror led by the secret police, known as **Cheka**, and its fanatical leader Dzerzhinsky. Officially, some 13,000 peasants were shot by the requisitioning squads, but later historians put the figure as high as 300,000. Labour camps were set up to remove anyone seen as a trouble-maker, along with their families. The Bolsheviks blamed the *kulaks* who had now been embedded in village life for over 20 years. The logic was that if there was not enough food, the *kulaks* must have hidden it. Lenin raged against them and demanded their deaths. The *mir* had been transformed into a genuine peasant organisation after the February revolution, but was now seen as a threat to the Bolsheviks and their plans for state control.

KEY TERMS

Red Army
The Workers' and Peasants' Army, set up by the Bolshevik government immediately after the October Revolution of 1917. Organised by Leon Trotsky, its task was to defend communist Russia against all opposition.

War Communism, 1918–21
A Bolshevik policy designed by Lenin to guarantee food for the workers and soldiers in order to win the Russian Civil War. It can be seen as a 'prototype' for Stalin's collectivisation policy a decade later and was very unpopular with the peasants.

Cheka
The secret police force set up after the October 1917 Revolution, tasked with finding and eliminating 'enemies of the state'. Under the leadership of Felix Dzerzhinsky, it performed its duties with fanaticism and succeeded in spreading terror.

The Bolsheviks, through the Statute on Socialist Land Organisation in February 1919, had reversed the Land Decree. The new law had declared peasant farming obsolete and had forced through more collective farms by converting all the available land that the gentry had owned. By 1921, some 16,000 had been set up, ranging from state-run farms (***sovkhozy***), of 100,000 acres, to small collective farms (***kolkhozy***) of around 50 acres, set up by peasants.

KEY TERMS

Sovkhoz* and *kolkhoz
The two main types of collective farms encouraged by the Bolshevik government.

A *sovkhoz* (plural *sovkhozy*) was larger and paid peasants a set wage. *Sovkhozy* were easier to control and were preferred by the government, but not many were created and they often failed.

A *kolkhoz* (plural *kolkhozy*) was slightly more independent, smaller and easier to set up, and became the dominant model. *Kolkhozy* mirrored some aspects of the farms that had been worked by serfs, in that peasants worked the collective fields in return for a share of the profits.

With this state intrusion into affairs that the peasants saw as theirs by right, it is no surprise that 1921 saw a massive increase in violent resistance to the Bolsheviks. In February 1921 alone, Cheka recorded 128 separate rebellions. Some peasants formed the so-called Green armies, such as Nestor Makhno's forces in the Ukraine, and fought anyone who threatened their area of land. This political anarchist fought for the area's independence and at various times fought the Reds, Whites and the Germans. In the Tambov region, starting in 1920, peasants led by Alexander Antonov fought back against the Bolshevik requisition brigades and kept the Red Army out for over a year. Even the sailors leading the 1921 **Kronstadt Mutiny** in Petrograd were ex-peasants, who knew the situation in the countryside and supported the various peasant wars.

KEY TERM

Kronstadt Mutiny, March 1921
A major rebellion at the naval base near Petrograd. Formerly committed supporters of the Bolsheviks, the sailors led an armed resistance against the Red Army. Among their demands was the return of the land to the peasants. The mutiny was viciously suppressed, with thousands killed on both sides.

The peasant reprisals against Bolshevik officials could be as gruesome as anything inflicted on them. People were decapitated, burned alive, drowned and eaten by dogs and rats in front of cheering crowds. Anything connected to the Bolsheviks was destroyed, from the state farms to schools to rural factories. Where possible, requisitioned grain was recaptured, to be joyfully returned to the people. The Bolsheviks promised rewards for informers, paid in salt, which was vital to preserve food over the winter, but this had little impact on the peasants' anger. The hatred between the government and peasants later helped to fuel tension under Stalin.

By March 1921, as a direct consequence of the **Civil War** and War Communism, the Moscow-centred Bolshevik government had lost control of the countryside. Half of the new collective farms were destroyed, and grain had virtually stopped moving from the farms to the cities, which encouraged further trouble and strikes in urban areas. Lenin could see that these peasant uprisings were more dangerous to the regime than any of the opposition forces, known as Whites, from the Civil War. The panic was clear when he announced that they seemed to be barely holding on.

The solution was to introduce the most controversial policy of Lenin's leadership. Russia had been devastated by seven years of war that had begun with the outbreak of the First World War in 1914, had continued with the Civil War, and was now out of control in localised uprisings. A new beginning would need a new economic policy to try to restore stability to a shattered country.

KEY TERM

Russian Civil War, 1918–21
A brutal civil war beween the new Bolshevik government, known as the Reds, and a loose coalition of both Russian and international opposition groups and nations, collectively known as the Whites. Though the Reds won, it cost millions of lives, economically destroyed the country, introduced institutionalised terror into Russia and triggered the 1921–22 famine.

How did the NEP change the status of the peasants?

Lenin realised that both concessions to the structure of peasant life and some economic liberalisation were vital for the Bolsheviks to regain control of Russia. He also needed to persuade a reluctant party that this was the right way forward. Trotsky preferred to intensify War Communism and crush the peasantry with the Red Army, but Lenin managed to convince the Party as a whole that a New Economic Policy (NEP) was required, even if it seemed at odds with communist ideology. Though the state remained in full control of heavy industry, transport and banking, as it had under War Communism, smaller businesses were allowed certain freedoms to encourage growth.

- For the peasants, the hated grain requisitioning would end. Instead, they would pay a tax in the form of grain, but at much lower levels than during the Civil War. They would be free to sell any surplus on the open market, usually in the cities.
- The ban on private trade under War Communism was lifted to allow a smoother flow of goods between the countryside and the cities. Shops were allowed, rationing was abolished and people could use their income to buy products.
- Small businesses were allowed to make a profit, particularly if they produced things the peasants wanted to buy. It was understood that the peasants would only sell food if there was something for them to buy.

It is easy to over-emphasise the capitalistic aspects of the NEP. Indeed, some contemporary European observers saw the situation as the beginning of the end of communism. However, it was only meant to be a short-term solution to get the economy running again. Lenin compared it to the necessary costs of Brest-Litovsk and said it was a policy that was required to reap the benefits later on. Zinoviev, a leading member of the **Politburo**, called it 'a temporary deviation, a tactical retreat'. Nevertheless, it took a lot of passionate debate to get the Politburo agreed on the policy. The scale of unrest in all areas of Russia convinced the upper echelons of the Party to endorse the NEP, as long as it was a temporary measure – though they were vague about what 'temporary' meant, with figures of around a decade not uncommon.

KEY TERM

Politburo
A small group of Bolshevik/communist leaders, as few as seven in the early years, created in 1917 to provide strong, central and continuous leadership. The Politburo was chosen from members of the Central Committee and in theory both were answerable to the Party Congress. However, in practice, it was the Politiburo that decided policy to be voted on by the Party Congress and therefore was the highest power in Russia. Known as the Presidium from 1952 until 1966, it lasted until the collapse of the Soviet Union in 1991.

How did the NEP affect the lives of the peasants?

The impact of the NEP on towns and the more industrial sectors of the economy is well documented, with profit proving to be a strong incentive for people to create various small-scale businesses. Many of these small market stalls were set up by peasants aiming to sell their produce.

SOURCE

From W. Duranty, *I Write As I Please* (1935). Duranty was a US journalist who was in Moscow at the time of the NEP. Though he was later criticised for his approval of Stalin, his observations on the impact of the NEP in Moscow reflect the reality at the time.

The city was full of peasants selling fruit, vegetables and other produce, or transporting bricks, lumber and building materials in their clumsy, creaking carts. Suddenly goods began to appear from unexpected corners, hidden or hoarded...

One morning at the top of my street I saw a man sitting on the sidewalk selling flour, sugar and rice on a little table... at the end of a week his 'table' had doubled in size and he was selling fresh eggs and vegetables. That was October and by mid-November he had rented a tiny store across the street, handling milk, vegetables, chickens and the freshest eggs and apples in Moscow... By the following May he had four salesmen in a fair-sized store, to which peasants brought fresh produce each morning... In July he added hardware. In October, after a year's trading he sold out... to buy a farm and live independently for the rest of his life... His enterprise stimulated scores of peasants to fatten chickens and little pigs, or plant vegetables, or fashion wooden bowls and platters and forks and spoons and produce clay pots and the rest of the village handcraft. In a single year the supply of food and goods jumped from starvation point to something nearly adequate and prices fell accordingly. This was the rich silt in NEP's flood, whereas the gambling and debauchery were only froth and scum.

The impact on the peasants has been less focused on, as it has been presumed that they simply got on with farming. The NEP can be seen as the removal of the mechanics and apparatus of War Communism rather than the imposition of anything new. Indeed, by 1923, this absence of policy had led to so much food arriving in the cities that prices were forced down, while the price of factory goods was inflated by their scarcity. As the respective prices crossed and then widened, a 'scissors crisis', as Trotsky called it, emerged. This caused some peasants to limit the grain sold to the state to try to raise prices. Instead, they fed it to cattle, stored it or sold it to private traders. The government lowered factory prices in line with food prices, so the crisis quickly passed. Cereal production increased by 23 percent from 1920 to 1923 and, as Source 6 shows, production had returned to nearly 1913 levels by 1926. In general, the agricultural results improved more quickly than the industrial ones, as the industrial base needed to be totally reconstructed after the Civil War years.

ACTIVITY
KNOWLEDGE CHECK

The impact of the NEP

1. Use Source 5 to demonstrate the relationship between cities and countryside at the time of the NEP.
2. Source 5 suggests a rapid development of capitalism. How do you think each of the following would react to reading this source?
   - a peasant
   - Lenin
   - a Party member and veteran of the Civil War.
3. How far did the Party consider the condition of the peasants in the decision to launch the NEP?

SOURCE 6 Agricultural production 1913–26, from Alec Nove, *An Economic History of the USSR* (1969).

	1913	1920	1921	1922	1923	1924	1925	1926
Grain harvest (millions of imperial tons)	80.1	46.1	37.6	50.3	56.6	51.4	72.5	76.8
Sown area (million hectares)	105.0	-	90.3	77.7	91.7	98.1	104.3	110.3

The return of many peasants from urban areas during the Civil War, as well as a population increasing after war and famine, meant the number of farms rose steadily from around 17 million before 1917 to 25 million by 1927, but these were still dominated by the 350,000 *mirs* that favoured strip-farming and avoided modern notions of crop-rotation. Advances that had been made under Stolypin had been lost, with 5.5 million households still using wooden ploughs and half of all grain harvested by sickle or scythe. Herein lay a problem for the government, in that the flag symbolised an alliance between workers and peasants. This union, known as *smychka*, needed the peasants to work for the benefit of the state. Despite the use of War Communism, the peasants had in general stuck with the Reds, as they felt that this gave them the best chance of retaining the land they had gained in 1917. To Lenin, it was important that the NEP kept the peasantry on the same side as the communist authorities.

Soviet officials, examining the period of the NEP, classified the peasants into four groups in descending quantities of wealth: the *kulak*, the middle peasant, the poor peasant and the landless labourer, though in reality each group widely overlapped the next. Many landless peasants actually owned some land but also needed to work on other peasants' land to get enough income to survive. Many middle peasants were in fact too poor to own a horse. Any peasant household that owned a couple of horses and cows and produced enough to eat could find themselves classified as *kulaks*. These groups were more about the Soviet authorities trying to create class warfare and enemies to unite against, than a reflection of rural reality. The *kulaks* were considered to make up five to seven percent of the peasantry, and it is true that their situation meant that their land or machinery could be hired out, or their food stockpiled to get a better price. The communist regime hoped that this would provoke jealousy among the other peasants and they used propaganda to this effect. However, the other peasants were as likely to aspire to be that *kulak*, even if it meant becoming part of a cursed class in the eyes of the authorities.

These more commercially-minded peasants provided the increased food production to feed the cities. Before 1917, the *kulaks* had produced 71 percent of the grain that went to market and Lenin, despite his actions against them in the Civil War, now realised the need to treat the peasants carefully and use a policy of co-operation and gradual mechanisation to enlighten them on the benefits of communism. In a 1924 speech honouring the recently deceased Lenin, the head of the State Publishing House, Meshcheryakov, asserted that Lenin had said that it was foolish to use coercion in relation to the peasantry and that persuasion was the only way to go. Though Lenin had hardly followed this road with War Communism, he hoped that the NEP would create a loyal class. The ideological power of communism would be equated with power of the tractor as it out-performed the traditional horse.

The state had some success in getting farmers to work in agricultural co-operatives where the state could promote newer farming techniques. Lenin had hoped this would be a first step towards a wider collectivisation of farms. By 1927, half of farms were in co-operatives or TOVs (loose producers' co-operatives). A TOV was a basic type of collective in which facilities and equipment were shared. Productivity increased, with yields rising by 17 percent from 1900 levels. But these small collectives were just adaptations that the *mir* integrated into its structure. It did not allow the state control that many communists wanted.

The traditional *mir* was far more dominant in the lives of the peasants than any Party-controlled organisation, such as the rural soviet. The Land Decree may have technically given the land to the peasants, but it was the *mir* that had taken it. The authorities had shocked the peasants with their actions during the Civil War, and there was an absolute lack of trust between the state and the *mir*. The Government reaction to the 1921 unrest demonstrated the true extent of co-operation in the early days of the NEP.

If the most serious peasant revolt was Tambov, then Tambov also highlights the approach of the state. As the NEP was beginning to take hold, the region was flooded with Red Army troops, freed up by the defeat of the Whites. During the summer of 1921, over 100,000 elite communist troops under Tukhachevsky, who had crushed the Kronstadt Mutiny, attacked rebel forces. Bombs, propaganda and poison gas were fired from guns and dropped by the air force to root out rebels. Fifty thousand peasants, including over 1,000 children, were put into new concentration camps. Whole village populations were shot or exiled to the Arctic as their villages burned. By the end of 1921, some 15,000 people were executed and 100,000 imprisoned or deported. It is no wonder the *mir* had little faith in the state. In the Ukraine, the Green leader Makhno allied himself with the communists to defeat the Whites, only to be crushed by the Red Army after the Civil War, though Makhno escaped to Romania.

The previous three years of terror and repression had left many scars. Bukharin, an up-and-coming Politburo member and economist, had remarked in 1921 that the government was making economic allowances to avoid any political ones. Nowhere was this as true as with the political repression of peasant unrest at the start of the NEP.

Part of the problem was that the victorious Bolsheviks failed to understand the countryside and felt threatened by it. The smallholding-based traditional *mir* had been strengthened by the consequences of the 1917 revolutions, while the Bolsheviks' urban and industrial powerbase had been largely wiped out by civil war. The force of peasant numbers cast an uneasy shadow in the minds of the Bolsheviks. If the NEP was to be temporary, the need to promote co-operation with the peasants must also be temporary.

Some improvements in living standards can be attributed to the NEP. Lenin's programme of electrification, which he saw as the basis for a modern communist society, brought power to peasant homes for the first time by 1927. Lenin hoped light bulbs would literally replace the light of faith in the peasants' lives. Hospitals, theatres and libraries began to appear. Some aspects of technological farming did filter down to the communes as dairy farming modernised and peasants experimented with more diverse market crops. Literacy rates continued to grow, most noticeably among younger peasants. By 1926, over half the population was literate, and over half were under 20.

SOURCE 7 The first electric light in the village, named 'Little Ilich-Light' by the peasants. Taken by an unknown photographer in 1925.

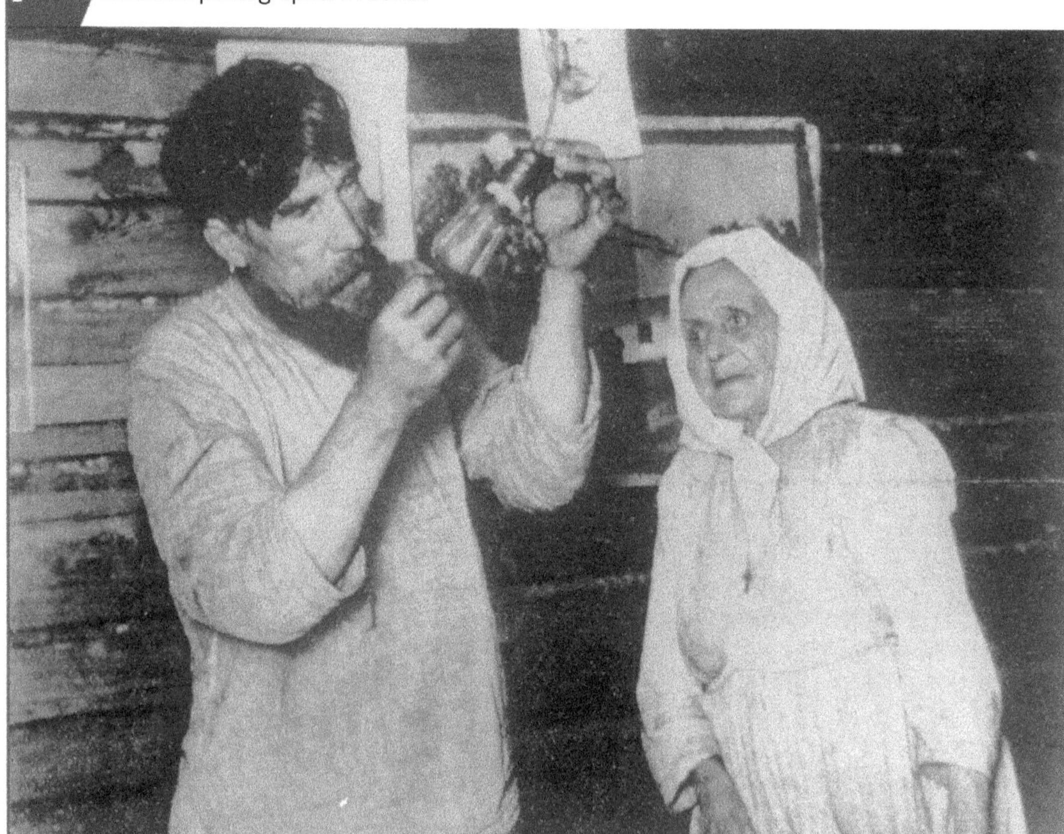

The generational gap that occurred in the *mir* during the NEP years provided an opportunity for the state to exploit. While the Party organisation floundered in the countryside, the ***Komsomol*** (a communist youth league) grew rapidly from 80,000 rural members in 1922 to over 500,000 by 1925 (three times the number of rural Party members). Though they took part in state campaigns against the rural Church and vocalised their despair at the elderly, most were young people who wanted to leave the rural life rather than stay and transform it. Many were ex-soldiers, who had seen the world and been tempted by its delights. These would only return, and with more troops, when it was Stalin's turn to take on the *mir*.

KEY TERM

Komsomol
A communist youth organisation, set up in 1918 for 14-28-year-olds, and seen as an important step in a career in the Communist Party. Stalin used these idealistic activists to implement Party policy and wage class war in areas such as the Church, education, shock brigades and the countryside, particularly in the period 1928-32, known as the Cultural Revolution. Sometimes their zeal and enthusiasm went further than even Stalin wanted, and their actions were subsequently reined back.

ACTIVITY
KNOWLEDGE CHECK

NEP results

1 How would you summarise the figures in Source 6? Make sure you note the impact of the famine.

2 How does Source 7 illustrate Lenin's maxim that 'Soviet power plus electrification equals communism'?

3 List all the problems created by War Communism. Think about the social, economic and political aspects. To what extent did the NEP solve these problems?

4 How would you compare and contrast a typical peasant of 1914 with one in 1927?

Collectivisation, 1928-32

How collectivisation came about

The decision to end the NEP was not based solely on economic reasons. In a summary of its impact, it would be fair to give a positive verdict. The peasants were growing more food, while the cities were producing more goods. Crises were dealt with and the worst excesses of the *kulaks* and *nepmen* (individuals who financially profited from the NEP), which so annoyed the Party faithful, were regularly restricted.

The Soviet leadership argued over extending the NEP. Bukharin warned that its premature end would create war with the peasantry; he felt the *mir* would allow change in its own time. Trotsky insisted that stricter requisitioning was the only way to guarantee the grain needed for export, and that the peasants should be forced into collective farming. This may have started as a debate about the pace of industrialisation, but it turned into an argument that was wrapped up in a fierce leadership struggle.

Lenin had died in 1924 without leaving clear instructions about his successor. The NEP, seen as part of Lenin's glorious legacy, was safe for a couple of years, but then it became the central issue in the fight for the leadership of the Party. Members of the Politburo made alliances, some determined to keep it, others to halt it immediately. To begin with, Stalin leaned towards the pro-NEP in order to build up support to counter anti-NEP politicians like Trotsky. On their removal by 1927, he immediately turned against the NEP, claiming that it and the peasants were a barrier to the desired change.

EXTEND YOUR KNOWLEDGE

Joseph Stalin (1879-1953)

Leader of the USSR from 1929 until his death, Stalin, meaning the 'man of steel', had a reputation for an extremely ruthless approach to rule. This was not helped by a paranoid personality that saw potential threats everywhere. As the focus of a cult of personality and the driving force behind a regime of terror, he faced very little opposition to his rule.

Stalin portrayed any affiliation to the NEP as a betrayal of the revolution, while he was presented as its saviour. The NEP was torn down in a bitter storm of violent language. The shortage of grain in 1927 was branded a *kulak* strike and an attempt to destroy the revolution. Stalin used the language of war in his class struggle 'to root out and crush the opposition of the exploiters'. To help him fight this battle, in which the economy was the weapon, Stalin stirred up the *Komsomol*. They had been too young to participate in storming the Winter Palace, or in the wars with the Whites, but were the perfect age for the next stage of revolutionary war against the capitalistic products of the NEP machine.

Stalin urged speed in ending the NEP, telling the country that 'We must make good this distance in ten years. Either we do it or we shall be crushed'. In short, to continue the NEP would be a concession to the enemy, even treasonous. The same would soon be said for those who opposed Stalin.

The economic decision to end the NEP was part of the justification for the shift in policy. The real reason was to further consolidate Stalin's power. The status of the peasants was merely one factor in a much wider game that Stalin was playing to win absolute power.

EXTEND YOUR KNOWLEDGE

The switch from rural to urban economy

There comes a time in the modernisation of a nation when the power underpinning the state swings from the rural economy to the urban industrial economy. In most European countries, this had been a gradual process. In Britain it began around 1750 with agricultural enclosure and the development of farming technology, leading unemployed farm labourers to seek work and higher wages in the labour-intensive urban mills and factories. Within a century, the cities ruled the nation, and the countryside existed merely as a producer of food. A poor harvest could be covered with grain imports bought with industrial profits. This was not a trouble-free process. Rural Swing riots and the Luddite factory disturbances in the early 19th century voiced the desperate plight of the workers, while the squalid living conditions and working practices of the textile mills led Marx to dream communism as an alternative. If the suffering that prompted Marx's work were the result of 100 years of change, what horrors would Stalin's decade conceive?

A taste of what was to come was launched in 1928 with Article 107 of the Criminal Code – a return to the techniques of War Communism. It was named the Ural-Siberian method, after the areas where it was first introduced. It involved quotas based on the class of peasants in a village: *kulaks* were expected to provide more grain. Resistance saw the quota multiplied by five; further resistance saw a year in a labour camp, or two years plus internal exile if the resistance was performed as part of a group. In March 1929, the Politburo approved the method and it quickly spread. The peasants' reaction can be seen by the 12,800 arrests on counter-revolutionary charges and another 15,500 on economic charges by November 1929, according to OGPU, as the secret police was now named. By December 1929, collectivisation was rolled out on a mass scale in time for the next spring's sowing.

The types of collectivised farms

It is important to see the mass collectivisation of the peasant farms as part of a dual approach to modernise Russia along with the massive increase in industrialisation. Though the focus here will be on the countryside, the cities also underwent a fundamental social transformation. The scale of planning and obsession with targets, which seemed to grow as anyone approached them, demonstrated the penetration of the state into every aspect of the lives of Russian citizens. Much of this was coerced, and the living and working conditions of factory workers were appalling. However, this industrialisation relied on a constant flood of labour from the countryside, and it is fair to assume that these labourers were fleeing the countryside rather than being pulled to the city. The workers also needed to be fed by grain from the countryside, and the surplus sold to provide investment to kick-start the industrial growth. To achieve this, Stalin was prepared to pay any cost, and indeed felt the extreme and inhumane cost would give him a political advantage. It is tempting to see the peasants on the collectivised farms as returned to their status before emancipation, a form of neo-serfdom, but it was much worse than life under the tsars. As serfs, the peasants at least had the local cohesion offered by the *mir*. Stalin broke the *mir* and enslaved the peasants who managed to survive.

The basic purpose of the collectivised farms was to provide food to the state at the lowest prices. There were three main types of collectivised farms by 1929.

- The TOV had grown in the later years of the NEP. These consisted of land individually owned by peasants who worked it together to share machinery and labour. These tended to be favoured by the peasants.
- In the *kolkhozy*, land, machinery and livestock were held by a group of 50–100 households and farmed collectively under the direction of the farm committee. Each household also had a private plot of land to grow vegetables and keep a number of animals.
- The *sovkhozy* were owned and run by the state. The peasants were merely paid a wage. These were often on a much larger scale, but had been largely neglected during the years of the NEP.

The state wanted to focus on creating *sovkhozy*, but it quickly became apparent that at this early stage it would be more efficient to create an agricultural infrastructure based on *kolkhozy*. Stalin's directives therefore focused on a single form of organisation which was obligatory and took no account of the variations in local conditions and environments that had played a fundamental role in previous agricultural developments. The ultimate socialist goal was to build large **agrotowns**. The co-operative and contented workforce would no longer need private plots or the security of the *mir*. Stalin was aware that this re-engineering of rural society would require considerable force.

KEY TERM

Agrotown (*agrogorod*)

Soviet planners and agricultural experts dreamed of huge agrotowns with collective fields and pastures. The workers (rather than traditional peasants) would live in tower blocks in a central town and be bussed out to the farms. The towns would have independent communist amenities and facilities, including schools, hospitals and communal apartments. Children would be raised communally. This ideal never saw the investment, or peasant desire, to get off the ground.

The first Five-Year Plan, to run from 1928 to 1933 (it was not only retroactive, but also planned to finish early, hence lasting only four years), announced a forecast for 15 percent of farms to be run collectively from a base of only 1 percent in 1928. There was a desire to persuade the peasants to join up, supported by an intensive propaganda campaign promising 100,000 tractors and pieces of machinery by 1933. The lure of the US Fordson tractor in particular was a popular incentive. However, the fear of a repeat of the 1927–28 grain shortage and its corresponding rationing, the fierce peasant resistance as a result of the initial collectivisation in the east and a lack of any tractors to fulfil the propaganda, meant voluntary participation rapidly became forced and expanded. The 15 percent target was reached by December 1929, at which point Stalin, against all expert advice, demanded mass collectivisation and, by February 1930, over 11 million households joined collectivised farms, pushing the total to a staggering 58 percent almost overnight (about 60 million peasants). To achieve this, Stalin declared the policy to dissolve the *kulak* class and generate such a climate of submissive fear that the middle peasants would do exactly as they were asked.

On paper, to reach nearly 60 percent collectivisation in just a few weeks over the oppressive Russian winter is a remarkable achievement, especially when relatively unplanned and ill provided for. The typical method would be to integrate force, terror and propaganda with an emphasis on whatever factor was required in the local circumstances. Urban activists, known as the 'Twenty-five Thousanders' were sent into the countryside to get the peasants to sign a register to call for their own collectivisation. These enthusiasts were anxious to join the revolutionary struggle and were extensively trained in class warfare, but were given only the briefest course in farm management. Shock brigades, OGPU, *Komsomol* and military support accompanied them to force the signatures, and each region was given a quota of *kulaks* to identify under any circumstances. Using the rhetoric of class war, the peasants could take any machines, land, property or livestock off the accused *kulak* to use in the new collective, and another village could duly be labelled collectivised. On paper, it was a stunning success, but the reality was a disaster in every respect.

SOURCE 8

Vasily Grossman describing how the activists would be enthused with class-hatred in order to catch and deal with kulaks. He later became the leading Soviet writer on the German Holocaust. This is from his book, *Forever Flowering* (1972).

They would threaten people with guns, as if under a spell, calling small children 'kulak bastards', screaming 'bloodsuckers!'... They had sold themselves on the idea that the so-called 'kulaks' were pariahs, untouchables, vermin. They would not sit down at a 'parasite's' table; the 'kulak' child was loathsome, the young 'kulak' girl was lower than a louse. They looked on the so-called 'kulaks' as cattle, swine, loathsome, repulsive: they had no souls; they stank; they all had venereal disease; they were enemies of the people and exploited the labour of others... And there was no pity for them. They were not human beings; one had a hard time making out what they were - vermin, evidently.

Reasons for the failure of the collectivised farms

Many local Party officials realised the impracticality of collectivisation. They understood the value of the *kulaks* as successful farmers to the community as a whole. Many middle or poor peasants likewise saw the contribution of the *kulaks* who had helped them get through difficult times or hired their labour to supplement their income. Even an unpopular *kulak* was part of the *mir*, a much stronger bond than any state-imposed organisation. Many *kulaks* rapidly shared out their property to disguise themselves as middle peasants. However, if the local Party officials were perhaps unwilling, the Twenty-five Thousanders made up for their lack of agricultural knowledge with an expertise in igniting class-hatred. While some poor peasants did denounce the *kulaks* in an attempt to gain their property or take revenge for a previous grievance, it was the urban activists who rooted out the desired number of *kulaks*. In January 1930, the government issued targets of 60,000 *kulaks* to be sent to labour camps and 150,000 to be sent into exile. OGPU then raised the targets to around five percent of peasant households. This was an order in which many activists sought to exceed their target.

The term *kulak* was soon extended to anyone who opposed the process, and backed by a decree in February 1930 which allowed the use of any necessary measures required. The aftermath witnessed entire villages removed and placed on trains or carts to be deported, and many did not survive the journey. Often the head of the household would be shot before the remaining family were expelled. The exact number of the exiled is impossible to calculate as many of the dead, particularly the young, were not recorded. A minimum of a million families, or six million individuals, were transported, but recent estimates suggest that it could be as high as an eighth of all peasants (around 15 million).

To begin with, the peasants tried to oppose collectivisation by attending meetings or writing letters, but this quickly turned to violence against Party activists and *kolkhoz* officials. Others turned to sabotage and deliberately slaughtered their own livestock and burned down their property, preferring the flames to claim it than the state. The number of cattle and pigs halved between 1928 and 1932, while sheep fell by two-thirds. Raids were attempted to recapture requisitioned grain, but any resistance was met with proportionately worse violence by Red Army troops and OGPU agents. Another 700,000 peasants were involved in riots and disturbances at the start of 1930 but, because they were largely confined to local areas, there was no general revolt against the system. Between 1929 and 1930, OGPU recorded 44,779 individual episodes of rural unrest. The speed of collectivisation over the winter of 1929–30 meant that the peasants' prime motivation was survival rather than political resistance.

Peasant women were often the most effective at resisting central policy. The communal aspects of collectivisation led to rumours that women would lose their children to the state crèches, their hair would be shaved to be more urban and 'worker-like', while they would also be forced into wife-sharing and sleep under the 'common blanket' (a 700-metre communal bed for the entire workforce of the farm). This gave women the motive, or the excuse, to hinder collectivisation where possible, especially as Party officials would often punish them less harshly because of their perception of peasant women as backward and illiterate. After a riot in the village of Belovka resulted in the burning of a Soviet building and the beating of officials, only the men were deemed responsible.

The Russian Orthodox Church, an anchor to the traditional faith and power of the *mir*, also helped resist the process of collectivisation. Soviet power began to be associated with the anti-Christ and the collective farm as 'the devil's mark'. Mass-collectivisation was clearly about more than economic productivity: it was a battle for the soul of the peasants. The state was relentless and, as households were forced into collectives, churches were also closed and turned into Party buildings.

Though levels of resistance were not a real threat to communist power and policy, they did threaten grain production. The most experienced and valuable peasants had been removed or killed, while over a quarter of livestock was slaughtered and mainly eaten by the peasants to spite the Party. By March 1930, it seemed unlikely that the peasants would begin sowing the seeds for a crop they would have no claim to. It was in these circumstances that Stalin wrote the article 'Dizzy with Success' in *Pravda*, the state communist newspaper, blaming local officials for taking the process too far, too quickly.

SOURCE 9

A Soviet propaganda poster from 1930. The slogan says, 'There is no room in our collective farm for priests and kulaks'. It was designed by Nikolai Mikhailov.

SOURCE

An extract from Stalin's 'Dizzy with Success' article in *Pravda*, No. 60, 2 March 1930. *Pravda* was the official newspaper of the Communist Party and was widely available and read.

By 20 February 1930 we had over-fulfilled the five-year plan for collectivization by more than 100 per cent... a tremendous achievement... but successes have their dark side, especially when they are achieved with relative 'ease' - 'unexpectedly' as it were. Such successes sometimes induce a spirit of conceit and vanity... people not infrequently become intoxicated by this kind of success...

They could have arisen only because some of our comrades have become dizzy with success and for the moment have lost clearness of mind and sobriety of vision. To correct the line of our work in the sphere of collective-farm development, we must put an end to these sentiments.

Stalin, like the tsars before him, was deflecting the blame away from the 'little father' at the top and towards the zealous local officials blindly drunk on ambition and unable to see the harm they were doing. By ridiculing the implementation of his own policy, Stalin hoped to get the peasants back on board and planting crops. Many peasants saw the article as the end of the policy and returned to their old methods, so by June 1930 the rate of collectivisation had fallen by over half to 24 percent. Stalin was accurate in stating that many officials competed with each other to meet their targets for collectivisation, and this resulted in staggering acts of inhumanity. It is also true that a practical lack of control meant that central government simply allowed the process to occur with a local dynamic. But it would be a serious mistake to read Stalin's posturing and insincere statements as evidence of his empathy with his people. The acknowledgement of the necessity of private plots and the suspension of the drive to the utopian communal agrotowns was merely stating the reality on the ground. The call for moderation was temporary and, once the roots of the new season's crop had taken hold, forced collectivisation began again, though at a less hasty pace. OGPU prepared 1,000 camps, each designed to hold 300 households, deep in the north as well as in remote parts of Kazakhstan. In September, a new target of 80 percent by the end of 1931 was announced and mass-collectivisation with all its associated horrors began anew.

The famine of 1932–33

The result of the '**dekulakisation**' of the countryside was famine in the years 1932–34. The urban activists' zeal was matched by their incompetence. There were not enough animals left to pull the ploughs, and the promised tractors were yet to be built. Excellent weather conditions had sustained good harvests in 1928–30, but a drought in 1931 saw grain production drop sharply.

KEY TERM

Dekulakisation
The process of removing any peasant who opposed Stalin's mass-collectivisation policy in the 1930s, as millions were 'liquidated'.

The famine was man-made and, some argued, deliberate. Despite the drop in grain production, the state procurements taken increased from 10.8 million tons in 1929 to 22.8 million tons by the end of 1931. This was enough to adequately feed the workers in the cities and export grain for profit abroad, but it left the peasants to starve. Indeed, even at the height of famine, around 1.7 million tons of grain were exported in 1932 and only slightly less in 1933. On 7 August 1932, a law was passed giving a ten-year sentence for stealing any grain, even a few ears of wheat. It was known as the Law of Seventh-Eights (because of the day it was passed) or the Five Stalks Law (after the amount needed to be classed as criminal), and the punishment was quickly increased to execution.

The scale of famine is hard to calculate because it was denied by the government and therefore, unlike 1921, there was no international aid, despite bumper crops in Europe and the USA. Some calculate the deaths from starvation and disease as 8.5 million, though other figures are lower.

The key areas affected by the famine were the Ukraine, North Caucasus and Kazakhstan, but all rural areas experienced severe food shortages. Unsurprisingly, many peasants fled to the cities, which grew by 50,000 every week between 1928 and 1932. In the years 1929–41, over 18.5 million made the journey. This put further strain on urban areas, as disease and food supplies worsened, resulting in a population floating from town to town to find food but avoiding the country. The reduction in the number of peasants on the farms likewise put pressure on the new collective farms to find labourers to work the fields. The solution was to impose internal passports to restrict movement.

EXTEND YOUR KNOWLEDGE

Holodomor – a Ukrainian genocide?

Some historians, such as Robert Conquest in *Harvest of Sorrow*, believe the Ukraine was singled out for special treatment because of Stalin's mistrust of the Ukraine over its nationalism and resistance to collectivisation.

Ukraine was known as the 'breadbasket' of Europe, and the state procurements for the region were excessive, despite falling production. Thousands of extra officials and military units were sent into the area to requisition grain, and Conquest claims that much of the grain they collected was left rotting while the people starved. Therefore, the famine was used to impose terror and obedience on the survivors, while removing most of the perceived troublemakers. Lazar Kaganovich, who oversaw the process in the Ukraine, believed that a few thousand deaths would teach those who remained to comprehend the power of the state. This deliberate famine, known as *holodomor*, is widely recognised by the Ukrainian government and the United Nations.

While it is true that the famine hit the area particularly hard and the communist authorities did very little to prevent the deaths or provide relief – even restricting any migration out of the area – there is little hard evidence to prove that it was a deliberate policy on Stalin's part, though it was clearly a man-made disaster. Soviet documents released after the collapse of the USSR in 1991 reveal a death toll of over 1.5 million, considerably higher than previously available Soviet figures, but far lower than other recent estimates, which range from 2.4 million to 7.5 million. The debate is not over the existence of famine, but over whether the Ukraine was targeted for special treatment, especially as other areas like Kazakhstan suffered in equal measure. Modern conflicts and disputes have coloured arguments from both sides.

EXTRACT

From *The Harvest of Sorrow* (1986). Robert Conquest is describing the aftermath of the deportation of the entire town of Briukhovetska, in the Armavir area, which formerly had 20,000 inhabitants. After an attempted uprising was put down by the Red Army, nearly all the survivors were removed except for the odd old couple. Conquest quotes the experience of a soldier as he enters a wrecked house months later.

'In the half a minute that I spent there I saw two human corpses. An old woman sat on the floor, her gray unkempt head on her chest. She was leaning against the bed, her legs were wide spread. Her dead arms were crossed on her chest. She died just like that, gave up her soul to God without uncrossing them. An old yellow arm extended from the bed and rested on the gray head of the woman. On the bed I could see a body of an old man in a home-woven shirt and pants. The bare soles of his feet stuck over the edge of the bed and I could see that these old feet had walked far on earth. I could not see the face of the old man, it was turned to the wall...

But there was, after all, one live inhabitant. A naked man with long hair and beard was fighting with some cats under an acacia, for possession of a dead pigeon. He had gone mad, but the soldier was able to piece together his story. He had been a Communist, and was Chairman of the local Soviet; but when collectivization came he had torn up his Party card and joined the rebels. Most of them had been killed but he had managed to hide in the malarial swamps among the Kuban's clouds of mosquitoes. His wife and children had been among the deported. He had somehow lived through the winter, and then returned to his old home – the last inhabitant of what had once been a large and flourishing settlement.'

During the 1930s, collectivisation became fully implemented into Russian agriculture, with around 70 percent of farms collectivised into *kolkhozy* by 1934, rising to 97 percent by 1940. The typical *kolkhoz* was defined by the 1935 Model Collective Farm Charter, which granted the use, though not ownership, of land for communal cereal crop production. Each household was allowed an acre plot where the few animals were kept. In theory, each peasant was credited with 'workdays' in exchange for their work on the collective farms. At the end of the year, the profits would be divided according to the number of earned 'workdays'. In reality, the deliberately low prices meant that no farm made any profits. The peasants received no wages and were as tied to the land as they had been as serfs.

While the model farms shown to the outside world might have new buildings, processing plants and communal facilities, the vast majority made do with existing buildings in various stages of ruin. The farm's chairman, usually from outside the area and rapidly replaced as the farm failed to meet targets, knew little of the technical aspects of farming. In the first five years of mass-collectivisation, the tractors were not delivered and yet the only new building was likely to be the Motor and Tractor Station (MTS). In theory, these were set up to hire out machines to the peasants, but actually they contained a political department to supervise the peasants, root out troublemakers and guarantee the maximum state procurement from the *kolkhoz*.

SOURCE 11 A photo showing a piece of propaganda called 'First Tractor', which aimed to show the joy of mechanisation during the early days of collectivisation.

SOURCE 12 Orphaned children from the famine caused by collectivisation.

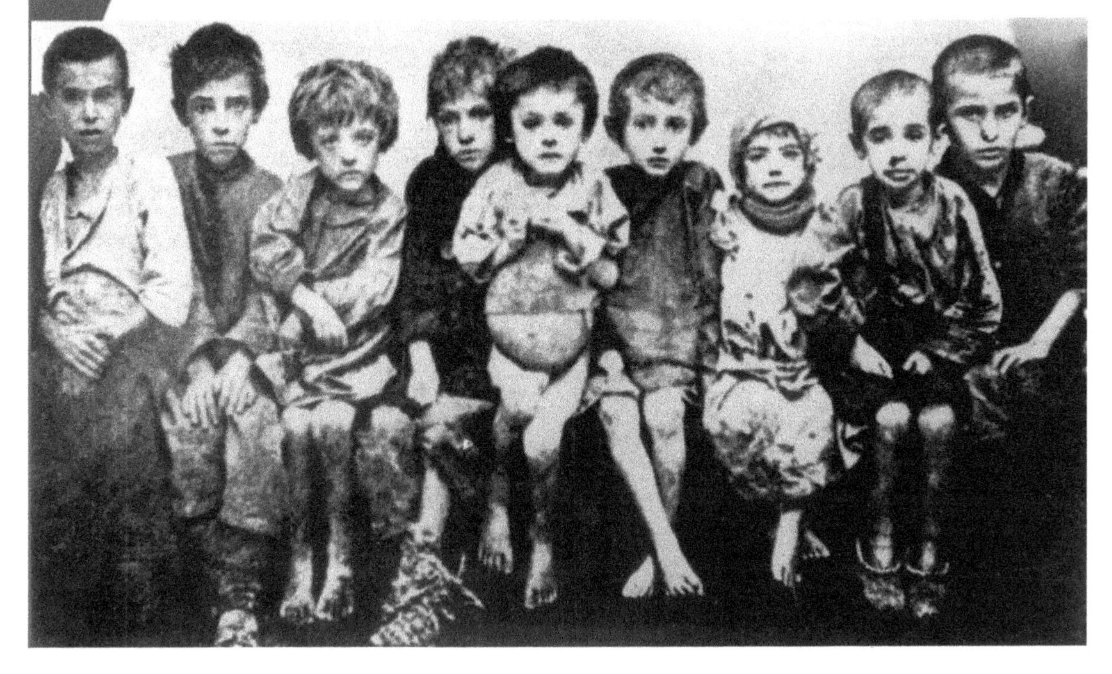

The grain quota was always excessive, and this was made worse in 1933 when 'biological yields' were introduced, based on the potential output of a fully-planted field. Theft, wastage and loss might reduce output by 20–30 percent and this, plus any failure in the harvest, had to be borne by the peasants.

For collectivised peasants in the early 1930s, life had changed completely. Famine and deportation had removed millions, while those who were left experienced a genuine fear of the state and deep-rooted apathy within the workplace. The *kolkhoz* became the state-sponsored community centre for the peasants, as the *mir* was abolished by decree in July 1930. Collectivisation had delivered food for industrialisation and Party control of the countryside.

During the Second World War, Stalin had confided to Winston Churchill that the atrocities of collectivisation had frightened him almost to breaking point, but he failed to mention the peasants' fear. It was the peasants who were broken, which of course was exactly the intention, as their needs were sacrificed for those of the cities. Stalin was seen by the Party as the only person able to dominate the peasants. The *smychka* (see page 23), even if it had only existed in wishful theory, was gone.

It was no surprise that when the Germans finally invaded in 1941, many of the peasants applauded the Nazis as liberators. It was an action that few peasants would live long enough to be able to regret.

The concession of peasant plots, 1932

The one aspect of a peasant's life where they could retain a sense of their connection to the earth was in the private plot. Stalin had been reluctant to allow the concession, but the fierce resistance that he slyly acknowledged in 'Dizzy with Success' meant some concession was required. Since 1932, when the plot was first allowed, it had become the only area where the peasants had a real incentive to work. As they received no financial wages to speak of, the food grown on the private plots was an important way to supplement their diet. The 1935 Model Collective Farm Charter, after much Party debate, confirmed what was allowed. The size was around an acre but in exceptional circumstances could be nearly two and a half acres. Livestock was fixed at a single cow, two young cattle, a pig with offspring, up to ten sheep or goats, unlimited poultry and rabbits and up to 20 beehives. The plots soon became the chief source of many products sold in the cities, such as milk, butter, eggs, honey, wool and meat, as well as fruit and vegetables.

Though the Party instinctively distrusted the private plots and resented the apathy for work on the *kolkhoz* compared to the enthusiastic farming on the profitable private plot, the plots were tolerated as they provided much-needed food. Stricter laws, such as that passed in 1939, which required more workdays on the *kolkhoz*, had little effect on the balance of production. The plots were restricted in size in 1939, but grew again due to the need for food during the Second World War, only to be curtailed afterwards. The relationship between the state and the private plot was tense. However, with the overwhelming focus on cereal production in the collective, the plots were essential. They should not be seen as a reward for the peasants, an attempt to make up for the brutality of the period. In 1932, stealing a handful of grain was punishable by death, while the same year saw the peak of the terror against the *kulaks* and the height of the famine. The private plots were necessary to prevent food shortages destroying the urban supplies as well as those of the peasants, so were often encouraged in times of crisis. By 1940, they made up about 3.5 percent of cultivated land. It is estimated that, by 1952, the cash a peasant earned from collective farming was only a quarter of that earned from their private plot, which was their only opportunity to subvert the process of collectivisation.

ACTIVITY
KNOWLEDGE CHECK

Collectivisation

1 Give a brief argument to justify the use of collectivisation under the following headings:

   a) to create a powerful communist country

   b) to further Stalin's power

   c) to represent the will of the people

   d) to protect the USSR from foreign invasion.

   Which one do you find the most convincing?

2 Using Source 8 and your own knowledge, explain why the Party activists were trained to this extent in 'class warfare'.

3 Were the actions described in the text and Source 8 necessary for collectivisation to succeed?

4 How does Extract 4 show both opposition to, and the process of, collectivisation in the early 1930s?

5 How does Extract 4 demonstrate Stalin's aims in the collectivisation programme?

6 Look at the economic, social and political impact of collectivisation. To what extent can it be seen as 'brutal but necessary'?

7 How would you compare and contrast a typical peasant of 1927 with one from 1932?

8 Using Sources 11 and 12 and your own knowledge, say how far the collectivisation of agriculture 1928-32 represented a break with the past.

9 Did the use of private plots show the failure of collectivisation and therefore of the ideology behind it?

The increase in *sovkhozy* at the expense of the *kolkhozy* after 1945

During the Second World War, the state was forced to make some concessions in order to provide food. Restrictions were lifted on the private plots and in some areas a 'link' system developed, in which officials gave responsibilities to small groups of peasants within the collective farm as an incentive to grow more. The changes helped to increase production enough to survive the war, but weakened the structure of collective agriculture. Therefore, after victory in 1945, Stalin began an economic reconstruction which reversed any of the small gains the peasants may have had. The link system was abolished, the powers of the MTS increased as an agency for government control and taxes were raised on the private plots, along with other restrictions intended to reduce their importance. Taxes on collective farms rose by a third in the years 1946–48. A drought in 1946 exacerbated the situation and brought famine, in which perhaps 100 million people went hungry and a million died of starvation and disease, particularly, and predictably, in parts of the Ukraine.

In this stagnant climate of post-war Russia, Stalin brought in the self-proclaimed expertise of Khrushchev to solve the problems of the collective farms. Khrushchev had been the first Party secretary for the Ukraine after the war, and Stalin made him secretary to the general committee with a brief to apply the agricultural knowledge he had acquired in the Ukraine. His initial plans for grand agrotowns failed and he was attacked in *Pravda*, but he continued to push for larger farm units. After Stalin's death in 1953, Khrushchev's forceful personality enabled him to claim the leadership in 1956, and he made a blistering attack on Stalin's policies, character and legacy in the 'Secret Speech'. He was now in a position to try his own policies and see what the 'wise peasant' could achieve.

SOURCE 13

From Khrushchev's speech to the Twentieth Party Congress on 25 February 1956. The speech became known as the 'Secret Speech' and attacked every aspect of Stalin's rule. This extract addresses the state of agriculture in the USSR since the end of the Second World War. Khrushchev was talking to a closed session of Party delegates.

All those who interested themselves even a little in the national situation saw the difficult situation in agriculture, but Stalin never even noted it. Did we tell Stalin about this? Yes, we told him, but he did not support us. Why? Because Stalin never travelled anywhere, did not meet city and *kolkhoz* workers. He did not know the actual situation in the provinces.

He knew the country and agriculture only from films. And these films dressed up and beautified the existing situation in agriculture. Many films pictured *kolkhoz* life such that tables groaned from the weight of turkeys and geese. Evidently, Stalin thought that it was actually so...

ACTIVITY
KNOWLEDGE CHECK

Khrushchev

Using Source 13 and your own knowledge, list the arguments Khrushchev gives to explain the failure of agriculture under Stalin.

EXTEND YOUR KNOWLEDGE

Nikita Sergeyevich Khrushchev (1894-1971)
Ruler of the USSR from 1956 until he was replaced in 1964, Khrushchev rose to prominence under Stalin, though he attacked Stalin's legacy in 1956 as he assumed leadership after a three-year struggle. He implemented some more liberal reforms domestically, but these were often ineffective. His erratic approach and failure at a domestic and international level, such as the Cuban Missile Crisis, led to his removal in 1964. He was quietly pensioned off until his death in 1971.

The *kolkhozy* had consistently failed to deliver what the government had expected, and Khrushchev could not resist the temptation to worry at the problem. This led to increasingly complicated solutions, which Khrushchev amended with a multitude of agricultural organisations.

The first programme was to continue the amalgamation of *kolkhozy* into larger farms. This process had started earlier and reduced their number from 250,000 to 124,000 in just a year from 1949 to 1950, and they would halve in number again by 1960. It was taken almost as an act of faith that the larger the farm, the larger the efficiency and yield. One *kolkhoz*, 'Gigant', was created from 84 single collectives and covered 333,000 acres. The logic was that this would not just improve the farm economically but would also increase the Party's political control. The smaller *kolkhozy* did not have enough Party members living in them to form a Primary Party Organisation (PPO), which was the smallest unit of the Party organisation. By combining the farms into larger units, there would be enough members to form a PPO and therefore strengthen the hold of the Party over the peasants from within the farm, as well as reducing the number of farms to actually control.

Khrushchev then aimed to further the Party's control of the management system, and attempted to replicate Stalin's Twenty-five Thousanders (see page 27). Out of 100,000 volunteers, some 32,000 were selected to be sent out to the farms, mostly as chairmen. Khrushchev had now extended his control from both above and below the farm. The process was completed with the decentralisation of Party power away from a regional basis, known as *raikom*, which had externally controlled all the *kolkhozy* in an area. This power was transferred from *raikom* to the individual MTS within a farm, bringing Party control much closer to the means of production with an Instructor Group (IG) set up in each MTS to spread communist dogma throughout the farm. Now the chairman, the IG and the PPO all worked together to control the *kolkhozy* from the inside. Khrushchev re-organised the Ministry of Agriculture to ensure none of his rivals could interfere in agriculture through the state bureaucracy.

However, the IG proved as unpopular as previous attempts to politically coerce the peasants, and under heavy criticism from the Presidium (as the Politburo was then known), Khrushchev dropped the IG in 1957 and the MTS in 1958, with all machinery now purchased by the farms. In 1961, Khrushchev tried again with a State Inspectorate of Procurements to oversee production, while the Ministry of Agriculture was further demoted to just research and replaced with Territorial Production Administrations (TPA), whose complex bureaucracy was a more covert attempt to politically control the farms. When this too ran into difficulty, Khrushchev began planning to purge officials and dismiss departments, but he was overthrown in 1964 before any practical changes could happen.

The trend towards larger farms continued deep into Brezhnev's tenure. By 1967, the *kolkhozy* numbered just over 36,000, with an average of nearly 420 households each. The *sovkhozy*, each being roughly twice the size of a *kolkhoz*, were favoured even more, because of 'the bigger the better' attitude which prevailed, and numbered almost 13,000 by 1967. Any new farm created in this period was nearly always a *sovkhoz*, and some *kolkhozy* were also converted, though the peasants complained bitterly as they found their private plots and their vital livestock reduced to the bare minimum. By 1978, the number of *kolkhozy* had fallen to 26,700, while *sovkhozy* rose to nearly 20,500.

Khrushchev had tried to continue Stalin's policy of establishing political control on the farms and reducing the peasants' status to an ever more subservient level. Like Stalin, he did not succeed and the policy had negative effects on production. The peasants, despite the suppression and the terror, still proved resilient in the face of external control.

EXTEND YOUR KNOWLEDGE

Leonid Ilich Brezhnev (1906–82)

Brezhnev was leader of the USSR from 1964 until his death in 1982. His rule saw the global influence of the USSR grow considerably, but it also saw economic and social stagnation within the country. He mainly reinforced the policy of increasing collective farms and he offered few initiatives to any agricultural policy.

Reduction of taxes on private plots and peasant households, 1953–54

Khrushchev took a new, and most un-Stalinlike, approach to incentivise the peasants to work harder. A series of measures was introduced to give the collective farms more independence in making decisions and more direct control of their potential profit. Khrushchev was proud of his peasant origins and enjoyed visiting the countryside. Taking the role of an interested country squire, he berated officials, encouraged farm chairmen and chatted to farm labourers in the warm language and manner of the peasants. He offered a broad range of ideas, with the aim of placing decisions at the local level.

- The state began to pay higher prices for their grain. On average, over a wide variety of crops, the prices paid rose by 25 percent between 1953 and 1956, while grain and livestock saw a sixfold rise in the same period. In a revealing use of terminology, the state procurements were rebranded 'state purchases', suggesting a new government relationship with the peasants based on co-operation. Any purchase above the original quota was paid at a significantly increased rate as a bonus to the workers, though after 1957 a single price in the peasant's favour was used to simplify matters.
- Costs of moving produce to market had been paid by the peasants on the farm. These were now reduced: the farm only had to pay for the first 25 km of transport costs, though this was often the highest proportion of the total because of a lack of paved roads around the farm. By the early 1960s, to give impetus to the flagging reforms, the state absorbed all the transportation costs.
- Overall taxes on farming profits were reduced. This resulted in a doubling of the average farm worker's income between 1952 and 1958, though it still lagged way behind industrial workers.
- The bioyields that had inflated the quotas by around 23 percent in the years 1933–37 were no longer used to calculate the potential output per field, leading to more realistic and lower quotas.
- The tax system was reorganised and made simpler, with all arrears cancelled, signalling a fresh start. Taxes were reduced and later abolished on the private plots, while the purchase quota was also removed, giving the peasants greater motivation to work on them. Private plots made up only three percent of land but accounted for 50 percent of a peasant's income, and amounted to 30 percent of all agricultural production. However, as the peasants poured their efforts into their private plots, the collective fields saw less attention. In a typical Khrushchev counter-reform, measures were then taken to apportion more time on the collective fields, such as punishing small crimes and delinquency by cutting the size of the private plot.

The state put loopholes into all its reforms. In good harvests, the quota could be raised, but they could not be lowered in a poor harvest. As with Stalin, the quota system remained and continued to be based on land, rather than the fairer basis of actual sown area. Complications also arose about how to calculate prices based on production costs over the previous five years. The calculation was structured around labour costs, but the farm workers had received no real wages, only work credits. To make matters worse, no data was available as the only economists who had studied it had been purged by Stalin in the 1930s. The solution was only reached in 1966 when *kolkhozy* were restructured into *sovkhozy* and began to pay a regular wage.

Another restriction was that farm chairmen and Party officials showed their loyalty by wringing the maximum out of the collective farms, leaving the peasants less time for their more efficient and profitable private plots. In the 1960s, Khrushchev, worried about the dominance of the private plots, reversed some of the reforms that favoured them. As part of this campaign, peasants had their dairy cattle 'donated' for them by the state to the collective farms and milk production crashed.

The peasants' status and living standards had started to increase during the early years of Khrushchev's rule, but this failed to have a large impact on the rural population. His flamboyant and unpredictable nature meant that Khrushchev continually tinkered and meddled in areas where he had convinced himself that he was an expert. Despite distancing himself from Stalin, he continued to impose Party control and maintained its apparatus in the expanding collective farms. It is true that Khrushchev preferred to incentivise the peasants rather than use Stalin's brutal repression. This would be the first time since the NEP that the carrot was chosen over the stick in dealing with the peasants. However, farms were stuck in the world of quotas, and any freedoms were severely restricted by the apparatus, making a poor return on the considerable financial investment. Apart from the size of the farm, the only real difference an observer might notice between a Stalin-era and a Khrushchev-era collective farm would be moderately happier peasants.

Khrushchev's reforms swung too wildly to lay the foundations for long-term success. In the early years, the peasant's private plot had been encouraged, but then as *kolkhozy* were turned into *sovkhozy*, the private plots were severely reduced, which reduced the availability of the more speciality items such as vegetables. Agricultural production rose steadily to 1958 but then decreased by two percent by 1963. There was no mass-murder of *kulaks* (partly because Stalin had already 'liquidated' them all) and no deportations, but his creation of vast *kolkhozy* and *sovkhozy* meant that entire villages were dismantled. Khrushchev genuinely believed he was creating a utopian centre complete with schools, shops and leisure facilities to rival anything in the West, but the investment was never there to fulfil his promises. The inefficiencies of the collective farms remained a constant, so no reform was far-reaching enough to make a decisive difference to the peasants' living standards.

ACTIVITY
KNOWLEDGE CHECK

Khrushchev's reforms

1. Make a list of all the ways agricultural policy under Khrushchev differed from agricultural policy under Stalin, and all the ways it remained the same.
2. Do you think Khrushchev changed Soviet agriculture or merely modified Stalin's design? Explain your answer.
3. For the period of Soviet control between 1917 and 1991, chart the periods of famine, migration and prosperity. Are there any links and common factors? Think about the extent of government involvement for each, or are these things independent of government actions?
4. To what extent could the peasants be seen as prosperous under Soviet control? Explain your answer.

In the two decades after the Presidium's 1964 removal of Khrushchev and appointment of Brezhnev, the only significant difference in agricultural policy was the reinstatement of the Ministry of Agriculture to protect the Presidium's interest. From now on, Soviet agriculture was amended and tweaked, but no more fundamental changes took place, and it slid into decline as output slipped further behind the plan. Brezhnev wished to improve the lot of the peasants, but his allegiance to the communist collective structure meant little could be done. Roughly 75 percent of collective workers lived below the poverty line in the early 1960s. Brezhnev did try to make the rural population equal to the rest of the people. In 1966, internal passports, removed in 1938, allowed the peasants the freedom to move, while collective workers became eligible for social security and pensions. Like many of the changes in the previous hundred years, it may have affected legal status but did little to improve living standards.

Only Mikhail Gorbachev in the mid-1980s saw the immediate necessity for a radical solution to prevent the stagnation in agriculture. He began the process allowing the private ownership of farmland in late 1990, but his ideas came too late to be put into practice before the collapse of the Soviet model.

A Level Exam-Style Question Section C

'Peasant farmers in both Russia and the Soviet Union never shook off the yoke of serfdom between 1855 and 1991.'

How far do you agree with this statement? (20 marks)

Tip

Section C questions always cover a period of at least 100 years. Therefore, your answer should include the whole period stated. It is not a matter of dense descriptive detail, but of looking at change and continuity over the whole period.

THINKING HISTORICALLY **Change (7a)**

Convergence and divergence

Political change in Russia, 1855–1991:

1855	1905	1917	1929	1956
Alexander II becomes tsar	Revolution and rise of Stolypin	October Revolution brings in Bolsheviks	Stalin becomes leader of USSR	Khrushchev's 'Secret Speech'

Peasant social changes in Russia 1855–1991:

1861	1906	1917	1929	1950s
Serf emancipation legally frees peasants	Peasants given power to leave *mir*	Peasants take control of the land	Mass-collectivisation begins	Push for *sovkhozy*, but private plot concessions

1 Draw a timeline across a landscape piece of A3 paper. Cut out ten small rectangular cards and write the above changes on them. Then place them on the timeline, with political changes above the line and peasant social changes below. Make sure there is plenty of space between the changes and the line.

2 Draw a line and write a link between each change within each strand, so that you have four links that join up the changes in the *political* part of the timeline and four that join the *peasant social* changes. You will then have two strands of change: *political* and *peasant social*.

3 Now make as many links as possible across the timeline between political change and peasant social change. Think about how they affected one another and how things can link across long periods of time.

You should end up with something like this:

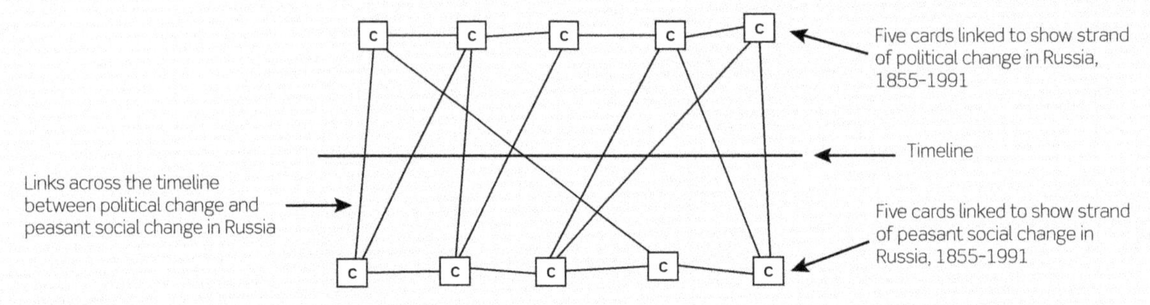

Answer these questions.

a) How far do different strands of history interact? Give two well-explained examples.

b) At what point do the two strands of development converge (i.e. when do the changes have the biggest impact on one another)?

c) How useful are the strands in understanding the reasons behind the control of Russian agriculture during the 18th and 19th centuries?

Conclusion

Though the 1861 emancipation liberated the serfs, the free peasants were burdened with redemption payments, while their work practices remained under the control of the local *mir*. 'Liberation' did not solve the problems of agriculture, but merely postponed them. It did not solve the land hunger of the peasants; approximately 60 percent had less than was needed to sustain a family, and the heavy redemption taxes left them dissatisfied and permanently in debt. The government reduced the payments in the 1880s and 1890s, but by 1900 the amount of debt arrears was greater than the annual payments. Famines, such as those in 1891, 1897 and 1901, were a regular threat. In the first years of the 20th century, Stolypin tried to create a wealthier class of peasant *kulaks*, free of *mir* restrictions and grateful enough to be loyal to the tsar. Any success was halted by his death and then reversed by war, as the peasants retreated into the traditional shelter of *mir* life.

The peasants grabbed their land in 1917, only for the Bolsheviks to take it back through War Communism in 1918. The respite of the NEP concessions, in which the peasants were largely left alone, was a chance for the *mir* to restore some cohesion to village life. As the NEP continued, there was a growing feeling among the Bolsheviks (now called the Communist Party) that the peasants, and the *kulaks* in particular, would hold the revolution back. If the *mir* could not be controlled, or converted, then the answer was to remove it, though this would certainly mean a civil war in all but name. In 1926, taxes were raised to limit profits, and state prices dropped by 20–25 percent on the amount paid for grain, with a six percent drop on other agricultural produce. In response, the peasants refused to release their stocks and either stored them, waiting for the dwindling supply to force prices up, or fed the grain to their livestock and themselves. By 1927, food was in desperately short supply in the cities as state purchases dropped by a half.

Stalin's collectivisation programme forced both his rivals and the peasants into submission. The *kolkhoz* replaced the *mir*, the *kulaks* were liquidated by terror and famine, and the peasants were reduced to being just another tool of the farm. By the 1950s, under Khrushchev's reforms, the farms grew into *sovkhozy* and the peasants were allowed more freedom on their private plots. However, the basic Soviet model of state-imposed prices and conditions of trade, of party control within the farm and its structure, meant that very little changed. The peasants suffered as each experiment failed to improve efficiency. Size was always the first choice, rather than any genuine attempt to tackle the lack of intensive farming ability.

The *mir* was never trusted to look after the peasants' interests as governments sought to increase direct control over the peasants and production of grain. This control was imposed from above, either in legal declarations of the tsarist period, or the more brutal and direct control of the *kolkhozy* and *sovkhozy*, which replaced the *mir*. The peasants' status as serfs was removed as they became technically free and then technically citizens of Russia and then the USSR. Yet under the tsar, poverty bound their freedom, and the Soviet state bound them to a land they still did not own or control.

Those peasants who burned with the fiercest land hunger perished through famine, while the *kulaks* who showed the most potential to improve were removed as potential threats. Force and terror were always preferred over economic independence. Even the incentives allowed by the NEP and Khrushchev were weak and offered reluctantly, often quickly being taken away.

Often the peasants' welfare was caught up in the violence and wider context of a power struggle as Stolypin vainly tried to steer the tsarist regime into the future, or as Stalin manipulated his way to the top, using a war on the peasants as a weapon for his own power.

Despite a century of uncertainty, famine and destruction of their livelihoods, the Russian peasants remained resilient and defiant. The briefest spell in 1917 and a few good years of the NEP showed how quickly they could bounce back and produce food. The image of the peasants putting their hearts and souls into their private plots, while the collective fields were harvested with apathy, reveals that they were farmers who simply wished to be left alone to nurture the soil they loved.

A Level Exam-Style Question Section C

How far do you agree that the government's need for political control over the peasants was mainly responsible for limiting changes to the peasants' living standards between 1855 and 1991? (20 marks)

Tip

Your answer should be dominated by a discussion of the stated factor, in this case the need for political control by the state. You should also examine other factors, such as the economic infrastructure of agriculture, the incompetence of management, the relationship between urban and rural areas. Weight should be given for each factor and the links between them should be explored.

ACTIVITY
SUMMARY

The changing status and condition of the peasantry

1. Construct two timelines, one to show how each period of reform and change brought positive outcomes for the peasants, the other one showing negative outcomes.
2. Try to extend this by weighing up the true impact and extent of each point.
3. How far do you agree with the opinion that there was a steady improvement in the lives of Russian peasants over the years 1855-1991?

WIDER READING

Corin, C. and Fiehn, T. *Communist Russia under Lenin and Stalin*, John Murray (2002)

Figes, O. *A People's Tragedy: The Russian Revolution 1891-1924*, Pimlico (1996)

Figes, O. *Revolutionary Russia: A History, 1891-1991*, Pelican (2014)

Hedlund, S. *Crisis in Soviet Agriculture*, Croom Helm (1984)

Lee, S.J. *Russia and the USSR 1855-1991*, Routledge (2006)

Lewin, M. *The Making of the Soviet System*, The New Press (1985)

Sixsmith, M. *Russia: A 1,000-year Chronicle of the Wild East*, BBC Books (2012)

Westwood, J.N. *Endurance and Endeavour: Russian History 1812-2001*, Oxford University Press (2002)

3.2 Agriculture and productivity: meeting the country's needs?

KEY QUESTIONS

- To what extent did reform and innovation increase productivity across the period 1861–1991?
- To what extent did domestic agriculture manage to feed the population between 1861 and 1991?

INTRODUCTION

Russia, whether imperial or communist, would always struggle to modernise its agricultural practices. Though reform and innovations were attempted, from railways to tractors, there was never enough investment in the right areas to really raise productivity. Yields seldom improved, and it was largely due to the increase in the area actually farmed, as opposed to the quality of farming, that most of the population were fed, most of the time. Russia was a diverse array of environments, in which the local peasants knew the land best. Yet, in the 19th century, the peasants were unwilling to change, as they were largely content to continue their traditional existence that had hardly changed since medieval times. Change was imposed from above, with little regard for local circumstances. Stolypin, the tsar's prime minister after 1905, and all the communist leaders after 1917, believed they knew best. Stalin, leader of the USSR between 1928–53, saw the peasants as counter-revolutionaries holding back industrialisation, while the more sympathetic Khrushchev, USSR leader between 1956–64, believed that only his grand visions would work. Both approaches fell short in solving the problem. No one comprehended, or cared, that it was the farms of the peasants themselves that needed to be the very bedrock of modernisation. There was no trust in the peasants' ability to innovate for themselves. Therefore, any reform was destined to fail without the co-operation of the people it was for.

These failures resulted in both a lack of food and a lack of range of agricultural products. Under the tsar, the cities went hungry first as the masses fled to the relative security of their peasant families. However, it did not take much for famine to spread across all areas. A summer drought, autumn winds, a winter freeze or spring floods were all capable of ruining a year's harvest and there would be no stored resources to supplement the poor harvest. Under the communists, the peasants went hungry first as the workers (the **proletariat**) had to be fed for ideological reasons as well as to keep industry running. However, the population was mainly eating bread, and the communists' obsession with grain eventually unbalanced the economy and forced the USSR to look abroad for grain. Over a century of meddling, interfering and tinkering with agriculture meant that Russia was no longer self-sufficient and the masses still queued for food.

KEY TERM

Proletariat
Originally a Roman term for those with little property, it was used by Karl Marx to describe the working class that he hoped would lead the revolution against capitalism. Therefore it refers to any urban worker.

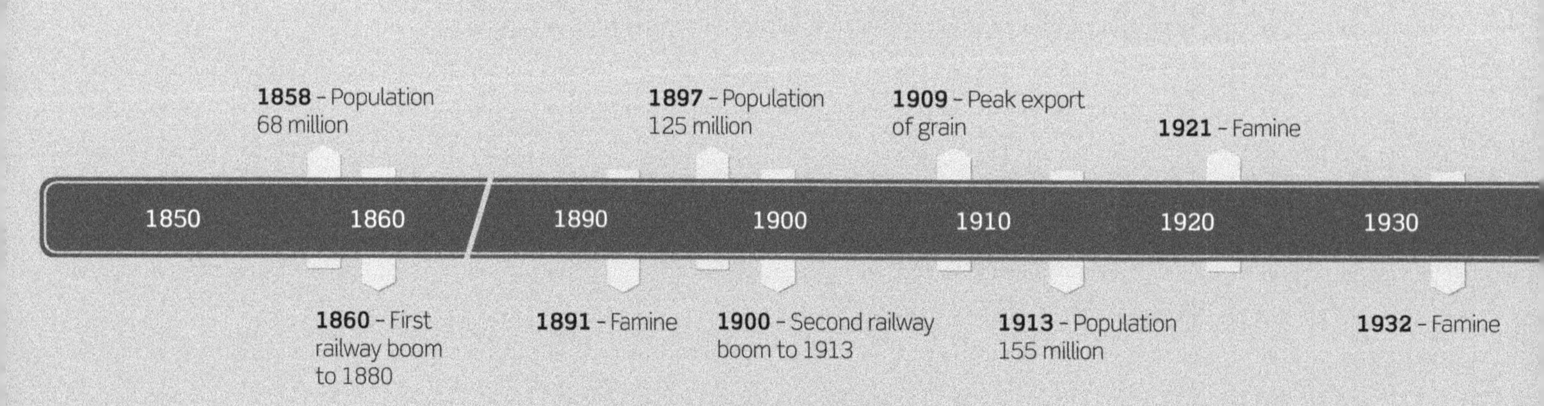

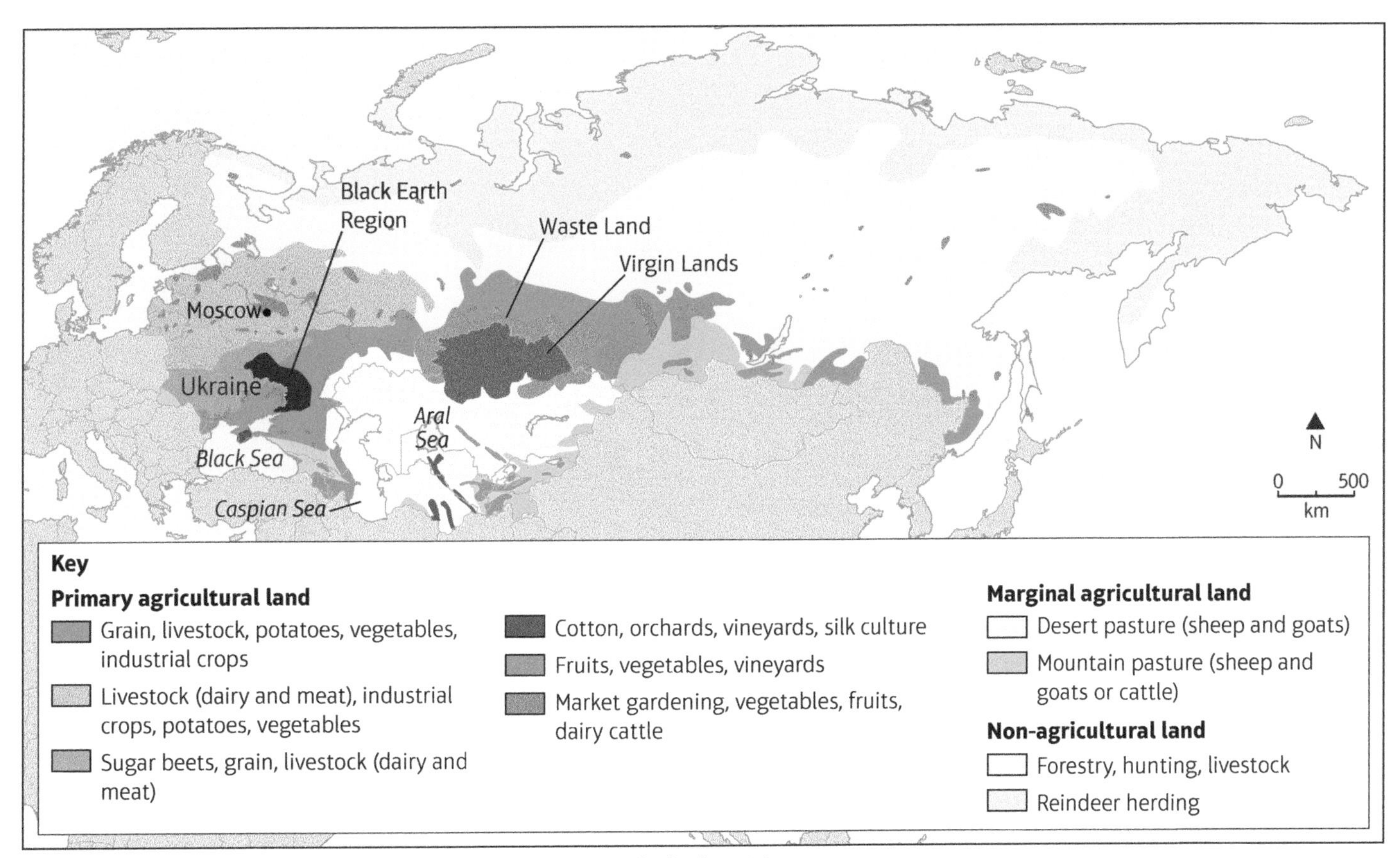

Figure 2.1 The main agricultural regions within the Russian Empire in the 20th century.

TO WHAT EXTENT DID REFORM AND INNOVATION INCREASE PRODUCTIVITY ACROSS THE PERIOD 1861–1991?

The backwardness of peasant agriculture in the 19th century

With the emancipation of the serfs, Alexander II wanted to trigger economic growth by modernising the agriculture of Russia. This would help restore a sense of prestige to the empire in the eyes of the world. However, the economic effects were blockaded by an embedded resistance to change by the peasants, expressed by the communal voice of the *mir*.

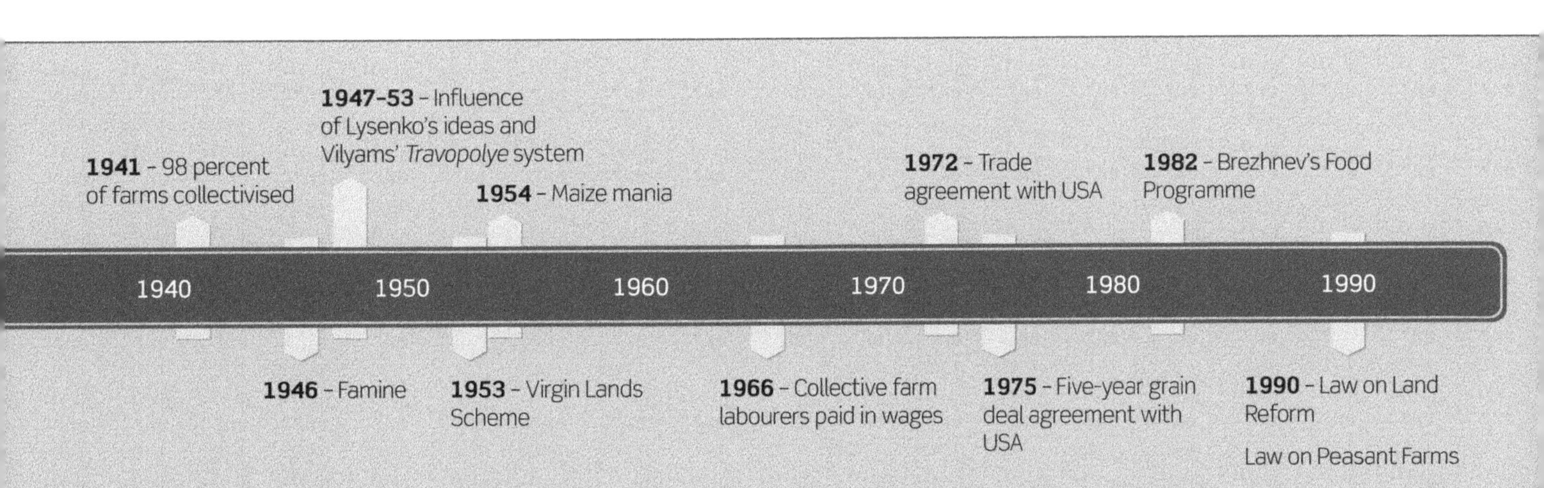

The farming practices used by the typical Russian village saw little change during the second half of the 19th century. Indeed, they had not evolved much in hundreds of years. Each village consisted of a few dozen to a few hundred huts, each with some three generations of peasants inhabiting it. The *mir* then apportioned an allotment which consisted of some 20–30 strips to each hut. The amount of land depended on the number of people or 'eaters' in the hut. There was an attempt to evenly distribute strips according to their distance from the hut and the quality of the soil. Therefore, every hut would receive some that were a long way from the hut and some of poor fertility. Each strip was calculated to be the length a horse-and-plough team could work before needing a break, which worked out around 170 metres long by eight metres wide in most agricultural regions. However, the exact amount varied considerably within Russia. In the south, along the River Volga, some strips were as far as 15 km from the hut and involved overnight camps to work them, while in the north some families were apportioned 50 strips, some too narrow for the plough to work effectively. Most peasant households still used the traditional wooden plough (*sokha*), which dug a shallow furrow at best (a maximum of ten centimetres deep), and only scratched the surface of the soil in the poorer agricultural regions. Seed was sown by hand, and a flail (a wooden staff with a heavy wooden stick swinging from it) threshed the grain as harvesting machines were almost unknown. A peasant toiling in the fields of Russia in 1870 looked almost identical to an English peasant in the 1300s.

EXTRACT

The historian Orlando Figes describes the way the Russian peasants, and the village elders and leaders of the *mir* in particular, are looking backwards to a past, rather than forwards towards new technologies and horizons. From *A People's Tragedy: The Russian Revolution 1891–1924* (1996).

The domination of the peasant patriarchs was not based on capitalist exploitation but on the fact that, by and large, this was an oral culture, where the customs of the past, passed down through the generations, served as a model for the collective actions of the village in the present and the future: 'Our grandfathers did it this way, and so shall we.'... on the whole the peasant patriarchs had an inbred mistrust of any ideas from the world outside their own experience. They aimed to preserve the village traditions and to defend them against progress. The 'old way of life' was always better than the new. There was, they believed, a peasant utopia in the distant past, long before the gentry and the state had imposed their domination on the village.

Everything about this agricultural set-up would hinder innovation. It was difficult for the landowner to implement new ideas. His own personal land was also in strips and the peasants supplied their own basic tools to work the land. The village elders were left to run the *mir* and it was not in the interest of the landowner to interfere with that process and thereby upset the very peasants he needed to work his land. These elders imposed conformity upon the village that naturally vetoed any change. For example, if

SOURCE

Russian peasants making hay near Moscow in the 1890s. The photograph was taken for a French magazine to highlight the costumes of Russian peasants. Hence the peasants are working at a higher density than would be usual, but it illustrates the basic tools used at the time.

a forward-thinking landowner did try to introduce new methods he would be politely listened to by the peasants, who would then ignore any instructions and continue as before. Their passive resistance eventually killed any innovation by apathy.

There were no hedges separating the strips of land, as the paths were needed for the hundreds of extra miles the peasants would walk each year to and from their respective strips. These paths took up an estimated seven percent of the arable land. With such an open-field system, all households must sow the same crop at the same time, to prevent the cattle grazing on the stubble of one fallow strip from eating the crops of another growing strip. Therefore all the peasants grew the same crop in the same area at the same time, in a three-crop rotation. One third of the land was dedicated to winter wheat, another third to spring wheat and the last third was left fallow. The rigidity of this system not only discouraged experimentation in crops but also meant that, for 33 percent of the time, all arable land was unused. Fallow fields were used for grazing cattle, but this did not make up for the loss of available land and produced little manure to renew the soil's nutrients. Although emancipation fundamentally changed the status of the peasants, it had little effect on farming practices.

* In many ways it is misleading to portray any village as typical, but the diagram does serve to illustrate some aspects of the structure of a village. In some cases, particularly in the south, the fields might be miles from some peasant houses, which were straddled along a dirt track.

Map 1. 1860

Key

- Strips worked by one serf household
- Serf house and surrounding plot
- † Church
- **M** Meadow; collectively used by all; vital pasture for animals

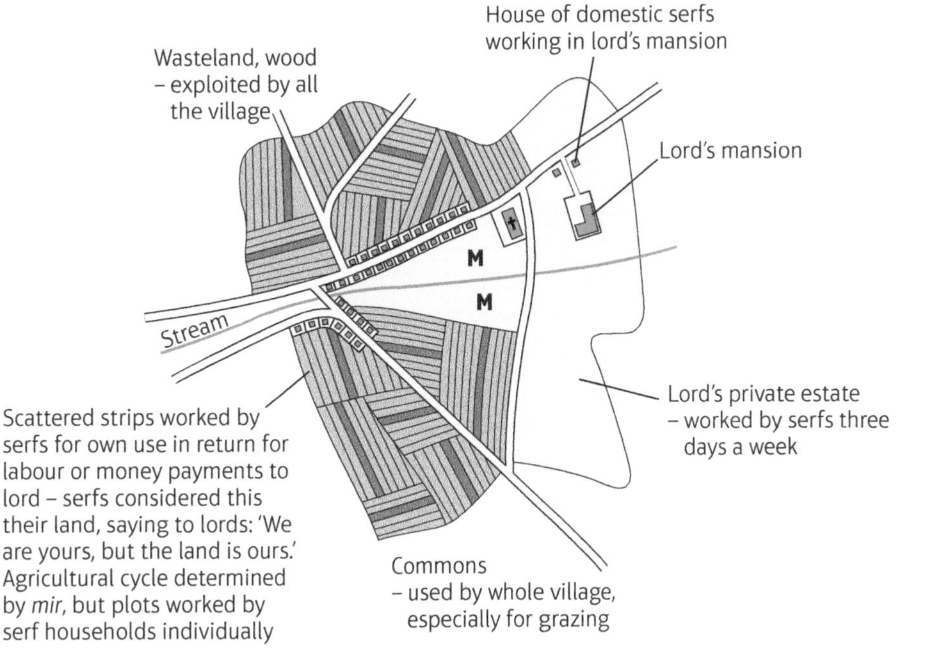

Wasteland, wood – exploited by all the village

House of domestic serfs working in lord's mansion

Lord's mansion

M

M

Stream

Scattered strips worked by serfs for own use in return for labour or money payments to lord – serfs considered this their land, saying to lords: 'We are yours, but the land is ours.' Agricultural cycle determined by *mir*, but plots worked by serf households individually

Lord's private estate – worked by serfs three days a week

Commons – used by whole village, especially for grazing

Map 2. 1875

Key

- 'Cut offs', i.e. land cut off from strips formerly worked by serfs and retained by lord as part of his estate – might be leased to peasants in return for rent or work on lord's estate
- **M** Meadow. Now usually formally owned by lord – some might be kept by lord for own animals' use; rest hired out to village
- **m** Part of meadow transferred to *mir*

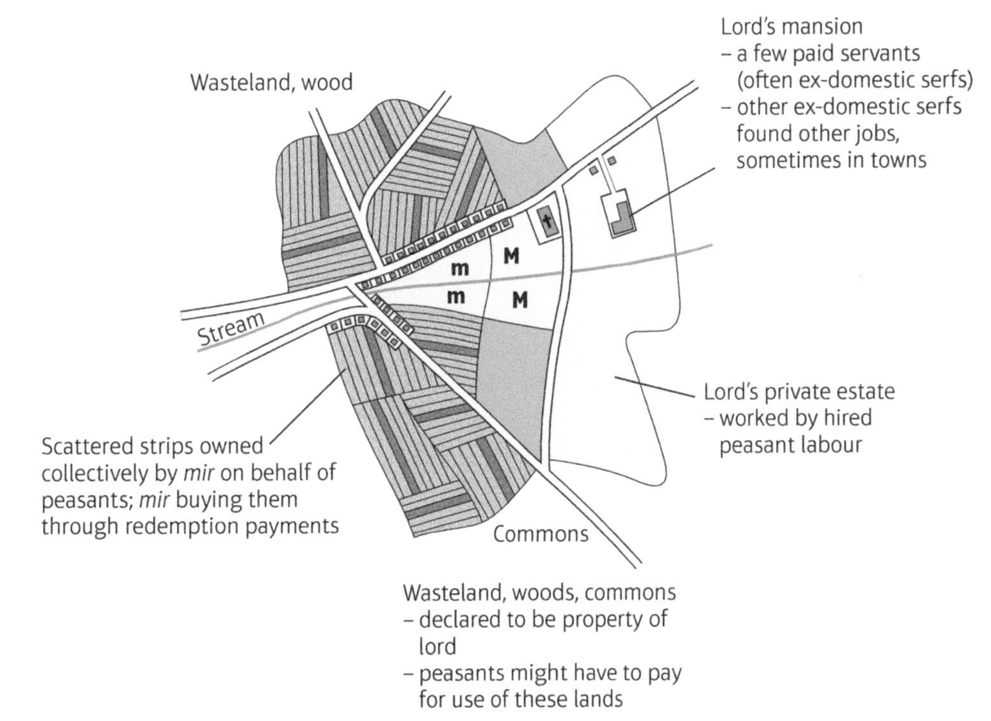

Figure 2.2 The limited impact of the Emancipation Edict on strip farming – comparing the situation in 1860 and 1875.

Strip farming and crop rotation blocked agricultural progress, as did the unusually brief growing season in most parts of Russia. The thaw in April started an intense period of farming that had to be completed before the November snows. This meant that co-operation between households was needed and each household tended to have large families in order to provide the labour to bring in the harvests on time. In periods when labour was not as needed, many family members moved into urban areas to find temporary work in small industries, before returning for the harvest. Communal co-operation and uniform farming would also help to share out the small quantity of seed, tools and livestock. Again, this reinforced the reactionary conformity of the system.

ACTIVITY
KNOWLEDGE CHECK

Peasant farming

1. Use Source 1 and Figure 2.2, as well as Extract 1, to write a paragraph explaining how the backwardness of peasant farming was cemented into the fabric of Russian society.
2. What solutions could be required to break this reluctance to modernise farming?

The years after emancipation saw a rapid increase in population. This was chiefly due to higher birth rates to provide labour in rural areas. In 1858, the population was 68 million, while by 1897 it was 125 million, with the majority of the increase in the rural districts of European Russia. This area saw a 50 percent increase in population, but no corresponding increase in resources. There was no incentive for the peasants to improve the strips of land if they were to be reallocated to someone else in a few years. This steadily reduced the average size of each peasant's holdings (see Figure 2.3), while the pressure raised prices and rents on the land at a time when a world surplus in grain meant that its price fell.

	1860	1880	1890
Northern Region	8.3	6.6	5.1
Central Agricultural Region	3.9	2.7	2.2
Ukraine	3.6	2.7	1.9
South West	3.2	2.3	1.5

Figure 2.3 The size of an average peasant holding (in hectares). It is estimated that 6.5 hectares was the minimum amount of land needed for survival in Black Earth areas (see Figure 2.1) where the earth is very fertile and produces high yields, with 8.7 hectares needed in non-Black Earth areas.

SOURCE

A frustrated Prime Minister Witte writing in his memoirs, published in 1922, about the inbuilt reluctance, from all areas of society, to change the peasant system of farming.

The defenders of the commune were loyal, respectable collectors of old rubbish, admirers of old forms because they were old; or police watchdogs who found it more convenient to take care of herds than of individuals; or the partisans of upheaval, who supported all that was easily shaken; and lastly the theoreticians, who saw in the commune a practical implementation of that last word in economic doctrine, the theory of socialism.

Finally, there was no genuine desire to challenge this conformity. The communal nature of the peasant agricultural system was popular not only with the peasants but also with the tsar and his advisers, who felt it preserved the essence of Russia and provided protection against a revolutionary landless proletariat.

The view that an overall shortage of land, heavy taxation and the attitudes and restraints of the *mir* held agriculture back and prevented it from creating a reliable production for the internal market or surplus for export can be challenged as too simplistic. Some peasants were able to purchase land, often through the **Peasant Land Bank**, and could diversify and specialise their production. Over 18.5 million hectares were purchased by the peasants through the bank between 1877 and 1905, though much more was rented by peasants. Those peasants who gained land would become the *kulaks* that Stolypin's reform after 1905 would encourage to leave the control of the *mir*.

KEY TERM

Peasant Land Bank
A state bank established in 1883 to lend money at low interest rates to peasants who wanted to buy land. In its early years, many peasants distrusted the bank as a symbol and tool of the state. After 1906, Stolypin made it easier to borrow money to encourage peasants to set up their own farms. It was liquidated by the Bolsheviks after the communist revolution of October 1917.

There were also organisations created to promote better agricultural techniques.

- The Free Economic Society had been created by a group of wealthy landowners as early as the 1760s and was independent of the government. After 1861, it compiled statistical evidence to compare different regions, to map soils and debate the influence of the *mir*. However, after 1895 its views were deemed too liberal and it was closed down in 1900. Despite publishing over 280 volumes of its findings, its actual impact on Russian farming was limited.
- Partly in response to the 1891 famine, a new Ministry of Agriculture was designed to improve methods. However, it only had a modest budget of around two percent of the state budget, and much of its work and any goodwill it harboured among the peasants was lost with the government's imposition of the hated Land Captains (see page 15).
- In 1896, the **Resettlement Administration** was set up within the Ministry of Internal Affairs to aid internal migration to Siberia to exploit new farmland. The construction of the Trans-Siberian Railway made this an easier trip, with 932,000

KEY TERM

Resettlement Administration
An initiative set up by the government in 1896 to actively encourage migration to Siberia. Previous 'temporary regulations' had been in place since 1881, but red-tape and a small budget meant measures were ineffective. The Resettlement Administration greatly improved the system, such as granting extra privileges and subsidies to migrants in 1896, 1899 and 1904.

peasants crossing the Ural Mountains within four years. The best land was quickly taken, though more migrants made the journey during Stolypin's time after 1906. However, it was not the amount of land farmed that held back Russian agriculture, but the production techniques and therefore the yields grown. The opening up of the Siberian lands did little to improve this. The peasants could, by and large, feed themselves, but the inefficient farming methods could not create the constant surplus needed for urbanisation or foreign markets.

Therefore, despite the best of intentions, any organised and governmental attempt to improve agriculture either floundered against the rock-like refusal of the peasants to change or it was not given the resources required to succeed.

EXTEND YOUR KNOWLEDGE

The most successful peasant farmers

The Cossacks, who numbered over three million by 1900, were a unique case in Russia. They were soldier-farmers, who would offer 20 years' military service to the tsar in exchange for nearly 81 acres of land. This was over four times the average state peasants' allotment and eight times the average allotment of former landlords' peasants. However the farms, though large, used many of the same techniques as other peasant holdings, and each Cossack had to provide his own horse in the army.

There were 11 Cossack forces spread out on the fringes of the empire. In peacetime, they devoted themselves to their land and even their villages were often outside the general structure of provincial administration. The tsars required their special services right up to the last days of the empire.

In conclusion, despite the fundamental change in the legal status and social conditions of the peasants in the latter half of the 19th century, economically it was largely a period of neglect and stagnation. By 1900, nearly 85 percent of the rapidly increasing population still were predominantly connected to the land and methods of agriculture remained largely unchanged. Incentives were not consistent or large enough to encourage innovation and reform. Though the average peasant controlled more land than a peasant in many other nations, the almost universal strip-farming and three-crop rotation method kept productivity at inefficient levels. The government was more concerned with social control than with creating an efficient agriculture capable of creating a surplus to fund industrialisation. Instead, the peasants were squeezed for their revenue, which would be taxed out of their income or taken as surplus at the expense of their food. This would then fuel the tensions that exploded in the unrest of 1905 and 1906.

The railways' impact on the larger estates of the gentry and nobility pre-1914

After 1905, the reforms of Stolypin finally focused the government's attention on agricultural reform and the desire to weaken the grip of the *mir* and allow the *kulaks* to prosper. However, on the whole, the larger estates of the nobility adapted to new techniques more quickly, and the development of the railways enabled them to take advantage of opportunities to increase trade.

The number of estates owned by the nobility declined in number after 1861 as many sold land to peasants and tried to find fortune and investment opportunities in the cities. The amount of land owned by the nobles fell from 120 million hectares in 1861 to just 35 million hectares by 1914, just ten percent of the arable land. There was even a Noble Land Bank created, which, like the Peasant Land Bank, aimed to encourage the nobility to keep and expand their land. The rural unrest of 1905 had persuaded many of the landowners that it was safer to sell their land than keep it. However, for some of the nobility who stayed, the rapid expansion of the railways helped to open up remote regions and transform the whole empire into a single market.

Though primarily used for developing industry and moving freight, such as cotton for the textile industry, the railways extended the cultivation of land in the Black Earth Region (see Figure 2.1) and the steppe (a wide area of grassland running across eastern Europe to Asia). Some landowners, more attuned to the changing markets and perhaps with more access to capital investment, began to hire labour and use more modern techniques to grow wheat for export through the port of Odessa.

Railways, often financed by foreign capital, saw a sevenfold increase in the 1860s, and then doubled in the 1870s. This was made possible by the fact that the government underwrote the debts of new railway companies while allowing the companies to keep any profits, as a way to encourage investment and building. This shows the intent of the government to introduce a planned railway system to promote both agriculture and industry, though it did leave them open to abuse when some railways made more from running at a loss through the guaranteed dividends from the government. By 1900, the government preferred state-owned and managed railways and the decade witnessed another boom in railway-building. Often new railways were demanded by the local nobility, in competition to the cities.

	Mileage	Freight traffic (million tons)
1866	3,000	3
1883	14,700	24
1903	36,400	76
1913	43,900	158

Figure 2.4 The growth of Russian railways and the corresponding amount of freight traffic on them. Of course, not all freight traffic was grain. In the 1870s, it accounted for between 27 and 42 percent, but this dropped to around 20 percent by 1900.

The new facilities offered by the railways were reflected in the rise in grain exports. In 1861–65, grain exports were worth 60.3 million rubles and this had grown to 305.9 million rubles in 1876–79. The late 19th century saw a levelling-off of exports due to falling prices caused by the development of the US prairies, but by 1905 exports had rapidly increased to 568.3 million rubles and peaked to their highest level at 749.4 million rubles in 1909.

The large estates of the nobility were chiefly responsible for this, especially in the steppes of the south as they adjusted most quickly to the new techniques. This can be seen in the rising demand for agricultural machinery. In 1900, farming machines were imported to the value of 28 million rubles; by 1908, it was 61 million, and 109 million by 1909. The demand also caused domestic production of machines, with 13 million rubles' worth of machinery built in 1900 and 52 million in 1912. Artificial fertiliser began to be imported: 108,000 tons in 1900 and 630,000 tons in 1912. Therefore, for the first time in Russia, modern professional farms with hired labour rather than peasants began to emerge on the estates of some of the nobility.

This was not repeated across the country, but only in the areas with close access to railways that could move the grain more effectively, where previously the navigable rivers were used. Some of the nobility simply failed to see the economic advantages the new railway would bring. The Kiev–Zhmerinka Railway tried to build a station a few hundred yards from the Bogdanov estate, but the landowner fiercely resisted as he believed the railway would disturb his sleep. In the end, the station was built ten kilometres away. For the peasants near a new railway, there was an opportunity to make a quick profit by selling grain to the railway labourers, sometimes at ten times the normal price. However, outside the large estates there was little provision for the peasant farms. There was no covered area to store the grain and so sacks were exposed to the weather and easily stolen. While some peasants welcomed the arrival of the railways, many others whispered a quiet prayer and fretted over this noisy interruption to the traditional way of life.

Some of the increases in grain output were down to the peasants selling their produce to middlemen, often months in advance of the harvest and at very high interest rates. This desperate bid to turn their strips into profit shows the inadequacies of the peasant-based agriculture compared with the rail-connected landed estates. As well as the agricultural technology, new crops were tried, such as potatoes, whose output rose from around six million tons in the 1860s to nearly 26 million by 1913, or sugar beet, of which nearly two million acres were sown in 1913, compared with just 270,000 acres in the 1860s. With changes in crops, there was the opportunity to change the strict three-crop rotation. Mirroring the developments in western Europe in the 18th century, fodder grasses and clover were planted to renew the soil's nutrients and allow more grazing for cattle, which provided more manure. These experiments tended to take place away from the grain areas of the central Black Earth Region, but progress was still slow, with multi-crop rotations in only 7.2 percent of arable land by 1924.

Change was gradual. While Stolypin's policy to free the new *kulak* class from the *mir*'s control and place them more under state control, met with limited success, the clearest improvements in agriculture belonged to the estates of the nobility that were serviced by the railways. Change then led to more change as new crops and more consolidated farming allowed experimentation and innovation. Some of these improvements filtered down to the *kulak* farms, but the onset of the First World War brought any innovations to a sudden stop. The *mir*, in its traditional role as a stable centre in a chaotic state, once more reasserted its control. The overwhelming demand was for grain to feed the workers and the army. Economically, this meant that the peasants gained during the conflict, both in the area under cultivation and in grain prices. However, despite these gains, the farms were worked by women and children or by old men, while any increase in savings was washed away by inflation and the absence of manufactured goods to buy.

This pattern of government pressure demanding grain and the peasants meeting the demand through sheer hard work only intensified during the next two decades. Any innovation was merely superficial, as it was the stick, rather than the carrot, that ruled. The Decree on Land may have given the land to the peasants, whose traditional outlook was more likely to limit reform, but the grain requisitioning of War Communism and the brutal terror imposed by Cheka and the Red Army squeezed the grain from the countryside.

Likewise, the relative peace of the NEP years allowed the peasants to restore their lands rather than introduce new techniques and agricultural methods. The formative year of Stalin's collectivisation policy might have consolidated the farms and ended the strip fields, but force and terror harvested the crops, not reform and innovation. It was only once the government had the unyielding control over the peasantry that any true attempts to reform and innovate could be stutteringly implemented.

The drive to modernise under Stalin

The fact that during the period of collectivisation, 1928–41, some 25 million peasants were forced to labour on 250,000 collective farms should not be seen as modernisation. Promises of tractors and machines were hollow for the first seven years, as the figures in Figure 2.5 show.

	1928	1929	1930	1931	1932	1933	1934	1935
% of land collectivised			23.6	52.7	61.5	66.4	71.4	83.2
Grain (million tonnes)	73.7	71.7	83.5	69.5	69.6	68.6	67.6	75.0
Cattle (million head)	70.5	67.1	52.5	47.9	40.7	38.4	42.4	49.3
Pigs (million head)	26.0	20.4	13.6	14.4	11.6	12.1	17.4	22.6
Sheep and goats (million head)	146.7	147.0	108.8	77.7	52.1	50.2	51.9	61.1

Figure 2.5 Agricultural production in the Soviet Union 1928-35 (estimates based on Soviet statistics). By 1941, 98 percent of land was collectivised. From *Years of Russia and the USSR, 1851-1991* (D. Evans and J. Jenkins, 2001). Reproduced by permission of Hodder Education.

Clearly, the initial results of collectivisation indicate the detrimental interference of Stalin and the government's policies. Even in 1937, the output from the private plots, the small acre or so of land that each peasant family was allowed to privately work, was greater than the collective's output. While the first period could be seen as a civil war against the peasants whose horrors and tragedies may have either been planned or stumbled upon, the latter half of the 1930s did see some improvement. While the talk of '**tractorisation**' never really led anywhere, more machines were available through the MTS and this did help raise levels of production.

Part of the problem, however, was Stalin's and the Party's belief that all that was needed for success were more tractors. The infrastructure required to look after the tractors was simply not given enough priority. By 1931, nearly 54 percent of all Soviet quality rolled steel was used to produce farm machinery, yet nearly 89 percent of collective farms had no tractors. Even when the tractors became more readily available, there was simply not the expertise or incentive to maintain them. The average tractor in the USSR lasted a mere five years before its destruction, while a tractor on a British farm could last ten years and still be in an operational condition. US tractors, like the John Deere Combine, were imported, but a combination of inferior oil and poor repairs meant they lasted only a third of their expected lifetime compared to the USA. Some MTS served many collectives. One in Kharkov Province had 68 tractors for 61 farms, some of which were over 40 km away. It is estimated that in September 1933, some 7,300 hours were spent just driving tractors to the workplace. It is not surprising that, in the 1930s, it is estimated that between 20 and 33 percent of all tractors were broken at any one time.

KEY TERM

Tractorisation
As part of the collectivisation of Russian agriculture, this was an ambitious plan to modernise the country's agriculture from the medieval period to the 20th century by supplying farms with modern machinery, including tractors. However, the number of tractors required, in terms of both quantity and quality, was never really met.

EXTRACT

From historian Robert Conquest's *Harvest of Sorrow* (1986), in which he uses two accounts to illustrate the inferiority of the MTS. The first is from an emigré, while the second is from a senior Soviet official.

The former tells of how, in February 1933 the whole administrative staff of the Machine Tractor Station in Polyvyanka was arrested, and tried for sabotage, in that the tractor and farm machinery were not in shape and the oxen and horses also in poor condition. The reason for the latter is obvious. For the former, there was no way to keep machines in good shape. There were no spare parts available, and the forges were unable to obtain fuel, iron or even wood.

The second, official account does not mention sanctions inflicted, but adequately tells of the troubles of the Krasnovershk MTS in the Odessa Province. In 1933 it should have carried out medium repairs on twenty-five tractors and twenty-five threshing machines. But it had only three workers and a smith's forge and anvil borrowed from a neighbouring kolkhoz [collective farm], besides having no spare parts at all.

SOURCE 3

A still from the film *Staroye i novoye* (*Old and New*), showing the new tractors of the agricultural collective. The propaganda film, directed by Grigori Aleksandrov and Sergei M. Eisenstein, aimed to show the appeal of collective farming. The state had a target of 100,000 tractors by 1933, but delivered less than half this number. The mechanised 'ballet' was absurdly misleading, but was effective in enticing the peasants to the farm, and there were examples of children being named 'Tractor' in their honour. Photographs of ecstatic peasants surrounding their first tractor as if welcoming returning heroes from some war became common pieces of propaganda.

The situation after the Second World War was even worse, with a severe shortage of both tractors and horses. In some cases, women, of whom there were 13 million more than men on the *kolkhozy* in 1945, found themselves literally harnessed to the ploughs.

Stalin's instinct for grand schemes and unrealistic mechanisation also ignored the importance of small-scale reforms which could dramatically improve results. Investment in fertilisers and pest control could have achieved significant results, but Stalin favoured certain 'scientific' doctrines which actually held agriculture back. The theories of Vilyams and Lysenko, based on pseudo-science and communist ideological reasoning, were used to dictate which crops should be planted.

Lysenko claimed he had developed a wheat which could grow within the Arctic Circle, a strain he called 'Stalin Branched Wheat', which played to Stalin's ego and ensured its widespread use. The results were predictably disastrous, but to criticise Lysenko was to criticise Stalin and therefore met with repression. Lysenko was promoted to be head of the Academy of Agricultural Sciences, while his predecessor died in captivity. Lysenko recovered from one denouncement by Khrushchev, but when his Marxist theory of hereditary plant genetics produced no results, while the western model produced new crops with higher yields, it marked the end of his career.

Vilyams, who was originally from the USA, developed the *Travopolye* system, which used grasses within the crop rotation that he claimed could be applied to replenish the nutrients in any soil. Though the system had some merit, Stalin's insistence on using it everywhere meant it failed more than it worked, and it also meant that any investment in artificial fertilisers was diverted and wasted. The sheer scale of both Stalin's ambition and failure in agricultural innovation can be seen in his scheme in the late 1940s and early 1950s to plant millions of trees in semi-arid regions to improve the climate of the USSR and to prevent soil erosion. Stalin felt he was powerful enough to transform nature, but the trees quickly died from lack of water.

Finally, there was a complete lack of reform or innovation in incentivising the peasants to work. Supervision had slipped during the extremes of the Second World War, and the private plots were important in supplying the food needed, while some collective land was allowed to revert back to peasant farms. There were even rumours that the process of collectivisation was to be abolished. This was untrue and control was hastily tightened, with all land collectivised and further powers decreed to the MTS. It has been calculated that a peasant working for 500 work days on a collective might only receive a sack of grain or three sacks of potatoes for their efforts, or 60 work days would result in a single kilogram of butter. This, logically, meant that peasants fell back on their private plots to earn money. More could be made from picking mushrooms and making illegal alcohol than working for the collective, yet the farm chairman had to coerce the peasants into the fields. A policy that encouraged the private plots should have improved the agricultural production in the USSR but, for Stalin, the collectives were more about control. Therefore, private plots were taxed, the state procurements applied to them were excessive and their livestock was restricted as Stalin focused on industrial recovery from the devastation of the war.

In conclusion, the process of collectivisation might have been a radical and momentous policy decision of enormous consequence to the status and livelihood of the peasantry, but it should not be seen as an attempt to innovate agricultural production. The bitter resentment of the peasants to their forced collectivisation resulted in resistance and outright opposition to Stalin, which in turn resulted in mass terror and genocide. Stalin would not forget this reluctance to embrace his policies. After 1945, both he and Party officials viewed the peasants with suspicion, a leftover from pre-revolutionary bourgeois attitudes. The core idea of applying force rather than innovation to produce higher yields, which would then feed the urban workers, remained and was reinforced by the war years. The peasants had been seen to be too eager to break free of state control and needed to be reined back in. Agriculture continued to be the most vulnerable sector of the USSR's economy and Stalin continued to fail in finding a solution to its problems. By 1953, the average peasant was once more little more than a serf. The restrictive practices of the land strips, the innate conservativism of the *mir*, and the uncaring, noble landowners may have all gone, but they were replaced by the uniform techniques of the collective, the control of the MTS and the unrelenting inhumanity of the state.

ACTIVITY
KNOWLEDGE CHECK

Soviet agriculture

1 List the problems faced by Soviet agriculture under Stalin.

2 Now rank the problems in order of seriousness in preventing the improvement of agriculture.

3 Write an introduction to explain why collectivisation failed to modernise Soviet agriculture. This should contain a clear argument.

Khrushchev's drive to boost productivity

In the last years of Stalin's rule, Nikita Khrushchev, then Party secretary of the Ukraine, was promoted to first secretary of Moscow and tasked with helping to plan agricultural policy. An indication of his preferred style of management can be seen in his unsuccessful attempts to create agrotowns (see page 26). The idea was criticised for being too expensive at the 1952 Party Congress and was abandoned. However, it showed that Khrushchev's approach was to try something bold, new and costly. Khrushchev's ideas, which his critics labelled 'hare-brained', would often enjoy brief success before they ultimately failed through a lack of support and planning.

The Virgin Lands Scheme

Khrushchev's agrotowns had been mainly ridiculed by Malenkov, who was a direct rival to Khrushchev in the struggle to replace Stalin as leader after 1953. Malenkov put agricultural reforms at the centre of his own bid for power by introducing popular measures to incentivise the peasants.

He increased procurement prices, tried to reduce taxes and encouraged the private plots. Khrushchev's attempt to steal back Malenkov's thunder was the Virgin Lands Scheme. Khrushchev publicised the real extent of grain failures since the end of the Second World War, thereby implicating Malenkov as part of the conspiracy to cover up the truth. As well as appearing to be the leader in all matters agricultural, it seemed that Khrushchev was willing to infer that the actual system was at fault for the poor performance of agriculture. Instead of blaming the weather or the structural ruins from the tsarist days, he seemed prepared to do something practical to solve the problems.

SOURCE 4

From Khrushchev's speech to the Leningrad Party Congress in April 1955, showing his new approach to agricultural policy. From Khrushchev: *The Man and His Era* by William Taubman (2003).

The people put it to us this way: Will there be meat to eat, or not? Will there be milk, or not? Will there be decent pairs of pants? This isn't ideology, of course, but what good does it do if everyone is ideologically correct but goes around without trousers?

His initial idea was to plough up at least 13 million hectares in two years, with at least an initial 2.3 million in 1954, and to grow grain. This would be in the so-called Virgin Lands, mainly on the empty steppe of Kazakhstan (see Figure 2.1, page 39). Land that was previously untilled or idle, in that it had been abandoned, would be cultivated in a grand plan to create the equivalent of the agricultural might of the North American plains. Despite opposition from his rivals for power, Malenkov and Molotov, as well as Party leaders in the area, who felt the land was better suited to sheep than grain, Khrushchev forged ahead and replaced any critical local Party officials with his own supporters. One such promotion was of Leonid Brezhnev, the man who would eventually lead the removal of Khrushchev from power.

Though Khrushchev's rhetoric downgraded ideology, the scheme relied on the ideological purism of its participants. Fuelled by zeal and enthusiasm, the farmers would be volunteers willing to head east. These were mainly *Komsomol* activists, and unfortunately many of the three million had little experience of farming and no experience of the potential hardships the wide-ranging climate would offer them. It was the lure of socialist adventure that would inspire the young to travel, though the promise of regular employment and the guaranteed wage on a state farm were additional motivations. The scheme became a campaign with the simple slogan 'Sow spring wheat in the new areas'. There was a genuine spirit that seemed to be echoed in Khrushchev himself as he raised the target to 30 million hectares and expanded the territory into West Siberia.

However, as well as the numerous volunteers from the West, the scheme also used many ethnic groups that had been exploited and deported by Stalin during the Second World War, such as Chechens, Volga Germans, Ingush and Crimean Tartars. During the de-Stalinisation era from 1956 (see page 138), some were allowed to return to their homelands, but the Tartars and Germans were seen as too important for the scheme's success and so were forced to stay.

SOURCE 5

Khrushchev describes the momentous achievement in resettling the volunteers for the Virgin Lands Scheme. From his autobiography, *Khrushchev Remembers* (1970).

We ourselves tried to make sweeping improvements in our agricultural system when we tried to resettle collective farmers on the Virgin Lands. You can imagine the difficulties that the Virgin Lands campaign posed for a family which had to be picked up and moved from the home where it had lived for generations. It was a great hardship for them, but we had to resettle many such families - Ukrainians, Belorussians, and Russians - thousands of kilometres from the graves of their ancestors. Enormous material expenditures went into the resettlement campaign. Among other things, we had to give credit loans and financial aid to the youths who went out to build settlements in the Virgin Lands. We became convinced that we shouldn't set up collective farms out there; a collective farm is an artificial organization; that is, it's not a real community, and it would have been too expensive to resettle people on collective farms. Therefore we decided on the alternative of state farms. While I was in leadership, our cheapest bread was grown by state farms on the Virgin Lands.

SOURCE 6

Propaganda poster encouraging 'volunteers' to participate in Khrushchev's Virgin Lands Scheme. The 1954 poster says, 'Come along with us to the Virgin Lands'. Note its focus on capturing the 'revolutionary spirit' of the scheme rather than advertising any agricultural aspect. The scheme was extensively promoted and glorified in novels, films and songs.

The scheme was not cheap, with over 5.3 billion rubles spent to harness the Virgin Lands. With such heavy investment in tools and tractors (some 200,000), which were often diverted from non-Virgin Lands sectors, the area ploughed just in 1954 was bigger than the cultivated land of England, France and Spain combined. The land was split into state farms of between 20,000 and 40,000 hectares each, and for the next four years it increased the grain production of the USSR from 81 to 144 million tonnes. In the meantime, Khrushchev became undisputed leader of the Party and the state.

However, the speed with which the project was undertaken proved to be its undoing. Enthusiasm replaced planning and no thought was given to the long-term effects of farming the land, either for the soil or its farmers. Grain was farmed intensively, with no rotation of crops, which caused the quality of soil to deteriorate. Droughts hastened the deterioration of the soil, which consequently dissipated the enthusiasm of the volunteers, many of whom drifted back towards an urban life. A lack of investment in fertilisers helped to exhaust the land further and the topsoil was quickly removed by the wind as large parts of Kazakhstan became dustbowls. Likewise, inadequate amenities were created for the volunteers, with particularly a lack of basic housing causing much resentment. The key factor to its varying degrees of success or failure seemed to be the weather, not surprising in an area traditionally prone to drought and more suited to livestock than grain.

- 1954: Thirty million hectares were ploughed, with nearly 15 million tonnes of extra grain produced by the 425 new state farms, or *sovkhozy*.
- 1955: The year saw a sharp drought, in which the area received only ten percent of its normal rainfall. The Kazakhstan harvest dropped by 35 percent, despite a doubling of the sown area. Political opposition to the scheme grew, but Khrushchev insisted that two good harvests out of five would be enough to be successful in both harvest and profit.
- 1956: Though many volunteers had returned west, 1956 proved to be a record harvest year, with grain output up by 90 percent on 1954–55 in the Virgin Lands and a 50 percent improvement on the USSR's total output. This prompted a visit to the area by Khrushchev to award medals and promote his own leadership ability.
- 1957: The harvest failed and there was a subsequent 40 percent reduction in the Virgin Lands' output.
- 1958 and 1959: There was very little expansion in ploughed land, but good weather caused two good harvests in a row, triggering a new wave of enthusiasm.
- 1960: The year saw considerable expansion of the scheme. Khrushchev combined five provinces in Kazahkhstan into a single administrative unit with a capital called Tselinograd (Virgin Land City). However, the harvest failed and as the soil finally became exhausted, a steady decline began.
- 1961–63: Sixty new fertiliser factories were built, at a cost of over 6 billion rubles, to try to replenish the soil, but it was too late and output continued to fall. Poor weather meant that out of 37 million hectares sown with grain, only seven million could be gathered. This caused a terrible harvest in 1963, meaning output was down over a third from the expected target. This, therefore, meant a lack of animal fodder, which led to a slaughter of animal livestock. The pig population fell from 70 million to 40 million. To avoid famine, the USSR was forced to import grain from North America and Australia. This helped to spark the political revolt that removed Khrushchev from power. An improvement in the 1964 harvest arrived too late to salvage his career.

Khrushchev had willed the Virgin Lands Scheme into being. In 1954, he had announced the crisis in agriculture, put forward the solution and called for the Russian people to implement it. The result was a quick fix. Initially, output did rise sharply, but at high cost in investment in creating the basic infrastructure. The lack of measures to raise production in existing farmed land meant that, when the scheme failed, there was nothing to back it up. Basic facilities were absent because local managers were either incompetent or just inefficient. A lack of drying and storage units caused many harvested crops to rot, which compounded the problems. Despite an average yield of around 20 million tonnes in Kazakhstan in the late 1950s, there was only storage capacity for 10 million tonnes. The real tragedy for Soviet agriculture is that the land was originally fertile and with intelligent innovation and professional management, it could have provided a considerable and, most importantly, consistent grain production. The reality is that the Virgin Lands Scheme never met its targets in any year, and it was the increased production in the established farmlands that did most to feed the population after 1960. Khrushchev had boasted that two good harvests in five would be enough. In the end, the years 1954–64 saw at least four good harvests in a decade, and proved him wrong.

Maize mania

One reason that a 40 percent good harvest rate was not enough was that the Virgin Lands Scheme went hand-in-hand with another of Khrushchev's 'campaigns'. It also showed the difficulties in directing control from the centre with little regard for local circumstances.

Soviet delegations to the USA sent back wondrous accounts of the cornfields of the Midwest, mainly due to a hybrid strain developed by Roswell Garst, an Iowa seed executive. Garst was invited to the USSR and befriended Khrushchev, who bought 5,000 tons of seeds. 'Maize mania' was born. With the ploughing of the Virgin Lands, the traditional lands in the West could be used to plant the maize corn that would provide fodder for livestock to satisfy the growing demand for meat. Khrushchev ordered that oats and barley, the usual fodder crops, should be replaced with corn, despite the fact that the USSR is much further north than the US corn-belt and the growing season is both too short and too dry for corn. He proposed expanding the area cultivated for corn from 4.2 million hectares in 1954 to 30 million by 1960, with about half the crop harvested early for silage and the rest for fodder.

Like the Virgin Lands Scheme, it started quickly, with 13 million hectares sown in the first year, and peaking in 1963 with 36 million hectares. Khrushchev earned the derogatory nicknamed *Kukuruznik* ('little corn-man' or 'corn-nut') and he grew the crop in his *dacha* home in Moscow. After his return from the USA, cornflakes were introduced as a breakfast use of maize, but they were seen as a western luxury and not to be squandered, so breakfast would be a bowl of milk with a few flakes.

SOURCE

A happy and proud Khrushchev speaking to the media on a 1959 visit to Roswell Garst's farm during a state visit to the USA.

Up to now, you Americans have worked better than we do. So we will learn from you. And once we've learned, we'll work even better than you do. So you will have to jump onto the running board of the train of socialism, which is about to leave for the future. Otherwise you'll be left far behind, and we will wave goodbye to you from the rear platform of the last carriage.

SOURCE 8

Khrushchev (centre) inspects a field of maize at a collective farm in the Orel region in 1962.

There was some resistance to Khrushchev's maize mania at local levels and so the sowing of maize was mandatory, with coercion where appropriate. The *Travopolye* grass rotation was abandoned, even though it was effective in the right conditions. Khrushchev had said that no system was equally applicable everywhere, but he ignored his own advice. Some farm managers resisted by growing maize where it could be seen from the road, but other crops out of sight. Fallow land was reduced, which worked well in areas of high moisture, but helped to destroy the soils in more arid areas. Likewise, grasses helped to restore soil in high-moisture soils, but for Khrushchev it was one-size-fits-all, and that size was maize.

The results were catastrophic harvests, with only the Ukraine producing a profitable crop of maize, while the European Russian fields failed to ripen. As the maize replaced the more traditional wheat and potatoes, there was an acute shortage of these crops. For a farmer to switch to maize was more a test of political loyalty than an economic or agricultural decision. This tended to make local Party officials take Khrushchev's already ambitious ideas to the extreme. He had spoken kindly of legumes, and within a year large areas of grain were replaced with beans. Novels and stories appeared, such as Abramov's *The New Life* (1963), which ridiculed the state's micro-management and blanket approach. By February 1964, with agriculture close to collapse, even Khrushchev began to blame local officials for planting unsuitable crops, but this attempt to pass the blame would not save him.

On a smaller scale, Khrushchev was more successful in helping to incentivise the peasants, with a policy that favoured the carrot over the stick. This can be seen in removing the MTS in 1958, the increase in state farms with their guaranteed wages and reforms of the private plots, raising procurement prices and lowering taxes. However, none of these policies was implemented everywhere, and loopholes allowed local farm managers to continue to manipulate the peasants, though on the whole, they were no longer exploited as they had been under Stalin. He also invested heavily in agriculture and managed to increase output, though at enormous financial cost.

It could be argued that these small-scale incentives could have been brought in by any leader after Stalin. The major policies, which are clearly the product of Khrushchev's flamboyant approach – the Virgin Lands Scheme and the cultivation of maize – were far more ambiguous, with their boomerang results and long-term damage. The micro-management had failed and the basic problem of Soviet agriculture – low productivity – remained. At the start of his Virgin Lands Scheme, Khrushchev had sent Leonid Brezhnev to Kazakhstan to help oversee the ploughing. In 1964, Brezhnev ousted Khrushchev from power and it was now his turn to tackle Russia's more persistent and difficult problem.

ACTIVITY
KNOWLEDGE CHECK

Khrushchev's agricultural policies

1. How do Sources 5 and 6 demonstrate the flaws in Khrushchev's approach to solving the USSR's agricultural problems?
2. Do you think this attitude can also be applied to his solutions to all the USSR's agricultural problems?
3. How could the Virgin Lands Scheme and 'maize mania' be made to work, or were they doomed to fail?
4. To what extent do you think that it was not Khrushchev's policies themselves that failed but their implementation by the state that caused the problems?

Attempts to boost productivity under Brezhnev and Gorbachev

Brezhnev

Like Khrushchev, Brezhnev saw himself as an expert in agricultural policy. He had learned that the outlandish 'campaigns' never maintained results after initial success, and that perhaps a more steady approach was necessary. Anyway, any new areas for agricultural exploitation had already been farmed and often ruined by Khrushchev's policies, so the emphasis was to improve the intensification of grain production. The organisation of farms was placed firmly within Party lines and under official supervision, which provided a steady if not spectacular basis. The local officials were often from urban areas and lacked the expertise or political will to challenge the existing system. Brezhnev began a series of small measures which focused on raising the incentive of the peasants rather than any radical reform and innovation.

- Procurement prices rose, especially in meat, while retail prices stayed low. This developed into a massive state subsidy system, but it helped to provide food for the masses. In 1981, the subsidy to collective farms amounted to $33 billion a year.
- In 1966, the workday system was replaced by a guaranteed, though small, wage and a yearly share in the bonus.
- Private plots were again encouraged, with Brezhnev winning a political battle to increase their size to 1.2 acres per household. By 1978, the plots provided a third of all eggs and meat and a quarter of all agricultural output, despite being only one percent of the cultivated land.
- Further investment went into fertilisers, using imported western technology to improve production.
- Brezhnev's Food Programme targeted the weak agricultural infrastructure by improving storage facilities, refrigeration and especially the provision of all-weather roads. He placed the young politician, Mikhail Gorbachev, in charge, who managed to avoid criticism when the programme failed to make any drastic improvements.
- Overall investment in agriculture increased to nearly 25 percent of total investment, which was a far higher figure than other countries, such as the five percent in the USA. However, the increase in expenditure only stabilised the production amounts. Eduard Shevardnadze, the Georgian first secretary, estimated that each ruble invested in agriculture created only 39 kopeks in return (there were 100 kopeks to a ruble). With 172 billion rubles planned for agricultural investment in the Tenth Five-Year Plan, it was a lot of wasted revenue.

Despite Brezhnev's tinkering in agriculture, there was no fundamental policy that addressed the key issues. The *kolkhozy* (collective farms) and the *sovkhozy* (state farms) failed to get the best out of the farming population, who accounted for 25 percent of the USSR's total workforce. New technology helped in the short term, but there were not the skilled technicians to maintain it. There was no overhaul of the collective system and any suggestion of such innovation usually meant dismissal from one's post. As before, the weather, rather than farming practices, was the dominant factor in the size of the harvests. Poor harvests in 1965 and 1967 saw an estimated 38 percent of peasants fall below the poverty line, while poor harvests in 1972 and 1975 threatened to bring back memories of famine.

At the same time, China was decollectivising agriculture to return to a system of co-operatives and household farms that were allowed to sell any surplus on the free market. Such an innovation, very similar to the NEP system (see page 20) of the USSR in the early 1920s, would have made a real difference, but it was not considered by Brezhnev. It was too ideologically distant from the Stalinist collective farm system he had grown up with. Though Khrushchev had distanced both himself and the USSR from Stalin in his 1956 'Secret Speech', it was a move away from the terror and personality of Stalin, rather than his economic policies. Brezhnev, who had actually taken steps to rehabilitate Stalin in certain places, was far too embedded to the idea of the collective to deviate away from it. Besides, Sino–Soviet relations were particularly hostile in this period, meaning there was no way the USSR would follow China. By 1980, agriculture, as with industry, had stuttered into stagnation. Fifty years of the collective farm seemed to have sucked the life out of the Russian peasants, and many villages rotted away or became home only to the elderly.

Gorbachev

One man who did recommend such a shift in autonomy towards the farm was Gorbachev, in a memorandum during May 1978. Though rejected, it gave hope that the situation might change in the 1980s. Gorbachev was a politician who had developed under Khrushchev rather than Stalin and was more prepared to bring in wide-ranging economic changes that later became known as *perestroika*.

On assuming power, Gorbachev set up the 'superministry', the **State Agroindustrial Committee**, in 1985 to run every aspect of the agricultural industry. However, any reforms were overshadowed by the rapid developments in the collapse of the industrial sector, the growing nationalism within the empire and the ending of the Cold War in foreign relations that would lead to the USSR's disintegration by 1991. Reforms and innovations did not have time to take effect before the system fell apart.

KEY TERM

State Agroindustrial Committee
Also known as *Gosagroprom*, this was set up in 1985 by Gorbachev to centralise all agricultural decisions under a single organisation in an effort to make reforms more universal and efficient to implement. It was part of his wide-ranging reforms to prop up the centrally planned economy. It only lasted until 1989.

It did seem that Gorbachev was open to the idea of the Chinese farming reforms and he told the annual Congress of Kolkhozy in March 1988 that these farms put the family in charge. However, it should be noted that this remark was edited out of the text version of the speech, indicating the sensitive nature of this move towards privatisation. A few thousand 'family farms' were set up, but they greatly depended on the co-operation of the local collective farm. There were strict limits to this reform. Land was leased, not sold, to the family and only family members could be employed.

By 1989 and 1990, the various republics within the USSR had gained some independence from Russia. Swept up in the rapid changes occurring within the USSR, Gorbachev suggested that referendums in the republics might be allowed to decide on private ownership. The November 1990 Law on Land Reform legalised private ownership of land by individuals, while the December 1990 Law on Peasant Farms began to define what private farms would be tolerated outside the collective framework. Land would be transferred from the *kolkhozy*, but there was surprisingly no rush to establish more family farms.

Many farmers felt that the infrastructure was simply not in place to support a small family farm, and that a lack of processing and market facilities would quickly bankrupt them. Secondly, there was a real fear that a private farm would lose any social services which had been provided by the collective farm in the preceding 60 years. As the USSR slipped towards a market economy, the entire framework of the country collapsed. Even in the years that followed the 1991 dissolution of the USSR, the collective farms, despite being privatised out of state ownership to the individual *kolkhoz*, still retained their household plots and dominated the agricultural system.

ACTIVITY
KNOWLEDGE CHECK

The collective farm after Stalin

1. Examine the changes to the collective farms made by Khrushchev, Brezhnev and Gorbachev. Do you think the inability of the Soviet leadership to ideologically free themselves from the collective farm meant the problem of low production would never be solved?
2. Could an intrinsic reliance on the collective farm system be applied to the peasants themselves after 50 years of collectivisation?
3. Was the import of grain, begun by Khrushchev but normalised by Brezhnev, an admission of the failures of the Soviet economic system?

In conclusion, the peasants had been repeatedly told what innovation they had to implement by the central authority, both tsarist or communist. The problem with agriculture has always been how to grow more food, but for the central authority this had not always been their prime concern in their approach to agriculture. In the 19th century, both peasant and master clung to the old ways – the peasant for the traditional security of the *mir*, the master simply to preserve the status quo and their privileged position within society. For much of the existence of the Soviet Union, any reform had choked on the ideological millstone that was the collective farm. This imposition from above, often with the idea of control rather than innovation, never granted the peasants any trust whatsoever. It was always the state that knew best and, whether its intentions were genuine or Machiavellian (scheming to further its own interests), it was always a blanket policy with no exceptions or considerations of local circumstances. Hence, Khrushchev's grand schemes were destined to decay and fail. Some change did occur, but it was forced by population growth or by technology, such as the railways, and its impact was always limited and usually painful for the peasants.

Innovation implies something new, but most reforms, or at least attempts to raise productivity, were more about meddling with the established system rather than experimenting with new approaches. The one completely novel idea, the collective farm, was more concerned with crushing the peasant as a political entity. The innovative aspects of collectivisation should have been the modernisation of the farm, but this never really happened.

The tinkering with the system, whether by Stolypin, Khrushchev or Brezhnev, again failed as they were afraid to change the system radically, and in the end the system itself met a slow death by inertia. It is no surprise that when the slightest amount of faith was placed with the peasants themselves, the results were beneficial. The peasants knew the land they worked, and when they were given the incentives to farm, the most successful changes and the most productive farming took place on their own household plots. Whether this was ever enough to begin to transform Russian agriculture is debatable. At most, the plots made up just four percent of land and, even as the USSR died, its leaders desperately struggled to hold on to the principle of collective farming. The vast size and range of the Russian farmland meant that no single approach to raising productivity would work. It failed, leaving a system that would always struggle to maximise its yields and feed itself.

A Level Exam-Style Question Section C

How far was the imposition of reform from the leadership of Russia and the USSR responsible for the failure to introduce innovation into agriculture between 1855 and 1991? (20 marks)

Tip

Be confident enough in planning your essay to challenge the statement within the question. In this case, you could argue that at certain periods it was only the authority of the leadership that had any chance of reform, while at others it hindered innovation. In a question that covers 130 years, there will be many changes throughout the period.

EXTRACT 3

From Chris Ward, *Stalin's Russia* (1993).

What happened between November 1929 and December 1931 cannot be grasped by reciting statistics... a socio-economic system in existence for five hundred years vanished forever. But the whirlwind which swept across the countryside destroyed the way of life of the vast majority of the Soviet people, not just the Russians... Early in 1930, countless individuals and families in entire regions and republics - the Russians, Ukrainian and Causasian grain districts - were stigmatized as kulaks, driven from their land, forced into collectives, exiled or shot. Central Asian cotton growers and sugar beet farmers in the Central Black Earth region suffered the same fate in 1931.

EXTRACT 4

From Robert Service, *A History of Twentieth-Century Russia* (1997).

Conditions in the countryside were so dire that the state had to pump additional resources into the country in order to maintain the new agrarian order... Yet Stalin could draw up a balance sheet that, from his standpoint, was favourable. From collectivisation he acquired a reservoir of terrified peasants who would supply him with cheap industrial labour. To some extent, too, he secured his ability to export Soviet raw materials in order to pay for imports of industrial machinery... Above all, he put an end to the recurrent crises faced by the state in relation to urban food supplies as the state's grain collections rose from 10.8 million tons in 1928-9 to 22.8 million tons in 1931-2. After collectivisation it was the countryside, not the towns, which went hungry if the harvest was bad.

EXTRACT

From Chris Corin and Terry Fiehn, *Communist Russia under Lenin and Stalin* (2002). Reproduced by permission of Hodder Education.

For the party, collectivisation was an essential part of its modernisation drive. The Party did not want a sizable sector of the economy to be dominated by the private market or to be at the mercy of the peasants who hoarded grain. In this sense, collectivisation was a political success. The Party gained control of the villages, and did not have to bargain with the peasants any more. It had established a system, using local soviets and MTS, of controlling the countryside and making agriculture serve the towns and workers.

THINKING HISTORICALLY Change (8a, b & c) (II)

Judgements about change

If two professionals were asked to track a patient's health over time, one might approach this task by measuring heart rate, weight and cholesterol, while the other might assess the patient's mental well-being, relationships and ability to achieve their goals. Both are valid approaches, but result in different reports. What is true in this medical case is true in historical cases. Measuring change in something requires: (a) a concept of what that something is (e.g. 'What is "health"?' 'What is an "economy"?'); (b) judgements about how this thing should be measured; and (c) judgements about what relevant 'markers of change' are (how we distinguish a change from a temporary and insignificant fluctuation).

Historians have differed in their accounts of the impact and success of Stalin's collectivisation policies. Read Extracts 3-5 about the impact of collectivisation and answer the following questions.

1 How do these accounts agree about the impact of collectivisation?

2 Do the historians all think of the impact of collectivisation in the same way, e.g. social, economic, individual?

3 Generalising from these examples, to what extent do historians' judgements about change depend on **what** historians decide to look at and **how** they decide to measure change?

TO WHAT EXTENT DID DOMESTIC AGRICULTURE MANAGE TO FEED THE POPULATION BETWEEN 1861 AND 1991?

To successfully feed a population, a government must fulfil two key criteria.

- First, enough food must be either grown or imported. This includes a range of products to enable a healthy diet for the population. The food producers, the peasants, must provide a surplus to feed those not economically engaged in food production.
- Second, the food must be distributed across the entire population. This includes geographical locations, not easy in such a vast empire, but also throughout both rural and urban locations.

In Russia, during this period, the emphasis of food distribution changed as the needs of the workers in the towns and cities grew ever more important, and this placed an increasing strain on the ability of the peasants to get enough supplies for their own use. More constant was the over-dependence of Russia on one particular crop. Russia measured its agricultural power in the amount of grain produced, just as it went on to measure its industrial might in the amount of steel forged. This lack of diversity continued to generate problems throughout the 20th century.

1861–91

The emancipation of the peasants did little to modernise the technological aspects of Russian agriculture. Therefore, the most significant trigger for food shortages remained the climate, and this had generated a fairly regular pattern of shortages over the previous centuries, with a drought occurring every 5–7 years and a famine every 10–13 years. The three areas most sensitive to the climatic fluctuations were central Russia around the Volga basin, the southern farmlands of the Urals and Ukraine, and the eastern steppes of Kazakhstan and Siberia. Nothing in the years following emancipation changed this and it could be argued that it made some matters worse.

The peasants still strip-farmed small plots of land within their *mir*. The population of Russia was growing more quickly in the countryside than in the cities: over 80 percent of the population could be classed as peasants. With more people needing a share of land, the size and therefore the yields of the plots in each *mir* diminished. The peasants mainly practised subsistence farming, growing crops to support their own households. Though this could include a more diverse range of crops such as rye, oats and potatoes, it was only for the use of the household. As the growing demand for food put ever greater pressure on the agricultural system, food shortages became more likely. Subsistence farming is particularly susceptible to famine, as each household is totally reliant on its own crops. The food for the cities, and the surplus grain needed for export, tended to be grown by the landowners' estates.

The freedom from serfdom was rightly seen as a humanitarian and moral improvement in the status of the peasants, but with no welfare system established to replace it, the peasants found themselves in a less secure system than before, which again made them vulnerable to poor harvests.

SOURCE

Scottish traveller and journalist Sir Donald Mackenzie Wallace commenting on the peasants' lack of security. He visited Russia during the 1870s, and this was first published in 1877.

Their burden and their privileges have been swept away together, and been replaced by clearly defined, unbending, unelastic legal relations. They now have to pay the market price for every stick of firewood that they burn, for every log that they require for repairing their houses, and for every rood [0.10 hectares] of land on which to graze their cattle. Nothing is now to be had gratis. The demand to pay is encountered at every step. If a cow dies or a horse is stolen, the owner can no longer go to the proprietor with the hope of receiving a present, or at least a loan without interest, but must, if he has no ready money, apply to the village usurer, who probably considers twenty or thirty per cent as a by no means exorbitant rate of interest.

In 1861, about a quarter of farms were not self-sufficient and provided no surplus at all. By 1900, this had grown to over half. Debt and the tax burden kept the peasants impoverished with minimal innovation. Even those who had borrowed money to buy land were held back by the mortgage payments. It was worse for those 750,000 who took one of the quarter-size 'beggar holdings' for free. These simply could not sustain even themselves and most fled the countryside and sold their land; up to 20 percent of the peasants in the Black Earth Region took this option. Even the nobles complained. A December 1861 petition to Tsar Alexander II commented that hired labour for their estates was unprofitable and the amount of grain on the market would decrease, as would the size of their estates.

Farming in Russia was living always on the edge. When crops failed, the peasants desperately tried to look after themselves and it was the cities that went hungry first. The majority in the cities maintained their close links with the countryside and would return to the relative safety of their *mir* to sit out a period of hunger. However, the famine of 1891–92 demonstrates how both government interference as well as inaction can quickly escalate a poor harvest into a full-blown famine.

The famine, 1891-92

It was the predictably vicious cycle of the weather that caused the initial shortages along the course of the River Volga down to the Black Sea. A dry autumn in 1891 delayed sowing the crops, while a freezing but snow-free winter killed many young plants. Icy floodwater destroyed more, as well as ruining the fodder for the horses. After a windy spring removed the topsoil, the dry summer started to kill an already weakened population and their livestock, with some areas having no rain for 100 days.

Even then, Russia still produced just enough grain to feed itself. But here the decision to export grain to provide capital in order to start the process of industrialisation was to prove disastrous. The surplus was mainly provided by the noble estates, but the agricultural infrastructure was too weak both to support exports and feed its own population. The surplus grain, even with the limited railway system that was set up to export abroad rather than distribute internally, could have been stopped from leaving the country if the political will had been there. With grain leaving the country, the people began to go hungry. Even then, the finance minister, Vyshnegradsky, did not ban grain exports until August 1892 and then gave a month's warning to allow the merchants to ship any reserves. Vyshnegradsky also began collecting the peasants' taxes immediately after the harvest. This forced them to sell more grain than normal at low prices, meaning they had none left in reserve. The government also censored any mention of the famine, delaying any relief. The crisis became a tragedy and around 500,000 died, mostly from cholera outbreaks triggered by the conditions.

Even the relief efforts, when they eventually came, failed to make any impact. The government asked people to create voluntary anti-famine organisations, rather than establishing a state-organised facility. Russia's famous author, Leo Tolstoy, volunteered, but the Orthodox Church refused to let any peasant accept his charity, as he had been excommunicated. The local ***zemstva*** loaned money to the peasants for food, but rules stipulated that only those who could repay it were allowed to take it. Therefore, the most needy received nothing. The government did provide horses to plough the fields in 1892, but the effects of that harvest would not be felt until 1893. Meanwhile, the starving made do with donated raw flour and a 'famine bread' made of moss, goosefoot weeds, bark and husks.

KEY TERM

Zemstvo (plural *zemstva*)
An organ of rural self-government in Imperial Russia, established in 1864 to provide social and economic services.

The famine highlights not only that the government had no action plan to deal with emergency food shortages, such as storage depots, distribution networks and state agencies, but also that it lacked a basic desire to recognise it as a problem. Hunger and starvation were facts of life. A poor harvest or a period of famine were not planned for. The peasants were left to cope; usually they could just scrape through, while urban workers had to flee or die. There was a government 'faith' that a poor harvest would be followed by a good one and that matters would return to the much desired status quo, such was the rhythm of life and death in 19th-century Russia. What truly mattered was that there was grain to export. Grain exports had increased from around 60 million rubles in the early 1860s to over 300 million rubles in the late 1870s. Even when competing grain from Canada and the USA lowered the prices and therefore the profits, more actual grain was exported to make up the capital. In the eyes of the government, the need to export grain far outweighed the need to feed the population.

From famine to the end of Imperial Russia, 1892-1917

These exports became more important as Russia stepped up its programme of industrialisation. The peasants paid for industry through grain and tax, both of which were in limited supply. Between 1893 and 1913, 20–33 percent of all Russia's wheat was exported. This constant squeezing of the peasants would explain the scale of the peasant uprisings in 1905. During the 1890s, Prince Kopotkin, the radical political activist, spoke of the normality of famine and the fact that a third of Russian peasants suffered from disease and hunger while ships piled high with grain set sail for foreign countries.

Russia became the largest exporter of grain in the world by 1913, with an almost eightfold increase in the amount exported since 1861, which amounted to 55 percent of all Russian exports by value. The early years of the 20th century were generally free of large-scale famine, though there was plenty of misery with each poor harvest. In general, though, agriculture kept up with population growth. The main reason for this was the expansion of cultivated land.

In particular, the planned economy of Siberia opened up by the Trans-Siberian Railway presented new opportunities to farm. With no history of the *mir*, the freer atmosphere of Siberia encouraged more high-value products as well as grain. By 1914, it provided half the meat for Russia's two most rapidly growing cities, St Petersburg and Moscow. This was important as Russia's lack of mechanisation kept its crop yields far below those of western nations (see Figure 2.6). In European Russia in 1911, there were only 166 tractors, compared with 14,000 in the USA.

	Wheat	Rye	Oats	Maize	Potatoes
Russia	803	964	928	1,321	8,729
USA	1,232	1,214	1,354	1,981	7,855
France	1,535	1,214	1,481	1,446	10,174
Britain	2,606		2,035		18,064
Germany	2,606	2,143	2,233		16,140

Figure 2.6 Comparative yields (kg per hectare),1911–15.

In many ways this period is similar to the preceding one. Agricultural methods changed little, while the population grew, reaching over 155 million by 1913 (with 78 percent in European Russia). The percentage of the population in the countryside remained remarkably consistent and the government remained equally indifferent to improving the quality and quantity of people's diet. Even Stolypin's deliberate attempts to reorganise agriculture and create the more independent *kulaks* had little effect. Several years of fine weather after 1905 helped to produce good harvests and keep the population fed, despite the odd setback, as in the harvests of 1906 and 1911. In the first decade of the 20th century, the peasants' prime concern was, as always, hunger for land or ownership, rather than food.

Despite two decades of industrialisation, the continuity with the past is clearly shown in the years of the First World War. The annual production of grain fell from 90 million tonnes in 1913 to 64 million tonnes in 1916. As the chaos of war cut exports and damaged the grain distribution network, the cities emptied out as people returned to their roots in the *mir* and turned to subsistence farming to keep them alive. Once more, it was the traditional *mir*, despised by the state, that would enable the rural population to be fed before, and often instead of, the city in times of crisis. Inflation made the problem more serious as the price of manufactured goods far outstripped the price of grain. Therefore, the peasants began to hoard their stocks. They ate more of it themselves, fed it to their livestock and turned it into vodka. In short, the peasants did anything they could with it rather than sell it to the market at a minimum cost. In August 1915, the government set up special councils to buy grain at set prices, but the peasants refused to sell. The first demand on any surplus was always the army, which also commandeered the transport network, making distribution to urban areas unreliable. Petrograd (St Petersburg), far from food-producing areas, suffered especially as refugees from the devastated Eastern Front tended to head there. By 1916, the decline in food production meant that even the troops struggled to maintain supplies. Once more, life was on the edge. It was left to troops to individually barter their coats and boots for food, as compulsory grain requisitioning brigades set up by the government failed. Though the government fell short of using outright terror, the peasants still refused to sell. Food distribution moved onto the black market.

Imperial Russia had always placed social control over genuine attempts to improve agriculture. The elite had never wholeheartedly supported industrialisation or they would have invested more to provide agriculture with a solid foundation and ensure the workers were fed. Crops would have been more diversified and yields improved. In its hierarchical vision of the world, hunger, even starvation, among the lowest tier was a price that could be paid to maintain the imperial system. This lack of empathy with both workers and peasants would prove fatal. The peasants struggled, but at least they were situated where the food grew; the workers in the cities felt the pangs of hunger more fiercely.

The communist and Stalinist state, 1917–53

The failure to distribute food, even though there was enough, underpinned the fall of the tsarist regime. The attempted solutions made matters worse. By keeping food prices low while the price of manufactured goods rose sharply, there was little motivation for the peasants to sell. In Moscow, the price of rye rose by 47 percent in the first two years of the war, but the price of boots rose by 334 percent and matches by 500 percent. The result was long queues at the food markets. In autumn 1916, women camped overnight outside bakeries in the hope of provisions. By the end of the year, it was estimated that the average woman was queuing for around 40 hours a week on top of her hours at work. The queues became a hotbed of political dissent.

It was women queuing for bread in Petrograd, as well as the hungry factory workers, who started the February Revolution of 1917 and the end of imperial rule. The Provisional Government repeated the same mistakes as the tsar, and was equally ineffective. Six months later, a drastic cut in bread rations in Petrograd created the perfect conditions for the communists. Hunger will always seed revolt.

However, the new rulers learnt the lessons. As Russia slipped into civil war (1918–21), the urban food crisis was the Bolsheviks' most serious problem. The average worker, so important in building the weapons of the inevitable war, was eating half the bread and a third of the meat they had eaten in 1913. For the first time in Russian history, it was the aristocracy, now labelled 'former people', who starved most quickly. They sold their possessions and joked about losing weight. The Bolsheviks did not care about them, but they did care about the workers fleeing the cities away from the weapon factories. Some workers left for good, but many spent days in the countryside looking to buy food, known as 'bagging'. Over 100,000 bagmen travelled each month, even taking over trains to get to the favoured destinations. The Bolsheviks blamed the peasants for hoarding grain. In a rehearsal for the terror of collectivisation, they declared a 'food dictatorship' and went after the peasants' grain under the political policy of War Communism (see page 21).

It was assumed that all peasants would hide grain and, although many did, the armed brigades took reserves of seed and food as a 'surplus'. In the battle for grain, the peasants were subjected to extremes of terror and violence. By the end of 1919, the brigades, each consisting of 75 men and at least two or three machine guns, even stopped trains to confiscate any food from passengers. The result was that both the Red Army and the workers were fed enough to keep going and eventually win the Civil War. Trotsky boasted of winning the war, but recognised that the cost was the destruction of Russia. But there was worse to come as the combination of drought, grain requisitioning and civil war caused grain production to halve in 1920 and 1921, resulting in a famine that killed five million people.

SOURCE 10

Lenin, in the summer of 1918, announcing the creation of a 'Food Army' of 76,000 'soldiers'. It was a declaration of war on the peasants just as violent as Stalin's 'liquidation' a decade later.

The kulaks are the rabid foes of the Soviet government... These bloodsuckers have grown rich on the hunger of the people... These spiders have grown fat at the expense of the peasants ruined by the war at the expense of the workers. These leeches have sucked the blood of the working people and grown richer as the workers in the cities and factories starved... Ruthless war on the kulaks! Death to all of them.

The Bolsheviks, under Lenin, continued their grain requisitioning until December 1921 and only stopped when the scale of peasant unrest forced them to consider the alternative policy of the NEP. The Bolshevik response to the famine is similar to that of the tsarist government in 1891. By the spring of 1921, about a quarter of the peasants were starving. The government banned all transport from famine areas in order to contain epidemics. Cannibalism was common, with thousands of reported cases. It was felt that eating a dead body was tolerated as the soul had left, so corpses in cemeteries were dug up. However, there were many cases of people being killed for food. Children were murdered and either eaten or sold at markets. There were even gangs of children killing adults for meat. One man, convicted of eating several children, said that it was accepted and that all the people ate human flesh, served by the several cafeterias in the village. The government, just as in 1891, denied any existence of famine. Despite the starvation, it continued to transport grain out of the Ukraine and even exported millions of tons abroad, to the disgust of international aid agencies.

Lenin had criticised charity organisations in the 1891 famine as being too sentimental, and therefore the state was very reluctant to set up any relief agencies. Indeed, it was left to private charities to fund relief, including the American Relief Administration (ARA), which by the summer of 1922 was feeding ten million people every day, despite constant harassment by the Bolshevik authorities.

EXTEND YOUR KNOWLEDGE

The thankless work of the American Relief Administration (ARA)

The ARA was set up by President Herbert Hoover to feed post-First World War Europe, but he extended it to Russia in 1921 after an appeal by the Russian author, Maxim Gorky.

The Bolsheviks allowed a voluntary body to be set up to help organise the ARA in Russia. This 73-member organisation, known as *Pomgol*, was created in July 1921 and was the only independent body ever established in communist Russia. Hoover offered aid as long as its activities were completely independent and all US citizens were released from Russian jails. A furious Lenin grudgingly accepted the aid, closed down *Pomgol*, and arrested nearly all its members, sending most into exile.

The ARA gave medicines and clothing, as well as the tools and seeds that enabled Russia to plant and harvest the crops of 1922 and 1923, thus escaping famine. The ARA spent $61 million in total, but received little gratitude or assistance from the Russian government. Instead the Bolsheviks interfered with ARA supplies, arrested relief workers and searched ARA trucks and trains. When the US public discovered that, as it gave supplies and money in the name of charity, the Russian government continued to sell grain abroad for funds, there was outrage. US fundraising immediately dried up and the ARA left Russia in June 1923. The Bolsheviks sent a formal brief letter of appreciation, which embarrassed the increasingly disillusioned Gorky, and was a key factor in his decision to leave Russia in the 1920s.

SOURCE 11

A Russian couple sell human parts on a market in the Samara province during the 1921 famine.

SOURCE 12

One of the consequences of the famine and the communists' lack of action was the packs of orphans scurrying through the streets. By 1922, some seven million orphans were living rough and open to abuse, addictions and crime. One observer noticed such a boy in a market square.

I myself saw a boy of about 10 to 12 years of age reach out, while being beaten with a cane, for a piece of bread already covered with grime and voraciously cram it into his mouth. Blows rained on his back, but the boy, on hands and knees, continued hurriedly to bite off piece after piece so as not to lose the bread. This was near the bread row at the bazaar. Adults – women – gathered around and shouted: 'That's what the scoundrel deserves: beat him some more! We get no peace from these lice.'

Crime rates grew as people stole food and then graduated to armed raids on granaries or fields of crops. The cities emptied as people fled to try to find food at source. Petrograd's population fell from 2.5 million in 1917 to just 600,000 by 1920 and, for those who remained, the death rate was 8–10 times higher than the birth rate.

The NEP was a temporary halt to the government's policy towards feeding its population, allowing the peasants to recover sufficiently to get Russia back on its feet before the onslaught of Stalin's collectivisation.

The catalogue of horror of the 1930s echoed and then built on the worst cruelties of the early 1920s. The famine in the 1930s was a deliberate policy of starvation rather than incompetence and a lack of compassion, but the driving force behind the government's actions was the same. The workers were fed before the peasants. The collective fields were planted and the harvest would be exported before the peasants ate. The peasants were seen as an obstacle to the communist utopia and must be paid to serve the cities, while their labour provided the capital for Russia's industrial transformation.

It is important to note that the peasants' intense, if ultimately futile, resistance to the collective programme did achieve one concession that had important consequences for the state's ability to feed its population. The private plots for each household, which Stalin finally allowed after 1932, were the intensely farmed gardens that would provide the vegetables, fruit, dairy, poultry and meat for the Russian population. Farmed by the peasants with more dedication, and the possibility of profit, their yields were 8–12 times higher than the collective fields. This was the sole reason why there was no more famine in Russia, with the exception of 1946 after the devastation and scorched earth of the Second World War. For Stalin, the private plots would remain a hated throwback to pre-revolutionary days and he could not recognise their intrinsic value. It seemed for a while that even these small allotments would become victims in an ideological war, but Stalin's death saved them.

By 1953, Russia was entirely self-sufficient in food production. Both range and quantity were limited, but the people did not starve. Strict government control of low procurement prices had delivered the basic food products, particularly bread, at low cost. However, this was becoming increasingly hard to afford as the bread was sold more cheaply than the cost of the ingredients. As Russia moved into the second half of the 20th century, the strains on the system only grew as the population and the new regime demanded a more diverse diet.

ACTIVITY
KNOWLEDGE CHECK

Famine

1. Compare and contrast the famines of 1891 and 1921. Think about the causes, the government's responses, and the impact of famine on society at the time and afterwards.
2. The famine of the 1930s was examined in Chapter 1. To what extent is the history of the Russian peasant 1855-1953 a catalogue of famines? How would you approach answering a question like this?

The Khrushchev era, 1956–64

In his bid to catch up with the USA, Khrushchev placed huge demands on agriculture. In 1957, he demanded a threefold increase in meat production. The consequences demonstrated that the authorities went a long way to hide the fact that they were struggling to feed the people. The truth was even kept from the leaders themselves, in an effort for local Party officials to prove their loyalty and climb the career ladder.

Alexi Larionov, the Party boss of the Ryazan region to the south of Moscow, promised that he would meet the new meat target within a year. This boast was much publicised by Khrushchev to 'inspire' other bosses to do likewise and Larionov was awarded the Order of Lenin. However, to fulfil his promise, Larionov slaughtered almost every cow in the region, both beef and dairy. He bought every cow reared on any private plot and bankrupted the region by buying meat from other regions. The target was met to great applause, but the next year's meat production fell to a fraction of the target and the people went without meat. The truth was exposed and an embarrassed Khrushchev fired Larionov, who promptly committed suicide.

The government, as always, was still largely dependent on the weather, and a sequence of bad seasons compounded by the poor management of the Virgin Lands Scheme and maize mania meant that the 1960 harvest contrasted sharply with the abundance of high-quality food products talked about in Party propaganda. Again, the issue was made worse by a refusal to accept the situation, while claiming that all was well. The population, freed from the idea of absolute totalitarianism and terror under Stalin, began to protest. Posters in the Siberian city of Chita in December 1960 proclaimed that Khrushchev was a blabbermouth and demanded to know where the abundance was that he promised.

Soon, the expense of feeding a population cheaply could not be maintained. In May 1962, Khrushchev announced a 35 percent rise in the retail prices of meat and poultry, and a 25 percent rise in the price of butter and milk. In 45 years, communism had inflicted many hardships on the people of the USSR, but at the least they had expected full employment and a reduction in consumer prices. There were immediate calls for strikes in Moscow, Kiev, Leningrad, Donetsk and Chelyabinsk. The situation was worse at Novocherkassk, in southern Russia, where around 10,000 strikers and protesters carried red flags and portraits of Lenin and Marx in a scene reminiscent of the Revolution or Bloody Sunday. As the demonstrators demanded cheap food, the authorities killed 16 locomotive workers. Later, over 100 protesters went on trial, seven of whom were sentenced to death. In a state supposedly free of Stalinist terror, this was a wake-up call for Khrushchev. Though his deputy, Kozlov, was overheard on the phone angrily demanding more food for himself, Khrushchev seemed to be more deeply affected by the disturbances. However, he did not allow the protests and repression to be reported.

An increasingly desperate Khrushchev looked for a panacea to the food problem, but the discredited ideas of Lysenko and Garst's wonder maize had failed. The new cure was fertilisers, but the failure of the grain harvest in 1963 both in European Russia and the drought-hit Virgin Lands meant that rationing was considered. Despite losing his temper over the idea at a Presidium lunch,

Khrushchev was forced to buy foreign grain. He cut the military budget in order to afford 6.8 million tonnes from Canada, 1.8 million from Australia, two million from the USA and even 400,000 on loan from Romania. At least, finally, the solution involved feeding the whole population and a new precedent was set.

SOURCE 13

Sergei Khrushchev reflects on his father's attitude to his failure to solve the agricultural problems and consistently feed the population. Sergei Khrushchev left Russia in 1991 to live in the USA and has written several books, which have tried to shed a positive light on his father's legacy. This is from his book *Nikita Khrushchev and the Creation of a Superpower*, published in 2000.

Father didn't understand what was wrong. He grew nervous, became angry, quarrelled, looked for culprits but didn't find them. Deep inside, he began subconsciously to understand that the problem was not in the details. It was the system itself that didn't work. But he couldn't change his beliefs.

ACTIVITY
KNOWLEDGE CHECK

Food supplies

1 How reliable do you find Sergei Khrushchev's analysis of his father's mistakes in Source 13?

2 What are the implications for the USSR's leaders after Khrushchev, according to Source 13?

Brezhnev: the import of western grain, 1972–79

Present at the Presidium lunch where Khrushchev had erupted with rage before accepting the need to buy in foreign grain was Leonid Brezhnev. In his possession were newspapers full of furious letters from members of the public complaining about the lack of food. He had feared showing them to Khrushchev, but he did at least learn from the reaction.

The 1970s were not a time of plenty in the USSR. Though the population was eating more than the people in really poor countries, they still had significantly less than rich countries (see Figure 2.7). Part of the problem was the reliance on potatoes and especially grain for cheap bread.

	Food consumption per head per year		
	USSR (1973)	USA (1972)	UK (1970)
Bread (kg)	145	65	73
Potatoes (kg)	124	66	103
Meat (kg)	52	110	76
Eggs (number)	195	321	283
Milk (kg, mainly as cheese)	307	254	216

Figure 2.7 A comparison of Soviet consumption levels with the USA and the UK. The figures for milk hide the fact that fresh milk was scarce in the cities and most of the USSR's milk consumption was in Soviet cheese. The lack of refrigerators severely hampered the storage of milk.

The USSR had always supplied its citizens with cheap bread, often at the expense of other food groups. The riots at the increase of food prices in the early 1960s just confirmed what the state already knew: bread must be available to all and at a low price. The result was that people queuing for long hours often returned with only bread, as that was the only product available. In fact, there was so much bread that it was bought to excess and fed to animals. The guarantee of cheap bread meant there had to be enough of it. Starting in 1972, Brezhnev was forced to import massive amounts of grain, mainly from the USA, to manufacture into the artificially-created domestic demand for cheap bread. The breadbasket of the world was reduced to importing its own grain. It paid for it with energy exports, increasingly supplemented with foreign credit when energy prices were low. More and more of the state budget went on subsidies to bridge the gap between the price of grain and the cheapness of bread, reaching $33 billion a year by 1981. Though extraordinarily inexpensive to buy, these costs made it the most expensive bread in the world to produce, especially as the price of imported grain went up. In 1970, a bushel of US grain cost $1.54, but by 1980 it was $4.45. Meanwhile, the price of bread had not risen from 20 kopeks a kilo since 1955. This money should have been spent on social improvement for Soviet citizens and the USSR continued its spiral into economic collapse.

Apart from bread and potatoes, all food products were ***defitsitnyl*** (in short supply). The opposite of this was ***nedefitsitnyl*** (not in short supply), unlike the West's plentiful or just normal. The very language of the time indicated that the queues remained. The only citizens with an uninterrupted supply of all types of food were the members of Soviet ***nomenklatura***, a privileged group of selected Party officials who had access to special shops that were kept hidden, if not totally secret, from the public.

KEY TERMS

Defitsitnyl* and *nedefitsitnyl
Local Russian terms for food products that were either 'in short supply' or 'not in short supply'. The Russian word for 'abundant' was rarely applied to food.

***Nomenklatura* system**
A list of Communist Party personnel, from which appointees were chosen for administrative posts. It formed an elite of public officials, or even a new privileged class. It was extremely important in the USSR and other Eastern European countries for ambitious individuals to get their names on the list.

Everyone else had to make do. In Moscow in 1976, despite the capital being given top priority for food, restaurants had to organise 'meatless days'. In Tula, workers refused to receive their pay as there was nothing to buy. This protest was put down by the state, after a few arrests, by announcing that Tula was a 'hero city' for its role in the Second World War and therefore qualified for extra food distribution.

Brezhnev began importing grain as part of the July 1972 trade agreement with the USA, with a plan to buy at least $750 million worth. However, disputes over the treatment of Soviet Jews saw the agreement cancelled in January 1975. The shortage of grain continued, particularly as feed for beef cattle, and by October 1975 a new five-year grain agreement was decided.

EXTEND YOUR KNOWLEDGE

Grain as a political weapon?

Many in the USA hoped that Soviet reliance on western grain would give the forces of capitalism political leverage in negotiations. While ratifying the US-Soviet trade agreements in 1975, the US Congress insisted on adding a clause to include 60,000 visas a year for Soviet Jews to emigrate to Israel. The Kremlin could not accept this humiliation, which led to the agreement being cancelled.

As the USSR bought more grain in the late 1970s, the USA hoped to wrest concessions from the USSR. However, the complex movement of grain could make its exact provenance hard to name. To the pleasure of US grain-trading companies, the export of grain to the USSR survived the end of the relaxed political relations known as *détente*. Even when the West imposed economic sanctions after the Soviet invasion of Afghanistan, restrictions applying to grain were quietly ignored and the USSR imported 34.5 million tons in 1979-80. Grain, it seemed, would not become a weapon, at least on the international front.

A run of bad harvests in 1975, 1979, 1980 and 1981 raised the spectre of popular uprising not just in Russia but in its Eastern European satellite states. As early as 1970, strikes in Poland sparked by the merest hint of food price increases had been enough to see the increases quickly withdrawn. It was clear that the need to import western grain was not simply an emergency and short-term measure, but an annual purchase designed to make up the shortfall in grain and help to ease political tensions.

Nikolai Baibakov, who headed **Gosplan** in 1955–57 and 1965–85, estimated that between 1971 and 1975 the Soviet Union's oil and gas bought $5 billion worth of food, rising to $15 billion between 1976 and 1980, and $35 billion in 1981–85.

KEY TERM

Gosplan

The State Planning Committee, whose task was to work out the economic plans based on directives from the political leadership. It was the nerve centre of the Soviet economic system.

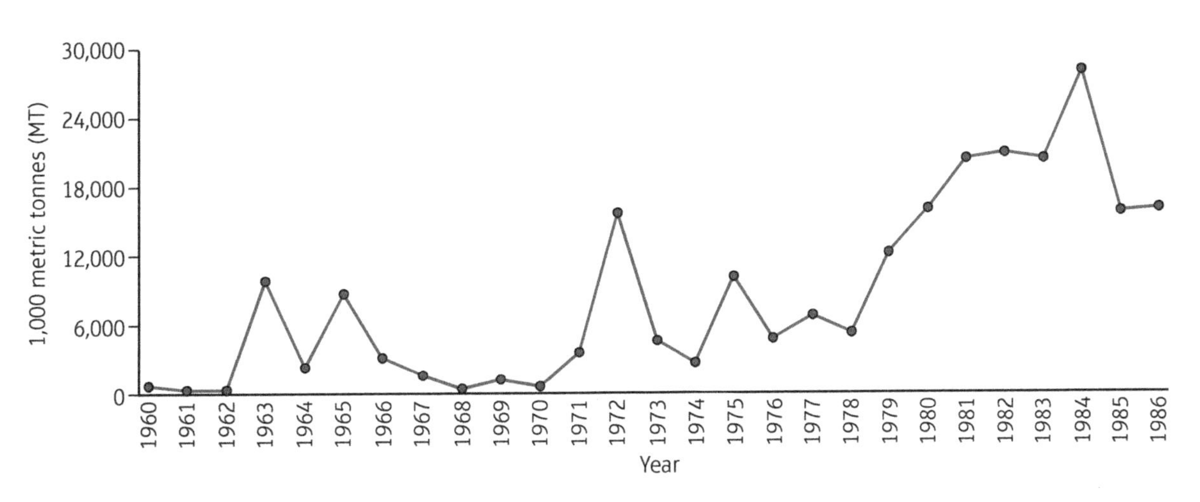

Figure 2.8 USSR imports of wheat, 1960-86.

To be fair, the Soviet diet did improve between 1965 and 1980 as consumption of meat rose by around 40 percent, and fish, vegetables and fruits all saw increases of over 30 percent. But this was not enough to satisfy demand. The collective farms still failed to produce the goods needed, and the importance of the private plots in supplying fruit, vegetable, pork and poultry was even more pronounced. In the less repressed atmosphere of the late 1970s, jokes could be heard on the streets, such as 'Why isn't there any flour in the shops? Because they've started adding it to bread.'

ACTIVITY
KNOWLEDGE CHECK

Khrushchev and Brezhnev

1. Working in pairs, each write a speech as either Khrushchev or Brezhnev, aiming to persuade the Russian people that you did more as leader to ensure that the masses were adequately fed.
2. After listening to your partner's speech, write a rebuttal attacking their version of 'history'.
3. Together, form a conclusion with a reasoned judgement on which period, 1956-64 or 1965-1982, saw the most progress in feeding the Russian population.

Throughout the 1980s, the shortages remained, especially of meat and dairy products, resulting in long queues waiting for possible deliveries in front of empty shops. The most reliable way to get meat was by buying rabbits and meat from peasants on the roadsides. Though no one starved in Russia during the last days of the communist regime, food was mostly limited to bread and potatoes, and getting hold of anything beyond the staples involved considerable patience and/or skill on the black market.

SOURCE 14 From Plutarch, *Parallel Lives: Lycurgus 24* (late 1st century AD).

Spartiates' training extended into adulthood, for no one was permitted to live as he pleased. Instead, just as in a camp, so in the city, they followed a prescribed lifestyle and devoted themselves to communal concerns. They viewed themselves absolutely as part of their country, rather than as individuals...

SOURCE 15 From Xenophon, *The Politeia of the Spartans VI* (early 4th century BC).

Lycurgus made it possible for someone to use another's servants in case of need, and established a similar system of sharing hunting dogs... similarly with horses... because they share in this way, even those who are not well off have some part in all the resources of the country when they need something.

EXTRACT

From Pamela Bradley, *Ancient Greece: Using Evidence* (1988).

The Spartans were taught a way of life. The system of training (*agoge*) was successful in that it achieved a stable city-state and produced courageous and loyal citizens, but it did not encourage resilience to cope with change. During the fourth century it became obvious that the Spartans were unable to adapt satisfactorily to changing conditions.

EXTRACT

From Paul Cartledge, *The Spartans: An Epic History* (2003).

The balance of power between Sparta, on the one hand, and the allies, on the other, was manifestly clear... Sparta was the *hêgemôn* or leader, and the allies were *summachoi*, that is committed to both offence and defence on behalf of and at the behest of the *hêgemôn*.

THINKING HISTORICALLY Cause and consequence (6c)

Connections

Sources 14 and 15 and Extracts 6 and 7 describe some typical aspects of Spartan society around 400 BC.

Work in groups or individually and answer the following questions.

1. Read Sources 14 and 15. How might these be seen as similar to the Soviet leadership's belief regarding the principles of communism?
2. Read Extract 6. How could you compare the Spartan aim of education with that of the communist regime 1917–91?
3. Read Extract 7. To what extent is the Spartan role with their Peloponnesian allies an earlier version of the relationship between the USSR and Eastern Europe between 1945 and 1989?
4. Why it is important for historians to see these links across time and be able to explain how causal factors can influence situations much later in time?

Conclusion

The central planned economy of the USSR had failed to meet the basic requirements of feeding its population. In the 19th century, the urban areas went hungry, unless the combination of poor climate and poor management resulted in a famine that none could easily escape from. Even then, Russia could always produce enough food, but it was either sidelined for export to raise investment or wasted through an inefficient distribution network. In the first few decades of communist rule, it was the turn of the peasants to feel the first pangs of hunger as priority went to the urban areas with their factories. Here, the famines took on a political aspect, as food became a weapon to aid control.

Under War Communism in the early 1920s, and again under the forced collectivisation of the 1930s, the state was breaking the peasants to serve the cities. Famine did little to limit the export of grain and only the private plots, reluctantly allowed by the state, kept the population alive. By the 1960s, the emphasis on grain not only revealed the lack of variety in the population's diet, but also began to unbalance the national economy. With yields failing to rise in the failed modernisation of agricultural practices, the USSR had to import grain to feed its people and livestock. This set the pattern through the stagnating Brezhnev years and continued until the end of Gorbachev's days.

Though the disintegration of the USSR is often portrayed within an atmosphere of an inevitable industrial collapse, it was the inability to build an economy with a strong agricultural foundation that prevented a balanced and stable economic infrastructure from developing. The inherent weakness at the heart of this command economy is reflected in its inability to provide a consistent supply of food to its whole population and a varied diet evenly distributed across the extent of the USSR. Bread queues and empty shops regularly sparked calls for change in 1991, just as they had done in 1917.

A Level Exam-Style Question Section C

How far was the October 1917 Revolution and the establishment of communist rule the key turning point in the inability of Russia/the USSR to feed its population in the years 1855–1991? (20 marks)

Tip

In a question that asks about a turning point, it is important to examine the situation before and after the stated event. You should also try to show how events afterwards are connected to the stated event, as well as keeping open the possibility of other turning points. Think about what would make a turning point 'key'.

ACTIVITY
SUMMARY

Agriculture and productivity: meeting the country's needs?

1 Split the period into the following sections:
- 19th-century tsarist Russia
- Stolypin's reforms
- early communist rule
- Stalin
- Khrushchev
- post-1964.

For each one, summarise the changes in agricultural practice and the State's ability to feed the people.

2 What issues place limits on reform, and what helps to promote reform in each period?

3 Discuss in groups the idea that the necessity for an autocrat, be it the tsar or the communist leadership, to maintain social control made it impossible to modernise agriculture and provide a surplus to feed the population.

4 Identify the periods of severest food shortages and famine. Were any of these truly preventable? Did the government's reactions merely make the famine's consequences worse, or was the government actually responsible for causing them?

WIDER READING

Conquest, R. *Harvest of Sorrow*, Oxford University Press (1986)

Evans, D. and Jenkins, J. *Years of Russia and the USSR, 1851-1991*, Hodder & Stoughton (2001)

Hanson, P. *The Rise and Fall of the Soviet Economy*, Longman (2003)

Hite, J. *Tsarist Russia 1801-1917*, Causeway (1989)

McCauley, M. *The Khrushchev Era 1953-1964*, Longman (1995)

Mosse, W.E. *An Economic History of Russia 1856-1914*, I.B. Tauris (1996)

Thompson, W. *The Soviet Union Under Brezhnev*, Pearson (2003)

3.3 The political reforms of Alexander II, 1855–70

KEY QUESTIONS

- How significant was the impetus to reform a result of the Crimean War?
- How effective were the reforms of the legal system and local government in the years 1855–70?
- To what extent was there greater freedom of expression in Russia in the years to 1870?

INTRODUCTION

Tsar Alexander II inherited a nation in crisis, and he could see that reforms were necessary to adapt Russia towards a modern Europe. The most important of his reforms was the emancipation of the serfs in 1861 (see Chapter 1), but this major change initiated connected reforms in the army, local government and the *zemstvo* system, justice and education. The tsar became known as Alexander 'the Liberator', an image he evidently enjoyed, as Source 1 shows. As often happens, the introduction of reforms led to demands for further and more radical policies, and protests grew. The limited freedoms provided the substance for revolutionary groups to feed on, and this era saw an increase in political violence, followed inevitably by political repression. While the revolutionary groups believed the reforms would erode the powers of the tsar, Alexander II did not. Although some of the revolutionary demands focused on a reduction of the tsar's power, he saw no link between his social reforms and a relaxation of his personal autocracy. His reforms certainly began the process of change, but he clashed repeatedly with a myriad agitational groups over the direction the change should take. A series of assassination attempts littered Alexander's reign before a final bomb ended his life, ironically just as he was finally conceding an element of political dialogue. His violent death abruptly ended Russia's experiment with reform.

By the time of Alexander II's coronation in 1855, the disastrous consequences of the Crimean War clearly identified the need for change.

1855 – Coronation of Alexander II

Fall of Sevastopol

1856 – Treaty of Paris ends Crimean War

1861 – Milyutin appointed minister for war

Emancipation of the serfs

St Petersburg University closed down

1862 – *Young Russia* proclamation

St Petersburg fires

1863 – January Uprising: Polish unrest

University statute

Corporal punishment in military abolished

1855 | 1856 | 1857 | 1860 | 1861 | 1862 | 1863

SOURCE 1

A contemporary Russian poster of Alexander II celebrating the emanicipation of the serfs in 1861. The image announces that the tsar is the source of all reforms in the early period of his rule. It also makes it clear that he should be acknowledged by a grateful and subservient population for all reforms.

1865 – Censorship enforced after publication

Student unrest

1870 – Municipal Regulations Act introduces *duma* to the towns

First university course for women

1864	1865	1866	1867	1868	1869	1870

1864 – Military administration reformed

Regulations for judicial institutions

Zemstva created in countryside

1866 – First attempted assassination of tsar

Reactionary Tolstoi replaces Golovnin at education ministry

The Contemporary and *The Russian Word* periodicals closed down

1869 – Student unrest

HOW SIGNIFICANT WAS THE IMPETUS TO REFORM AS A RESULT OF THE CRIMEAN WAR?

How did the conclusion to the Crimean War create the circumstances for the reforming attitude of Alexander II?

The contradiction of a forward-looking ruler in a backward country could not be more evident. The new tsar was 36 years old, well educated in both military and academic disciplines, and groomed for leadership. He had travelled, won awards for bravery, and his more tyrannical father had trained him for leadership with appointments on various committees discussing many aspects of Russian life, ranging from serfdom to railways. During his father's absences, it was Alexander who continued the routine of state, and was therefore more than prepared to rule. With regard to 1850s Russia, Alexander was very much a modern man. However, his nation was in disarray.

While Russia could hold its own against Turkey, once the war widened to include France and Britain the Russian deficiencies were clearly exposed. The military incompetence of the French and the British was more than matched by the incompetence of the Russian generals. The 1854 defeat at the Battle of Alma was followed by a costly year-long siege at Sevastopol on the Crimean peninsula, in which the Russians were forced to withdraw from this largely symbolic fortified base. One of the first humiliating acts Alexander II had to face was to negotiate surrender and sign the Treaty of Paris to bring the war to a close – he may have been a new tsar, but he was one in charge of an old country.

It was not the cost of defeat that harmed Russia; it was what the defeat represented that shocked the political elite within the nation. Casualty rates had been high, with over 400,000 dead and around 80,000 wounded. Most of the deaths were from disease and the appalling conditions, rather than any military action. The Treaty of Paris did not excessively punish Russia, though it did not allow a Russian naval fleet in the Black Sea. All sides realised that inept generals, poor military and communications infrastructure and the need for an increasingly technological armoury were indications that changes were needed, at least on a military front. For Russia, the far bigger blow was that it was diminished as a European power.

In 1812, Russia had devastated the main French army, and as part of the coalition it had forced Napoleon out of power and into exile. In 1855, it could no longer defend a homeland base against an enemy from the other side of the continent. An army of 1.8 million soldiers with 171,000 reserves and 370,000 militia could not defeat its rivals. Part of the problem was that the sheer size of the empire meant the army was spread too thinly across its land, with only 100,000 troops spared for the defence of Sevastopol. The diversity and constant unrest among the provinces and regions continually demanded that troops were sent out in every direction. Added to this was the cost in training and supplying the army. Equipment was out of date and the supply chain riddled with corruption. The state arsenals contained only half the weapons they were meant to. Russian bravery was wasted by the lack of quality officers. In short, the army was not professional enough to fight a modern war, and it lacked the initiative to enact its own reforms.

Before the Crimean War, the intellectual debate over the future of Russia was argued between the slavophiles, who idealised a Russian-dominated Slavic world, and the westernisers, who felt that the traditional Russian way could hold back progress and therefore a more European model was required. The Crimean War was proof of Russian backwardness, and therefore maintaining a Russian-centred outlook would only maintain the status quo. The consequences of the war, as well as the more European education of Alexander II, seemed to encourage a more westernising attitude to a reforming society. His ascent to the throne was greeted with widespread enthusiasm and a consensus of opinion for change. However, the possibility of European-style politicisation of the nobility and gentry was a vain hope. Tsar Nicholas I, from his deathbed, may have apologised to his son for the poor state of Russia, but he also urged him to hold on to everything. Alexander II might have truly empathised with the Russian people, but they were his people, not their own. The autocracy would remain.

One person Alexander II did take advice from was his younger brother, the Grand Duke Konstantine Nikolaevich. He had headed the imperial navy and realised that a new type of official was required, who was prepared to implement change when and where it was needed. He promoted like-minded people and this slowly began to spread into other government departments. The generally uncensored *Naval Review* magazine (*Morskoi sbornik)* encouraged ***glasnost*** throughout the 1850s. Despite being under surveillance by the tsarist secret police (known as the **Third Section**) during

KEY TERMS

Glasnost
A Russian term meaning openness and transparency in government. More commonly associated with the 'New Political Thinking' of Mikhail Gorbachev in the 1980s and the democratisation of the USSR, in fact it has a much longer history.

Third Section
Set up by Nicholas I in 1825 after the Decembrists' Revolt, with 16 officers, it effectively acted as the tsar's secret police. By 1855, it had 40 officers. It was replaced by the *ochrana* in 1880. It is sometimes referred to as the Third Department.

the reign of his father, Nikolaevich became Alexander II's chairman on the Council of State. This marriage of bureaucracy and autocracy drove forward the reforms of the 1860s.

SOURCE

A slavophile view of Russia in 1855 by Konstantin Aksakov, a writer and critic. He urged Alexander II to restore the feudal parliament known as the *Zemsky sobors*, based on Russian landowners and last seen in 1682. Here he blames the influence of Peter the Great, who reigned 1682–1721, for leaning the new Russian Empire towards Europe. Aksakov became radically anti-European.

The people called for political power, elected a Tsar, and entrusted their fate to him; then they peacefully laid down their arms and dispersed to their homes. Russia's history contains not a single instance of a revolt against authority and in favour of political rights for the people... Under Peter there began that misfortune which is still with us today. In the West there is this constant enmity and rivalry between State and people, who fail to understand the relationship that exists between them. In Russia we have never had that enmity and rivalry. The Russian people remained true to their outlook and did not encroach upon the State; but the State encroached upon the people, forcibly changing their ways and customs... Thus was destroyed the ancient union between land and the State. Let us re-establish the ancient union between government and people, state and land, upon the lasting foundation of truly basic principles.

EXTRACT

From Geoffrey Hosking's *Russia and the Russians: A History* (2001), in which he describes the view of Vissarion Belinsky, the leading proponent of the westernisers' view in the 1840s. In his *Survey of Russian Literature* (1847), Belinsky proposes that the spirit of individuality that has been present in Russia since the days of Peter the Great is essentially a European tradition. His survey, along with Konstantin Kavelin's *Survey of the Juridical Way of Life of Ancient Russia*, published in the same journal in 1847, came to be seen as the manifesto of the western view.

Russia, he pointed out, belonged to Europe, 'by its geographical position, because it is a Christian power, because its civic culture is European, and because its history is already indissolubly linked with Europe.' Nor, as an undoubted power of international standing, need it fear being swamped by European innovations: it could absorb and assimilate them without damaging its own distinctive essence, just as 'the food ingested by a human being is transformed into his flesh and blood and maintains in him strength, health, and life.'

ACTIVITY
KNOWLEDGE CHECK

Slavophiles and westernisers

1 How do Source 2 and Extract 1 differ in their analysis of Russia's situational problems?

2 What do they imply are the possible courses of action that could be taken?

3 Using your own knowledge, how do the circumstances created by the Crimean War give credence to Belinsky's view rather than Aksakov's?

How did Tsar Alexander II reform the military after the Treaty of Paris, 1856?

All of Alexander's chief advisers in the first half of his reign were military men. His brother was in charge of the navy, General Rotovstev tackled the emancipation of the serfs, while Dmitry Milyutin was minister for war from 1861. It was Milyutin who pushed through the army reforms against aristocratic opposition. Even when the tsar relied more on reactionary advisers in the latter half of his reign, Milyutin remained and General Loris-Melikov pressed for political concessions to gain a loyal base among the general population.

EXTEND YOUR KNOWLEDGE

Dmitry Milyutin (1816–1912)

As a professor of military history, Dmitry Milyutin had analysed the causes of the Russian defeat in the Crimean War. Alexander II made him minister for war in 1861. He was a sincere supporter of liberal reform and was responsible for all the reforms to the military.

Following the assassination of Alexander II and unable to work with the reactionary Alexander III, Milyutin retired to his Crimean estate in 1881.

Many of Alexander's political reforms were needed as consequences of the emancipation of the serfs in 1861, and the military reforms were no exception. However, the Crimean War made it obvious that some immediate reform was necessary, even before the serfs were freed. The war exposed some of the basic inadequacies of the Russian army.

Military service had been for 25 years, almost a life sentence for a conscripted peasant. Many landlords used the army to take the most troublesome or unproductive of the peasants off their estates, and the state used recruitment as an alternative to exile. Even for the sons of the lower nobility, the education and training were insufficient to create talented officers and replace experienced ones. The poor quality of reserves meant that mobilising a large force in times of crisis and war was hard to enforce.

Alexander II, in 1856, closed down the garrison, or cantonist, schools which had been training soldiers' children since the early 18th century. These schools were brutal and spartan, and pupils as young as eight had been taken into service during the Crimean War. It was not an efficient method of supplying a modern army, so all pupils under the age of 20 were discharged from the army, though the process took three years to complete. Any military settlements, which had been set up during the 1820s after the Napoleonic Wars to create soldier communities, were abolished for similar reasons. The settlements that had attempted to integrate the worlds of the peasant and the soldier to provide a ready supply of troops had failed due to lack of investment and were deeply unpopular with the soldiers. In 1859, the length of military service was reduced to 15 years in the army, 14 in the navy, both with around ten years as a reserve.

The appointment of the energetic Milyutin in 1861 saw a planned and comprehensive reform of the military. He understood that the way to provide high-quality troops for war, without the expensive cost of a large army during peace time, was the European model of universal conscription for a brief time, with a longer period in the reserves. He also admired the way the European military allowed a degree of mingling of different classes to create a sense of nationhood. His reforms tackled several areas.

Conscription

Throughout the 1860s, the period of service continued to drop, even if not backed by law, and many soldiers left after 7–13 years. Each year the military took in around 100,000 recruits (a rate of four in every 1,000 eligible males), of which 80 percent went into the infantry. The new conscriptions still caused problems; Poland's 1863 January Uprising against Imperial Russian rule was triggered by forced conscription of Polish youths. However, by 1870, the strength of the reserve had risen from 210,000 to 533,000 soldiers. In April 1863, corporal punishments such as running the gauntlet were abolished.

> **KEY TERM**
>
> **Franco-Prussian War, 1870–71**
> A war between France and the German Confederation headed by Prussia. A swift series of decisive military victories by Prussia's conscripted army led by a professional elite proved influential in military tactics. Orchestrated by Chancellor Bismarck, the war culminated in the unification of Germany.

The success of the Prussian army in the **Franco-Prussian War** inspired many in Russia to copy the Prussian-style universal conscription. This support enabled Milyutin to pass the 1874 law for universal service for all males from all social classes. All males aged 20 that year would be registered and a quarter chosen by lot to serve about six years full-time and nine years as reserves (or seven years full-time and three as reserves for the navy). Reserves would be expected to attend summer camps and courses to maintain effectiveness, providing a well-trained reserve core in case of emergency. Milyutin acknowledged that exceptions regarding status and education would also be needed.

Young men who were their families' sole providers were excused, while better-educated recruits had their service length reduced, meaning that a university degree would result in just six months' service, secondary education 18 months', and primary three to four years', while a university-educated 17-year-old could 'volunteer' for a short period of three months (one year for secondary; two for primary) and then become an officer in the reserves. Milyutin realised that this would encourage young men to remain in education as long as possible, which would benefit the nation as a whole. He believed that not only would educated men be quicker to train, but that it would be foolish to remove them from society for too long and waste their talents. Therefore, there was an element of social engineering in his reforms as he sought to emulate the western powers.

It was this aspect that instigated the fiercest opposition to his reforms from the nobility. Previously, the nobility, as volunteers, constituted nearly all of the officer class. Now non-volunteers would be conscripted along with everyone else, and even volunteers would be forced to mix with non-noble officers. The nobility, often through the Minister of Education Count Dmitry Tolstoi, complained bitterly to the tsar and in the press. Alexander II noted that aristocratic women resented the changes the most, as they could not accept their children mixing with peasants, while Milyutin despaired at the stubborn resistance to his common-sense and practical reforms. The effectiveness of the Prussian army convinced the tsar to back Milyutin.

Military administration

In 1864, the administration of the military was decentralised away from St Petersburg into a system of local military districts, each led by a commander. By 1871, European Russia had around ten districts, Asiatic Russia had three and the Caucasus had one. This freed the general staff in the capital to focus on larger concerns, while also allowing for a more rapid mobilisation on a regional scale.

Military education and training

The cadet corps which had provided a poor-quality, if free, education for the sons of the nobility, were replaced with military gymnasiums. These taught a wider curriculum of academic subjects facilitated by civilian teachers. Special military schools were created for future officers, and progymnasiums offered a more general four-year course. The less prestigious two-year military cadet or 'iunker' schools were also set up to cater for non-noble recruits. By 1880, some 56 military schools of all these types were running and a decent standard of education was required for all officers, whereas in the Crimean War only one third of officers had had a military education. At the highest level, academies for general staff, engineering, artillery, medicine and military law were created. These were set at an increasingly professional level, with graduates fast-tracked for promotion and key positions. The educational policy meant that despite the continuing power of patronage from the tsar and aristocracy in promoting untrained officers, there was a professional officer core throughout the many regiments.

Thus, the character of the army gradually changed through the 1860s, as ceremonial drill and parade practice were replaced by target shooting, fencing, gymnastics and combat training. Corporal punishment and discipline were restricted and the soldiers often found their lack of schooling balanced by a broader education within the army.

Weapons

Military equipment was slightly improved as it was easier to provide newer examples of technology for a smaller army. However, long borders and the rapid obsolescence of weaponry meant that equipping troops would remain acutely expensive for the state, and this was never satisfactorily resolved. In the 1860s, about a third of all government expenditure was on the military; despite a budget bigger than any other European nation, the proportion spent on each individual soldier was less because the army was so large compared to other European powers. Russia also lacked the industrial infrastructure to deliver up-to-date military hardware, a problem that would remain until the Second World War nearly a century later.

In conclusion, the military reforms pushed through by Milyutin against considerable opposition did transform the spirit of the military in the 1860s and 1870s, as gradually a system based on meritocracy began to take hold among the officer class. However, membership of the elite core of officers remained the privilege of the aristocratic families who enjoyed the tsar's blessing rather than military experience. They therefore possessed very little training. The new emerging graduates were snobbishly referred to as 'pheasants', while lower officers who were often quite professional were still regarded as inferior. In 1877–78, the new military system was tested in a brief war with Turkey. Despite success, and noticeably better organisation than during the Crimean War, it was a victory of the weak over the weaker, rather than a display of military might, and certainly did little to impress other European nations. Training was still insufficient, senior leadership inept and the army underfunded.

These lessons went unlearnt as Milyutin was quickly retired once Alexander III became tsar in 1881. Privilege and the cadet corps were brought back, while civilian teachers and gymnasiums were removed. In general, the essence of the reforms stayed, improving administration and conscription, while they did not threaten the tsar's overall control as he continued to put close friends and family at the head of each military section. With no progression over the following decades, the impact of the cluster of reforms in the 1860s was severely limited, as the 1904 war with Japan would prove.

SOURCE 

The Russian minister of the interior, Valuev, admiring the recent Prussian victories over France in 1871, and reflecting on the reforms of military service in Russia.

Military service is a form of national elementary education. The habit of military order, the concept of military discipline, are not lost when active service ends.

SOURCE 

From *Punch* magazine, 21 February 1863, *A growl for Poland*, by John Tenniel. Russia, represented by the bear, had launched a campaign of conscription in Poland. Lord Napier, the British ambassador at St Petersburg, commented that it was designed solely to confine the potential for Poland's revolution within the Russian army. After some 2,500 young men had been conscripted by Russian police agents and soldiers in one day, there was a Polish rebellion. Here, the bear brandishes a gun at the shackled Poland, while John Bull and the British bulldog look on, preserving British neutrality.

PUNCH, OR THE LONDON CHARIVARI.—February 21, 1863.

A GROWL FOR POLAND.

Mr. Bull. "AH, OLD DOG—YOU'D LIKE TO HAVE ANOTHER RUN AT THAT BEAR, WOULDN'T YOU; BUT IT WON'T DO THIS TIME."

ACTIVITY
KNOWLEDGE CHECK

Military reforms

1. Compare how Sources 3 and 4 indicate the usefulness of military reforms beyond purely military efficiency but for social and political ends. Compare the tone as well as the inferences.
2. How useful is Source 4 to a historian studying the impact of Milyutin's military reforms?
3. To what extent do you think Milyutin was a successful minister for war in Russia? Think about how he could be judged, both by his contemporaries as well as his legacy.

HOW EFFECTIVE WERE THE REFORMS OF THE LEGAL SYSTEM AND LOCAL GOVERNMENT IN THE YEARS 1855–70?

Before Alexander II, the system of justice was riddled with corruption and opaque proceedings, and blocked by bureaucratic obstacles. Cases could last for years, even decades, while poorly trained judges sat in socially segregated courts in which the poor had little hope of justice. There was a vast array of courts in which judges examined only written evidence in closed sessions and were heavily reliant on the police for their information. With over half of judges illiterate, this did not make for an efficient and fair process. The judges would never see the defendant, and this gave little opportunity for the written evidence to be challenged. It was the court secretaries who best understood the system and they were notorious, along with the police, for their willingness to take bribes to support their standard of living. An example of the institutionalised misconduct was the fact that the local inhabitants would have to pay a fine to the police if a murderer was not found.

The verdict of a case was highly influenced by social class. A man's evidence was more valuable than a woman's, while evidence from a noble or priest carried more weight than that from anyone else. When a defendant was found guilty, the punishments were cruel and severe, as set out in the code of 1845. Typically, the standard sentence of hard labour in exile in Siberia was accompanied by vicious corporal punishments, and often ended in a slow and agonising death. Legal reform had been a key demand in the 1825 Decembrist uprising against Alexander II's father and, with the emancipation of the serfs, the basic inequality of the system could no longer be tolerated by either the masses or those within the legal system who desired reform.

Between 1858 and 1860, draft reforms were formulated based on European models, and in 1862 the tsar approved their implementation into the judicial institutions. These reforms were centred on three basic principles: an open and transparent system, the use of juries and independent courts. While the details were being worked out, parallel legislation was introduced to limit the possibility of police corruption by creating special magistrates to investigate suspected criminal offences, while corporal punishments, such as the lash and branding, were eliminated and the birch much restricted. The reforms were remarkable in that these concepts were new to Russia and had no links to the traditionally autocratic system.

The new judicial system was eventually implemented for civil and criminal cases, and punishments were formalised through the November 1864 Regulations for Judicial Institutions, which formalised the earlier draft reforms, while a new code of 1866 reduced the harsh excesses of previous punishments.

The new courts

The new courts were open to the public and in all cases the 'controversial' trial was introduced, where there was oral dialogue between prosecution and defence as each pleaded their case. The defence was made by a lawyer, who had been professionally educated and trained, and a lawyer would be appointed by the state if the accused could not afford one. A special court investigator examined the more serious cases, and the decision of guilt was decided by a jury of 12 local men selected by lot.

A new, elected official, the justice of the peace, investigated less important cases and tried to conciliate the two parties to avoid the use of the court. This represented a fairer and more accessible system than had previously been available to many in the towns and cities, and provided many with their first experience of democratic, if diluted, elections as the justices were elected for a three-year term by the *zemstvo*, the local council.

More important cases were heard at the county level, where justices of the peace met with special honorary justices. For the most important cases at the district court, government-appointed judges sat in court. Courts of appeal were situated in the largest city of each district. Previously the highest court was the 'governing senate', but its powers were reduced to a final court of appeal to reverse a decision only if it violated legal procedure and not for political reasons. Senators were still directly appointed by the tsar, but the tsar and his government could only appoint judges from a group selected by the courts, and they enjoyed complete independence and could not be removed. This was a genuine shift away from autocratic power. Judges were well paid, to discourage bribery.

Some of the new judges were the best of the old ones, untainted by corruption, while most were young university-educated professionals who quickly won great popularity as crowds flocked to see the most interesting cases and the most eloquent lawyers. More important was the fact that the average person felt for the first time that the justice of the peace gave each individual a true sense of equality and justice before the law, as everyone, whether noble or peasant, was addressed in exactly the same manner. Public access to the courts, as well as to the more professional judges, meant that corrupt or false evidence was much harder to present, and trials progressed more quickly. The affairs of every court were reported in the official journal, *Government Messenger* (*Pravitel'stvennyi Vestnik*), an indication of how sympathetic to legal reform the autocracy was under Alexander II.

While many aspects of the jury system mirrored the West, such as voting by secret ballot, the final decision was based on a majority rather than a unanimous vote, as it was felt that the will of a few should not hold back that of the majority. Juries did sometimes act in the spirit of the public consciousness rather than impartial justice: if they felt a punishment was too harsh for the crime, they would find a guilty defendant innocent, or guilty of a lesser crime.

The impact of legal reforms

There were a few restrictions and exemptions from the reforms. Church and military courts were excluded, and the state retained the right to exile an individual without trial if it felt that this would prevent a crime. This was mainly used for political reasons, and a special state department was set up in 1872 to enforce it. In addition, a judicial official could only be accused of corruption with the agreement of his superior. However, the principles of 1864 were so universally accepted and popular that even the more reactionary and repressive tsars that followed Alexander II found it difficult to use these clauses and loopholes.

The most serious defect of the new legislation was the fact that peasants' cases were held in separate courts, known as ***volost*** courts, created after the 1861 emancipation. The law applied in these courts was based more on custom than written, legal definition and highlighted the fact that the peasants were a class apart from the rest of Russia. The 1864 reforms specifically required the *volost* courts to continue. Therefore, some 80 percent of the population was excluded from the benefits of the legal reforms.

While the judicial system presented a fundamental change in Russian legal proceedings and proved popular with the common citizens it applied to, the most important and arguably far-reaching consequence of the reforms was the creation of a new class of professional lawyers.

These defence attorneys, or ***advokatura***, had their own organisation based purely on merit. These Bar Councils, of which there were three by 1874, in St Petersburg, Moscow and Khar'kov, upheld a genuine faith in the rule of law and enjoyed freedom of speech while in court. This helped to maintain professional conduct and ensure that standards would be continued. The tsar had felt uneasy over the creation of a class of lawyers, as he was concerned that the Bar would attract liberal thinkers. This did indeed happen, as lawyers were trained in rhetoric and persuasion, and came into contact with all social groups. They naturally became the voices and leaders of reform and even of revolutionary ideas. Both Kerensky, who eventually became the leader of Russia after the February 1917 Revolution, and Lenin, who became the leader of Russia after the October 1917 Revolution, were members of the Bar Council.

More immediately relevant to the common citizen, the position of justice of the peace gave people a trustworthy method of challenging the imposition of authority through the courts. Many of these justices became valued members of the community, which was resented by many supporters of absolute autocracy, as can be seen by the fact that Alexander III was quick to abolish the position.

KEY TERMS

Volost **(plural *volosti*)**
After the 1861 emancipation of the serfs, this became the main unit of peasant local self-rule. Each *volost* was made up of several *mirs* (see Chapter 1). The chiefs of the *mirs* that made up the membership of a *volost* formed an assembly that elected a chief (or elder) of the *volost* and a *volost* court to deal with local crimes.

Advokatura
Defence lawyers who found employment in the new open courts. Over the next few decades, the Bar Councils proved to be a talking-shop for reform and a breeding ground for new and revolutionary ideas.

Response to the reforms

Along with a more professional and generally reform-minded personnel staffing the courts, the openness and debate within the court allowed radical and political ideas to be aired in court and then published in the *Government Messenger*. In addition, the government was allowing an independent group to judge people who had been arrested for political acts. This was a perfect opportunity for revolutionaries to air their views, as for example in 1871 when Sergei Nechaev, an anarchist who had organised the assassination of an innocent student, used the court, as did his followers, as a platform for their ideas rather than to defend themselves. Sometimes political defendants were let off by juries who saw their actions as youthful, if misguided, idealism.

EXTEND YOUR KNOWLEDGE

The case of Vera Zasulich (1878)

Vera Zasulich, the 28-year-old daughter of an army officer, had attempted to murder General Trepov, the governor of St Petersburg, and had shot and wounded him in front of several onlookers. The minister of justice, Count Palen, requested a guilty verdict from the judge, but was ignored. The defence lawyers argued that Vera had been upset by Trepov's brutal actions, such as flogging a political prisoner who refused to remove his hat. Details of Zasulich's life on the fringes of the revolutionary movement were revealed, along with reports of over-zealous police supervision of her. Her sensitive nature was discussed by witnesses. Despite her clear guilt, the jury acquitted her, to loud applause from the court. The authorities immediately demanded her re-arrest and a retrial, but her supporters quickly got her out of the country, where she became a Marxist revolutionary.

Vera Zasulich survived, but Count Palen was sacked and the judge lost any chance of promotion. The conservatives were disgusted that the will of the government in such a clear breach of law should be disregarded, and even some liberals were alarmed that the notion of justice could be tainted by political considerations, even if it was in their favour. The trial had been twisted by clever, liberal lawyers and a willing public to be a damning verdict on Trepov and the authority of the state. Anxious not to repeat the mistake, the government transferred all trials concerning violence against officials to military courts.

The government could not tolerate the courts challenging its authority, and although it could not reverse the direction and spirit of the legal reforms, piecemeal action was taken throughout the 1870s, and especially in the 1880s under Alexander III, to limit the freedom of the courts. In 1874, the Bar Councils were limited to the three already set up, while unqualified lawyers were allowed to practise. This created a two-tier system, but the state hoped it would curtail the legal profession's liberal influence. In 1889, the powers of the justices of the peace in rural areas were given to the hated Land Captains (see page 15), who now policed the countryside, while Jews were refused admission to the Council.

Although these measures chipped away at the reforms, they did not dismantle or replace them. The new courts were thoroughly successful in their application of justice, despite being a clear break from the traditional structures of Russian society. As well as modernising the legal system, the reforms brought forward the idea that the law was for the benefit of everyone and not just the state. The masses could receive a sympathetic response to their grievances, and the atmosphere created by the reforms encouraged a generation of lawyers to be more open in their views. Indeed, one prominent lawyer of the time, V.D. Spasovich, likened the lawyer's role after 1864 to a chivalric knight, with more political freedom than the press.

EXTRACT

From historian J. McManners in *Lectures on European History 1789–1914* (1966) commenting on the reforms of Alexander II.

Tocqueville's* famous dictum, the most dangerous moment for a bad government comes at the point when it tries to reform, was proved right again. Half measures aroused the demand for full measures, and a glimpse of the shadow, whetted by imagination which yearned for reality. By dabbling in freedom, the autocracy had demonstrated its own obsolescence without being able to adapt itself to the new age.

* Alexis de Tocqueville (1805–59) was a French historian whose most famous works were *L'Ancien Régime et la Révolution* and *Democracy in America*.

ACTIVITY
KNOWLEDGE CHECK

Legal reforms

1 McManners, in Extract 2, warns that the reforms would inevitably create calls for more, further-reaching reforms. Do you think this is necessarily true?

2 If the legal reforms caused political problems for the autocracy, why did Alexander II introduce reforms which clearly broke with the Russian tradition to which the tsar's authority was central?

3 Alexis de Tocqueville wrote about the American Revolution of the late 18th century. Why might it be dangerous for historians to apply universal ideas across different countries and periods? Try to support your ideas with examples from your own knowledge and reading.

How did Tsar Alexander II reform local government within Russia?

The *zemstvo* statute of 1864

The size and geographical variety of the Russian Empire meant that well-organised local governments were needed to ensure the efficient operation of the government. Before Alexander, local government was split into three levels which found it hard to work together. There were 50 provinces headed by a governor who was considered to be the voice of the tsar. Each province was divided into districts of around 200,000 people, but there was no district administration and very few qualified officials. At the most local level were the rural districts (*volosti*), where the local nobility dominated the serfs. After the 1861 emancipation, this needed changing, as the nobility had no legal control over the peasants.

Each village (peasant commune or *mir*) became part of a *volost*. There were 10,000 *volosti*, each covering an area with a diameter of around 25 miles. There was no way any central authority could directly control every aspect of life, so the *mir* controlled day-to-day life, with the village or district elder responsible for enforcing the regulations. Each group of ten households sent a representative to the *mir*, one of whom was elected elder. Despite many efforts by subsequent government policies and political programmes, the *mir* dominated at the most local and personal level until Stalin's mass-collectivisation of the 1930s.

There was growing demand for change at higher levels too. There was very little infrastructure to run the social requirements at a local level, especially in rural areas. Public education and hospitals were barely developed, while fire prevention, roads and bridge repairs were haphazard or non-existent, relying on the goodwill and co-operation of local landlords. Westernising nobles admired the political sway of the English squires of the time and desired a similar system. In 1862, some of the nobility of the Tver province called for an end to the traditional privileges such as tax exemption and automatic state positions, while 13 nobles went further and called for a classless elected assembly. Their calls were met with prison sentences and a law restricting the discussion by noble assemblies to only local matters. However, with each provincial governor weighed down with paperwork, handling around 100,000 documents each year, reform was desperately needed to allow local government to function.

On 1 January 1864, the *zemstvo* statute was a solution to the idea of self-government at both provincial and district levels. For the district *zemstva*, the nobility, townsmen and peasants each elected their own representatives. The elections were set up to give the nobles and peasants around 40 percent each, despite the vast differences in their numbers. The townsmen and Orthodox clergy made up the rest. In 1864, some 13,000 deputies were elected to the district *zemstva*. The provincial *zemstva* were elected from members of the district ones, and favoured the nobility even more, at over 70 percent of the assembly. Initially just 19 provinces had them, though this quickly grew to 34. Both types had a chairman who was always a member of the nobility, and both had an executive to run the *zemstva* on a daily basis.

Although the nobility had greater weight in the assemblies at the *zemstva*, the meetings were organised so that all classes sat as equals and, perhaps surprisingly, the atmosphere was usually calm and businesslike, rather than a resentful standoff between former masters and former serfs.

SOURCE 5

D.M. Wallace, an Englishman who had lived in Russia for many years and was an acute observer of Russian life, reported his observations on the *zemstvo* assembly of Novgorod province in the late 1860s, which were published in his book *Russia* (1905).

What surprised me most in this assembly was that it was composed partly of nobles and partly of peasants - the latter being decidedly in the majority - and that no trace of antagonism seemed to exist between the two classes... The discussions were carried on chiefly by the nobles, but on more than one occasion peasant members rose to speak, and their remarks, always clear, practical and to the point, were listened to with respectful attention.

SOURCE 6

Midday Break for the Local Authorities (1872) by Grigoriy Grigoryevich Myasoyedov (1834–1911). It portrays a typical *zemstvo* having lunch after 1864.

ACTIVITY
KNOWLEDGE CHECK

The district *zemstvo*

How useful to a historian are Sources 5 and 6 in investigating the organisation of the district *zemstvo* between 1864 and 1870?

The work and importance of the *zemstva*

Though the nobility dominated the district *zemstvo*, the peasants had most to gain, as public health and education were the key interests. The *zemstva* set up medical assistants and then doctors. At first, the peasants did not trust the poorly-equipped medical staff, but this began to change as the *zemstva* received more funding for medical care and duly spent more – around 20 percent of their budget – on health care. Assistance was free, though a few doctors charged for the actual medicines. By 1870, the *zemstva* employed 613 doctors, and this figure continued to grow sharply over the next few decades. The *zemstvo* doctor became an honoured member of the local community.

The other honoured member was the teacher, and the *zemstva* played a vital part in promoting rural primary schools. Most education for the peasants' children was practical and aimed at getting the young used to the dealings of agriculture and trade, as well as dealing with the authorities. Farm work always took precedence and was organised at the level of the *mir*. Therefore the *zemstva* tried to support mutual aid societies to deliver summer courses and libraries, as well as offering help in an emergency. By the 1870s, the number of primary schools had expanded greatly, rising to 23,000.

The creation of the *zemstva* was an undoubted success, but most of their work became apparent after 1870. A range of activities, including financial assistance, theatres, public health and education, were important aspects of *zemstvo* work. The seeds for all their future work were planted in the late 1860s.

If the social impact would eventually become increasingly positive, there were also political impacts that were more mixed, depending on your point of view. The *zemstva* can be credited with bringing more professional people from a non-noble background into the countryside, such as teachers and doctors, but also statisticians, clerks, book-keepers and the like. For example, in Tver, the *zemstvo* employed just 17 professional people in 1866, but 669 by 1881. These people had no fixed place in the class system and they were known as ***raznochintsy***. Proud of their humane efforts in bringing skills to the countryside, they saw the need to reform the state politically in order to further their work. They became the 'third element' (after the official bureaucracy and *zemstvo* deputies) and developed into a powerful liberal force. Again, it was the reforms of Alexander II that began this process.

KEY TERMS

Raznochintsy
A new class of professional, skilled employees who worked through the *zemstva* in the countryside. Like the *advokatura*, they would promote a general trend towards reform. Also known as the 'third element'.

Obshchestvennost
A rather vague concept, similar to the idea of a new political consciousness. It refers to the period of the reforms of Alexander, which introduced the notion of wider political participation in Russia. Once introduced, it could only be limited by repression, and was never completely subdued.

This force was not a revolutionary movement, although these were emerging at the same time. It was a collective feeling made up of educated, politically and socially aware individuals who wanted change. They were not an organised group, and they did not demand social transformation, but wanted to introduce moderate change independently of the government. They saw the *zemstvo* as the beginnings of a national assembly. This momentum for practical change became known as ***obshchestvennost***. Though the *raznochinsty* were criticised by more radical groups for being too limited, the government became increasingly worried by the constant pressure they applied.

Indeed, the government appeared to regret the political awakening the *zemstva* had caused, almost as soon as they were created in 1864. Article 6 of the Act that set them up promised full independence to the matters the *zemstva* would cover, while Article 9 gave the provincial governor the right to veto any *zemstvo* decision seen as against the interests of the state. Clearly, what the tsar could give with one hand, the other hand could take away. Restrictions over funding and tax were quickly put into place. The central bureaucracy became progressively worried about losing its powers to the *zemstva*. Likewise the *zemstva*, spurred on by the third element, saw the limits of their powers but had no means of widening them. The tsar and the autocratic bureaucracy had seen the necessity for change, but were not prepared to follow the reform to its logical conclusion. Changes to the *volost*, the districts and the provinces would naturally lead to changes in the structures of the national government, but Alexander II was adamant that this would not occur. The number of provinces with a *zemstvo* was never more than 50 percent, as the government, understanding its potential for political agitation, did not allow 'troublesome' provinces, particularly on the European borders, to have them, such as in Polish provinces which had rebelled in 1863 over conscription and resulted in 4,000 people sent to exile. The government would not allow ethnic majorities to gain any political or social control over Russians.

Therefore, the creation of the *zemstva* caused political frustration in the long term, but the social impact in improving the lives of the rural communities should not be overlooked. In the cities, with perhaps more concentrated potential for unrest, the changes were more limited.

The municipal statute of 1870

In the 1860s, the government examined the structures of 595 municipalities, or cities, and found that only around 15 percent were industrial or commercial centres. The rest were populated by peasants, who supplemented their incomes with urban employment, returning to their farms at peak times. By 1870, there were 700 government-defined cities, but only five had more than 100,000 inhabitants (St Petersburg, Moscow, Warsaw, Odessa and Kishinev) and just 11 had between 50,000 and 100,000. The emancipation of the serfs, the creation of the *zemstva* and the growing industrial economy all encouraged the government to implement similar changes in the cities, resulting in the June 1870 Municipal Regulations Act.

Urban self-government was through the municipal council, or city *duma*, made up of at least 30 deputies. The franchise was based on a Prussian system where voting was restricted to those who paid taxes. This qualification was then split into three brackets according to the amount of tax each paid, and each bracket elected a third of the deputies. This meant that a small group of wealthy taxpayers carried the same political weight as many middle-income taxpayers and thousands of low-income taxpayers. For example, in St Petersburg, the 202 voters of the top bracket elected the same number of deputies as the 705 voters of the second and 15,233 of the third.

The idea of the municipal *duma* was to work in conjunction with the *zemstva* in local administration, public works, emergency food supply, promoting public health, welfare and cultural institutions, as well as submitting reports on local requirements to the government. The municipal *duma* also elected a mayor and members of the city council, though the mayors needed to be confirmed by the government. Like the *zemstva*, its independence was restricted by various amendments allowing the governor to overrule any particular decision he felt needed overruling. The municipal *duma* was also not allowed to control the city police, which remained under central government.

However, like the *zemstva*, much good work was achieved in social areas and the infrastructure of the city, such as street lighting, rubbish disposal and drainage. Though practical in nature, it demonstrated to the people of Russia that they were able to run their own lives in new institutions based on the principles of democracy and wider participation. Members' knowledge of local conditions made the municipal *duma* a more efficient agent in improving local lives than a central government official based in St Petersburg could have been. The municipal *duma* were more elitist than their country *zemstva*, but both contributed to the atmosphere of *obschestvennost* that prevailed in late 19th-century Russia. This aspiration to serve the country was given extra focus and the opportunity to be expressed by the reforms to the universities (see page 78) and the press (see page 81).

SOURCE 7

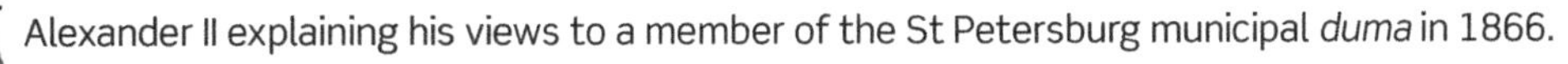

Alexander II explaining his views to a member of the St Petersburg municipal *duma* in 1866.

I suppose you consider that I refuse to give up any of my powers from motives of petty ambition. I give you my imperial word that, this very minute, at this very table, I would sign any constitution you like, if I felt that this would be for the good of Russia. But I know that, were I to do so today, tomorrow Russia would fall to pieces.

ACTIVITY
KNOWLEDGE CHECK

The intentions of Alexander II

1. What does Source 7 imply about Alexander II's fears and attitudes towards reforms and the rule of Russia?
2. From your own knowledge, which area of military, judicial or local government reforms could potentially be the most dangerous to the autocracy of the tsar? Explain your answer.

A Level Exam-Style Question Section B

To what extent did the legal and local government reforms of Alexander II allow greater participation in politics by the Russian people in the years 1855–70? (20 marks)

Tip

Make sure you cover both legal and government reforms, and that you give a clear judgement on their extent (the amount of change the reforms actually caused, not just what they were).

TO WHAT EXTENT WAS THERE GREATER FREEDOM OF EXPRESSION IN RUSSIA IN THE YEARS TO 1870?

With his reforms of the military, judicial and local government, Tsar Alexander II had either adapted Nicholas I's old system in an attempt to improve some of the apparatus of ruling Russia, or adopted a more western approach, new to Russia, to completely relaunch some institutions for a modern Russia. However, to an observer of the two tsars, the clearest difference would be in the freedom of expression laws. Nicholas I's heavy use of censorship and distaste for universities were replaced by a more open and relaxed attitude towards the press and an encouraging sentiment for higher education. It was not a smooth transition, and Alexander II never successfully solved the dilemma, common to all autocracies, of the state improving education without teaching the population to question the state. This led to a rapid increase in radicalisation and revolutionary ideas, particularly among the new young intelligentsia. Their ideas turned violent and resulted in several attempts on the life of the tsar, and a repressive political response from the shocked Alexander.

The significance of the university statute, 1863

On Alexander's accession to the throne, all of Nicholas I's restraints on university life were abolished. Foreign teachers were allowed and universities were open to all students of any social background, though the peasants were yet to meet the necessary academic qualifications for higher education. The universities set up societies, public lectures and reading rooms. In the late 1850s, the students embraced the literary and political criticism of Russia's leading contemporary writers, in particular the following.

- **Alexander Herzen** was a Russian writer living in exile, mainly in London, who published many criticisms of the Russian authorities as well as social novels such as *Who is to Blame?* (1846). He created the Free Russian Press in London and his works were smuggled into Russia after 1855. He was seen as the leading spirit behind the emancipation of the serfs with his 'Liberty and Land' campaign for peasant rights. He was later seen as the 'father of Russian socialism'.
- **Nikolay Chernyshevsky**, son of a priest and influenced by Herzen, was a revolutionary thinker and publisher of periodicals such as *The Contemporary*. He was a graduate of St Petersburg University, and his 1862 novel *What is to be Done?*, written in prison, presented a portrait of a political activist totally committed to revolution. It was seen as a manual for young radicals.
- **Nikolay Dobrolyubov** was also the son of a priest. As a student at St Petersburg in 1853, he ran an underground democratic movement and fought against the university's administration. He worked with Chernyshevsky and other radicals, and wrote several volumes of criticism, but died of tuberculosis in 1861 at just 25.
- **Dmitry Pisarev** was another graduate from St Petersburg University. From 1861, his political writings emphasised complete independence in thought. He spent 1862–66 in prison. On his release, he continued writing, but drowned in 1868.

These writers helped create a *Zeitgeist* (spirit) of anti-autocracy and an angry impatience for change. In an effort to train the new elite who would run the tsar's state, the students became fiercely critical of its actions.

The tsar moved quickly to tighten up on student actions. Admiral Putyatin, a man with a reputation for discipline, was minister for education, and he at once began to enforce identity cards for students, but this did little to stop the young discussing current affairs. This can be seen in the reaction to the state's suppression of the 1861 peasant uprising in Bezdna. The peasant leader, Anton Petrov, had interpreted the Edict of Emancipation as equality of all people, and the resulting uprising had left dozens dead. As the government prepared further reprisals, students gathered and openly discussed government policy. At Kazan University, in the same province of Bezdna, some 400 students held a memorial for the dead. Ten were expelled and a professor who had participated with them was sent into exile.

In 1861, Admiral Putyatin discussed matters with the head of St Petersburg University (a general), and the rector of the university (a colonel), and they devised a military solution. Blaming the influx of poor students as the root cause of the rebellion, they ended scholarships for the poor, and forced everyone to pay for their education, when previously some 65 percent had had subsidies. All student meetings were banned and students' identity cards now carried information on their attitude and grades. When the students returned from summer vacation, they found the new rules were in force and poor students were locked out.

After six years of relative freedom under Alexander II, the students were not prepared to accept this, and they had lost the fear the previous generation had under Nicholas I. The disturbances that followed saw St Petersburg University closed down twice in 1862 and the students openly demonstrating against the university authorities. The situation began to spiral out of control, and the army was only held back from mass-whipping the students by the intervention of the tsar's brother, Grand Duke Konstantin Nikolayevich. Still the violence left some students in hospital, while 270 others were imprisoned at the Fortress of Peter and Paul. Nevertheless, the unrest and riots spread to six more universities, including Moscow.

The situation calmed when the tsar's brother persuaded Alexander II to replace Putyatin with the more liberal Golovnin as education minister. Golovnin re-opened the university and allowed expelled students to return. He then began to prepare legislation for wider reforms. At face value, it would appear that the students had won and their protests had delivered further reforms. However, this would be misleading. The reforms of Alexander II, especially in university education, were ad hoc and the tsar was often steered by whomever he was consulting with. A more liberal adviser would result in a calmer, more progressive programme, but reactionary advice would result in a more repressive programme. Another repercussion of the 1861–62 student protest was the 'publication' of *Young Russia* by Peter Zaichnevsky, who had been arrested for his participation in unrest at Moscow University. From his prison cell, he organised a violent proclamation against the tsar.

SOURCE

From the manifesto *Young Russia*, written in prison by Peter Zaichnevsky in 1862. It was smuggled out and distributed by the underground press, coming to the attention of the secret police, or Third Department. Another pamphlet, also smuggled out of prison, called the peasants to take up weapons and overthrow the state. Both were signed by the Central Revolutionary Committee of Young Russia, which consisted of Zaichnevsky and some fellow prisoners.

We need not a divinely anointed tsar, not an ermine mantle that hides hereditary inability, but an elected elder who receives a salary for his service. If Alexander II does not understand this and is not willing to voluntarily cede to the people, the worse for him...

There is only one way out of the oppressive situation - revolution, revolution bloody and inexorable, revolution that must radically change everything, everything without exception, all the foundations of contemporary society, and destroy the adherents of today's order. We are not afraid of it, even though we know that rivers of blood will flow, that there might be innocent victims. We will have just one cry; 'To the hatchets!' and then attack in the squares, if the vile blackguards dare to come out, attack them in their houses, attack in crowded city alleys and towns! Remember that those who are not with us are against us, and those who are against us are our enemy, and enemies must be obliterated by every means.

The extremist violent rhetoric of *Young Russia* shocked and infuriated the tsar. So, although the formulation of liberal reforms to the universities continued, the student unrest and hardening views caused the tsar to tighten political control. The Third Department started to reappraise its performance and began imposing greater control and surveillance. The tsar's close adviser, Count Peter Shuvalov, renounced his liberal views and became a reactionary politician responsible for curtailing many of the reforms throughout the 1870s.

In May 1862, a series of fires in St Petersburg was perceived by the state as a further sign of student unrest; more young people were arrested and publications closed. Despite the vague origin of the fires, they gave the authorities an excuse to clamp down on student activities. For the first few years of the tsar's reign, the reactionary military officers and state officials had remained in the background, fondly remembering the ways of Nicholas I, but this saw them more openly defending the autocratic tsar, the Orthodox Church and a sense of nationalism. As the tsar gathered the liberal side to begin work on the series of reforms from the military to the *zemstvo*, he gathered the 'retrogrades' under the leadership of General Mikhail Muravyev to viciously put down the Polish rebellion of 1863, when over 22,000 Poles were imprisoned and executed.

It was during this climate of anxiety over the apparent radicalisation of students that reforms for the university were also drafted. This shows the contrasting pressures not only within Russia but also on the tsar himself. There was a recognition of the need to reform and modernise, yet there was concern about where these reforms would lead. On the one hand, the tsar wished to retain absolute autocracy, while on the other his instinct was to reform according to a European model and to avoid harsh measures.

EXTEND YOUR KNOWLEDGE

The strange case of the St Petersburg fires

The fires that began in St Petersburg in May 1862 were presented in the newspapers as having been caused by revolutionary students. This prompted a series of repressive measures. However, an investigation by the St Petersburg police and the Third Department found no group of arsonists, but only a poor Jewish man in Odessa, who was subsequently hanged. Another fire was found to have been started by three drunk, rather than radical, students. The daily fires seemed to be the result of a combination of hot weather, wooden buildings and a lack of water for fire-fighting. Similar fires in the summer of 1860 had been blamed on the Poles.

The minister of internal affairs, Valuyev, suggested in his diary that the fires and the ranting of *Young Russia* had the intended consequences, implying that they could have been organised to frighten the tsar. The episode revealed widespread anti-student feeling. General Milyutin, brought in to fight the fires, recalled how students were attacked in the street and that the phrase 'rebel student' was common among the poor.

In June 1863, Golovnin put forward the university statute, which the tsar had taken a personal interest in drafting, even to the extent of sending officials to European universities to search for useful ideas. From Germany came the key idea of granting all universities autonomy in their affairs, while from France came the idea of a single curriculum with annual exams for all universities. Each university would be run by a council that would oversee teaching, degrees and publications. The final power would thereby free the university from any general censorship. The council was made up of the university staff, while the dean, rector and other high positions were elected to the council by the staff, though the dean's appointment had to be confirmed by the minister of education and the rector's by the tsar. A university court made up of three professors was established to deal with student offenders. Subsidies were restored to around 40 percent of students, and teachers' salaries were raised. Student organisations and student representation were not recognised.

The interest in higher education promoted by the 1863 statute saw new universities opened in Odessa (1864) and Warsaw (1869), and the groundwork was laid for one in Siberia. Another seven specialist higher-education institutions were also created by the end of the tsar's reign in 1881, ranging from archaeology to agriculture and from forestry to philosophy. In 1865, there were 4,125 students at Russian universities and, by 1880, this had grown to 8,045, with about 46 percent from noble families and 35 percent the children of clergy, who were often the most prominent radicals. However, there was a wide demographic spread from all income brackets compared with European university intakes, though students from peasant backgrounds remained a tiny minority, with only 2.9 percent as late as 1880.

With the rise of higher education, it is only logical that education would need improving lower down, to feed the universities with able students. The *zemstva* and the Church organised many primary schools, but the government did much to improve secondary schools, with classical gymnasiums providing an eight-year academic grounding, and real gymnasiums being more vocational-based with an emphasis on modern languages, science and mathematics. Pupil numbers doubled between 1855 and 1865. Importantly, there was also a great deal of achievement in creating educational opportunities for women for the first time. There were girls' gymnasiums for 4,000 pupils in 1864 and for 27,000 by 1875. As the girls finished secondary school, the first few university courses for women began in the 1870s, in Moscow under Professor Gerié and under Professor Bestuzhev-Riumin in St Petersburg. The first medical courses were created in St Petersburg, which later evolved into a medical institute for women. In this area, Russia was ahead of many European nations.

Alexander II seems to have been balanced awkwardly on a narrow path. Unsure whether to follow it towards reform or reaction, he tried to do both in order to keep his autocracy and modernise Russia at the same time. This indecision caused him to veer one way then the other in response to a crisis. General Muravyev's savage repression was felt to be too much by Alexander II, so he forced through his quick retirement. However Alexander's mood changed when, in April 1866, Dmitry Karakozov, a former student of Kazan and Moscow Universities, shot at the tsar in St Petersburg. Though the tsar was unhurt, the assassination attempt immediately raised questions about revolutionary groups using the universities as recruiting grounds, and once more the tsar veered away from reform.

EXTEND YOUR KNOWLEDGE

Assassination attempt 1 (4 April 1866)

Dmitry Karakozov was the son of a minor noble. His expulsion from both Kazan and Moscow Universities led to a suicide attempt. He then became involved in his cousin's revolutionary group, the Ishutin Society, which had been set up to organise student sewing co-operatives. The inner circle of the group, known as Hell, chose the enthusiastic Karakozov to kill the tsar. He wrote a proclamation of his ideas to the governor of St Petersburg, which was lost in the post.

Seeing the tsar outside the summer garden, he tried to fire a pistol at him, but his elbow was knocked by a peasant, Osip Komissarov, a hatter's apprentice. This was later cited as evidence of the common people's love of the tsar, though Soviet historians claimed it was a fictional event. Karakozov was arrested and imprisoned, while Komissarov received a large pension and a place at the imperial court. (His boorish character soon proved embarrassing and he was quietly removed to the countryside.)

In prison, Karakozov converted to the Orthodox faith and begged for mercy, but was executed in September 1866. When asked by the tsar personally what he wanted to achieve by his act, Karakozov simply replied, 'Nothing, nothing.'

The liberal Golovnin was replaced by the Orthodox leader Dmitry Tolstoi, who believed that the spirit of revolution was being fermented in schools and universities, especially in science classes. Science was therefore replaced at secondary level by classics, and the entrance exams for the universities were made much harder. The idea was to make the exam content so dense with facts and quotations, that only those students totally dedicated to study, rather than more open investigative minds, could qualify. Indeed, only about a third of those entering the secondary gymnasium graduated. Obedience and good behaviour would be rewarded over free thought.

Tolstoi hoped to control the universities by restricting their intake rather than reversing the 1863 reforms. However, St Petersburg University was specifically punished, as he imposed a total ban on all student organisations no matter what their intent and function. He hoped this would prevent any potential political discussions from escalating into opposition. The disciplinary power of the university courts was placed in the hands of the police, while police and state inspection and surveillance of all schools was increased. Interestingly, Tolstoi's education changes were rejected by the Council of State by 29 votes to 19, but the tsar upheld the minority and Tolstoi's measures became law in 1871.

In conclusion, the government treatment of universities, and of the education system in general, was a mixed affair. There seemed to be a trend towards European-style reform and expansion of the education system, but at the same time the limits to reform demonstrated the duality of the tsar's thinking. He would create the circumstances to allow independence, then react sharply when it was implemented. A clear example of this can be seen in the education of his son. Alexander II had enjoyed travel and a liberal education under the guidance of the poet Zhukovsky, but he chose Konstantin Pobedonostsev, a professor of civil law, as his son's tutor. Known later as the Grand Inquisitor, and as head of the Orthodox Church, Pobedonostsev ardently supported autocracy and valued faith over reason. He became a leading reactionary and reversed many of Alexander II's reforms after 1881 when his former student became tsar.

While the universities tested their new autonomy and the state reacted, the students regularly took to the streets in what became almost a tradition of student life, with serious unrest in 1865 and 1869. These students graduated into a world where the high educational standards of Russian universities, especially in science and technology, fostered a sense that real improvements in Russia's economy and society were within reach. However, they found that the hierarchical and bureaucratic service they entered discouraged any innovation. This built up their frustrations as their idealism was met with resistance. However, an outlet to vent their rising anger could be found in the periodicals of the new intelligentsia that were emerging from the academic world. This was helped by the tsar's attitude to censorship and the free press, which again was somewhat contradictory and ambiguous.

SOURCE 9

A diary entry of A.V. Nikitenko in response to the attempted assassination of Alexander II in 1866. Nikitenko was a professor and government censor who had been born a peasant serf, but won his freedom and job on the grounds of his intelligence. It is somewhat ironic that this extract rails against the very qualities that made him. It was published later in A.V. Nikitenko, *Dnevnik* (1956).

Nothing harms our independence of thought as much as the passion for reading that is spreading so powerfully among us. Reading decisively kills decisiveness, and the power of acting according to one's reason. This latter gets used to the mainstream of the river of alien thoughts which carries it along, not permitting it, or hardly permitting it, amid the movement of words, to use its own strengths.

ACTIVITY
KNOWLEDGE CHECK

University reforms

1 How does Source 9 demonstrate the establishment's fear of the spread of education?

2 How might the sentiment expressed by Nikitenko be applied to the tsar himself in regard to his attitude and reforms of education, especially in the universities?

The significance of the new press regulations of 1865

Linked with the reforms of the universities was a relaxation of the censorship laws after the reign of Nicholas I. The period 1855–65 saw the rise of the new intelligentsia of mixed social origin, which expressed itself in a wide range of periodicals. This new generation of radicals, known as *shestidesiatniki* ('generation of the 1860s') spread its ideas through the two main militant periodicals.

- *The Contemporary* (*Sovremennik*) published most of the leading writers of the day and was led by Chernyshevsky and Dobrolyubov. It focused on social and political questions answered from a populist or socialist perspective.
- *The Russian Word* (*Russkoe Slovo*) was led by Pisarev and espoused a philosophy that would become known as nihilist. This was an idea from Ivan Turgenev's 1862 novel *Fathers and Sons*, in which the character Bazarov devotes himself to experiment and science to further his medical knowledge, thereby rejecting all traditions. Politically, to be a nihilist is to accept nothing on faith or authority unless proved by reason.

In 1855, there were about 140 periodicals, or 'fat journals' as they were called, of which about 60 were published by government departments (though they often commented on other matters, such as the education articles that appeared in the *Naval Review*), and another 60 dealt with specialist academic studies. Only about 20 discussed current affairs, and these were closely monitored. Some of these periodicals and government departmental newspapers were popular because they were the only way to get accurate information on current affairs. For example, the Ministry of War's *Russkii Invalid* newspaper was the most reliable public source on the Polish Rebellion of 1863, but Milyutin was also able to use it to promote his military reforms (as well as his anti-Polish and anti-Catholic dogma).

The tsar understood the need to allow some discussion of the changes he was introducing, so he often ignored the censorship laws that were still theoretically in place. The press particularly attacked the factors that had caused so much incompetence during the Crimean War, such as supplies and corruption. By 1863, censorship was transferred from the Ministry of Public Education to the Ministry of Internal Affairs, and work was done to simplify the multi-level censorships of Nicholas I's reign, whereby a publication would need approval from several offices before it could be published.

In April 1865, new press regulations were introduced. The idea of pre-publication interference by several groups was stopped, as now censorship would only be applied after publication. In other words, it was largely up to publishers to police their own writers. The new rules applied to periodicals, academic articles, all works over 160 pages and all translations over 320 pages. As always, there were loopholes, or institutions too stubborn to change; in this case both the Church and the army insisted that any article that discussed their interests should be submitted to their institutions for censorship.

The Ministry of Internal Affairs had the power to punish periodicals that over-stepped the unwritten boundary between state and publishers. The minister of internal affairs, Valuev, could issue fines, withdraw advertising and issue warnings. Three warnings meant closure of the periodical for six months, extended permanently if the Senate Court agreed. Indeed, within two weeks of the 1865 law, one newspaper received a warning for discussing Russia's finances, as the state claimed this could affect Russia's international credit reputation. Valuev, a man with a liberal reputation, used this power and he, and his successors, issued 177 warnings and 52 orders to cease publication between 1865 and 1880.

The most important of these orders came as part of the backlash against the 1866 assassination attempt when both the well-established *The Contemporary* and *The Russian Word* were shut down in in the same year. Neither journal had expressed direct support for the assassination, but their liberal views were seen as potentially damaging in encouraging sedition. However, as censorship now took place after publication, it enabled other periodicals to take up the mantle, and *Notes from the Fatherland* (*Otechestvennye zapiski*), edited by the poet Nikolay Nekrasov, had great influence over the next two decades before it too was closed in 1884. If a journal was closed, another sprang up ready to publish. Radical writers might find many new homes, if an editor was bold or had financial backing. Politically daring publications could often sell out before the censor stepped in. Sometimes the courts saved the periodicals, which caused Valuev to remove censorship cases from the provincial courts. A few journals were returned to the old pre-publication checks, while others were allowed to sell only to established subscribers. The minister could ban discussion on certain topics, but these reactions tended to be spontaneous and ineffective, like baling out water instead of fixing the leak. The ban was often too late, or the publication only banned after it was published, making it meaningless. The result was that publishers produced journals (531 by 1880), newspapers (89 by 1894) and books (from 1,020 titles in 1855 to 1,836 in 1864) in greater numbers and on an ever greater range of topics.

SOURCE 10

A photograph by Sergei Lvovich Levitsky showing the most popular contributors to *Sovremennik* (*The Contemporary*) in 1856. From left to right: Ivan Goncharov, Ivan Turgenev, Leo Tolstoy, Dmitri Grigorovich, Alexander Druzhinin and Alexander Ostrovsky. The period between 1852 and 1862 is considered to be the most brilliant in the history of the journal. Its owner, Nekrasov, managed to strike a deal with its leading contributors, whereby their new works were to be published exclusively by him. As regards to ideology, *Sovremennik* grew more radical together with its audience and it had a circulation of over 7,000 by 1861.

ACTIVITY
KNOWLEDGE CHECK

The periodicals

How far does Source 10 demonstrate how difficult it was for the government to try to censor publications and radical ideas?

The impact of the new press

Periodicals and the easing of censorship were particularly important due to Russia's unique circumstances. They were the only way to get a message or opinion across the empire. The periodicals helped to link individuals from cities to rural towns, and established a series of political networks which greatly aided the growth of political parties in future decades. It is no surprise that Lenin closed down all non-Bolshevik periodicals within a year of coming to power.

It would be wrong to suggest that all the periodicals presented a united radical front. Conservative periodicals such as the *Russian Messenger* (*Russkii Vestnik*) published works by great writers such as Leo Tolstoy, Fyodor Dostoevsky and Ivan Turgenev. Many radical writers spent a good deal of effort criticising each other. Herzen was demeaned as old-fashioned for refusing to endorse revolution, while Pisarev's vision of an educated elite creating a good society was twisted, and the label 'nihilist' was applied to anyone who rebelled violently against authority. However, these debates drew in new thinkers. Some became revolutionaries, others conservatives, but both detested the ones in the middle. This forging of new political thinkers and the fact that their ideas could, and would, be published, made the 1860s the start of a golden age for Russian political thought.

Despite occasional infighting among writers and radical thinkers, the reforms of freedom of expression helped to reinforce the impacts of the other reforms. The press often worked with the independent universities, creating an atmosphere that encouraged political participation. This could occur in the *zemstva* and more open legal proceedings. The overall result was a political awakening, or *obshchestvennost*, of the whole of society. As society became more literate, with 55–60 percent literacy in St Petersburg and 40 percent in Moscow by 1860, newspapers became a more important source of information. New printing technology and distribution via the railways allowed ideas to spread. The revolutionaries and the radicals might have been the most visible, vocal and violent of the new intelligentsia, but many educated people were convinced that Russia was proudly unique in its multi-ethnic and part-Asian make-up. They felt its social problems could be solved by collective rather than individualistic means, and therefore the reforms played an important part in evolving a national identity. This would take time, but that was something Alexander II did not have.

THINKING HISTORICALLY **Cause and consequence (7c)**

The value of historical explanations

Historical explanations derive from historians who investigate the past. Differences in explanations are usually about what the historians think is significant. Historians bring their own attitudes and perspectives to historical questions and see history in the light of these. It is therefore perfectly acceptable to have very different explanations of the same historical phenomenon. We judge historical accounts by looking at how well argued they are and how well evidence has been deployed to support the argument.

Approach A	Approach B	Approach C
The process of reform is caused by decisions taken by politicians. It is imposed from the top by great men. Ordinary people fall into line and do whatever they are told.	The pressure for reform stems from mass movement of similar people with similar ideas. The small aspects of commonality all combine to cause reform.	The trend towards reform within a modernising society is inevitable. The great movements of history point us to this fact.

Work in groups of between three and five. (You will need an even number of groups in the class.)

1 In your groups, devise a brief explanation to explain the causes of reform in Russia after 1855. Your explanation should be 200-300 words long, and should match one of the approaches above. Present your explanation to another group, who will decide on two things:

a) Which approach is each explanation trying to demonstrate?

b) Considering the structure and the quality of the argument and use of evidence, which is the best of the three explanations?

2 If you choose a 'best' explanation, should you discount the other two? Explain your answer.

Conclusion

In many ways, Alexander had little control over the reforms. The Crimean War had necessitated the need for basic political reforms in the military, legal system, education and the press. The Russian army could not compete with modern European armies. The new conscription reforms weakened the landlords' control over the peasants, so some form of local self-government was needed, as well as a new legal structure to run the empire. These new organisations and institutions needed a modern professional staff and officials, who would be educated at independent universities. At these universities, a hungry student body sought, discussed and published ideas on how to take the reforms further in periodicals that, to the tsar and his government at least, escalated their radical ideology.

This was not planned, or even truly desired, by Alexander II. Despite a genuine wish for reform, he wanted to limit their impact and stop the reforms creating a dynamic of their own. He steadfastly refused to change the basic structure of his country's society. This would have involved a change in the political nature of Russia and a direct threat to his rule. The result was that all his reforms were restricted in an effort to control their impact to maintain the tsar's autocracy.

Alexander II liked to be known as the 'Tsar Liberator', but when his people wanted genuine liberty and publicly voiced their displeasure, he retreated and sought the assurances and reactionary stance of those connected with his father's rule and ideas, such as the High Church. He could not, and never wanted to, let go of his autocracy, yet he could not comprehend why anyone, especially those who had apparently gained from his reforms, would express a desire for more. Like many sheltered dictators, he could not understand why the public were not grateful for what he had granted them. He had wanted the reforms to strengthen his hold on power and failed to see why they never could.

Part of the problem was that a lot of the details, of both reform and reaction, were worked out by others, like Milyutin and Konstantin Nikolaevich or Dmitry Tolstoi and Pobedonostsev. These more determined characters drafted the Acts and then persuaded the tsar to add his name. As they sought to out-manoeuvre the other side, a sense of a coherent and reasoned plan was lost. The reforms suffered from a lack of a single vision as they were muddled and watered down in hundreds of committees. Therefore, they always seemed to promise more than they delivered, and the false hope and frustration were expressed in the increasing radicalism of the period. The tsar, and the Third Department, were well aware of this, as the radicals had the apparatus to make their views known.

Part of the cost of tolerating new ideas is the advancing of political extremes. If the tsar had wanted the waves of reforms to secure his popularity, then he was fatally disappointed. The ideas of *Young Russia*'s 1862 demand for bloody revolution did not dissipate with the reforms. In 1868, the revolutionary newspaper *The People's Cause* (*Narodnoe Delo*) published by Bakunin, the 'Apostle of Anarchy', continued the call for violent overthrow. As he worked from the relative safety of Europe, Nechaev formed secret revolutionary cells within Russia and published *The People's Vengeance* (*Narodnaya Rasprava*). His imprisonment for murder inspired many others such as Tkachev and the Land and Liberty group. This last group splintered, and one half became the People's Will (*Narodnaya Volya*) terrorist group, which plotted to kill Alexander II in 1879 and 1880, and succeeded in 1881.

It would be too narrow a viewpoint to suggest that the reforms of the 1860s made Russia a more desperate and politically violent state. All the reforms constituted significant change, but the effects were long-term. The idea that a person, usually educated, but of any social origin, could begin to participate in local government, or to aspire to a university education and professional career, was a fundamental shift in the political climate of the empire. The *obshchestvennost*, or political consciousness, gave a generation of Russians the drive to get involved, which even Alexander III's repression could not extinguish. Students were educated at institutions every bit as good as those in Europe, and would often work as *advokatura* in a legal system that was among the most progressive in the world. Or they would find work through the *zemstva* as *raznochintsy* or the 'third element' that spread the idea of reform further into the countryside. There may have been loopholes and restrictions to every reform act, and each reform was created in isolation, but at least there was action.

It may be tempting to view Alexander II, basically a good-natured individual, and his reforms as the first steps on a path towards a European constitutional monarchy (and that may have been the ultimate intention of some of the advisers), but it was certainly not the path that Alexander himself would choose. Student protests and fires, Polish uprisings, radical literature and terrorist cells and eventually assassination attempts all gave impetus to the opponents of reform. All the reforms had limits and restrictions that retained autocratic control. These limits may have dampened the impact of the reforms, but they did not halt or reverse it. The reforms helped to create the framework of a new civil society, and despite the tensions, they allowed the opportunity for many to desire more.

The impact of the reforms must have been considerable first to promote such a backlash in the aristocracy, and then to ignite a wave of more extreme views. As Alexander II breathed his last tormented breaths, watched by his son and grandson, the next and final tsars, so too did the hope of any state-instituted reforms achieved through peaceful process.

SOURCE

From *Russia under Alexander II*, by Dr Julius Eckardt (1836–1908), collected in the volume *Modern Russia* (1870). Eckardt was a German journalist, and later a Senate secretary and diplomat; his politics and economic views can be described as broadly liberal. When this book was published, Eckardt was working as a journalist for a German magazine with a special interest in the Baltic and Russian world. His book was originally published in Germany. Here he is commenting on the start of Alexander II's reign.

But although the young Emperor had been trained in strict military discipline, and from his youth had been accustomed to spend the greater part of his time in military trifling; it was still well known that he had no lack of inclination for employment in the affairs of the state, and he recognised the duty of rulers, not only towards God, but also towards the nation. He was considered honest and straightforward. But more than this Alexander had always exhibited more gentle and large-hearted feeling, and greater accessibility to foreign views than Nicholas...

The troublous years, from 1853 to 1855, had in many respects opened his eyes to the errors of his father, to whom he clung with childlike reverence, and who in his eyes was to the last the model of a great ruler... Without the experiences of these years of warfare, Alexander would perhaps have trod in the footsteps of the old policy; trained as he was in the strict traditions of the autocracy... It was characteristic enough, that Alexander, in spite of his clear conviction for the necessity of numerous reforms, in spite of his insight into the deep evils of old state of things, for years retained the servants of his father... Easy enough was it, indeed, for the new sovereign to pass as a Reformer. A witty Russian, strikingly remarked at the time, that if Nicholas had forbidden his subjects to appear in the streets, and if Alexander had only revoked this prohibition, he would have immediately been regarded by the Russians as one of the most free-minded monarchs of his day... The revocation of the law of 1849, by which the number of students was limited to 300 at each university, the abolition of high fees for passports for foreign travel, the ready concession for new journals and newspapers; the abolition of those miserable schools, in which the sons of soldiers and non-commissioned officers were obliged to be placed... all sufficed to transport the nation into an ecstasy of enthusiasm, which increased day by day, carrying with it even the most obdurate pessimists. The government soon went further and set about actual reform.

A Level Exam-Style Question Section A

Study Source 11 before you answer this question.

Assess the value of the source for revealing reasons and attitudes towards the implementation of political reform in Russia under Alexander II.

Explain your answer using the source, the information given about it and your own knowledge of the historical context. (20 marks)

Tip

It is important to realise that all Section A questions require a dual focus. In this case, you are asked to assess the source in relation to both the reasons for, as well as the attitudes towards, the reforms in Russia. Both must be addressed in the answer.

SOURCE

Peter Chaadaev was a leading figure in Moscow society. In the 1830s, he wrote about the backwardness of Russian life, claiming that this was why the nation had contributed nothing to civilisation. He had blamed the Orthodox Church as a stagnating factor and had been officially declared insane as a result. Though he partly recanted these views, he returned to a similar vein during the Crimean War.

Talking about Russia one always imagines that one is talking about a country like the others; in reality this is not so at all. Russia is a whole separate world, submissive to the will, caprice, fantasy of a single young man, whether his name be Peter or Ivan, no matter – in all instances the common element is the embodiment of arbitrariness. Contrary to all the laws of the human community, Russia moves only in direction of her own enslavement and the enslavement of all neighbouring peoples. For this reason it would be in the interest not only of other peoples but also in that of her own that she be compelled to take a new path.

SOURCE

Alexander reacts to the Address of the Assembly of Moscow Nobility, 1865, which asked the tsar 'to complete the structure of the state by convoking a general assembly of elected persons of the Russian land for the consideration of needs common to the whole state.' Alexander firmly stated that it was his task alone.

Such deviations from the order of things established by the laws in force, can only make it more difficult for me to fulfil my plans; in no case can they assist the achievement of the purpose to which they may be directed.

EXTRACT

From the historian W. Mosse, *Alexander II and the Modernisation of Russia* (1970).

Alexander proved himself not only a disappointing 'liberal', if indeed that term can be applied to him, but, more seriously, an inefficient autocrat. While he would not give his educated subjects the constitution for which they clamoured, he failed to use to advantage the autocratic powers which he felt impelled to retain. He merely succeeded in proving that a pseudo-liberal autocratic is an unhappy hybrid unlikely to achieve political success. The narrow principles of Nicholas I or Alexander III, for whom Alexander's problems did not exist, proved, on a short term view, more effective than the unsuccessful attempt to combine authority and freedom.

ACTIVITY
KNOWLEDGE CHECK

The influence of Alexander II on the reforms

1 How do Sources 12 and 13 reinforce and challenge each other in their views? Remember to use the caption of the sources as well.

2 Study the view in Extract 3. How far do you agree with the sentiments expressed in it? Is it a fair reflection about the impact of Alexander II as an individual?

ACTIVITY
SUMMARY

The reforms of 1855–70

1 For each of the following groups, make two lists or spider diagrams to show how they benefited and how they suffered as a result of the political reforms in the years 1855–70:
- Alexander II and the imperial court
- the nobility
- the middle class
- urban workers
- peasants
- the army.

2 Rank the reforms covered in this chapter in order of importance. Explain your thinking.

3 Research some of the radicals and periodicals mentioned in the section on censorship, and show:

a) how they expressed their views

b) how they differed from each other.

4 To what extent would it be a fair assumption to conclude that Alexander II sowed the seeds of his own destruction by embarking on his programme of Great Reforms?

5 Can an autocrat ever modernise and reform a society without creating a threat to their own power?

WIDER READING

Hite, J. *Tsarist Russia 1801-1917*, Causeway Press (1989)

Hosking, G. *Russia: People & Empire 1552-1917*, Fontana Press (1998)

Pipes, R. *Russia under the Old Regime*, Penguin Books (1995)

Pushkarev, S. *The Emergence of Modern Russia 1801-1917*, Pica Pica Press (1985)

Radzinsky, E. *Alexander II: the Last Great Tsar*, Free Press (2005)

Westwood, J.N. *Endurance and Endeavour: Russian History 1812-2001*, Oxford University Press (2002)

3.4 Revolution and reform, 1904–06

KEY QUESTIONS

- How important was the Russo-Japanese War as a stimulus to reform and revolution?
- What was the significance of Bloody Sunday in 1905?
- How effective was the tsar's repression of opposition in the towns and countryside?

INTRODUCTION

'A small victorious war to stop the revolutionary tide.'

This was the 1904 recommendation from Plehve, minister of the interior, to Tsar Nicholas II. The result was a war with Japan in which Russia was confident it could rapidly secure victory and use the resulting wave of nationalism to shore up support. What followed was a series of military disasters both on land and at sea, which humiliated Imperial Russia and acted as a catalyst for a cascade of protests throughout 1905. Triggered by the massacre known as Bloody Sunday, the 1905 Revolution nearly overwhelmed the tsar as workers went on strike, peasants across the empire burnt their landlords' farms and sections of the armed forces mutinied. It was the year that first brought Leon Trotsky to the nation's attention, as revolutionary groups seized the opportunity to play a role in the new Soviets.

It seemed as if the imperial autocracy was disintegrating as protests sprang up across the empire. However, these protests were more spontaneous than united, while the tsarist support remained firm. The aristocracy, Church and bureaucracy kept faith in their ruler. The army stayed loyal enough to hold back the protests and allowed the secret police to do their work. The tsar was forced by his supporters into a response to the crisis, and managed to survive. Hastily granted concessions offered just enough political power to just enough groups to divide the opposition into inaction. The military, brought back from defeat against Japan, could viciously repress the unrest and dismantle the soviets before they could take root. Learning to divide and conquer, by 1906, the tsar was confident enough to reverse some of the political concessions and once more impose his control, helped by able politicians such as Stolypin. There followed a decade of rule in which Nicholas II was more secure in power than he had been in the decade before 1905.

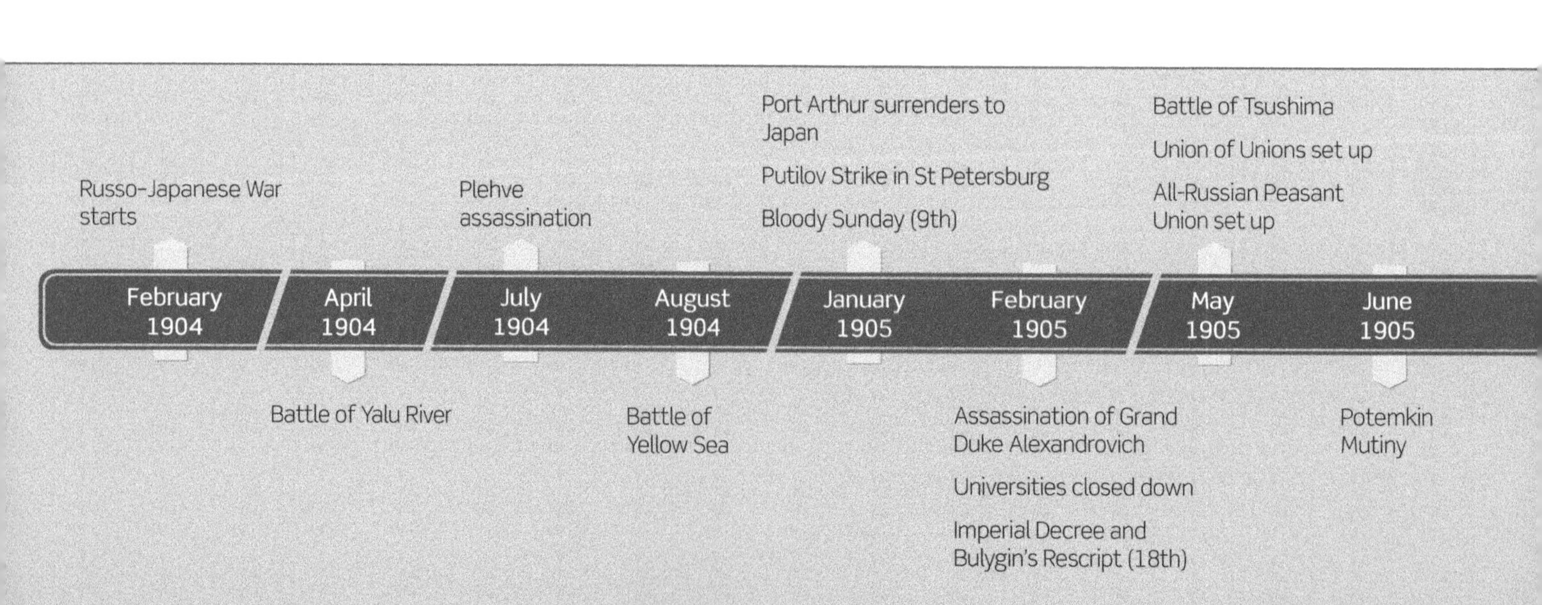

HOW IMPORTANT WAS THE RUSSO-JAPANESE WAR AS A STIMULUS TO REFORM AND REVOLUTION?

The Russo–Japanese War, 1904–05, illustrated both the ineptitude of Russia's military forces and the arrogance of its leadership. The war, which ironically Tsar Nicholas II had hoped would boost his rule, only roused rebellion. It focused the discontent already present over the tsar's lack of political reforms and unflinching faith in his family's autocracy. The disastrous course of 1904 only encouraged revolt, while the Russians' capitulation of 1905 combined with the general unrest within Russia to prompt 'the year of revolution'. Nevertheless, defeat enabled the more reform-minded Count Sergei Witte to gain influence, so some reform was introduced because of the war.

Initially, the war was used by Nicholas and his minister of the interior, Plehve, to stop any rebellion and reform, despite going against the advice of the majority of his advisers, including the ministers of war and of foreign affairs. The tsar had previously encouraged anti-Semitic feelings and pogroms, such as the killing of 50 Jews in Kishinev in April 1903, to distract the population and rally the majority around him. He now believed that a war would further ignite nationalist feeling and deflect attention from domestic problems such as demonstrations, illegal strikes and an economic slump.

SOURCE

Minister of finance, and later prime minister, Count Witte, writing about the tsar's decision on war with Japan. The tsar was not favourable towards Japan; in 1891 he had been travelling in Japan to mark the start of the construction of the Trans-Siberian Railway, when an assassination attempt saw his face slashed and permanently scarred by a sword. From the *Memoirs of Count Witte,* translated by A. Yarmolinsky and published in 1921.

At heart, His Majesty was for an aggressive policy, but, as usual, his mind was a house divided against itself... He became involved in the Far Eastern adventure... because of a hidden craving for a victorious war... Suffice it to say that he alone is to be blamed for that most unhappy decision...

ACTIVITY
KNOWLEDGE CHECK

The Russian government and the start of the Russo-Japanese War, 1904

1 How does Source 1 support the sentiments of Plehve, the minister of the interior, that the war was meant to prevent reform and revolution?

2 What does Source 1 imply might be a problem with using a war for this purpose?

August 1905	Treaty of Portsmouth ends Russo-Japanese War
September 1905	Universities reopen; Moscow printers' strike
October 1905	General Strike called; St Petersburg Soviet set up; October Manifesto
November 1905	Trotsky Chairman of St Petersburg Soviet; St Petersburg Soviet closed down; Moscow uprising crushed
January 1906	United Nobility forms
April 1906	First national *duma*; Russian Constitution with Fundamental Laws
July 1906	First *duma* dissolved; Stolypin prime minister; Vyborg Manifesto
November 1906	Stolypin's land reform passed by decree

It quickly became clear that Japan was not to be a quick pushover. Any public enthusiasm was lost as news reached home of the humiliation of the Russian military. The Russian army was defeated at the Battle of the Yalu River in April 1904, while an entire navy (one of three Russian fleets) was routed at the Battle of the Yellow Sea in August. It was a small step for many in Russia to equate the ineptitude of the military commanders (one commander at the Yalu River retreated in the wrong direction) and the ineptitude of Russia's leadership. Indeed, it was an appointee of the tsar who had overridden the Russian commander Kuropatkin's initial call to retreat, causing the army to be lost. Russian morale was dealt a crushing blow, and worse followed with the surrender of the Russian harbour and naval base at Port Arthur on 2 January 1905.

SOURCE

Japanese print showing naval action at Port Arthur, 1904. The Russo–Japanese War was a technological one; at the Battle of the Yellow Ship, steel ships fired missiles at each other from a distance of up to eight miles. The war highlighted that Russia lacked the technology to fight and the leadership to win against a Japan well-equipped and trained by western European powers.

The fall of Port Arthur, well fortified and manned by the empire's best engineering troops, had the greatest effect on provoking demands for revolution within Russia. The Russian people found it hard to accept that an Asian military force could ever be the equal of a European power, even a fleet whose ships and admirals were made and trained in England, and whose army was modelled on the Prussian system. The loss of the port was comparable with the fall of Sevastopol in 1855. However, instead of forcing the tsar to seek reform, it triggered an angry ignominy among already discontented workers in St Petersburg. There is a clear link between the failures and ineptitude of the Russian military leaders and the growing discontent within Russia. Stoessel, the commander at Port Arthur, had surrendered the port without consultation, and the next day the Putilov Iron Works in St Petersburg called a strike, which 150,000 workers quickly joined. As the news filtered back to the capital, it intensified the discontent among all classes, bringing a new wave of anti-government demonstrations. It was by no means the only cause, not even the most dominant one, but the shame of defeat triggered anger in St Petersburg. Almost immediately, a demonstration at the Winter Palace was planned for the following Sunday and the year of 'revolution' began.

It was not just the national ignominy that helped stir the mood for revolt. The defeat at the Yalu River had hurt Russia's ability to raise credit from Europe, while Japan's success had the opposite effect. This meant that Russia had to export grain in order to raise funds to pay for the war, and slipped into a payments deficit while food shortages in the cities increased, directly contributing to the discontent already fostered by poor harvests. The Russo–Japanese War was a technological war, particularly in its naval battles, and the huge casualty rates (between 40,000 and 70,000 Russians died) surprised both sides. The need for equipment and men to compensate for the losses strained Russia's economic abilities. Therefore, the Russo–Japanese War up to the surrender of Port Arthur should not be seen as the sole factor behind the unrest of 1905, but as one which exacerbated many economic problems that already existed in Russia, and one whose shock focused discontent on the tsar's autocratic rule. The incompetence of the war reflected the incompetence of the system.

An example of this can be seen in the activities of the Union of Liberation, a radical organisation set up in 1902 and formed from frustrated *zemstva* members, Third Element and intelligentsia figures who wanted to establish a constitutional monarchy, with a *duma* elected by the 'four-tail formula' of universal, direct, equal and secret suffrage. The Union was set up in Switzerland, but the aftermath of the military disasters of 1904 encouraged it to campaign more openly in Russia. 'Liberation banquets' provided an opportunity to raise money from invited guests as well as making speeches to spread their demands. Despite its non-violent outlook, by October 1904, the Union was meeting revolutionary groups in Paris to identify common goals, such as a constituent (constitutional) assembly, which suggested a tsar-free system. Hence the war was a catalyst in drawing rebellious groups together and instilling a confidence in them that their messages would be appreciated by the Russian people.

Likewise in Finland, the people were furious when Nicholas II increased the **Russification** process of the province and abolished the autonomous local state secretariat. The result was an increase in unrest in Finland and the assassination of the governor-general in July 1904. During the war, the Japanese exploited this sentiment by using Finland as a route to supply arms to Russian revolutionaries in an attempt to destabilise the Russian government. Finland serves as an example of how the Russian government desired national unity in time of war, but the repressive measures to ensure conformity only increased the antagonism between an increasingly educated minority and the imperial forces of Russia. Though the Japanese plan largely came to nothing after a shipment of rifles they had funded was wrecked off the coast of Finland, it did help to foster anti-Russian activities in Finland. This must have genuinely concerned the Russians as, unusually for this period, Russia responded by restoring Finland's constitution and halted the Russification process for over two years.

In Poland, some political leaders such as Józef Piłsudski travelled to Japan in 1904 to buy weapons for another Polish uprising. He offered to collaborate on sabotage and intelligence-gathering, though Japan turned down his idea of forming a Polish Legion from Polish prisoners of war. This again shows how the war was able to centre and concentrate anti-Russian or anti-government feelings.

While the course of the war in 1904 stimulated revolt, the consequences of the final defeats in 1905 and the resulting Treaty of Portsmouth are less clear. Once again the Russian army was forced to retreat after the Battle of Mukden, while in May the second Russian navy, having sailed all the way from the Baltic, was devastated as it arrived at the Battle of Tsushima. Five thousand Russian sailors and eight battleships were lost in Russia's worst naval defeat. Though this ended the fighting, it confirmed the belief that change was needed.

KEY TERM

Russification
A social policy favoured by Alexander III and Nicholas II to have the whole empire dominated by Russian culture rather than local cultures. This included the use of the Russian language in schools, conscription into the Russian army, even changing architecture to a more Russian style. It proved very unpopular and helped focus local nationalist and separatist feeling in the provinces.

SOURCE

Vladimir Kostenko, a ship's engineer on board the Russian ship *Orel* during the Battle of Tsushima, recalls the impact of the naval encounter. From V. Kostenko, *Na Orle v Tsushime* (On board the *Orel* at Tsushima: Memoirs of a Participant in the Russo–Japanese War of 1904–05), published in 1955.

While there is no doubting the bravery and dedication of our sailors, all their heroism and self-sacrifice counted for nothing. Our best ships went down one after another in agony and flames. Only now do we see what an unparalleled crime was committed by those who so heedlessly sent us to our deaths. Our decrepit, degenerate tsarist monarchy was blindly hoping for a miracle, but instead it begot the catastrophe of Tsushima. It is tsarism that has been smashed by the guns of Admiral Tōgō! It is tsarism that bears the shame of this defeat. Tsushima stands as the boundary between two eras of our history, the final, indisputable demonstration of the bankruptcy of the whole absolutist system!

SOURCE

The 1906 poem 'Our Tsar' by Konstantin Balmont, a leading Russian Symbolist. This poem is unusual in its directness, as the Symbolists normally used metaphors. Balmont became involved in protests in 1905, reading his poetry on the barricades. He fled to Paris in December 1905 to avoid arrest. Police records indicate that he was seen as a politically dangerous activist. 'Khodynka' in line 11 refers to the stampede which killed nearly 1,400 people celebrating the coronation of Nicholas II in May 1896. Published in K. Balmont, *Polnoe Sobranie Sochinenii* (1976).

Our Tsar means Mukden,
Our Tsar is Tsushima, a bloody stain;
The stink of gunpowder and smoke,
Where reason goes dim.
Our Tsar is blind poverty,
Prison and firing squads.
Tsar of the gallows, doubly low,
Who makes promises he dare not keep;
A coward who thinks with a stammer.
But just you wait: the hour of reckoning is near.
He whose reign began with Khodynka
Will end it on the scaffold.

ACTIVITY
KNOWLEDGE CHECK

The early impact of the Russo-Japanese War

1 How do Sources 3 and 4 demonstrate the links between military performance and political agitation?

2 How valuable are Sources 3 and 4 to a historian investigating the impact of the Battle of Tsushima on the political feeling in Russia? Think not just about the reaction but about the extent of radicalisation. Also reflect on the origin of both sources in your answer.

KEY TERM

Potemkin
A Russian battleship and part of the Black Sea fleet. Its sailors mutinied against its officers in June 1905 because of low morale caused by harsh conditions and the disastrous war with Japan. The Russian authorities quickly got the ship back, but the mutiny was of great symbolic value to revolutionaries in Russia.

Tsushima particularly increased discontent among the military. With two fleets gone, it took only a month for the final fleet based at Odessa in the Black Sea to mutiny on the battleship ***Potemkin*** in June 1905 (see page 97). The conduct of the naval officers in the war and at Tsushima highlights the brutal treatment dealt out to the sailors, as well as the inequality of society.

SOURCE

A Russian sailor who survived the Battle of Tsushima writes in 1907 about life in the navy during the Russo-Japanese War. From A. Zaterty, *Za chuzhiye grekhi* (1907).

These noblemen's sons, well cared-for and fragile, were capable only of decking themselves out in tunics with epaulettes. They would then stick their snouts in the air like a mangy horse being harnessed, and bravely scrape their heels on polished floors, or dance gracefully at balls, or get drunk, in these ways demoralizing their subordinates. They didn't even know our names. Corporal punishment was forbidden on paper only, for decency's sake: the sailors were beaten for all kinds of reasons, and often. It was considered the natural order of things. There was no way of complaining... We were compelled to eat rotten biscuits and stinking decaying meat while our officers fatted themselves with the best food and drank the most expensive wines.

With the end of the fighting, there was nothing to distract the sailors, and the *Potemkin* was stuck in the Black Sea, festering with revolutionary sentiments.

The events in the Far East in 1905 also prompted a congress of delegates of *zemstva* and municipal *dumas*, under a leadership of liberal aristocrats, including at least four princes, to petition the tsar for change. They met in late May and warned the tsar that the war was leading towards the destruction of both the empire and the monarchy. The congress urged the tsar to take responsibility for action.

In contrast to his reaction to the mismanagement of the war in 1904, the tsar, against the advice of his chief adviser, General Trepov, accepted the presentation of the congress and allowed Prince Sergei Trubetskoy, a Moscow University professor, to present their plans for democratic freedoms, including freedom of speech, the press, and assembly, as well as an extension of democratic elections. The tsar agreed in principle to the creation of an elected body, but insisted that the traditional bond between the tsar and the people would remain. He was not ready for a complete change, but the significance of the stimulus to reform that emerged out of Tsushima was the grudging acceptance by the imperial court that change had to happen. It was just a question of how small a change they could get away with.

Tsushima effectively finished the war. This helped to provide the possibility for reform through the discussions to formally end the war. The August 1905 Treaty of Portsmouth dealt with the defeated Russians with surprising moderation. Russia had to concede land to Japan including Port Arthur, half of the island of Sakhalin and southern Manchuria; it also had to acknowledge Korea as being under Japan's sphere of influence, but it did not have to pay reparations to Japan. Indeed, there were riots in Japan at the perceived injustice of the treaty, as the Japanese felt they were being treated as the defeated nation rather than as outright winners. The reason Russia did so well was largely due to the fact that the tsar sent Sergei Witte to negotiate the terms. The most internationally recognised and experienced of the Russian statesmen, Witte had been sidelined by the tsar in 1903 because many aristocrats saw him as too much of a moderniser with his earlier industrialisation programme. They feared that further reforms might follow.

The relatively lenient terms gave the tsar support when he most needed it. He made Witte a count on his return to a Russia in turmoil during September, and Witte took the lead in defusing the tensions that ran through 1905, when he announced the creation of a national *duma* in the famous October Manifesto. The Russo–Japanese War gave Witte the platform for a political comeback, and his work on the Treaty of Portsmouth and the October Manifesto not only promoted the greatest reform of the period, but also ensured that the tsar would remain. This was aided in a more sinister and familiar way by the returning armies from the East, who enforced the tsar's rule with repression and terror.

EXTEND YOUR KNOWLEDGE

Count Sergei Witte (1849–1915)

Count Sergei Witte was an influential politician, who had led the industrialisation of Russia in the late 19th century for Alexander III and Nicholas II. As minister of finance, he was sacked by Nicholas II, who despised him, in 1903. However, his comeback after the Russo-Japanese War saw him create Russia's first national *duma* and he became, in effect, prime minister. Attacked as both reactionary and revolutionary, he was dismissed when the *duma* met, as the tsar no longer needed him. He opposed Russia joining the First World War. He died in 1915, predicting revolution.

In conclusion, though the campaign of the Russo–Japanese War was similar to that of the disasters of the Crimean War, the immediate effects were subtly different. While the Crimean War pushed a reform-minded tsar to begin a series of progressive changes, the disasters of the war with Japan had greater impact on the demands of those opposing the tsar. It angered many to openly resist the tsar for the first time, and tended to make their demands more extreme. In summer 1905, Polish demonstrators calling for independence shouted 'Long Live Japan', while the list of aims in the petition of the marchers on Bloody Sunday in January 1905 included an end to the Russo–Japanese War. The desire for the tsar to implement reform was taken further by many with a desire to replace the tsar himself. However, the defeat of Russia by the summer of 1905 had persuaded even Nicholas II that some concessions were necessary, as well as bringing Witte back into influence. Witte went on to play a major role in saving tsarism during the crisis of 1905.

The effects of the Russo–Japanese War should not be seen in isolation. The discontent of the peasants and workers, the frustration of the intelligentsia, nationalist feelings in the provinces, and the violence of the revolutionaries were all present before the outbreak of war, and remained afterwards. The war was a catalyst for the political views within Russia, adding fuel to an already fierce fire.

ACTIVITY
KNOWLEDGE CHECK

The impact of the Russo-Japanese War

1 Draw a table comparing the effects of the Crimean War and the Russo-Japanese War on the period immediately following them.

2 Draw a table with two columns headed 'Revolt' and 'Reform'. Add evidence to each column regarding the impact of the Russo-Japanese War.

3 If the war had not happened, would it have been necessary to reform the imperial system?

4 'If the Russian people demand change, then it is revolt. If the tsar allows it, then it is reform.' To what extent do you think the concepts of reform and revolt are merely down to the perception of the observer? In pairs, prepare a debate arguing for each side of this topic. Then write a conclusion that offers a clear and reasoned judgement on your findings.

A Level Exam-Style Question Section B

How far did the Russo–Japanese War stimulate revolt within Russia in 1904–05? (20 marks)

Tip

A good answer will always give a balanced response and look at both sides of the argument. In other words, how far it did and how far it did not. A better answer will also attempt to look at changes within the time period given in the question. In other words, was the impact of the war different in 1904 compared with its impact in 1905?

WHAT WAS THE SIGNIFICANCE OF BLOODY SUNDAY IN 1905?

The classic account of Bloody Sunday is usually presented as follows: on 9 January 1905, Father Gapon led around 150,000 unarmed people to petition the tsar at the Winter Palace in St Petersburg. Carrying religious icons and shouting slogans of support for the tsar, they were met at the palace by lines of soldiers. The imperial guard opened fire on them, killing and wounding perhaps 1,000 people. Rage at the tragedy led to nationwide strikes and uprisings as 1905 became the year of revolution.

In this version, Bloody Sunday is often taken to be the trigger for the 1905 revolution. While this presumes that 1905 actually was a revolution, it is also inaccurate to see the event as a trigger which by implication marks the event as the starting point. Student unrest had been common since 1900, while liberal opposition worried that the tsar's refusal to grant any political concessions would provide ammunition for more revolutionary and violent groups. Their concerns were confirmed in the form of the Social Revolutionaries (SRs), who formed a fighting detachment in 1902, using assassination as their method of protest. They killed one minister of the interior in 1902, and the second one, the hated Plehve, in 1904. Therefore Bloody Sunday occurred in the context of a build-up of political agitation. In particular, the number of strikes had been increasing by an average of 176 a year between 1895 and 1905. A strike that began in Vladikavkaz in 1902 included 225,000 workers in southern Russia within a year, and resulted in the government banning all worker organisations by the end of 1903. Ironically, the event that caused the regime so much trouble was created by the regime. While independent trade unions were illegal in Russia, since 1901 the police had created labour unions. This form of 'police socialism' was the idea of Zubatov, head of the Moscow ***ochrana***, who hoped to integrate the workers into the umbrella of imperial rule as well as allowing the police to infiltrate and spy on potential troublemakers, particularly violent groups such the Social Democrats or Social Revolutionaries (SRs). Though Zubatov had been discredited by 1904, as more radical workers joined the unions only to use them for subversive ends, the St Petersburg union simply switched allegiance to a church-based union. This was the Assembly of Russian Factory and Mill Workers of St Petersburg, led by Father Gapon and aided by the St Petersburg *ochrana*, to whom Father Gapon provided information on the more dangerous radicals. Indeed, it is most probable that Gapon was an *ochrana* agent; though this was not unusual for its day, it does not necessarily dismiss his desire to reform.

KEY TERM

The *ochrana*
The Department for Protecting the Public Security and Order (abbreviated to *ochrana*) was set up in 1880 to replace the Third Section. It acted as the secret police in Imperial Russia. It was also known as the 'guard department'. It was formed to combat terrorism and left-wing revolutionary activities, often using covert operations and agents to penetrate suspected organisations.

EXTEND YOUR KNOWLEDGE

The appropriately strange world of Father Gapon

The ambiguous role of Father Gapon neatly symbolises the chaotic, double-dealing and dangerous world of Russian political and reform movements in the 1900s. He demonstrates that nothing is ever straightforward, nothing is ever as it appears on the surface and motives are never clear-cut. He first became a priest not because of a religious calling, but in order to win the approval of the father of a woman that Gapon wished to marry. Becoming a priest also offered the chance to further his job prospects after poor behaviour saw his university career cut short. On the death of his wife, he moved to St Petersburg, where the appalling conditions of the urban workers prompted his missionary zeal to improve their lives.

There is evidence that, as well as police sponsorship, Gapon received aid to set up his union from the Japanese spymaster Akashi Motojiro, who was eager to sow revolt. However, Gapon was not just a tool for the police or others, but harboured a genuine desire to move Russia towards a constitutional monarchy. During the violence of Bloody Sunday, he was saved by his friend Rutenberg and managed to escape, heavily disguised, to Europe. As the SRs sang songs blaming Gapon for his betrayal and for deliberately leading workers to their death, he was treated as a celebrity in the West. He was fêted by many radical politicians, including Lenin, for he had managed to inspire the workers to rise up - something that the Marxist revolutionary groups had failed to do at this point. He wrote his autobiography, *The Story of My Life*, and in 1906 returned to Russia. There, he supported Witte's reforms and continued to liaise with the secret police. In March 1906, he attempted to join the SRs. One story goes that he attempted to recruit his friend Rutenberg as a police informer, but was overheard and was immediately hanged by three other SRs. Another story has the three SRs as police agents and Gapon being murdered on police orders. His body was found a month later.

Father Gapon was a charismatic priest, and both a drinker and a gambler. Witte, who witnessed Bloody Sunday, wrote that while Gapon worked as a police informer and spy, he believed he was striving for the workers' best interests. It was not uncommon for political leaders to exist on both sides, while trying to further their own cause. In an age of violent and varied political groups, one way to survive was to be involved in all of them. The portrayal of Father Gapon often depends more on the perspective of the writer than the reality of his life. It would be too simple to judge him as a saint or a sinner; perhaps he was just a complex man with sympathy for the workers, but over-optimistic about his own abilities.

The actual events of Bloody Sunday have been coloured, or tainted, depending on your point of view, by later regimes' use of the tragedy for their own ends. The event was recreated and filmed in 1925 for the film *Devyatoe yanvarya* (*9 January*). For the benefit of a Soviet audience, it was portrayed as the communist workers' revolution cut down by the tsar's orders.

The historical truth is more uncertain. The Putilov Iron Works had gone on strike in early January and this had quickly spread to over 150,000 workers across the city, spurred on by the demand for an eight-hour working day and the news of the surrender of Port Arthur. Gapon saw the strike as an opportunity to present his petition to the tsar. Despite a warning two days earlier that the assembly was banned, it went ahead. The demonstration ranged in size from the official figure of 3,000 to perhaps as many as 50,000, but it was not a call for revolution. Workers, women and children wore their Sunday-best, held religious icons and sang songs of loyalty to the tsar – more a plea for help than a scream of revolt. However, some 10,000 troops had been brought in, and confusion in their ranks led to shootings and cavalry charges throughout the city over the next three hours, as opposed to the single attack outside the Winter Palace as often portrayed. Many of the dead were not even participants in the procession. Gapon's group was fired on at the Narva Gates, but most died later at Troitskaya Square. Sources vary in the number of casualties, with official figures of 96 dead countered by anti-government sources of 1,000. An accurate figure may have been around 200. What is important is that peaceful and loyal civilians were fired on by the tsar's troops, though Nicholas II was not at the Winter Palace at the time and did not order the killings. That night, workers rioted in the streets, looting and starting to construct barricades, but the cold night caused them to withdraw.

A hastily appointed governor compounded the problem by sending a delegation of loyal workers to the tsar to beg forgiveness for their actions on behalf of all workers, and then expelling the demonstrators from the city, which spread the details of the atrocity across the empire.

A Level Exam-Style Question
Section A

Study Source 6 before you answer this question.

Assess the value of the source for revealing reasons for discontent and methods of revolt in Russia during the period 1904–05.

Explain your answer using the source, the information given about it and your own knowledge of the historical context. (20 marks)

Tip

It is important to have a fully integrated answer. Do not see the historical context, or your own knowledge, as separate from the content in the source. Try to explore links between the two, especially as close reading and drawing inferences from the source can provide you with several reasons to discuss.

SOURCE

From the Workers' Petition written by Father Gapon and signed by 135,000 workers. It was to be presented to the tsar at the Winter Palace by Father Gapon on 9 January 1905, but the events of Bloody Sunday meant that it was never delivered. The petition contained other demands, including basic civil liberties, improvements in working conditions such as an eight-hour working day, tax changes, transfer of land to the people and an end to the Russo-Japanese War. From G. Gapon, *The Story of my Life, by Father Gapon* (1906).

We are not recognised as normal human beings, but are dealt with as slaves who have to bear their bitter lot in silence. Patiently we endured this; but now we are being thrust deeper into the slough of right-lessness and ignorance, are being suffocated by despotism and arbitrary whims, and now, O Tsar, we have no strength left. The awful moment has come when death is better than the prolongation of our unendurable tortures. Therefore, we have left work, and informed our employers that we shall not resume it until they have fulfilled our demands...

O Emperor, there are more than three hundred thousand of us here, yet we are all of us human beings only in appearance and outwardly, while in reality we are deemed devoid of a single human right, even that of speaking, thinking, and meeting to talk over our needs, and of taking measures to better our condition. Any one of us who should dare lift his voice in defence of the working class is thrown into prison or banished. O Tsar, is this in accordance with God's commandments, in virtue of which you are now reigning? Is life under such laws worth living?...

Russia is too vast, her wants too manifold, to admit of bureaucrats alone governing her. It is absolutely necessary that the people should assist, because only they know their own hardships...

... give orders without delay to representatives of all classes in the land to meet together. Let capitalists and workmen be present; let officials, priests, physicians, and teachers all come and choose their own delegates. Let all be free to elect whom they will, and for this purpose let the elections to the Constituent Assembly be organised on the principle of universal suffrage. This is our principal request, on which everything else depends...

... if you are not responsive to our petition, we will die here on this square before your palace... For us there are but two roads, one leading to liberty and happiness, the other to the tomb. Point, Sire, to either of them; we will take it, even though it lead to death.

The significance of Bloody Sunday was twofold. First, it seeded a cascade of sympathetic strikes across the empire, which spread from the workers to the intelligentsia and to sections of the military as well. Secondly, it changed the way the people viewed their tsar. They no longer saw him as a leader to save them from a crisis, but as the person responsible for the crisis.

By the end of January, over 400,000 workers were on strike in industrial centres throughout Russia. However, the effect was limited, as the strikers were not collectively organised, and were only united in their anger over Bloody Sunday. The spontaneous nature of their protest was partly due to the lack of strong leadership. The main revolutionary leaders, such as Lenin of the Bolsheviks or Martov of the **Mensheviks**, were all in comfortable exile and not yet ready to risk a return to Russia. The non-Russian parts of the empire saw more pronounced signs of discontent. In Poland, hit economically hardest by the war with Japan, some 6,000 workers went on strike in Łódź, and the next day a general strike of 70,000 was called. Warsaw saw 100,000 on the streets, and in response, Russian troops killed 93 people. In Riga (in Latvia), some 15,000 strikers met with more imperial violence and another 70 died, with the Russian governor boasting of having successfully crushed the 'insurrection' with his decisive action. Here and in other provinces, such as Finland, Georgia and the Caucasus, outrage at Bloody Sunday mixed with the passion stirred by nationalism, so that almost their entire population was involved in protest. It is estimated that around 50 percent of the industrial workers in European Russia, and over 93 percent in Poland, went on strike during 1905.

KEY TERM

Menshevik
A member of a revolutionary communist group in Russia. After the abdication of the tsar in 1917, the Mensheviks were willing to work with both the Provisional Government and the other communist groups.

To the masses, the tsar had been affectionately known as the 'Little Father', a patriarchal figure protective of his empire and subjects. He was the single person who could cure society's ills. Problems were to be blamed on his advisers or the landed gentry, but never on the tsar himself. Bloody Sunday transformed this view. As the images of the tsar held up by the protestors lay bullet-ridden in the St Petersburg snow, the tsar's reputation lay just as shattered. The embedded deference was gone. From now on, to the masses, he was 'Nicholas the bloody' and only his removal, or even his death, could save Russia. Students once more took to the streets and went on strike, with 3,000 protesting at Moscow University, where they burned portraits of the tsar and brought out the red flags of revolutionary intent. The government felt it had no choice but to close the gates on all higher-education institutions, which merely freed the students to engage in further political action.

The strikes brought on by Bloody Sunday did not necessarily bring about fundamental and direct change, but they did politicise the workers remarkably quickly and taught them that they had the organisational ability to strike at short notice and with considerable impact. Most strikes started for economic reasons such as animosity over sacked workers or a reduction of wages, but they could suddenly turn political, and the workers would apply this lesson later in the year. Perhaps more significant is the irreconcilable change in the people's perception of the very essence of the tsar. Workers and intellectuals alike called for an end to autocracy at any cost. On 4 February, less than a month after Bloody Sunday, the Grand Duke Sergei Alexandrovich, the tsar's uncle and close friend, was blown to pieces by an SR bomb in Moscow. This was the first leading member of the tsar's family to be killed since the assassination of Alexander II in 1881, and it profoundly shocked Nicholas.

A final effect of Bloody Sunday was that it increased the reactionary nature of the tsar's inner advisers on the State Council. After his murder in 1904, Plehve was replaced as minister of the interior by the more liberal Prince Svyatopolk-Mirsky. The war with Japan had made Nicholas wary of the rising tensions within Russia, and now the majority of his advisers were moving towards the drafting of concessions. This apparent drift towards reform caused some advisers to cry with joy, while others reacted with concern, such as the elderly Pobedonostsev, who still preached the total autocracy of Alexander III. Dmitry Trepov, the Moscow chief of police, resigned from the State Council in disgust on 1 January 1905, a week before the shootings. Two days after Bloody Sunday, Svyatopolk-Mirsky stepped down and Trepov was subsequently recalled to power as governor-general of St Petersburg. He was hated by the public, who saw him, with just a little exaggeration, as a dictator. However, he held great sway over Nicholas II, even after he lost his political role as part of the October Manifesto. Therefore, a liberal and influential section of the tsar's advisers lost power while the autocratic faction was strengthened, at least in the short term, as a result of Bloody Sunday. Tsar Nicholas' reaction to Bloody Sunday was seen by some of his advisers as a series of poor decisions. Sergei Witte later wrote in his 1921 memoirs that it was 'a mixture of cowardice, blindness and stupidity'.

EXTEND YOUR KNOWLEDGE

Trust no one

Edvard Radzinsky, in his influential 1992 biography of Nicholas II, *The Last Tsar*, suggested that there was a 'camarilla' (inner clique) of reactionary, autocratic advisers, including Pobedonostsev and Trepov, who deliberately created Bloody Sunday to scare the tsar against reform as well as taking the opportunity to put the workers in their place. They persuaded the tsar to refuse the petition and leave St Petersburg for his summer palace at Tsarskoe Selo. There is even a suggestion that the Grand Duke was murdered by them to begin to manipulate Nicholas II out of power and replace him with a more suitable tsar, Grand Duke Nicholas Nikolaevich, cousin to Alexander III.

However, the evidence for all this is circumstantial and, as Radzinsky pointed out, even though Russians love a good plot, what actually happens, whatever the scale of the event, is down to someone's mistake, stupidity or laziness.

SOURCE

The student Kerensky writing to his parents two weeks after Bloody Sunday. He witnessed the shooting at Nevsky Prospekt where soldiers fired on the crowd as the protesters sank to their knees and crossed themselves. Kerensky grew up to lead the Provisional Government which overthrew the tsar in 1917.

I am sorry not to have written to you earlier, but we have been living here in such a state of shock that it was impossible to write. Oh, 'these awful days' in Peter [St Petersburg] will remain for ever in the memory of everybody who lived through them. Now there is silence, but it is silence before the storm. Both sides are preparing and reviewing their own forces. Only one side can prevail. Either the demands of society will be satisfied (i.e. a freely elected legislature of people's representatives) or there will be a bloody and terrible conflict, no doubt ending in the victory of the reaction.

SOURCE 8

The recollections of a Bolshevik who was at Bloody Sunday, quoted in Orlando Figes' *A People's Tragedy: The Russian Revolution 1891–1924* (1996). Here he describes the immediate reaction of people who were involved in the massacre.

I observed the faces around me and I detected neither fear nor panic. No, the reverend and almost prayerful expressions were replaced by hostility and even hatred. I saw these looks of hatred and vengeance on literally every face - old and young, men and women. The revolution had been truly born, and it had been born in the very core, in the very bowels of the people.

SOURCE

Part of the speech by the tsar to the delegation of loyal workers who had arrived ten days after Bloody Sunday. Nicholas donated 50,000 rubles to the victims' families. Published in *Pravitel'stvennyi Vestnik* (*Government Gazette*), No. 15, 20 January 1905.

I have asked you here so you can hear my words directly from me and tell your friends what I have to say... I know your life as working people is not an easy one. Lots of things need to be improved and put right... I would ask you please to have patience... But you know it is wrong of you - criminal, in fact - to come in a mutinous crowd, as you did, to tell me about your needs and desires... I believe in the good intentions of the working people - and in your lasting devotion to me - so I am nonetheless willing to pardon you for what has happened.

ACTIVITY
KNOWLEDGE CHECK

Reactions to Bloody Sunday

1 Using Sources 7, 8, 9 and your own knowledge, say what the different reactions were from different groups within Russia to the events of Bloody Sunday.

2 In your opinion, which are the most important reactions? Explain your reasoning.

3 What do these reactions suggest might be the consequences for the stability of the Russian system over the course of 1905?

The months following Bloody Sunday consisted of an overlapping series of strikes, rural unrest, mutinies and political unions. Occasionally they were co-ordinated, but usually not. Often it was like a relay with a baton of discontent being passed on to a fresh impetus as the earlier one faded. There was a chain reaction which applied pressure by sheer weight of numbers rather than united will.

The tsar, pulled this way and that by his conflicting advisers, managed only to appear indecisive. On a single day, 18 February 1905, he managed three contradictory decrees. The first, the Imperial Decree, denounced all participants in rebellion as arrogant revolutionaries and called for the country to unite behind their tsar; the second decree invited ideas for improvement to the situation to be submitted to the government, which was ironic as that was what Father Gapon had tried to do. The third was almost an answer to the second: known as the **Bulygin Rescript** after the new minister of the interior, it promised to draft a new elected body that could consult with the tsar on legislation, as well as some other freedoms and reduced peasant redemption payments. To the people of Russia, it was unclear whether the tsar was cleverly playing for time, hoping a delay would somehow restore the traditional order, or simply had no control over the situation. His diary reflected mainly on inconsequential matters concerning his routine, and blamed the gathering storms on foreign spies. However, a consultative assembly was not now going to satisfy the increasingly radical mood of the country. As news of the tsar's actions filtered down, reports came in about Russia's military defeat at Mukden, and the unrest intensified and began to spread into the countryside.

KEY TERM

Bulygin Rescript
Published the day after the assassination of his uncle in February 1905, this was the tsar's promise to allow the peasants further concessions, including a consultative assembly, freedom of speech and a reduction in redemption payments.

Rural areas in 1905

The events of Bloody Sunday were discussed in the countryside, but in the main, the rural areas retained their deference to the tsar. It was their hunger for the land that ignited their passion, and saw a wave of petitions drawn up after the tsar's request for ideas. Issues of taxation, redemption payments and education were all added to the agenda, rather than the definitive political rights that the urban workers were demanding. As the petitions failed to have an effect or find an audience, each peasant community banded together to take on the local authority. This was the *mirs* taking the mutual responsibility, as well as the law, into their own hands. The target was usually the produce and property of the local landowner, which would be carefully packed up and transported back to the village on up to 700 carts. The affair would often end with the manor being burnt to the ground, after being carefully raided of all its useful and removable objects. There was even a case of a grand piano being broken up and the ivory keys shared out among the villagers. In 1905, it is estimated that over 3,000 manor houses were burnt, some 15 percent of all manors, and the rural night sky glowed with their flames in a phenomenon known as 'red cockerel'. During the month of the harvest, the unrest died down, but began again in earnest as the October Manifesto was published and the grain was gathered.

This destruction, vandalism and blatant stealing of the landowners' property dominated the concerns of Russia's rural elite, but the peasants also organised their own unions and co-operatives. This was particularly true of the largest villages, which tended to have schools and therefore the teachers, and other third-element professionals, who were heavily involved in setting up unions and co-operatives. Some, such as the Sumy Republic in Kharkov province, went as far as setting up independent peasant republics. These tended to be more political and wished to integrate the world of the village into national politics through elected bodies. The **Markovo Republic** effectively ruled part of the Volokolamsk district, just 80 miles from Moscow, for nearly a year. It had an elected government and president and set up, among other organisations, a school, an agricultural society and a theatre. It was destroyed by government forces in July 1906.

KEY TERM

Markovo Republic
A self-proclaimed peasant state set up in October 1905, which held out against the government until July 1906. Its existence highlights the tsar's weakness during this period of turmoil, especially in rural areas.

Indeed, between January and October 1905, the army was used 2,700 times to put down peasant disturbances. With the vast majority of the infantry made up of peasants, the military at a local level was often reluctant to suppress rural unrest. Units refused to carry out their officers' orders and many mutinies occurred, with even the Cossack (see page 43) cavalry involved. However, these were local mutinies, not insurrection against the state. They were self-contained, and in only one case did they link with the workers. This was at Chita and Krasnoyarsk on the Trans-Siberian Railway, where soldiers returning from the war with Japan mutinied and joined a workers' strike to form a workers' and soldiers' union based at the railway station. This was in November 1905, when the chaos of the year was starting to decline, and after a couple of months, special troops arrived to restore order by the familiar method.

Military mutinies

The government was also able to deal with most military rebellions quickly, as they were usually directed at officers and therefore isolated from other revolutionary groups. The unrest by many soldiers could almost be seen as peasant revolts, suspicious of both urban workers and the government officials, and only choosing to revolt when they felt they could win. If not, then the soldiers obeyed their orders and suppressed other rebellions.

Even the most famous mutiny on the battleship *Potemkin* in June 1905 is little more than the most high-profile case of a disconnected rebellion which failed even to encourage the support of other military units. With morale low after the Battle of Tsushima, the trigger was the sailors' refusal to eat maggot-ridden food. The captain threatened to have them shot, causing the crew to rebel, murder their officers and set sail under a red flag to Odessa, a city paralysed by a workers' strike. Eisenstein's 1925 film movingly showed the epic tragedy unfold, as government troops marched down the steps that led to the docks, firing on the desperate crowd. Two thousand died and 3,000 were wounded, but the guns of the *Potemkin* did not sound in support of the workers. The link between mutinying crew and striking worker was simply not there. The battleship failed to stir support from the rest of the Black Sea fleet, though one ship briefly mutinied in support, and loyal ships chose not to fire on the *Potemkin* when they had the opportunity. The ship eventually docked in Romania and its sailors sought refuge. As a revolt the *Potemkin* was a minor threat but, as an 11-day public spectacle, it was a significant embarrassment for the tsar. The mutiny, along with other examples of military insubordination, showed that, though not revolutionary, the armed forces could not be totally trusted.

A less well-known incident was the Sevastopol Uprising of November 1905, where Naval Lieutenant Commander Pyotr Shmidt led a fleet-wide mutiny of the Black Sea fleet with over 8,000 sailors, compared with around 10,000 loyal to the regime. After a 90-minute gun battle, the rebels capitulated. Shmidt was arrested and executed in March 1906, but was later remembered as a hero in Soviet Russia. Though they were great dramas, the various mutinies did little to further the cause of reform.

Union of Unions

Meanwhile, in May 1905, national organisations of professionals such as lawyers, engineers and professors sent representatives to Moscow to create a joint 'Union of Unions'. Their demand reaffirmed the 'four-tail formula' as the basic foundation of a constituent assembly. This added a third radical body complementing the work of the Union of Liberation and the *zemstva* groups. The Union of Unions is a manifestation of how the intelligentsia and professionals were starting to coalesce around a central idea. For example, members of the Union of Liberation and *zemstva* groups had recently formed the **Constitutional Democratic Party**, or the Kadets, who would play an influential role in the years to come. The chairman of the Union of Unions, Milyukov, was also the leader of the Union of Liberation. This more singular approach focused clearly on a constituent assembly as the solution, presenting the authorities with a genuine threat. Most of the responses across the empire had been forthright yet unco-ordinated; now the Union of Unions had the potential to draw them together. This national voice can be seen in the headline of a leading liberal newspaper on 21 May 1905, which foreshadowed the sentiment of Mikhail Gorbachev speaking about communist Russia some 80 years later: 'We can no longer live like this,' became the slogan of the opposition. The threat of a united opposition meant that some of the tsar's more liberal-inclined and pragmatic advisers saw the need for some concessions before the opposition united to a degree where they could not be controlled.

KEY TERM

Constitutional Democratic Party (Kadets)
A liberal political party largely made up of professionals and intellectuals. After 1905, the Party continued to push for political reform and would go on to make up a significant part of the Provisional Government after the 1917 February Revolution. However, most of its leaders would be forced to emigrate, mainly to Paris, after the communist victory in the civil war during 1921.

Linked to the Union of Unions was the All-Russian Peasant Union, which attempted to consolidate the national peasants' views to address all their grievances in one organisation. Originally just a collection of village assemblies called by the Moscow nobility to allow the peasants to express loyalty to the tsar and support for the war with Japan, in May 1905 it denounced the authorities and set itself up as the All-Russian Peasant Union. It held two congresses in the summer of 1905 and November 1905, and it is estimated that it may have had up to 5,000 branches with 200,000 members in total. It was heavily influenced by the SRs, whose views on peasant ownership of the land were eagerly supported, though the union never supported the armed overthrow of the tsar. It had many links with the Union of Unions, who carried out much of its organisational work. However, steady repression of the peasants in late 1905 and the promise of concessions in Witte's October Manifesto saw the union fall apart, despite the protestations and encouragement of the SRs. The link between the intellectuals and the masses was never solid enough to threaten the power of the autocracy.

The General Strike and the creation of the soviets

The impetus for the need for concession was given an extra boost by the events of August and October. Bulygin's Rescript was published, but the assembly it promoted would only be allowed to consult with the sacrosanct autocracy. This was no longer enough to satisfy anyone. The government tried to pacify the universities by re-establishing their independence, and though this stopped the student protests, it turned the lecture halls into political meeting rooms attended by all, except a reluctant police. By late September the Moscow printers went on strike and joined the students. The typically violent police response saw the strike extend to St Petersburg, including the railway workers who were affiliated with the Union of Unions. The railway unions, with their transport links, were the best organised and connected in Russia and, by early October, the whole empire had ground to a halt. They were joined by millions of other employees, from bank staff to actors, shop workers to lecturers. With the General Strike starting to be organised by the Union of Unions in their political demands, combined with the rising panic as the basic amenities started to fail across the nation, it looked as if a disciplined and focused radical opposition was moving to force power from the tsar.

Much of the discipline of the General Strike came from the newly formed **St Petersburg Soviet**. This grew out of the idea of the Union of Unions and on 17 October around 200,000 workers elected over 500 representatives, mostly metalworkers, from nearly 100 factories. It quickly became dominated by the three leading socialist parties: Bolsheviks, Mensheviks and SRs. It published its own newspaper *Izvestiia* (*The News*), with editorials written by Leon Trotsky, who took over as chairman in November. A Menshevik at that time, he had recently returned from exile. The soviet saw itself as a workers' government and an alternative to the authority of the tsar, and it even formed a militia to help organise strikes and distribute food. However, its immediate impact was limited to St Petersburg in late 1905. The impact of the soviet was greater after its demise, and its legacy was exaggerated and claimed by later revolutionaries. The Bolshevik leader, Lenin, who had returned to Russia in early November, was never allowed to speak to the soviet. The October General Strike was not called by them and Trotsky actually missed the start of the strike. However, they were good at self-publicity.

KEY TERM

St Petersburg Soviet
A workers' council, or soviet, set up in St Petersburg. Its exact origins have been disputed by the people involved, but it helped to organise the General Strike of October 1905 and Trotsky first rose to prominence within it.

SOURCE 10 From *1905*, Leon Trotsky's memoirs reflecting on the role of the St Petersburg Soviet in the October Strike. He wrote this in 1925.

As the October strike developed, the importance of the soviet grew literally hour by hour. The industrial proletariat rallied around it and the soviet united the revolution around itself. It resolved to transform the working class into a revolutionary army... A tremendous wave of strikes swept the country from end to end, convulsing the entire body of the nation. Every striking factory elected a representative and, having equipped him with the necessary credentials, sent him off to the Soviet. The Soviet was the axis of all events; every thread ran towards it, every call to action emanated from it.

ACTIVITY
KNOWLEDGE CHECK

The St Petersburg Soviet in 1905

1. How does Source 10 support the idea that the role of the St Petersburg Soviet has been romanticised as its participants looked back? Why do you think Trotsky might be particularly guilty of this?
2. While Trotsky may have exaggerated the soviet as 'the axis of all events', how could the importance of the St Petersburg Soviet be assessed?

EXTEND YOUR KNOWLEDGE

Violence for violence's sake

Not all the violence of 1905 can be attributed to political revolution. There was a sharp rise in criminal violence, such as muggings, vandalism and drunken riots. The lack of police also often resulted in mob rule, whose beatings and lynchings added to the atmosphere of wild violence. A mass amnesty at the start of the year had seen the jail population fall by a third, and this may have added to the sense of chaos.

The historian Orlando Figes, in his detailed and eloquent book, *A People's Tragedy*, argues that many historians have been swayed by the Soviet-created myth of workers on the barricades, when in fact much of the so-called political unrest degenerated into simple violent riots of looting and criminality. He goes on to say that the violent acts were part of the integral make-up of workers' and peasants' unrest, as expressions of their hatred towards both the wealthy and the authorities. This was a problem at the time for the revolutionary political parties, as they could not control this aspect of people's behaviour. The image of a vulgar, drunk, violent 'hooligan' did not sit comfortably with the Bolshevik image of the heroic proletarian worker standing up to autocracy.

As the idea of a soviet quickly spread to over 50 other industrial towns, they did allow a degree of co-operation between the workers and intelligentsia and worked more along the lines of village assemblies than traditional workers' organisations. However, a lot of their work was improvised and inconsistent. The soviets were created as a consequence of the strike, and they developed to control certain aspects of the strike, but many found it hard to maintain the spontaneity that created them. It was the escalating problems of the General Strike rather than the activities of the soviet that caused the authorities the most concern. When Moscow's water system malfunctioned, strikers were blamed for apparently contaminating the water. Law and order were starting to break down. The tsar turned to Witte to save Russia, while he himself spent the autumn hunting, safely removed from the chaos.

The significance of the October Manifesto

Count Witte proposed an October Manifesto which would install three basic principles into a Russian constitution to be introduced in 1906:

- freedoms, such as speech and assembly, for all of the Russian population
- extension of suffrage to the whole population in order to elect a state *duma*
- all legislation to be agreed upon by the state *duma*.

The idea was to enshrine real participation by both the population and the *duma* into the running of the country. However, despite the support of the majority of the advisers and even the normally reactionary Trepov, Nicholas II still searched for a way out and asked his uncle, the Grand Duke Nicholas, to act as dictator.

In a desperate effort to convince Nicholas II of the seriousness of the situation in October, the Grand Duke produced a revolver and threatened to kill himself if Nicholas did not agree to Witte's plan. This somewhat theatrical gesture seemed to persuade the tsar that concession rather than repression was the answer, though he whined about it in private letters, as he saw it as a personal betrayal. Witte wrote later that he felt the tsar, despite the finality of its wording, saw the manifesto as a temporary measure to placate the country so that autocracy could be re-established. He would be proved right.

The initial reaction to the manifesto was one of jubilation. Nine months from Bloody Sunday, the crowds once again gathered in front of the Winter Palace, but this time in peaceful victory and joy. Fifty thousand people crowded in front of Moscow's Bolshoi Theatre as songs were sung to celebrate the move towards a western-style constitutional monarchy. The first heady days saw political meetings held in the open, newspapers pushing for reform and a sense of genesis for a new Russia. This feeling was extended to the peasants, when two weeks later an Act reduced by half all redemption payments for 1906, and cancelled them altogether from 1907.

SOURCE 11

Demonstration 17 October 1905, by Ilya Repin, 1907–11. Repin painted many leading political figures of the period, such as Witte and Pobedonostsev, as well as writers, artists and common people. One of the best-known Russian painters of the 19th century, he was a major artist of the 'Russian national style'. He retired to Finland after the 1917 Revolution.

EXTRACT

From Geoffrey Hosking's *Russia: People & Empire 1552–1917* (1997), in which he focuses on the immediate reaction to the October Manifesto. Here, he refers to the Black Hundreds. These were ultra-nationalistic gangs who were fiercely loyal to the tsar and autocracy in general. They were often violent and particularly anti-Semitic.

The greatest moment for the St Petersburg Soviet came on the day after the October Manifesto, 18 October, when huge crowds from all strata of society thronged the streets and squares to celebrate Russia's liberation from autocracy. For a brief moment the workers enjoyed the enthusiastic support of propertied society. From the balcony of the university building Trotskii, who was gaining a reputation as the soviet's most brilliant orator, harangued the assembled multitudes, urging decisive action to complete the victory over Tsarism. Political demands were approved by acclamation: an amnesty for all political prisoners, abolition of the death penalty, the dismissal of Trepov (Governor-General of St Petersburg), the removal of the army from the city and its replacement by a people's militia. For a short time, St Petersburg became a huge and rebellious village assembly, euphoric and carried away by the collective mood. But by evening fighting had broken out, involving Cossacks or the newly formed Black Hundreds gangs. The crowds dispersed, having achieved little beyond sonorous declarations of principle.

ACTIVITY
KNOWLEDGE CHECK

The October Manifesto

1 What can you learn from Source 11 and Extract 1 about the days after the October Manifesto?

2 What does this suggest about the nature of political feeling in 1905?

The days after the manifesto also saw many political protests against the tsar transform into anti-Semitic riots and pogroms (massacres of Jewish people). Again, Kishinev saw another massacre of its remaining Jewish population and this was repeated in a wave of over 690 pogroms during October. In Odessa, over 800 Jews were killed and 100,000 made homeless as the police helped organise and orchestrate the murders. Trepov had edited pamphlets calling for the destruction of Jews, while the ministry of the interior had partly financed the pogroms. When Witte tried to intercede on behalf of the Jewish population, the tsar blocked him. Nicholas felt that the disturbances of 1905 were largely the fault of the Jews, and this was his vengeance. The authorities now used a general anti-Semitic sentiment to shore up loyalty.

Politically, the manifesto had the desired effect. The General Strike quickly subsided, and the soviet lost its support from the whole of society, as many in the country felt their demands had been met. Liberals, who essentially agreed with the manifesto enough to work with it, became known as **Octobrists**. They numbered around 20,000, mostly middle-class supporters like businessmen or landowners. Less conservative liberals, like the Kadets, lacked confidence that Witte would be able to deliver the reforms. They refused to join the first cabinet government that Witte set up in October, though several other liberals did join.

The October Manifesto had weakened and split the opposition sufficiently for the threat of a revolution to have passed. It was not the end of the violence, or of strikes, but it was the end of the possibility of a collective attack against the regime. It would now be much easier to subdue the divided opposition.

KEY TERM

Octobrist
A non-revolutionary reformer or politician willing to work with the tsar's government towards the idea of a constitutional monarchy following Witte's October Manifesto. This helped to ease the revolutionary feeling from the General Strike of 1905.

To what extent did the October Manifesto offer real reform?

Witte, the most experienced and internationally respected Russian politician of the time, spent months negotiating a mainly French loan to stabilise the economy. Despite tense mediations – as when the US bankers, Rothschild, withdrew their support in response to the tsar's refusal to improve conditions for Jews in Russia – an agreement was reached. A loan of nearly a billion rubles, the largest foreign loan ever at that point, was secured in February 1906. This allowed Russia to recover any losses due to the war with Japan and the chaos of 1905. Witte saw it as the highest achievement of his political life and the climax of his career. This sentiment was evidently shared by a grateful Nicholas II, who nevertheless, or perhaps because of this, now felt able to sack Witte at the first opportunity.

The opportunity did not take long to arrive. The October Manifesto had set out three basic principles, but it was more than six months before the constitution was created to supposedly put them into practice. Technically, it marked the end of the autocracy and the start of constitutional rule, with power shared between the tsar and an elected national *duma*. The reality was that, by this time, the tsar felt secure enough to remove many of the concessions in the **Fundamental Laws** of 26 April 1906.

Under these amendments, the tsar buttressed his autocratic rule in the following ways.

- He granted himself the power to veto any decision made by the elected *duma*.
- He strictly regulated the laws surrounding freedom of speech.
- He retained the sole right to appoint ministers.
- He had the power to dissolve the *duma* at any time.
- Article 87 allowed the government to bypass the *duma* completely to enact a law if the situation merited it. The definition of the situation was left to the tsar.

In any case, the tsar personally renewed the membership of the upper house each year, which always gave him an institution with which to block the national *duma* without having to rely on his veto. Even then, the first *duma* returned was not to his liking; the US ambassador noted how socially mixed and indifferent to the tsar it was. The *duma* was organised to give dominance to the landowners. They were a class bruised from the events of days of 1905 and nights of the 'red cockerel', and they formed a pressure group, the United Nobility, in St Petersburg to directly lobby the ministers. For the first *duma*, the peasants voted in large numbers for whoever promised them land, which helped the Kadets to become the largest party with 179 seats. Sympathisers of the SRs (who boycotted the election) came second with 94 seats, while the Octobrists won only 17 seats and right-wing parties just 15. The success of the radical parties was largely due to the rural vote, but the tsar steadfastly refused any concession on land reform. He sacked Witte and replaced him with the conservative Goremykin, about whom Witte said that his only good feature was his whiskers. The failure to find a compromise on the issue of land meant that, after 73 days, the first national *duma* was dissolved and Goremykin resigned.

In retaliation, members of the dismissed first *duma* travelled to Finland and signed the Vyborg Manifesto to campaign against conscription and taxes. The Russian masses failed to act beyond a couple of protests and the tsar's new and more dynamic prime minister, Stolypin, arrested the leaders and sentenced them to brief terms in jail, which conveniently barred them all from standing for another election. The elections of the second *duma* were, therefore, more inclined to follow

A Level Exam-Style Question Section B

To what extent were the events of 1905 an attempted revolution against the power of Tsar Nicholas II? (20 marks)

Tip

In trying to sum up the totality of a major event, it is important to think not just about the actual events, but also about their causes and climax. The advantage of hindsight means you can work backwards to explore how the end of the events shines light on the significance of what preceded it. You should avoid giving a chronological narrative of the period.

KEY TERM

Fundamental Laws
The Act that brought in the new Russian constitution in 1906. It was a revision of the earlier Fundamental Laws or set of Laws for the Russian Empire of 1832. It set in legislation the relationship between the tsar and the *duma*, and remained in place until the monarchy was abolished in September 1917.

the advice of the tsar. In the event, the second *duma* in February 1907 was not loyal enough, as it opposed Stolypin's land reform and criticised the tsar's imperial army. It too was dissolved, the electorate again manipulated and finally a third *duma*, with the Octobrists this time as the main party, was elected to the satisfaction of Stolypin, if not quite of the tsar himself.

Finally, in November 1906, when Stolypin introduced his famous land reforms to break the grip of the *mir* and create a broader social base of loyal imperial support with the creation of the *kulaks*, he did it by invoking Article 87, though it was hardly an emergency. The concessions promised in 1905 arrived with so many loopholes that they had almost no political effect. The peasants and workers who had participated in the first two elections soon lost interest in a political process they were now cut off from.

The October Manifesto had produced a nationally elected *duma* for the first time in Imperial Russia. Despite its limited power and influence, despite the interference in its procedures by Stolypin and despite the indifference and distaste the tsar felt towards it, the *duma* gave a voice and political experience to many for the first time. The October Manifesto had set up the political organisation that would replace the tsar when he finally fell in February 1917. It could also be argued that the concessions wrought out of the October Manifesto brought the tsar just enough support to have his final 12 years of power and not be overthrown in the tumultuous events of 1905 and 1906.

The October Manifesto, although neutered by the fundamental laws, gave the tsar and his supporters the opportunity to restore autocratic order within Russia using the traditional, brutal methods.

SOURCE

Extracts from the Russian constitution of 1906 which became known as the Fundamental Laws. The constitution totalled 124 articles split over an introduction and 11 chapters. It was written by Peter Kharitinov, the deputy state secretary of the state chancellory in St Petersburg, and ratified with the signature of Tsar Nicholas II on 23 April 1906. The original draft was amended to strengthen the tsar's position in relation to the new state *duma*. The tsar's signature officially transformed Russia from an absolute monarchy to a constitutional one.

A. From Chapter One: The Supreme Autocratic Power

4. The All-Russian Emperor possesses the supreme autocratic power. Not only fear and conscience, but God himself, commands obedience to his authority.

7. The Sovereign Emperor exercises the legislative authority jointly with the State Council and the State Council and the State Duma.

8. The Sovereign Emperor enjoys the legislative initiative in all legislative matters. The State Council and the State Duma may examine the Fundamental State Laws only on his initiative.

9. The Sovereign Emperor approves laws; and without his approval no legislative measure can become law.

10. The Sovereign Emperor possesses the administrative power in its totality throughout the entire Russian state. On the highest level of administration his authority is direct; on subordinate of administration, in conformity with the law, he determines the degree of authority of subordinate branches and officials who act in his name and in accordance with his orders.

12. The Sovereign Emperor alone is the supreme leader of all foreign relations of the Russian state with foreign countries. He also determines the direction of foreign policy of the Russian state.

13. The Sovereign Emperor alone declares war, concludes peace and negotiates treaties with foreign states.

14. The Sovereign Emperor is the Commander-in-chief of the Russian Army and of the Fleet. He possesses supreme command over all the land and sea forces of the Russian state...

15. The Sovereign Emperor has the power to declare martial law or a state of emergency in localities.

17. The Sovereign Emperor appoints and dismisses the Chairman of the council of Ministers, and Chief Administrators of various departments....

B. From Chapter Nine: On laws

86. No new law can be enacted without the approval of the State Council and the State Duma, and it shall not be legally binding without the approval of the Sovereign Emperor.

C. From Chapter Ten: On the State Council and State Duma

99. Duration of the annual session of the State Council and State Duma and the lengths of recess during the year are determined by decrees of the Sovereign Emperor.

A Level Exam-Style Question Section A

Study Source 12 before you answer this question.

Assess the value of the source in revealing the extent to which the tsar successfully navigated the crisis of 1905 and his attitudes towards political reform.

Explain your answer using the source, the information given about it and your own knowledge of the historical context. (20 marks)

Tip

When assessing the value of a source, think about who the author was, who the intended audience was and the nature of the source. All these will give a different weight to a source's validity. A person might be more open in the wording of a private letter, but more guarded in a public proclamation. The message to an educated elite would be delivered in a different tone and vocabulary from a message to the masses.

HOW EFFECTIVE WAS THE TSAR'S REPRESSION OF OPPOSITION IN THE TOWNS AND COUNTRYSIDE?

The closing of the St Petersburg and Moscow soviets

The October Manifesto succeeded in draining sections of support, particularly middle-class support, away from the General Strike and the St Petersburg Soviet. The government believed it had a good opportunity to close down the St Petersburg Soviet in November 1905, when Trepov ordered the arrest of its chairman (he was replaced by Trotsky). A few days later, Trepov sealed the soviet's building and arrested some 200 of its delegates. Trotsky was sentenced to exile in Siberia, but quickly escaped to England. The closure of the St Petersburg Soviet came just after Lenin's return to Russia. He, and other Bolshevik leaders, urged insurrection against the government.

Moscow, the location of the largest surviving soviet, heard their call. They issued a second general strike in late November, and the most radical supporters prepared bombs and organised military-style training, mainly in the Presnia textile district. Former members of the St Petersburg Soviet joined them and even tried to manufacture chemical weapons to cause policemen to fall asleep so their weapons could be stolen. Not all actions of the strike were so surreally absurd, as barricades were constructed, often with the help of students and the middle-class incensed at artillery being used against the workers in their city. The strike appeared to be transforming into an open war against the authorities. This was a war, or **Moscow Uprising**, that was encouraged by Lenin with little thought of the result.

KEY TERM

Moscow Uprising, December 1905
The urban climax to the year 1905 as thousands of workers fought to overthrow imperial rule. Despite being brutally repressed, it helped to foster revolutionary attitudes among the workers over the next decade.

SOURCE 13

Lenin discussing the possibility of an armed uprising in mid-November 1905. This was published by V. Zenzinov in his memoirs. He was an SR and present in Moscow in 1906. He writes that Lenin was overheard making the comment.

Victory? That for us is not the point at all!... We should not harbour any illusions, we are realists, and let no one imagine that we have to win. For that we are still too weak. The point is not about victory but about giving the regime a shake and attracting the masses to the movement. That is the whole point. And to say that because we cannot win we should not stage an insurrection - that is simply the talk of cowards. And we have nothing to do with them.

However, Lenin was not doing the fighting and, as the authorities bombarded the Presnia district day and night, over a thousand civilians lay dead in the street. The rebels surrendered and the strike was called off. Most victims were guilty only of being in the wrong place at the wrong time. Lenin escaped arrest and returned to further years in exile. The Moscow Soviet had done a lot of work in co-ordinating resistance and training workers' militias, but they were no match for the government forces. They met for the last time on 15 December, just before the most concentrated bombing began. The devastation of Presnia forced the closure of the Moscow Soviet. The commander of Presnia's fighting unit, Zinovy Litvin-Sedoy, issued a final message to his fellow workers as the uprising surrendered, warning of the violent repression that would follow. His prediction proved well-founded.

The repression in the towns and countryside

The Moscow Uprising failed as each segment of the uprising was only prepared to look after its own isolated area. It had no national support, and not even the majority of Muscovites backed it. The government, however, under the new minister of the interior, Pyotr Durnovo, followed up the suppression with savage reprisals, in a cruel effort to teach all a lesson and restore order. Suspected socialists were rounded up and sent into long exile or simply executed. Children were beaten to instil obedience in their parents. Durnovo wrote letters to provincial governors during December 1905 demanding that rioters should be shot and their homes destroyed rather than waste time and energy going through the actual process of an arrest and trial. In the Baltic provinces, during the first half of 1906, pacification was brutal: 1,200 people were executed, thousands flogged and tens of thousands of houses destroyed. The soldiers' pillaging, shooting and raping added countless crimes to the government's response, all with the approval of the tsar, who specifically praised the commanding officer. Drunken Cossacks violated daughters in front of their parents, and forced entire villages to kneel while being whipped by soldiers on horseback. The atrocities continued for as long as it took to break the peasants' spirit. Peasants were hanged with no official charge or trial. It is estimated that 15,000 people were executed, 20,000 shot or wounded and 45,000 deported between the October Manifesto in 1905 and the first national *duma* in April 1906. The troops were aided in this, not only by the *ochrana*, but by the newly created **Black Hundred** gangs. These were extremist pro-tsar bands whose appetite for violence was sanctioned by the police and government. Their so-called 'defence' of Russia usually resulted in attacks on intellectuals, students, socialists and particularly Jews.

KEY TERM

Black Hundred
A collective term for a number of imperialist and nationalist groups intent on fighting any revolutionary organisation. Formed from a wide range of social groups, they committed numerous acts of violence against anyone they perceived as disloyal to the tsar. Their membership peaked in 1905 and 1906.

SOURCE 14 Russian troops watching the deliberate burning of a rebel farm in the Baltic provinces, 1906.

ACTIVITY
KNOWLEDGE CHECK

The repression of the towns and countryside

1 What do Source 14 and the information in the text tell us about the nature of the Russian government?

2 What alternative strategies could the authorities have used to quell the unrest?

3 Read Source 13 and the information about Durnovo. Is there any difference between Lenin and Durnovo?

Unrest flared up regularly throughout 1906. The Sevastopol naval mutiny hinted that there was unrest to come, but the lulls between the outbursts of unrest gave the government an opportunity to tighten its controls, with unreliable officers and troops dismissed and many newspapers closed. Rural violence flared up again in the summer of 1906 as the first *duma* failed to deliver the reforms the peasants wanted. The methods of rural unrest were the same, with managed arson attacks as frequent as the year before. The difference was that, by this time, all the troops had returned from the Russo–Japanese War and the government was in a much more stable and secure position than in 1905. The repression intensified; the unrest was cut short.

In conclusion, the government was able to impose its control on society with increasing terror, partly because the flames of unrest were episodic and isolated. This enabled the forces of repression to ruthlessly eliminate each one before moving to another. For revolutionary leaders like Lenin, this was a sharp lesson: the workers were capable of revolting without the control and direction of the revolutionary parties. Indeed it seemed clear that the parties had failed completely to inspire a mass worker uprising, as the events in Moscow showed. The October Manifesto was by no means universally popular, but it did enough to weaken and split the opposition to the tsar. Once the regime was able to begin to get the upper hand, it could target ringleaders and specific areas with more force. There were only ten official executions during 1905, and even alternative estimates were little higher, but this figure rose to over 200 in 1906, then 600 in 1907 and 1,300 in 1908. These numbers include only those who were legally arrested, tried and executed, and not the countless unrecorded deaths as revolts were put down.

By December 1905, Witte had urged a more aggressive army reaction to unrest, though the fairly progressive military court procedures meant the hundreds of extra cases were taking their time to pass through the system. By the summer of 1906, the new prime minister, Stolypin, introduced the much quicker field court martial to try protesters, carefully selecting judges who were not trained in the law. The result was both fast trials and executions. Despite protest in the *duma*, '**Stolypin's necktie**' as the noose was nicknamed, was effective in reinforcing autocratic control, though this did not stop the revolutionary SRs from trying to assassinate Stolypin. Both Witte and Stolypin had a liberal reputation regarding their modernisation policies and aspects of their political ideologies, but not for their views of repression and terror. So-called liberal politicians could be as indifferent to the human condition and the plight of the masses as any tyrant.

KEY TERM

Stolypin's necktie
A contemporary nickname given to the hangman's noose, referring to the speedy trials in special courts and subsequent execution of political radicals. These were set up by Stolypin and resulted in over 3,000 deaths between 1906 and 1909.

EXTEND YOUR KNOWLEDGE

What's in a name?
In a session of the *duma* in 1907, Kadet Party member Rodichev called the hangman's noose 'Stolypin's efficient black Monday necktie'. Stolypin immediately challenged him to a duel. Rodichev apologised, but a shortened version of the nickname stuck.

The railway carriage that took political prisoners to Siberia after 1905 was referred to as 'Stolypin's car'. These carriages are still used for transporting prisoners in Russia, and are still named after Stolypin.

In 1907, the second national *duma* was dissolved by the tsar, and the electoral legislation amended to restrict the suffrage of non-propertied classes and to therefore produce an electoral result more favourable to the tsar. The event is, not surprisingly, referred to as 'Stolypin's Coup'.

Conclusion

For revolutionaries like Lenin and the Bolsheviks, there were lessons to be learned. The events of 1905 are often presented as a rehearsal for the Bolsheviks' own revolution in 1917, but that view inflates the significance of revolutionary groups in 1905. Despite the range of disturbances in 1905 and 1906, the revolutionary groups remained separate and unco-ordinated. Workers went on strike, peasants took revenge on landowners, some military units mutinied, the intelligentsia demanded the four-tail formula, nationalists fought for independence. The revolts were loud, violent and passionate, but they were not united. Lenin saw the need for a single organisation to take control, but in 1905 this had not been achieved, though the short-lived St Petersburg Soviet showed that it was possible, and more favourable circumstances might have allowed some centralised control of workers and uprisings.

The activities of the soviets made it appear that some unity of purpose was going to evolve, as shown in St Petersburg during the October General Strike. The government survived for two key reasons: first, the imperial military forces stayed loyal, despite occasional and localised mutinies, so that the option of repression was always available; secondly, the government learnt to 'divide and rule'. They granted, with the tsar's reluctant approval, just enough concessions in the national *duma* to split the revolutionaries from the liberals. Once these were weakened, the tsar could increase the terror, which decreased the opposition.

But the concessions could not be withdrawn completely. The results of 1905 should not be seen as totally negative. The constitution of 1906 could be seen as a new start with new freedoms that could not be repressed out of existence and memory. Political discussion was heard in the streets and printed in the newspapers. Though power was still in the ineffectual hands of the tsar, the national *duma* did broaden the participation in national debate. Fear and ruthless repression had won the day for the tsar's autocracy, but trust in his ability to rule was gone. Russia, outside the imperial court, had a liberal essence that had not been there before. Trotsky reported seeing it in the guards and officials of his prison in St Petersburg, where he was treated well and allowed access to political writings.

Though they were disillusioned, workers were more politicised. They were frustrated but not defeated. The peasants' deference to the tsar, lost after the brutality of 1905, was mirrored in their lost deference towards the landowners. This change in attitude scared some educated liberals towards reactionary views, as the peasants were seen as so unruly. The mob became a dark spirit to fear, as if the desperate need for political participation was just violent hooliganism.

The tsar survived by applying a 'carrot and stick' approach of concession and repression. This worked because of the weakness of the opposition and the fact that the aristocracy and the majority of the army remained loyal. It is inaccurate to describe 1905 as a revolution, rather it was a collapse from which imperial authority managed to recover. The tsar's weakness met with extensive unrest in both urban and rural areas, but they were not sufficiently co-ordinated to be considered a revolutionary movement. By the end of 1906, Nicholas II was secure as tsar, but quieter times disguised the nation's true feelings towards the autocracy. The majority accepted the tsar, but as a single factor in a constitutional monarchy. Nicholas, never a politically astute man, believed that the relative calm after 1906 was a confirmation of his own infallibility. He failed to see the damage that the events of 1905–06 had done to the imperial core. If, and when, another crisis engulfed Russia, the rage towards 'Nicholas the Bloody' would return. Though the tsar survived, many felt he was doomed.

THINKING HISTORICALLY Change (8a, b & c) (I)

Imposing realities

1 Explain why the conversation in the image above could not have happened.

The shape of history is imposed by people looking back. People living through 'history' do not always perceive the patterns that later historians identify. For example, some people during the industrial revolution may have understood that great change was taking place, but would not have understood the massive economic, social and political consequences of industrialisation.

2 Consider the beginning of the 1905 Revolution:

a) Who would have made the decision as to when the 'Revolution' began?

b) Could anyone have challenged this decision?

3 Explain why someone living at the start of the 20th century would have been unable to make a judgement about the beginning of a new era.

4 Who living at the present time might see the start of the 1905 Revolution as an important event?

5 What does the image tell us about the structure of history as we understand it?

A Level Exam-Style Question Section B

'The failure of the 1905 Revolution was due more to the weakness of the opposition than to the actions of the tsar and the government.'

How far do you agree with this statement? (20 marks)

Tip

It is important to address both sides. You may bring in additional factors or views, but the focus in the answer must target the stated factor, or factors, in the question. Be confident enough to query the question, for example whether 1905 was a failure or even a revolution, but try to integrate this into the body of the essay, exploring the impact of the two views.

ACTIVITY
SUMMARY

Revolution and reform, 1904–06

1 Which do you think was more important in causing the events of 1905, the Russo-Japanese War or Bloody Sunday? Give reasons for your choice.

2 a) Chart the activities of the following groups in the years 1905–06:

- workers
- peasants
- intelligentsia
- revolutionary groups.

b) Which had the greatest influence on furthering the opposition of the tsar in 1905–06?

3 Make a list of actions that Witte performed in the period.

a) If he was so important to the tsar, why was Nicholas so quick to remove him from power?

b) Who else can be credited with 'saving' the tsar?

4 Do you feel that the events of 1905 made a real difference to Russia? Explain your reasoning.

WIDER READING

Figes, O. *A People's Tragedy: The Russian Revolution 1891-1924*, Pimlico (1996)

Hite, J. *Tsarist Russia 1801-1917*, Causeway Press (1989)

Hosking, G. *Russia: People & Empire 1552-1917*, Fontana Press (1998)

Pushkarev, S. *The Emergence of Modern Russia 1801-1917*, Pica Pica Press (1985)

Radzinsky, E. *The Last Tsar: Life and Death of Nicholas II, the Last Tsar*, Free Press (2005)

Westwood, J.N. *Endurance and Endeavour: Russian History 1812-2001*, Oxford University Press (2002)

3.5 The end of the Romanovs and the triumph of the Bolsheviks, 1916–18

KEY QUESTIONS

- How did the experience of war in the years 1916–17 act as a stimulus to revolution?
- What were the reasons for the October Revolution in 1917?
- How did the Bolsheviks consolidate power during 1918?

INTRODUCTION

'Again, that fat-bellied Rodzianko has written me a load of nonsense, which I won't even bother to answer.'

This was the tsar's response to a desperate telegram sent by his president of the *duma* on 27 February 1917. He was speaking to his minister of the court, Frederiks. Three days later Nicholas II had abdicated, ending not only a 300-year Romanov dynasty but the whole imperial autocracy as well.

The failure of the Russian military to defeat the German army was clear by 1916. The deprivations caused by the First World War meant that 1917 saw momentous change in Russia. At the start of the year, the country was subject to Romanov rule, even though the tsar was personally weak, as shown by his reliance during 1916 on the mystic Rasputin. But a politically confident *duma*, combined with the deprivations caused by the First World War, meant that Nicholas would lose hold of power.

Though the Bolsheviks saw the February Revolution as a stepping stone for the October Revolution, the collapse of the Provisional Government was by no means inevitable. Consisting largely of the remnants of the fourth *duma*, the Provisional Government had opportunities to consolidate power, but a lack of authority and support from the Russian people, as shown by the rivalry for control by the newly relaunched **Petrograd** Soviet, was intensified by the decision to continue the war with Germany. By October, the government, now led by Kerensky, was simply too weak to retain power.

The opportunity was open for a small, determined group to seize power in an ambitious revolution. The Bolsheviks, led by Lenin and organised by Trotsky, were prepared to take a chance. Once in control of Petrograd, they faced the greater challenge of maintaining and reinforcing their power – plunging Russia into a brutal civil war more destructive than any of the battles of the First World War.

KEY TERM

Petrograd
St Petersburg. Founded by Peter the Great in 1703, St Petersburg was the imperial capital of Russia. In 1914, to avoid its German connotations, it was renamed Petrograd. Later, in 1924, it became Leningrad in honour of the leader of the communist revolution, before once more returning to St Petersburg in 1991, after the fall of the communist government.

December 1916
Unions of Zemstva and Towns closed
Murder of Rasputin

February 1917
Protests grow in Petrograd
Duma ignores tsar's order to stop meeting
Petrograd Soviet created

March 1917
Provisional Government set up
Order No. 1 issued by Soviet
Tsar abdicates

April 1917
Lenin returns to Russia
Lenin's *April Theses* published

June 1917
Congress of Russian Soviet
Kerensky Offensive launched

July 1917
July Days revolt
Lenin flees to Finland
Kerensky is prime minister

August 1917
Kornilov Affair

September 1917
Bolshevik majority in Petrograd Soviet
Trotsky is Petrograd Soviet chairman

HOW DID THE EXPERIENCE OF WAR IN THE YEARS 1916-17 ACT AS A STIMULUS TO REVOLUTION?

War can place a severe strain on a country's ability to rule itself, and losing a war can be fatal. Military ineptitude had forced the tsar to reform after the Crimean War (see Chapter 3), while military disasters heralded the wave of protests during 1905 and forced him to adopt a new constitution (see Chapter 4). The First World War would have even worse effects on Russia: a larger war with larger defeats would have greater consequences.

The majority of Russians may have greeted the war with patriotic enthusiasm, but some had other motives. Revolutionary leaders, such as Lenin, welcomed the war as an opportunity to promote their ideology if the war went badly for Russia. The same fear of failure was echoed by Durnovo, the former minister of the interior who had so brutally repressed the peasants after the uprising of 1905.

SOURCE

A memorandum from Durnovo to Tsar Nicholas II in February 1914. Durnovo, then a member of the Council of State, believed that conflict between Germany and Britain should not expand to engulf Russia. He, and other right-wing thinkers, believed Germany was a model of a conservative, constitutional monarchy. He was opposed to the majority liberal view which looked towards France and Britain for alliances.

The trouble will start with the blaming of the Government for all disasters. In the legislative institutions a bitter campaign against the Government will begin, followed by revolutionary agitations throughout the country, with socialist slogans, capable of arousing and rallying the masses, beginning with the division of the land and succeeded by a division of all valuables and property. The defeated army, having lost its most dependable men, and carried away by the tide of the primitive peasant desire for land, will find itself too demoralised to serve as a bulwark of law and order. The legislative institutions and the intellectual opposition parties, lacking real authority in the eyes of the people, will be powerless to stem the popular tides, aroused by themselves, and Russia will be flung into hopeless anarchy, the issue of which cannot be foreseen.

Once the fighting started, it went badly for Russia. Defeat followed defeat, as at Tannenberg or the Masurian Lakes, while an 'ammunition famine' left supplies in a desperate situation. In September 1915, the tsar took over personal command in the West and, against his ministers' advice, left Petrograd for the front. His absence left a power vacuum that was filled by the tsarina and Rasputin, which undermined confidence in imperial rule, especially as the *duma* had been closed down.

In 1916, despite the army's 1,500,000 casualties and another million held as prisoners, the Russian navy was in satisfactory shape in the Baltic and Black Seas, and increased production had eased the shortages of supplies and ammunition. The allies in general struggled through the spring, with French losses at Verdun and a Russian defeat by Germany in the North at Lake Naroch but, by the summer, Russia attacked Austria in what was known as the 'Brusilov Offensive' after the Russian commander.

October 1917: October Revolution; *Sovnarkom* set up; Decrees on Peace and Land

November 1917: Decree on the Rights of the People of Russia; Decree on Workers' Control and abolition of army ranks; Elections to the Constituent Assembly

December 1917: Cheka created

January 1918: Constituent Assembly is dissolved

February 1918: Germans begin hostilities again; Workers' and Peasants' Red Army officially created

March 1918: Treaty of Brest-Litovsk ends Russia's participation in the First World War

May 1918: Start of Civil War

July 1918: Murder of tsar and his family

Brusilov's success was voided by the tsar's lack of action: on the advice of his wife and Rasputin, Nicholas refused Brusilov's requests for support. Brusilov understood the incompetence of the tsar's favourite advisers when he heard that the elite imperial guards had been ordered into an open swamp by their commander, Bezobrazov, where they were slaughtered by German aircraft. As the finest soldiers of their generation sank into their muddy graves, Brusilov was confirmed in his view that a new system of government was needed. Nicholas had hoped that his taking over of command would directly inspire the troops, but his inexperience and nervous lack of charisma only lessened morale.

This view that political change was necessary was beginning to be accepted in Petrograd, where there was suspicion of a 'Black Bloc' of pro-German advisers who wanted peace or even betrayed Russia. Suspicions, fuelled by rumours, fell on the tsarina (who was German-born and the niece of the kaiser), Rasputin and also Stürmer, who had been rapidly promoted to a series of top posts such as prime minister, minister of the interior, foreign minister and supreme minister for state defence. By 1916, Stürmer was virtual dictator of Russia, while the tsar was at the front, and therefore to be suspected of German sympathies was greatly damaging to the regime. Despite no evidence other than German-sounding names, these rumours grew as they reached the front line and further demoralised the troops. To oppose the tsar and his court was becoming a patriotic act.

By late 1916 and into 1917, military activity slowed down, but some six million troops were posted on four Russian fronts. Though adequately supplied, they were not as well trained or equipped as the Germans they faced. In three years of war, 1,700,000 had died, some 5,000,000 had been wounded, 2,500,000 had been taken prisoner and 3,000,000 were sick. The tsar could now be blamed for this.

SOURCE 2 Russian prisoners being guarded by German soldiers on the Eastern Front during the First World War.

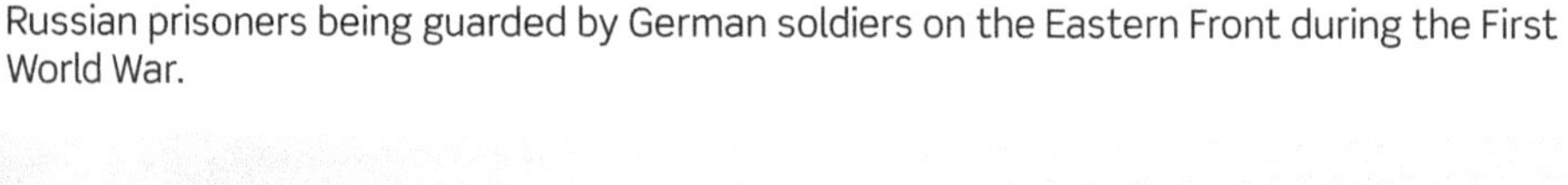

SOURCE

A speech by Kadet Party leader, Pavel Miliukov, at the opening of the *duma* in November 1916. The deputy of the *duma* warned Miliukov that the speech called for revolt. In response to the speech, the tsar removed Stürmer, but his replacement called for a further focus in the war to win victory, and further advisers were revealed to be favoured by the tsarina and Rasputin.

We have lost faith in the ability of this Government to achieve victory, because, as far as this Government is concerned, neither the attempts at correction nor the attempts at improvement, which we have made here, have proved successful... And, if we have formerly said that our Government had neither the knowledge nor the ability which were indispensable at the moment, we say now, gentlemen that this present Government has sunk beneath the level on which it stood in the normal times of Russian life. And now the gulf between us and that Government has grown wider and impassable...

The poisonous seed of suspicion is already yielding abundant fruit, and, from one end of the Russian land to the other there are spreading the dark rumours of treachery and treason... these rumours reach high and spare none... Painful, terrible suspicions, sinister rumours of treachery and treason, of occult forces fighting for the benefit of Germany and striving, through the destruction of national unity and the sowing of dissention, to prepare the ground for a disgraceful peace, have reached a point where it is generally felt that an enemy hand is secretly influencing the course of our State affairs...

Today we see and understand with this Government we cannot legislate, any more than we can with this Government, lead Russia to victory... We are telling this Government... "We shall fight you; we shall fight with all legitimate means until you go!"

And, does it matter, gentlemen, as a practical question, whether we are, in the present case, dealing with stupidity or treason? When the Duma keeps everlastingly insisting that the rear must be organized for a successful struggle, the Government persists in claiming that organizing the country means organizing a revolution, and deliberately prefers chaos and disorganization. What is it, stupidity or treason?

...And, therefore, gentlemen, for the sake of the millions of victims and the torrents of blood poured out, for the sake of the achievement of our national interests,... in the name of our responsibilities to that nation which has sent us here, we shall fight on until we achieve that genuine responsibility of government.

A Level Exam-Style Question Section A

Study Source 3 before you answer this question.

Assess the value of the source for revealing the reasons for discontent in Russia, and the attitudes of the opposition against the tsar.

Explain your answer using the source, the information given about it and your own knowledge of the historical period. (20 marks)

Tip

A good answer will interrogate the evidence of the source in relation to both enquiries with confidence and discrimination. This might involve showing a range of ways the source could be used, such as by distinguishing between information and claim or opinion.

By 1917, some contemporary observers, such as Winston Churchill, who became British secretary of state for war in 1919, or Sir Alfred Knox, the British military attaché, believed that Russia had overcome its military problems and was emerging as a considerable force out of the winter of 1916–17. However, this ignores the economic, social and political impact of the years of war.

Economic impact of the First World War

Although agriculture could cope with the demands of war, as farms could be worked by women, the elderly and the wounded, by 1917 there were supply problems to the cities as the railways failed to cope. Poor administration meant that supplies for civilians slipped down the list of priorities, leading to acute shortages of food and fuel over the winter of 1916–17. Although industry was able to meet the basic demands of the army, a shortage of skilled workers and an inability to repair machinery led to a decline in manufactured goods. The treasury had secured loans to pay for the war, but some 40 percent had to be covered by printing paper money to help cover the 14.5 billion rubles spent on the war in 1916 alone. With less trade possible and less tax available – the ban on vodka had cost the government 700 million rubles – the government relied more and more on printing money.

These three factors – shortage of food, shortage of goods and an abundance of paper money – drove prices up as inflation far outstripped wages. For example, the average wage in Petrograd in October 1916 had risen around 100 percent since 1914, but the average rise in the price of key consumer goods was 300 percent. People queued all night for bread, only to be told that a lack of flour or fuel meant none would be available. On 23 February 1917, International Women's Day, women workers in the Vyborg district of Petrograd formed a mob to rally against the useless queuing. When the police violently put down the mob, the protest grew to include factory workers from the Putilov steelworks. Cossacks were ordered to disperse the mob, but forgot their whips. The protest was joined by students and even army officers, singing revolutionary songs and slogans. The general of the Petrograd garrison issued orders for violent reprisals, but not before sending a message to the tsar, informing him that fresh snow and clear skies gave the city a festival feel.

Political impact of the First World War

At the start of the war, two important organisations were created to aid the mobilisation of resources. The All-Russian Union of Zemstva, led by Prince Lvov, was set up to help soldiers and refugees, and by 1916 it had grown to a vast organisation. The smaller All-Russian Union of Towns served the same function in the cities. Together, as *Zemgor*, they co-ordinated private industry to meet the needs of the military. With 8,000 affiliated institutions and hundreds of thousands of employees, Lvov was the head of an unofficial government. However, they faced bureaucratic obstacles, as when their 80,000-strong unarmed labour brigades, which dug trenches and graves, were forced to disband for being too much of a private army. This pushed Lvov, not unlike Brusilov, towards a more progressive ideology of self-government without a tsar. He, like many, saw this as a reward for service in the war effort.

Many members of the liberal, educated and propertied classes reached the same conclusion. It was clear that the system of government was collapsing. Within the *duma*, a coalition of six central parties formed a Progressive Bloc to call for moderate reform. Its politicians were dismissed, but the public welcomed its demands. By December 1916, the authorities closed down the congresses of both the Union of Zemstva and the Union of Towns, causing even the United Nobility, who represented Russia's most conservative viewpoint, to call for changes, while remaining loyal to the monarchy. By the end of 1916, the tsar and his government were isolated from all sections of political society.

The constant turnover of ministerial posts was a big problem. Ministers were fired for holding contrary views to the tsar, then their replacements were fired for being unpopular. Talented politicians lasted no longer than incompetent ones. The talented and respected minister of war, Polivanov, who had solved the ammunition famine by working with organisations such as *Zemgor*, was dismissed in March 1916 to the horror of most observers, because the tsarina saw *Zemgor* as revolutionary. He was replaced by General Shuvaev, who admitted that his loyalty to the tsar considerably outweighed his abilities.

In the three years of war up to February 1917, there were four prime ministers, six ministers of internal affairs, three ministers of foreign affairs, four ministers of war, four ministers of agriculture, three ministers of transport, four ministers of justice and four heads of the Orthodox Synod. The aristocracy and the educated classes saw their confidence in the autocracy greatly diminished, as no one remained in office long enough to sort anything out.

The murder of Rasputin

It is convenient to see Rasputin as the cause of the tsar's downfall, but this would be overstating his importance. Rasputin was a mystic faith healer, who had gained imperial favour by being able to heal, or at least control, the haemophilia of the tsar's son, Alexei, who was heir to the throne. Once embedded in the royal court, Rasputin found influence through his close relationship with the tsarina. On one occasion, the tsarina impelled the tsar to take total control and dissolve the rebellious *duma* and, to aid his strength, she urged him to use Rasputin's comb on his hair. The *duma* backed down and Rasputin's reputation with both tsar and tsarina grew. The patronage of Rasputin seemed to be the quickest route to political promotion, if only in the short term, as it proved for Alexei Khvostov, who was interior minister from September 1915 to March 1916. Khvostov quickly turned against his ally and became involved in a plot to murder him after accusing both Rasputin and the tsarina of being German spies. Khvostov was forced to resign and was banished to his estate. The tsarina had helped to foil the plot, an act that only brought her and Rasputin closer together and gave him more prestige.

The evidence of Rasputin's influence has probably been exaggerated either in gossip, which he was largely keen to foster, or by accounts written after his death by those with an anti-imperial agenda. An attempt had been made to kill him by a minister he had favoured but then discarded. He was also offered a large bribe to return to Siberia, but the tsarina had manipulated the situation to keep him close. This increased rumours of his sexual relations with the tsarina and other aristocrats, both male and female. Talk of his drunken orgies circulated quickly and perhaps grew in the retelling.

The motives behind the plot to assassinate him are unclear. Prince Yusupov and his co-conspirators, all favourites of the tsar, claimed they were trying to free the tsar from both Rasputin's hold and the tsarina's influence. However there were more personal reasons behind their actions after Rasputin had allegedly tried to seduce the homosexual, but recently married, prince. Rasputin's eventual murder, for it took several attempts, in the early hours of 17 December 1916, was celebrated among the Petrograd aristocracy. The murderers, however, despite public standing ovations, were exiled by the tsar, and thereby avoided both a court case and an inquest. The murder actually drew Nicholas II closer to his domineering tsarina, who continued to dismiss and appoint ministers. Nicholas II, perhaps aware of his detachment from society, spent the winter of 1916–17 at his country retreat.

EXTEND YOUR KNOWLEDGE

The stuff of legend – Rasputin's murder(s)

Rasputin's death only enhanced his dark reputation. Invited by Prince Yusupov on the promise of a potential seduction of the prince's beautiful wife, Rasputin was plied with cakes and wine, all poisoned. When these had no effect, he was shot and appeared dead. Yusupov claimed that Rasputin then awoke, screamed and lunged at him. Rasputin was then shot several more times and beaten and kicked to death. Weighed down with iron chains, the body was dumped through a hole in the ice of the River Neva. Other accounts indicate that a single bullet to the forehead killed Rasputin instantly.

Rasputin the invulnerable monk, despite being neither a monk or invulnerable, has become a staple of the horror genre and the personification of evil. In a famous letter to the tsar, Rasputin apparently warned that if he was killed by peasants, the regime was safe, but if killed by the aristocracy then the tsar and his family were doomed within two years, and Russia would be torn apart for 75 years.

An in-depth investigation by the Bolsheviks after they had taken power found no real evidence of Rasputin's alleged affairs with the tsarina and other aristocrats. They removed his body from its grave at the tsar's country palace, burnt it in a forest and scattered the ashes in the wind.

In life, Rasputin had helped to focus resentment and exasperation on the regime. His murder did not reverse or reduce this feeling. The Rasputin affair is a symbol of the tsar's weakness, for a stronger personality would have stamped out Rasputin's influence as well as any public outcry.

The murder of Rasputin changed relatively little. The war continued to go from bad to worse, while ministers were appointed and dismissed in equal measure. The murderers had hoped their actions would free the tsar from Rasputin's grip, but they had over-estimated exactly what Rasputin's influence was. The tsar became more determined to resist change and banned four Grand Dukes from Petrograd for advocating political reform. While he lived, Rasputin had at least deflected some of the political criticism away from the tsar and onto himself, but his death merely exposed the tsar's ineptitude.

SOURCE

A cartoon icon in the style of N. Ivano from 1917, entitled *Rasputin's orgies at court*. It shows the lavish lifestyle of the imperial court as Rasputin indulges in sexual play above the throne. In secret, Russians are imprisoned, tortured and executed, all on his orders.

SOURCE

An anonymous satirical verse from July 1916, commenting on the decadence of the aristocracy as they drank, gambled and partied away their fortunes. This hedonism was a reflection that they sensed the end, not only of the tsar's regime but also of their way of life.

We do not take defeat amiss, And victory gives us no delight

The source of all our cares is this: Can we get vodka for tonight?

The victories we can do without. No! Peace and quiet is our line,

Intrigues and scandal, evenings out, Trimmed up with women and with wine.

We only want to know next day, What Ministers will be on view,

Or who takes who to see the play, Or who Cuba's sat next who [*sic*]:...

And does Rasputin still prevail, Or do we need another saint,

And is Kshesinskaya* quite well, And how the feast at Shubin's went:

If the Grand Duke took Dina home, What kind of luck MacDiddie had –

Oh, if a Zeppelin would come. And smash the whole of Petrograd.

* The names refer to the trivialities of court life. For example, Kshesinskaya was a ballerina who had been linked to Nicholas II.

Reasons, events and significance of the February Revolution

While the social and political elite proved important in the consequences of the February Revolution, the workers and soldiers played a key part in triggering the crisis that removed the tsar. Both had lost any enthusiasm for the war, and the hardships led to a sharp increase in industrial strikes. Some 35,000 workers went on strike from August to December 1914. This rose to 553,000 in 1915 and to 1,086,000 in 1916, of which 310,000 strikers were considered to be politically rather than economically motivated. This was particularly the case in Petrograd, where the military garrison housed 160,000 soldiers of mainly peasant origin, who had little training and little to stop them getting restless.

Against this background, the February 1917 protests in Petrograd began, with queuing women, factory workers and the garrison troops joining forces. At this point, Rodzianko sent his desperate telegram begging for advice and action from an ill-informed and indifferent tsar. In the end, the tsar prorogued the *duma*, meaning its activities were stopped though it was not dissolved. The *duma* carried on meeting, with leading socialist Kerensky calling for the tsar's removal. By 27 February, the soldiers' mutinies had turned the protests more violent as the pleas for bread became shouts for revolt.

This same day, the Petrograd Soviet, based on the 1905 version, was created with the Menshevik Chkheidze as chairman and Kerensky as vice-chairman. As more troops joined the protests, including the elite Semeonov Guards, the soviet became the Soviet of Workers' and Soldiers' Deputies. By the next day, Petrograd was under rebel control, and on 1 March the executive committee of the *duma* formed a Provisional Government with Prince Lvov as president, Miliukov as minister of foreign affairs, the Octobrist

Guchkov as minister of defence and Kerensky as minister for justice. All tsarist ministers were arrested.

The new government instituted an amnesty for political prisoners, extending civil rights to the army, an end to religious and national discrimination and the preparation of a constituent assembly by a universal secret ballot. On the same day, the Petrograd Soviet issued Order No. 1, commanding workers and soldiers to follow only its orders. This started the disintegration of the army.

When the tsar tried to send loyal troops into Petrograd, rail workers blocked and delayed their trains, though it is unlikely the troops would have fought fellow Russians. The tsar then tried to reach his palace by train to quell the uprising, but rail workers redirected the train so that it met up with Guchkov and Shulgin, who had been sent by the new government to get the tsar to step down. On 2 March 1917, Nicholas II abdicated in favour of his brother, Grand Duke Michael, who wisely did not accept.

In conclusion, the tsar's power fell away before he realised the danger he was in. He was a weak man in a powerful job, who seemingly allowed his dominant yet politically short-sighted wife to manipulate policy. Even in the eyes of his ardent supporters, he seemed to fulfil the Russian peasant proverb that 'it is a sad home where the cow instructs the bull'. It was the tsarina, more than Rasputin, who cut the nobility away from the tsar. A natural reactionary, Nicholas II could never endorse the gradual move to a more progressive system of constitutional rule. By taking command of the troops at the Front, he both highlighted his poor political and military judgement and precipitated governmental chaos in the capital. The war also negatively affected the estates of the aristocracy, depriving them of labour and trade, so they lost faith in their leader and began to look elsewhere for a regime they could participate in. Unlike 1905, the tsar had lost his key pillar of support. On his somewhat pathetic downfall, the Provisional Government largely consisted of the aristocratic leaders of the *duma*. In this respect, the February Revolution was a revolution from above.

The workers and peasants played a key role. The war had intensified their hardship, particularly in the cities, bringing the masses onto the Petrograd streets in the coldest days of winter. Their discontent was not unusual, as shown in 1905, but the army's refusal to violently repress the protests was unique. Both aristocratic officers and peasant soldiers had had enough.

The simultaneous emergence of the Petrograd Soviet as a direct rival to the Provisional Government demonstrated to many, including the revolutionary groups somewhat overcome at the speed of events but anxious to take advantage of new opportunities, that the masses would not necessarily defer to the new government. Another old proverb said that 'the fish stinks from the head down'. Maybe the whole head had yet to be cut off?

A Level Exam-Style Question Section B

To what extent was the downfall of the tsar due to the First World War? (20 marks)

Tip

Think about the vocabulary you use to articulate the degree of the extent. Avoid words like 'huge' or 'great', but choose words which indicate a more sophisticated and analytical depth, such as 'catalyst', 'fundamental', 'underlying', 'intrinsic', 'proverbial', 'integral', 'central'.

The end of tsardom, the Provisional Government and relations with the Petrograd Soviet

Tsar Nicholas II had been removed because he had lost authority and support. The problem for the Provisional Government was that they had never had them in the first place. The decision to continue the war kept the government weak, just as it had the Romanovs. Not only did this intensify the mainly economic problems of industrial conditions, unemployment, food and fuel shortages, it also gave revolutionary groups, such as the Bolsheviks, Mensheviks and SRs, greater opportunities to exploit and target specific groups, such as workers, peasants and soldiers. Free from tsarist repression, they could now work more openly on the masses, who were hungry for further reform and change.

The Petrograd Soviet

The Provisional Government set up its assembly chamber in the right wing of the Tauride Palace, once used by Catherine the Great. Meanwhile, gathered in the left wing of the same palace, the Petrograd Soviet noisily discussed how a workers' dictatorship should be established. There was much internal disagreement as these revolutionary groups argued over its exact nature. The soviet, whose 2,000–3,000 members squeezed into the palace, could reasonably claim to be the elected voices of the masses, had an element of control over the workers, peasants and army that the Provisional Government did not. This gave rise to the notion of dual power (*dvoevlastie*), but this term implies working together. In fact, the two houses were clear rivals, with the Provisional Government constantly seeking the soviet's approval to pacify the masses, while the soviet itself was too cautious to take power for itself. It was also not a relationship of equals, as the Order No. 1 demonstrated.

SOURCE

From the Petrograd Soviet's Order No. 1 from 1 March 1917. It effectively gave the soviet control over the military and therefore prevented the Provisional Government from running a complete state. There were seven terms in total, including a ban on titles for officers and saluting while off duty.

1 In all companies, battalions, regiments, depots, artillery positions, cavalry regiments, other military service units and on the ships of the navy immediately to elect committees of selected representatives of the lower ranks of the above-mentioned military units.

3 In all of their political actions military units are subordinate to the Soviet of Workers' and Soldiers' deputies and their committees.

4 Orders of the Military Commission of the State *Duma* must be obeyed, except when they contradict orders and decisions of the Soviet of Workers' and Soldiers' Deputies.

5 All types of arms like rifles, machine-guns, armoured vehicles and others must be at the disposal and under the supervision of company and battalion committees and in no case to be given to officers even when they ask for them.

ACTIVITY
KNOWLEDGE CHECK

The First World War and the February Revolution

1. Durnovo is remarkably prophetic in Source 1, and seems to be predicting a series of revolutions. From your own knowledge, why do you think the tsar ignored it and favoured war with Germany?
2. How do Sources 2 and 3 highlight the problems Russia faced as a consequence of the First World War?
3. There was no evidence of the 'treachery' that Miliukov implied, but what evidence, from your own knowledge, was there of 'stupidity'? What could have been done differently? Would it have helped?
4. What impression do Sources 4 and 5 give of Russia in 1916?
5. Evaluate the usefulness of Sources 4 and 5 in investigating the political situation in Russia during the First World War. Support your ideas and explanation with your own knowledge.
6. Examining each of the terms in Source 6, why did Order No. 1 pose such a severe threat to the new Provisional Government?

Initially, other soviets sprang up spontaneously across the country, but neither the Petrograd Soviet nor the Provisional Government had real control of the provinces, who generally ruled themselves, largely through an inter-group co-operation not seen in Petrograd. However, during April 1917, the All-Russian Conference of Soviets held in Petrograd aimed to co-ordinate the actions of the soviets and gave the Petrograd Soviet the weight of a national organisation. The nature of the Petrograd Soviet also changed during the course of 1917. The Mensheviks split into factions while the SRs failed to deliver the peace that their peasant supporters demanded. Likewise, the SRs failed to elicit middle-class support, such as the Kadet Party, who saw the soviet as too radical. This led the soviet to become increasingly dominated, or inspired, by the ideology of the Bolsheviks, led by Lenin, who did not want to co-operate with the middle-class 'bourgeois', nor with the 'bourgeois' Provisional Government. Therefore, the Petrograd Soviet, increasingly hostile to the Provisional Government, acted as a competing authority, whose control of soldiers and key services such as railways and postal deliveries meant the Provisional Government was constantly undermined but had to tolerate it.

WHAT WERE THE REASONS FOR THE OCTOBER REVOLUTION IN 1917?

The importance of the Petrograd Soviet, Lenin and Trotsky

The impact of Lenin

Lenin had stated, just before the outbreak of the First World War, that revolution was unlikely in Russia in his lifetime. Though the war proved him wrong, the Bolsheviks had played little part in the fall of the tsar and the early days of the Provisional Government and Petrograd Soviet. By February 1917, they had only around 20,000 members, confined to a few large cities, especially Petrograd and Moscow, and their leaders were mostly in exile. Following the abdication of the tsar, these leaders were desperate to return to Russia.

SOURCE

From documents released by the German state archives in 1957. They are a series of telegrams released between German diplomats in Bern, Switzerland, and the Berlin Foreign Ministry, dated 23 March 1917. Winston Churchill later compared the German aim to a biological attack, infecting and destroying everything.

Leading revolutionaries here wish to return to Russia via Germany... Please send instructions... In Germany's interests for radical wing of revolutionaries to prevail in Russia... arrange train transportation for them... provide money... We must try to create utmost chaos... facilitate the triumph of the extremist and another shattering upheaval... then military intervention by us will guarantee the collapse of Russian power.

SOURCE

From Lenin's speech as he arrived in Finland Station, Petrograd on Locomotive 293 on 3 April 1917. This was a single-carriage, sealed train provided by the Germans for Lenin, his wife, and 30 other radicals. Despite arriving just before midnight, he was greeted by soldiers and workers drunkenly waving red flags and cheering their approval. Lenin was not a gifted speaker at this stage, and it was reported he had a high-pitched voice and struggled to pronounce the letter 'r'. He stood on the bonnet of a car and was then escorted with a military band to Bolshevik headquarters. The train remains on display as a trophy of the Bolshevik revolution.

The Russian revolution created by you has opened a whole new epoch... the worldwide socialist revolution is dawning; European capitalism is on the brink of collapse. Soldiers, comrades! We must fight for a socialist revolution in Russia! We must fight until the total victory of the proletariat! Long live the worldwide socialist revolution!

Lenin was making it clear that the Bolsheviks would not co-operate with other socialist groups. Unlike the Mensheviks, he believed that a strict Marxist version of communism could be adapted to the unique circumstances of Russia. Marxists felt that history followed an inevitable pattern, and that after a feudal period of aristocratic rule, an industrial period would emerge. In this, the middle class, or *bourgeoisie*, would exploit the workers and this would trigger the revolution. With no large middle class in Russia, Lenin felt that the capitalist stage of history could be skipped and the revolution brought forward. He also believed that the workers were few in number and would not be politically educated enough to lead a revolution. The answer was that a small, elite group, the Bolsheviks, would do it for them and prepare the ground for communism to evolve. However, the Bolsheviks were not in a strong position in April 1917, with very little representation in the soviet, and there were serious factions within the Bolshevik Party, with Lenin denouncing the more conciliatory approach of other members like Stalin. Lenin made his ideological approach to revolution absolutely clear in his *April Theses* (see Source 9).

Lenin needed to convert his blueprint for revolution into a functional timetable to implement a takeover of power. While the *April Theses* offered an ideological justification for their view, Lenin, who was as much a practical politician as a theorist, devised slogans that were accessible to the masses and perfectly in tune with the radical mood of a war-weary nation. 'All power to the soviets!' showed that Lenin understood that true power lay in the soviets, and his aim was to take them over. 'Peace, Land, and Bread!' was a powerful piece of Bolshevik propaganda that summarised the desires of the three groups that the Bolsheviks needed on board: the soldiers wanted an end to the war, the peasants hungered for land reform, while the workers strove for better conditions and control of their destiny.

SOURCE

From Lenin's *The Tasks of the Proletariat in the Present Revolution*, or *April Theses*, printed in *Pravda*, No. 26, on 7 April 1917. In the first thesis, Lenin refers to 'revolutionary defencism' which, in this case, means justifying the First World War as a defence of the newly formed Provisional Government. The purpose of the *April Theses* is not just to point out Lenin's view to the other Russian parties and people, but also to make the Bolshevik agenda clear to other Bolsheviks.

1) In our attitude towards the war, not the slightest concession to 'revolutionary defencism'...

In view of the undoubted honesty of those broad sections of the mass believers in revolutionary defencism who accept the war only as a necessity, and not as a means of conquest, in view of the fact that they are being deceived by the bourgeoisie, it is necessary... to explain the inseparable connection existing between capital and the imperialist war, and to prove that without overthrowing capital *it is impossible* to end the war by a truly democratic peace, a peace not imposed by violence.

The most widespread campaign for this view must be organised in the army at the front.

2) The specific feature of the present situation in Russia is that the country is *passing* from the first stage of the revolution—which, owing to the insufficient class-consciousness and organisation of the proletariat, placed power in the hands of the bourgeoisie—to its *second stage*, which must place power in the hands of the proletariat and the poorest sections of the peasants.

[...]

This peculiar situation demands of us an ability to adapt ourselves to the *special* conditions of Party work among unprecedentedly large masses of proletarians who have just awakened to political life.

3) No support for the Provisional Government; the utter falsity of all its promises...

4) Recognition of the fact that in most of the Soviets of Workers' Deputies our Party is in a minority, so far a small minority, as against a *bloc of all* the petty-bourgeois opportunist elements...

The masses must be made to see that... our task is, as long as *this* government yields to the influence of the bourgeoisie, to present a patient, systematic, and persistent explanation of the errors of their tactics, an *explanation* especially adapted to the practical needs of the masses.

[...]

5) Not a parliamentary republic... but a republic of Soviets of Workers', Agricultural Labourers' and Peasants' Deputies throughout the country, from top to bottom....

6) ... Confiscation of *all* landed estates.

Nationalisation of all lands in the country, the land to be disposed of by the local Soviets of Agricultural Labourers' and Peasants' Deputies....

7) The immediate union of all banks in the country into a single national bank, and the institution of control over it by the Soviet of Workers' Deputies.

A Level Exam-Style Question Section A

Study Source 9 before you answer this question.

Assess the value of the source for revealing Lenin's attitude towards the Provisional Government and the Bolsheviks' particular solutions to these problems.

Explain your answer using the source, the information given about it and your own knowledge of the historical context. (20 marks)

Tip

It is essential to plan your answer, even under the time restraints of an exam, as it enables you to focus on analysis immediately. The essay should follow the structure of the plan, and therefore the plan should be driven by the source, not your own knowledge. Build the plan and the essay around the source; do not make the source fit your own knowledge.

Lenin's ability to sum up a cause or a moment in a rhetorical masterstroke and political theatre can also be seen in his initial move for power. In June 1917, at the Congress of Russian Soviets, the other socialist and communist parties argued that it was too early for a revolution and that no party existed that could take on the Provisional Government. Lenin suddenly declared '*Yest' takaya partiya!*' ('There is such a party!') Even if their drama has subsequently been embellished by years of communist rule, as Russia fell apart over the summer of 1917, these words were a rallying cry for the masses eager for change. They also brought Trotsky into the Bolshevik Party. Though sympathetic to both Menshevik and Bolshevik ideas, Trotsky agreed with Lenin's urge for an insurrection. Trotsky had returned to Petrograd from New York in May and it was clear that an alliance would be made, with Lenin offering him a seat on the editorial board of ***Pravda***. Though Trotsky still desired an amalgamation of socialist interests, a concept utterly rejected by Lenin, he could see that the reality of dual power was that neither the Provisional Government nor the Petrograd Soviet had true authority in the country. Over the next few months, he became an ardent supporter of Lenin and rose to be his closest companion, to the bitter resentment of some other Bolsheviks such as Zinoviev, who had held that position for over a decade. Trotsky's qualities, which had so impressed Lenin, would truly come to light in the weeks before the Bolshevik takeover, but meanwhile it was apparent that Lenin did not yet have as much control of the situation as he would have liked.

KEY TERM

Pravda (*The Truth*)
The official newspaper of the Bolshevik Party. Set up in 1912 and closed by the authorities in 1914, it re-opened in March 1917 with Stalin as one of its editors. It had sales of around 40,000, of which half were in Petrograd. However, copies were passed from hand to hand, making readership figures higher. It later became the official newspaper of the USSR.

ACTIVITY
KNOWLEDGE CHECK

The impact of Lenin

1 Should the evidence in Source 7 affect a judgement on Lenin's role in the history of Russia?

2 How does Source 8 not only reinforce the sentiment expressed in Source 7, but also highlight the target audience for Bolshevik propaganda?

The Provisional Government's difficulties and mistakes

Following orders to move to the front line of the war against Germany, and roused by Bolshevik propaganda, the military garrison in Petrograd started to mutiny. They were joined by sailors from the Kronstadt naval base. The Bolsheviks' leaders had cancelled street demonstrations in June, but these protests in July seemed to escalate out of their control. As 250,000 people with Bolshevik flags and painted banners flocked to the Tauride Palace, they demanded that the soviet take over. However, Lenin was resting in Finland, and other leaders, such as Zinoviev, were also unavailable. Eventually, it was left to Stalin to order 20,000 Kronstadt sailors into the city, but when it became clear that the Provisional Government was preparing to counter the revolt, the Bolshevik leaders disowned the protest. It quickly became disorganised and slipped into violence and looting. Trotsky even had to rescue an SR leader who had been seized by angry sailors. As Lenin distanced himself from the revolt, calling it premature, the Provisional Government sent in loyal troops to disperse the crowd by the usual violent methods. One Bolshevik regiment even ended up defending the Palace from another Bolshevik faction of armed Putilov workers. In the chaos, no one seemed to know quite what to do and, more importantly, no one was prepared to take a leadership role.

The fiasco of the July Days was a disaster for the Bolsheviks. Lenin went into hiding, shaving off his beard to aid his disguise. The Provisional Government issued warrants for the Bolsheviks' arrest, banned *Pravda*, and saw, somewhat prematurely, the Bolsheviks as little more than a spent force led by German spies. Kerensky, a man of considerable charisma, replaced Prince Lvov as head of government by the end of July. Lvov had been in power just four months, but that had been enough to turn his hair completely white. To Lenin and the Bolsheviks, the dead bodies in the streets of Petrograd proved that the Provisional Government were as much the enemy of the people as the tsar was, but the July Days were a low point for the Bolsheviks under Lenin.

SOURCE 10 One of a series of photographs taken on 4 July 1917 on Nevsky Prospect, Petrograd, during the July Days coup. People carrying banners with Bolshevik slogans were shot by government troops. Other protesters ran for their lives, away from the heaps of bodies.

SOURCE

The journalist Nikolai Valentinov describing Lenin. Valentinov knew Lenin well and, despite never joining the Bolshevik Party, played an active role in politics during Lenin's lifetime. He died in France in 1964 and his reminiscences were published in *Encounters with Lenin* (1968).

He would be gripped by a state of rage, of ferocious passion, a frenzy of enthusiasm and extreme nervous energy... but then would come a sudden drop in his spirits, a sort of exhaustion, a very obvious wilting and depression... Looking back, it's clear that these two alternating states were the psychological essence of his behaviour.

SOURCE 12

Vladimir Dmitrievich Nabokov, a liberal Kadet member of the Provisional Government and father of the novelist Vladimir Nabokov, comparing the government and Bolsheviks in the aftermath of the July Days. He ended up in exile, where in 1922 he was killed by tsarist officers as he successfully prevented their assassination of Miliukov, his political opponent. Published in *The Memoirs of Vladimir D. Nabokov: V.D. Nabokov and the Provisional Government, 1917*, edited by V.D. Medlin and S.L. Parsons (1976).

The Provisional Government could have used [the July Days] to eliminate Lenin and co. But it failed to do so. The government simply made concessions to the socialists... The Provisional Government had no real sense of real power. This was a struggle between two forces: on the one side, those public elements that were sensible and moderate, but - alas! - timid and unorganised; and, on the other, organised immorality with its fanatical absolutist leaders... The Lenins and the Trotskys are completely indifferent to the fate of individuals. 'When you chop down a forest, chips must fly' is their convenient answer to every question.

The failure of the Provisional Government to fully utilise the July Days can be seen as one of a series of mistakes and misjudgements which eventually combined to give power to the Bolsheviks, despite the Bolsheviks' claim that they took it. These mistakes prevented the new government from gaining the authority and support it required.

The key mistake was the failure to end the First World War. Though the fighting spirit of the Russian front-line troops was surprisingly high during 1917, the rear garrisons, awaiting their turn and contemplating their future, were most open to Bolshevik propaganda. The Provisional Government hoped that by honouring its alliance with Britain and France, it would gain financial support from western governments. Kerensky, in particular, believed that defeat in the war and the consequent treaty with Germany would prove fatal to any government in power. He earned his nickname as the 'persuader-in-chief' in oratorical displays which would leave him in a state of sweat-drenched exhaustion and incite his audience to kiss his uniform, his car and the ground he walked on, as women donated their jewellery for the war effort. He hoped, and pleaded, that the troops would fight willingly for democracy, rather than having to be ordered by an autocratic tsar. In June and July, the Russian attack known as the Kerensky Offensive, led by General Brusilov, had some initial success, especially the section under the command of General Kornilov. However, German reinforcements quickly routed the Russians, causing huge numbers of soldiers to desert, with many murdering their officers on the way (over two million deserted in 1917). As they returned home, they reflected that the Mensheviks and SRs, who had previously enjoyed their support, had backed the offensive, while the Bolsheviks had offered 'peace'. The government created 15 all-women garrisons, with the First Women's Death Battalion under Maria Bocharyova sent to the front to encourage, or shame, male soldiers to fight, but these had little effect.

The disintegration of the army meant the Provisional Government had lost its key method of enforcing order if the situation required it. The continuation of the war also ruined any chance of consolidating much-needed support. While the tsar might have had his pillars of the aristocracy and army, the Provisional Government needed to construct its own pillars. To gain legitimacy and the potential support of the middle class, the Provisional Government had promised to hold elections for a constituent assembly. However, the war had led to delays and further delays and therefore the government remained a series of self-appointed coalitions. At least the tsar could claim tradition, or the soviet an elected right to rule, but the Provisional Government had no claim at all.

The Provisional Government also refused to deal with land reform, believing it to be a matter for a constituent assembly they had yet to call. The peasants therefore turned to the SRs, particularly the more left-wing radical branch who aligned themselves with the Bolsheviks. For the government, redistribution of land was impossible during the war, but the peasants started to take land for themselves. Peasant soldiers, anxious not to miss out, deserted in even greater numbers. The government sent in punishment brigades to prevent this, but this just made the peasants' resentment worse. By the time the government announced that elections for a constituent assembly would take place in late November 1917, it was too late to prevent its own collapse.

The war also continued the fuel and food shortages, which affected the workers in the cities particularly harshly as inflation, food shortages and unemployment continued after the February Revolution. The failure of the railways meant that fuel was not available for many factories: 568 factories closed in Petrograd between February and July, at a cost of 100,000 jobs. As resources were restricted, strikes broke out as workers tried to gain control and the Provisional Government, under pressure from industrialists, did not interfere to improve conditions. Any new laws, such as an eight-hour working day, were at the behest of the soviet, not the government. Wages had increased, roughly doubling in the last year, but this was nowhere near the increase in the price of food and manufactured goods: cotton, shoes, candles, firewood and charcoal had all increased by over 1,000 percent since the start of the war. These were the very commodities that were needed during October 1917 as Russia plunged into another harsh winter. Instead, the daily bread ration for a manual worker in Petrograd fell from 675 grams in March to just 110 grams by October. Petrograd was ripe for a change.

Finally, despite Kerensky's many qualities of leadership, he made some serious errors of judgement. The worst took place at the end of August 1917 and became known as the Kornilov Affair, after the disciplinarian general who had replaced the moderate Brusilov as commander-in-chief. It seems Kerensky ordered Kornilov to impose martial law on an increasingly restless Petrograd. There was a rift between the two men, perhaps worsened by poor communication, and Kerensky denounced Kornilov as a counter-revolutionary, since he feared Kornilov was about to eliminate him and take over as dictator. This gave the Bolsheviks the opportunity to recover from the July Days, as they organised the defence of Petrograd with their Red Guards, supplied with weapons by a panicking Kerensky. Meanwhile, anyone associated with the Provisional Government, including the Mensheviks and SRs, was tainted with Kerensky's ambiguous role in calling Kornilov to Petrograd in the first place. Soldiers, seeing the affair as an officers' plot, murdered their superiors in their hundreds. The Bolsheviks rode the wave of popular support as the saviours of Petrograd and won large majorities on many soviets, with Trotsky becoming president of the Petrograd Soviet in late September – they now had new weapons that they were not going to hand back. The Kornilov Affair showed that even a military general, feared by the left and a hero to the right, was not sufficiently secure with his own troops to restore order. It also showed that the Provisional Government with Kerensky, now living in the Winter Palace, was not fit to rule. It was only a question of who would take the initiative and replace them.

In the months after the Kornilov Affair, which demoralised all right-wing groups in Russia, the country fell apart. Violence increased in the countryside; conditions worsened in the cities. Kerensky had set up a pre-parliament to fill the void before the coming election in November. In late September, with a majority

EXTRACT

From *Endurance and Endeavour, Russian History 1812–2001* (2002) by J.N. Westwood, in which the historian gives his view on the impact of the First World War on the Provisional Government.

The war made almost inevitable the end of the Provisional Government. To keep the Revolution under control would have been near-impossible in any case, with the sudden release of the enormous social pressures accumulated by centuries of autocracy. To fight the war and conduct the Revolution simultaneously was a hopeless endeavour. Yet if the government had decided to end the war on unfavourable terms at this time it would probably have been overthrown, because too many Russians would have rejected such a defeat. Pride, patriotism, and the lure of territorial gain still had their effect, while most socialists believed that surrender to the Germans would mean the Kaiser would triumph over the Allies and then be free to send his armies to suppress the Revolution.

in the Petrograd and Moscow Soviets and Trotsky as Petrograd chairman, Lenin felt it was time for a takeover. He was worried that Petrograd might fall to the Germans, and that the Bolsheviks, less popular in rural areas, would be less represented in any constituent assembly. If his call for 'all power to the Soviets' was to be realised, it must occur in October. It was in his timing that Lenin showed his acute skill. He had to fight resistance from Party members who wanted the Congress of Soviets to take over, and who felt that the takeover must appear a more legitimate transfer than any seizure of power. This last point was not important to Lenin, and he had to persuade Trotsky and bully others to get his way. It was an open secret in Petrograd that the seizure was imminent.

Kerensky's response was lacklustre, perhaps backed by over-confidence in his own cult of personality and under-estimating the Bolshevik support, whose membership in October was only 300,000 (though it had been just 10,000 during the February Revolution). Kerensky decided to send the Petrograd garrison to the front line of the war to remove them from the city. This backfired, as they mutinied and joined the Military Revolutionary Committee (MRC), a force set up and controlled by Trotsky to defend the Petrograd Soviet in October. Here was Trotsky's chance to show his skill and energetic organisational ability. On 23 October, the MRC took over the Peter and Paul fortress, overlooking the Winter Palace. As Kerensky clumsily tried to restrict the MRC, the Bolsheviks used it as their excuse to act. On 24 October, Trotsky organised the final *coup d'état* by using his Red Guard to seize key points in the city such as bridges, railway stations, power stations and telegraph offices.

While life the next morning appeared as normal, Trotsky planned the arrest of the Provisonal Government and, in the early hours of 25 and 26 October, the Red Guard, prompted by the guns of the *Avrora* battleship, entered the Winter Palace and rounded up the few remaining figures of the Provisional Government, who were in the imperial family's breakfast room. The illiterate Red Guard made the officials write up their own arrest papers. The military cadets and 200 members of the Women's Death Battalion had almost all left, leaving the famous gates unguarded and open. What became known as 'the storming of the Winter Palace' was in fact a small scuffle as any resistance melted away into the darkness. In a day of revolution, 18 people were arrested and two were killed.

The key moment was on 26 October as the Congress of Russian Soviets gathered. Instead of condemning the takeover, the Mensheviks and SRs walked out in protest, leaving just the Bolsheviks and a few left-wing SRs, who could now stamp an 'official' approval to a Bolshevik government. At this point, Lenin arrived. As the rival deputies left, the words of Trotsky's speech filled the hall, 'You are miserable bankrupts, your role is played out; go where you ought to be – into the dustbin of history!'

In many ways, the *coup d'état* was largely the work of Trotsky, and his skills as an orator and organiser, and his unflagging enthusiasm, would prove vital in the years ahead. However, it was Lenin who saw the opportunity for a small party to take power, and who persuaded the party to take the very real risk. Though the Provisional Government had collapsed, it would not need many troops to defeat the Red Guard, and the other factions within the soviet could muster far more support than the Bolsheviks.

Kerensky slipped away from Petrograd on the morning of 25 October. Every action he had taken only exacerbated the situation and gave popular support to the Bolsheviks. Even his personal charm and reputation were under attack, with rumours of love affairs, drunkenness, morphine addiction and transvestism. While the tsar was a weak man in a powerful job, Kerensky was a powerful man in a weak job whose support fell away. He even had to borrow a car from the US embassy to flee the city.

EXTEND YOUR KNOWLEDGE

History is a flexible judge of the past

There has been much debate over whether the October Revolution was a popular revolt or a *coup d'état*. The debate shows that historians' political views often cast their own shadow over accounts of events.

The Soviet view (1917–91) saw the revolution as a popular uprising of workers, who created the soviets and were guided by the Bolsheviks. The western view, dominant after 1945 when a Cold War emerged between the USA and the USSR, portrays a more hostile view of a minority, who carried out a *coup d'état* and imposed a totalitarian system. Most historians of this liberal view see it as a disaster for Russia.

By the 1970s, revisionist historians highlighted the role of the common people by looking at history 'from below'. These structuralist historians, such as Sheila Fitzpatrick, see workers, soldiers and peasants as setting the scene for the Bolsheviks. More recent (post-revisionist) historians, such as Robert Service, attempt to combine the views by acknowledging the importance of Lenin and the *coup d'état*, while focusing on the local levels that helped to facilitate the situation as the masses became more radical.

Part of the problem is the way the Bolsheviks later portrayed and distorted the revolution in film, image, theatre and text. More people were shown to have died in Eisenstein's film *Battleship Potemkin* than in the actual event. The propaganda may be clearly false, but this does not mean the opposite must be true. Another danger is categorising historians according to their views. The solution is to study the evidence they provide, as well as alternative views, and always to be aware of the context a historian is writing in.

SOURCE

A summary of Trotsky's role in 1917, written by Stalin in *Pravda*, 10 November 1918. Stalin and Trotsky later became fierce rivals and this text was removed from Stalin's collected works. Elsewhere, Trotsky himself had written that he had managed to take over Russia with the participation of just 25,000–30,000 people.

All practical work in connection with the organisation of the uprising was done under the immediate direction of Comrade Trotsky, the President of the Petrograd Soviet. It can be stated with certainty that the Party is indebted primarily and principally to Comrade Trotsky for the rapid going over of the garrison to the side of the Soviet and the efficient manner in which the work of the Military Revolutionary Committee was organised.

EXTRACT

From Orlando Figes, in *A People's Tragedy: The Russian Revolution 1891–1924* (1996), discussing the personal qualities of Kerensky in September 1917. He compares Kerensky's actions to those of the Mensheviks and SRs in the Petrograd Soviet, whose revolutionary camaraderie with the Bolsheviks meant they did not put up enough resistance once it was clear that the Bolsheviks would take power.

Kerensky's own conduct was equally short-sighted. During the final weeks of the Provisional Government his behaviour began to resemble that of the last Tsar: both men refused to recognize the revolutionary threat to their own authority. With Nicholas such complacency had stemmed from hopeless despair and fatalistic resignation; but with Kerensky it was rather the result of his own foolish optimism. Kerensky's nationwide popularity during the early days of the revolution had gone to his head. He had come to believe in his own 'providential calling' to lead 'the people' to freedom and, like the Tsar confined in his Winter Palace, was sufficiently removed from their real situation not to question this faith. Like Nicholas, he surrounded himself with devoted admirers who dared not speak their mind, and kept his cabinet weak by constant talk of reshuffles. He had no idea of - or no wish to know - the true extent of his own unpopularity.

ACTIVITY
KNOWLEDGE CHECK

The October Revolution

1. How does Source 10 demonstrate the instability of the period between the two revolutions of February and October 1917?
2. Use Source 11 to explain why Lenin withdrew his support for the Bolshevik rebels in the July Days. How valid do you think this view is?
3. Nabokov gives his very clear opinion of the difference between the Provisional Government and the Bolsheviks in Source 12. Do you think this view is accurate and fair? Would the Provisional Government have fared better if they had been prepared to 'let chips fly' more?
4. Do you think, like Extract 1, that the Provisional Government was in a no-win situation? Was victory in the First World War the only way the Provisional Government could survive?
5. Using the ideas in Source 13 and Extract 2, as well as your own knowledge, say which view carries more weight in explaining the reasons for the success of the October Revolution.

A Level Exam-Style Question Section B

How accurate is it to say that the reason there were two revolutions in 1917 was because of a failure of leadership? (20 marks)

Tip

It is important that the two revolutions are not merely described, but also that the factors that caused them, e.g. issues of leadership, authority, legitimacy, support and impact of the First World War, are compared together in an integrated answer.

EXTRACT

From Robert Service, *Lenin* (2000), describing the qualities of Kerensky.

[He was] the real master of the modern technology of politics in 1917.

EXTRACT 4

From Orlando Figes, *A People's Tragedy: The Russian Revolution 1891–1924* (1996). Here he is describing Kerensky's speech to the soviet on 2 March 1917, in which he asked for approval of his decision to join the Provisional Government.

'I speak, comrades, with all my soul, from the bottom of my heart, and if it is needed to prove this, if you do not trust me I am ready to die,'... Now Kerensky turned to ask them whether they approved of his decision to join the government, offering to resign from the soviet if the answer should be no. But there were wild cries of 'We do! We do!' and, without a formal vote, his actions were endorsed. It was a brilliant coup de théâtre. What might have been the moment of his downfall had in fact become the moment of his triumph. Kerensky was now the only politician with a position in both the government and the Soviet. He was the undisputed leader of the people.

THINKING HISTORICALLY Evidence (6b)

The strength of argument

1 Read Extract 3.

a) What is weak about this claim?

b) What could be added to it to make it stronger?

2 Read Extract 4.

a) Is this an argument? If yes, what makes it one?

b) How might this argument be strengthened?

3 Now read Extracts 2 and 4 together, both from the same book by Orlando Figes.

a) How does the addition of Extract 2 give a more rounded view of Kerensky and therefore strengthen Orlando Figes' interpretation of Kerensky's abilities?

b) Reading Extracts 2-4 together, how could you sum up Kerensky's abilities?

c) What elements make a historian's claims strong?

EXTEND YOUR KNOWLEDGE

A thread through history: the life of Alexander Kerensky (1881-1970)

Kerensky's father was a teacher who taught Lenin. Kerensky trained as a lawyer and was involved in representing victims of the 1905 repression, an act that saw him jailed as a suspected militant. His work on reporting the details on the savage government repression on the Lena Goldfields strike of 1912 saw Kerensky elected to the fourth *duma* as a leading socialist of the Trudovik socialist group and later the more widespread SRs. During 1916, he attempted to limit the influence of Rasputin. Though not involved in the murder, he ordered the removal of the body for burial in an unmarked spot in the countryside, but the truck broke down and the order was not carried out.

His reputation as an orator helped secure him a leading role in the Provisional Government in 1917. Sir Bruce Lockheart, the British consul in Moscow, witnessed a June 1917 speech by Kerensky in the Bolshoi Theatre, where women threw roses and jewellery onto the stage. To his rivals and political enemies, his charisma was reminiscent of Napoleon Bonaparte, who turned the French revolution into a dictatorship. Kerensky left Russia during the October Revolution, and lived in Paris, Australia and the USA, where he died. Russian groups in the USA refused to bury him, as they felt he had allowed Russia to fall to the Bolsheviks, so his body was flown to Britain, where his sons lived, and he was buried in London.

Though his life is somewhat eclipsed by Lenin and Bolshevik rule, Kerensky was a remarkable individual at the centre of the dramatic events in revolutionary Russia.

HOW DID THE BOLSHEVIKS CONSOLIDATE POWER DURING 1918?

Concessions and violence

Now that the Bolsheviks had grabbed power, the crowds discovered the vast wine cellars of the Winter Palace. A drunken mob intent on violence and looting took to the streets around the palace, forcing the Bolsheviks to pump the wine and liquor onto the road, where the crowds drank some of the finest alcohol in the world from the gutters. In the end, the Bolsheviks used machine guns unsuccessfully to hold the people back. When the drink finally ran out, after several weeks, the people awoke with an almighty hangover. However, for the Bolsheviks it was worse: they had to work out how they could consolidate their power over a whole country, when they were forced to shoot at their own supporters.

The fundamental problem for the Bolsheviks was the same as for the tsar and the Provisional Government. Eventually they would need to implement measures to achieve enough authority and support to extend control, but in the chaos resulting from October, the first task was to survive. The fact that they managed to do this is a testament to their political skill and desire for power, even at the expense of their ideology.

Dissolving the Constituent Assembly and setting up Cheka

Lenin was prepared to pay any price to hold on to power. Although this would cause rifts within the Party in the 1920s, it enabled the Bolsheviks to fight and win a civil war that they knew was inevitable.

Petrograd fell with little bloodshed, but other cities saw more fighting. In a couple of weeks, Moscow and 14 other provincial cities were firmly under Bolshevik control, and a further 28 cities by the end of January 1918. However, the Bolsheviks had almost no control over rural areas, and no power to stop separatist groups from dissolving the empire. This was seen when an order for the army to negotiate a ceasefire with Germany was ignored until the Bolsheviks dispatched some Red Guards to murder the chief-of-staff, Dukhonin. Lawlessness and anarchy created a violent atmosphere, as people took revenge on anyone they saw as the enemy; in one town, 50 military cadets were thrown into the furnace of a metal factory. Lenin knew that control of the countryside would have to wait. The fact that resistance to the Bolsheviks was not more widespread is partly because most places had no Bolsheviks to resist, and partly because of the opposition's belief that the Bolsheviks would collapse on their own. The Mensheviks and SRs were content to wait for a constituent assembly, only days away, in which they were confident they would win, while the forces of the Provisional Government, or those who still supported the tsar, were in disarray and posed no immediate threat.

With an uncertain majority in the soviets, the Bolsheviks could claim some legitimacy, and they immediately started passing emergency decrees on a range of issues, all designed to capture the support they desperately needed, especially among the peasants. Some of the most important were:

- the Decree on Land (October 1917), which ignored communist ideology on nationalisation, and instead gave the land to the peasants; this decree copied the SRs' policy on land
- the Decree on Peace (October 1917), which called for an immediate truce and a fair peace with Germany; it did not dictate any terms, which came later
- the Decree on Workers' Control (October 1917), which authorised the workers to supervise their managers, and in effect take control of the factories
- the Decree on the Rights of the People of Russia (November 1917), which allowed different nationalities of the old Russian Empire the power to determine their own government
- the Decree on abolishing ranks in the army (December 1917), which set up soldiers' committees to elect officers

While other decrees separated Church from state, gave in principle equal rights to women and set up special people's courts with elected judges, the similarity between the key decrees is that they just legitimised what was already happening: the army had stopped fighting, the peasants had taken the land, the workers controlled the factories and the empire was already split. These paper decrees, as they became known, were an attempt by the Bolsheviks to take credit for what had already occurred. They would all cause problems for the Party later on; for example, they would have to reintegrate the empire (with Russian dominance) by force during and after the Civil War of 1918–21, but they worked in that they convinced the masses that the Bolsheviks were on their side and were, at least, more worth supporting than the others, who might take their rights away.

The Congress of Soviets also approved the new government known as the Council of People's Commissars (*Sovnarkom),* made up exclusively of Bolsheviks with the few left-wing SRs. *Sovnarkom* ruled by decree, bypassing the Petrograd Soviet, though many other soviets could still rule by themselves. Even in Petrograd, the government had to use armed force to compel the state bank to hand over money, and to break civil-service strikes. *Sovnarkom* was a clear indication that the Bolsheviks were not going to share power. This was confirmed when the railway workers' union went on strike. The Bolsheviks initially agreed to compromise, as the railway was needed to hold back a counter-attack by Kerensky. However, when this failed to materialise, the Bolsheviks turned on the union, making Bolshevik dominance clear to all.

Despite the concessions of the paper decrees, it is evident that the Bolsheviks were prepared to use the stick as well as the carrot. Measures to repress opposition began as soon as the decrees. Lenin stated that all parties that had opposed the Bolsheviks were 'counter-revolutionary' and therefore freedom of the press was banned for the sake of the revolution. This unpopular move caused some Bolsheviks to resign, but was reinforced as gangs arrested editors and smashed printing presses.

Other political suppression began, with the Kadet Party outlawed and two of its leaders killed, and various Menshevik and SR leaders arrested. Lenin labelled anyone who offered an alternative view a *burzhui* (bourgeois counter-revolutionary), though the term applied not just to the middle class but to all whom the workers blamed for their problems. By encouraging class warfare with the unofficial slogan of 'loot the looters', Lenin could use their hatred to bring them closer to his side while intimidating others into submission.

Lenin needed to do this as he knew the Bolsheviks would have to allow the elections to the Constituent Assembly. He had repeatedly called for them before October, ridiculing the Provisional Government for postponing them, and by November the Bolsheviks were in no position to stop them. The elections took place over two weeks in November, and Lenin's fears proved justified. The SRs with their peasant support base won 370 out of 707 seats, the left-wing SRs 40 seats, the Mensheviks 18 seats, and the Bolsheviks 175 seats with just 24 percent of the vote. The SRs together had 53 percent of the vote. Though this shows that the October Revolution was not the result of popular support, it does not show that the Bolsheviks held clear majorities in urban areas.

For Lenin, unwilling to compromise over sharing power, this was an obvious threat to Bolshevik rule. The electoral commission, accused by Stalin of forging the results, were arrested. When Bolshevik propaganda directed against the commission failed to change public opinion, reliable Bolshevik troops were moved into the capital. The Constituent Assembly was allowed to meet on 5 January 1918, but Bolshevik troops blocked the entrance the next day. Demonstrators who marched in support of it were shot at from the rooftops. Lenin declared the Constituent Assembly redundant and a product of the bourgeoisie, unlike the soviet, and by implication the *Sovnarkom.* With the assembly dissolved, the threat from the left was temporarily removed. Though there was little outcry from the rest of the country, perhaps because of the little Bolshevik influence there, it meant that the only avenue for protest open to the SRs and Mensheviks was civil war.

On 7 December 1917, a decree was passed creating the Extraordinary Commission for Combating Counter-Revolution and Sabotage (Cheka). The Bolsheviks now had their own secret police, confirming Lenin's view that a reign of terror, as in France in the 1790s, would be required after the revolution. The fanatical Dzerzhinski was put in charge and headquarters were set up in Lubyanka Street, Moscow. It would become a bureaucratic centre of torture and execution.

SOURCE

From *Pravda*, 25 December 1917, printing the advice of a leading Cheka official.

Do not demand incriminating evidence to prove that the prisoner has opposed the Soviet government by force or by words. Your first duty is to ask him to which class he belongs, what are his origins, his education, his occupation. These questions should decide the fate of the prisoner.

Over the next year, Cheka widened its activities to deal with whole sectors of communities, not just individuals. The criteria for arrest were the same, with the key factor being who they were (or knew, or were related to) rather than any crime committed. Both Cheka and the Bolshevik leadership felt that the price of many innocent lives in the pursuit of a single guilty one was worth paying. The reason for this step up in terror was that, through early 1918, the opposition was starting to challenge the Bolsheviks. One trigger for this discontent was the long-awaited peace treaty with Germany: the Treaty of Brest-Litovsk.

EXTRACT 5

Edward Acton, in *Russia: The Tsarist and Soviet Legacy* (1995), summarises the first few months of Bolshevik rule.

The peasants were authorized to parcel out private land as they saw fit, despite Bolshevik preference for the nationalization of land and immediate steps towards collective farming. Even in the factories, where Bolshevik influence was most deeply rooted, the widespread assertion of direct control by workers went far beyond anything the Party leadership considered compatible with economic recovery. And despite Bolshevik conviction that for the minority nations to break away from Russia now that she was in truly revolutionary hands would be a backward step, the government had to proclaim the right to do so. The People's Commissioners were in no position to resist or direct the tide that had swept away Kerensky. No Russian government had ever been more responsive, to pressure from below, or less able to impose its own will upon society.

ACTIVITY
KNOWLEDGE CHECK

Early Bolshevik consolidation

1. According to Source 14, what was the primary function of Cheka? What does this reveal about Lenin's view on Bolshevik rule?
2. Make a list of the evidence that supports and challenges the view presented in Source 14.
3. How far do you agree with Acton's view in Extract 5 of a weak Bolshevik government in the first three months of its rule to 1918?

Making peace with Germany and the creation of the Red Army

Lenin had delayed the treaty for as long as he could, in the vain hope that the Bolshevik Revolution would inspire a worldwide revolution, starting in Western Europe, and enabling the war to end on favourable terms for Russia. It was clear that this was not going to happen and German impatience was threatening to restart the war. Were this to happen, the German army would be virtually unopposed as they marched towards Petrograd, thereby ending the Bolshevik revolution completely.

The Bolsheviks were divided over peace talks. The majority, under Bukharin, wanted to continue a revolutionary war against Germany, while Trotsky wanted 'Neither war nor peace', which meant delaying any treaty for as long as possible. Lenin, in a minority, realised that the Germans would continue to advance and that Bolshevik forces needed to be free to face opposition within Russia. Trotsky's view held out for a couple of months before the Germans recommenced hostilities on 18 February 1918. In five days, with minimal troops, they advanced 150 miles by train and car, more than they had in three years of war. This forced the Bolsheviks, by a small majority, to back Lenin, with Trotsky switching to Lenin's view to avoid a split in the Party, as Lenin would have resigned.

A German thrust to take Petrograd caused Lenin to respond with troops, a plea to the western allies for aid, operations to move the capital to Moscow (causing panic in Petrograd) and the decree on 'The Socialist Fatherland in Danger!', which urged the working class to join the Red Army. Germany, having shown its strength, then introduced the harsh terms of the treaty. The Bolsheviks had to accept them, in spite of cries of betrayal from many, including the left-wing SRs who walked out of the *Sovnarkom* forever. Lenin, believing that any delay in accepting the treaty would prove fatal to the Bolsheviks, struggled to persuade the Central Committee. He felt that the Germans would simply advance into Petrograd and expel the Bolsheviks from power, but not everyone in the Party could accept this view. In the end, the committee voted seven to four, with four members abstaining, including Trotsky, who was more worried about the Party splitting than the Germans advancing. To Trotsky, it was vital for the Party, a small minority, to remain united. However, Bukharin did resign over the issue.

Economically, the Treaty of Brest-Litovsk pushed Russia back hundreds of years, as it lost all its territories in Western Europe (see Figure 5.1): up to 55 million people, 32 percent of its farmland, about 55 percent of its industry and 89 percent of its coal mines. The treaty helped to focus opposition to Bolshevik rule, as it was a patriotic rallying cry that went beyond any political ideology. To Lenin, however, it was the ultimate example of his uncompromising attitude that any sacrifice was worth making to consolidate power. With the few SRs having left the government, the Bolsheviks now ruled alone. Lenin knew that civil war was inevitable regardless of the treaty. Any unity forged by the anti-treaty feeling would soon dissipate in the field of war, and it would never surpass the motivation of the Bolsheviks in the Civil War – win or die. The treaty marked the point where it was clear that this would be a revolution particular to Russia, with a policy that was to be called 'Socialism in one Country' and a new capital in Moscow, safely away from the West.

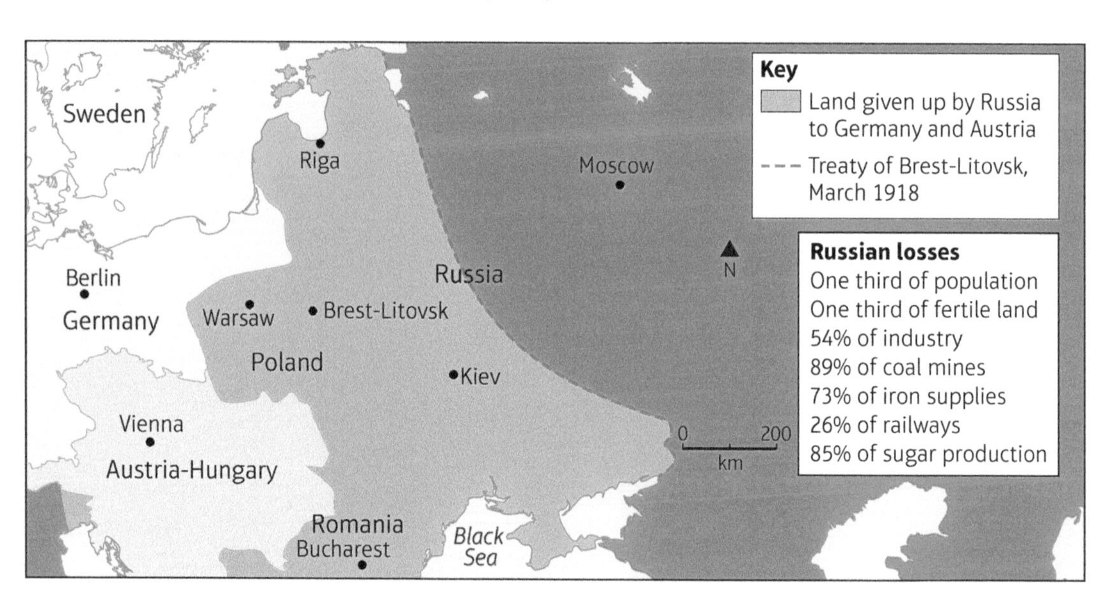

Figure 5.1 The effects of the Treaty of Brest-Litovsk, 3 March 1918.

The Bolsheviks needed a fighting force to win the approaching civil war. The MRC and Red Guards were not up to the task, so in late January and early February 1918, the Workers' and Peasants' Red Army had been created, with extra volunteers from the workers encouraged by the 'Fatherland in Danger' decree.

Trotsky's appointment as commissar for war in March 1918 meant that his vision would shape the Red Army. There were not enough dedicated revolutionaries, but he enlisted 50,000 tsarist officers who knew how to command and were keen for employment. Trotsky reversed an earlier decree and brought back pay differentials, ranks, saluting and the death penalty. Political commissars were put into each unit to keep an eye on the men and ensure the officers' loyalty. The scale of the Civil War meant that conscription targeting the peasants was introduced by June 1918. By 1919, the Red Army had three million soldiers, and by the end of 1920 it had five million, though desertion rates were almost as high as the numbers joining.

These measures were unpopular, and some Bolsheviks resigned, but Trotsky had Lenin's support. Conscription caused some peasants to revolt. The political commissars, always fanatical Party members and perceived to be from Jewish backgrounds, were often hated for anti-Semitic reasons, while officers, seen as *burzhui*, were often murdered. Despite all this, Trotsky's passion and unrelenting energy managed to create a Red Army that was better than the forces it would oppose. The Red Army was one edge of the Bolshevik sword; the other was the terror applied by Cheka. The use of terror increased sharply in the effort to survive the Civil War and as a response to the shooting of Lenin in August 1918 by the SR Fanny Kaplan.

SOURCE 15

Dzerzhinsky, speaking at a press interview in July 1918. His words were noted by fellow Bolshevik Karl Radek and recorded in his 1933 work *Portrety i Pamflety*.

The Cheka is not a court. The Cheka is *the defence of the revolution* as the Red Army is; as in the civil war the Red Army cannot stop to ask whether it may harm particular individuals, but must take into account only one thing, the victory of the revolution over the bourgeoisie, so the Cheka must defend the revolution and conquer the enemy even if its sword falls occasionally on the heads of the innocent.

As winter turned to spring in 1918, civil war erupted as a diverse opposition, collectively called the Whites, faced a core of Red forces in central Russia. The Whites were aided by foreign powers, such as Britain, France, the USA and Japan, all with their own interests, while Poland waged a war within a war for independence. There was even a Czechoslovak legion which had been stranded in Russia after the Treaty Brest-Litovsk and that became embroiled in the fighting. Some peasants formed independent armies, loosely called the Greens, and fought anyone who threatened their land. Yet the Bolsheviks, through Lenin's uncompromising stance and Trotsky's talent for military organisation, through inspiration and fear, were able to face the challenges and use their civil war conquests by 1921 to control Russia and its empire. The cost to Russia was staggering, in millions of lives and a devastated economy, but the five months following October 1917 showed that the Bolsheviks' greatest strength was their willingness to pay any price for victory. By 1918, they were on their way to imposing a dictatorship, and had laid the groundwork for all that followed under Lenin and then under Stalin.

At a more personal level, this can be seen by Lenin's decision in July 1918 to murder Tsar Nicholas II, the tsarina, their five children and four servants. They were shot and stabbed in the basement of a house in the town of Yekaterinburg and their bodies doused with acid. There could be no going back.

A Level Exam-Style Question Section B

'In a single year Russia had lost a tsar only to have it replaced by a Red one.'

To what extent do you agree with this view? (20 marks)

Tip

Think about aspects of continuity and change to give both sides of the argument. It is important that your conclusion has a clear and reasoned judgement. Try not to sit on the fence.

SOURCE 16

Statement made by Fanny Kaplan to the Cheka on 30 August 1918. She was executed four days later.

My name is Fanny Kaplan. Today I shot at Lenin. I did it on my own. I will not say from whom I obtained my revolver. I will give no details. I had resolved to kill Lenin long ago. I consider him a traitor to the Revolution. I favoured the Constituent Assembly and am still for it.

EXTRACT 6

From Orlando Figes, *A People's Tragedy: The Russian Revolution 1891–1924* (1996).

Although Kaplan had always denied it, she was at once accused of working for the SRs and the Western Powers... It later emerged at the SR trial in 1922 that Kaplan had been recruited by the SR Combat Organisation, an underground terrorist outfit not officially connected with the SR Central Committee but supported by some of its members who remained in Moscow. The Combat Organisation assassinated the Bolshevik Commissar Volodarsky on 20 June. It also tried to murder Trotsky on his way to the Eastern Front; but he foiled the plan by changing trains at the last moment.

EXTRACT

The case of Fanny Kaplan was re-examined by the historian Dmitri Volkogonov in his biography *Lenin: Life and Legacy* (1994). He highlighted several puzzling aspects to the case.

No one had actually seen Kaplan, as distinct from a woman's hand, fire at Lenin. Kaplan, moreover, had very poor eyesight; she could hardly see anything close up... the Cheka did not receive the Browning (a type of gun) that had been thrown to the ground after the shooting, for a full three days. Yet a Browning was found in Kaplan's handbag when she was first searched. Whose revolver, then, was it that was handed in?

A further significant detail is that pages 11, 84, 90 and 94 of the file relating to the shooting were missing when it was checked on 26 June 1963.

Oleg Vasiliev (a journalist) has suggested that there was no assassination attempt at all, merely a fake show.

It is more likely that it was not actually Kaplan who fired the gun. In the aftermath of the shooting, the authorities were not concerned to carry out a thorough investigation. There were only a few brief interrogations, and there was no trial. The 'Kaplan attempt' gave the Bolsheviks the excuse they wanted to launch massive, overwhelming state terror. It enabled them finally to deal with their recent allies, the Left SRs, whom they now felt to be a hindrance. Terror provided them with their last chance to make power the monopoly of one party.

THINKING HISTORICALLY **Evidence (6c)**

Comparing and evaluating historians' arguments

On 20 August 1918, Lenin was visiting a factory in Moscow. His wife had asked him not to go because of tension in the city. Earlier that day, Uritsky, chief of the Petrograd Cheka, had been assassinated by an SR terrorist. While at the factory, Lenin was shot three times by Fanny Kaplan, another SR assassin.

According to later official accounts, Kaplan was arrested on the spot by angry workers, but radiogram reports immediately after the event suggested that she was one of several people arrested. Kaplan was nearly blind and mentally unbalanced. It is unclear whether she was working alone or part of a greater campaign by a more organised group. After a brief interrogation by the Cheka, Kaplan was shot.

Although close to death, Lenin survived, but the shock had important consequences.

1. Compare Extracts 6 and 7 and identify factual statements or claims where both agree in their view of Source 16. Think beyond the shooting and consider the consequences as well. List these points.
2. Look carefully at the historians' language. Do both use equally cautious language in their claims, or is one more confident and assertive than the other? Is one (or both) over-claiming?
3. Are the two historical accounts equally credible, or are there reasons to prefer one account to the other? What other conclusions could there be?
4. Is Kaplan's guilt or innocence historically important, or is it only the consequences that matter?

Conclusion

During 1917, Russia had three main rulers: Nicholas II, Kerensky and Lenin. Though individually their trials and circumstances were different, all needed to solve the problem of the First World War. Their particular leadership skills largely dictated their approach and the degree of success they achieved. The tsar, believing he was divinely blessed to rule, was so ineffectual that even his closest supporters saw the need for change. Kerensky's lack of authority and support of the Provisional Government meant he was unable to have any real effect. He under-estimated the workers' and peasants' loathing of the war, and was just as deluded in thinking that a new government would change the war. Only Lenin, with a callous ruthlessness towards anything that blocked the Bolshevik rise to dominance, was prepared to try something new to end the war. Of course, this was not for peace, but to ignite a new internal war. The tragedy is that a leader with such a single-minded refusal to compromise was needed to solve the First World War, but then that same fanaticism was unleashed on Russia itself.

ACTIVITY
SUMMARY

The end of the Romanovs and the triumph of the Bolsheviks, 1916–18

1 For the three main sections of this chapter – the tsar, the Provisional Government, the Bolsheviks – list the specific problems they faced and how they solved them (or attempted to).

2 **a)** Was the abdication of the tsar due more to his own weaknesses or to the strength of the members of the Provisional Government in February 1917?

b) Was the Bolsheviks' seizure of power due more to the weaknesses of the Provisional Government than to the strengths of the Bolsheviks in October 1917?

3 In what ways did Trotsky's role in the October Revolution complement that of Lenin?

4 The historian Robert Service has commented that by the end of 1917 there would have been a socialist government regardless of Lenin.

a) Do you think the Bolsheviks could have taken power without him?

b) If they had not taken power, what is the possibility that the SRs or the Mensheviks would have done so?

WIDER READING

Carr, E.H. *The Bolshevik Revolution 1917-1923*, Vol 1, Pelican (1950)

Figes, O. *A People's Tragedy: The Russian Revolution 1891-1924*, Pimlico (1996)

Fitzpatrick, S. *The Russian Revolution*, Oxford University Press (1994)

Sixsmith, M. *Russia: A 1,000-year Chronicle of the Wild East*, BBC Books (2012)

Westwood, J.N. *Endurance and Endeavour: Russian History 1812-2001*, Oxford University Press (2002)

Khrushchev and attempts to reform the Soviet system, 1956–61

KEY QUESTIONS

- What was the impetus for Khrushchev to try to reform the Soviet system?
- Why did Khrushchev initiate de-Stalinisation through his 'Secret Speech' in 1956?
- How deep were Khrushchev's reforms to the administration?

INTRODUCTION

A period of significant reform which changes the direction of a regime, or even initiates a change in the regime itself, is usually the result of a considerable, often painful, event in a nation's history. Alexander II's modernising reforms were born in the defeats of the Crimea; the 1905 revolts emerged from the disasters in the Russo–Japanese War; while the First World War both ruined Russia and ended the rule of the Romanovs and the Provisional Government. It can be argued that the militarised and institutionalised terror of the communist rule, started by Lenin and perfected by Stalin, was created from the desolation of the Civil War. However, the reforms introduced by Khrushchev, though they date only a few years from the devastation of the Second World War, have their origins not in war, but in the death of a single man.

Stalin died a prolonged death, suffering a stroke that took days to kill him as bodyguards, advisers and doctors looked on, too afraid to act. With his eventual death, as the Russian people went into shock, his closest advisers quickly formed a collective leadership. Like the collective leadership that brought Stalin into power after Lenin's premature death, what followed was a complex series of plots and manipulations that would bring Khrushchev into power. Like Stalin, he seemed the least likely to emerge as supreme leader. But he had learnt from Stalin himself how to place key supporters in the right positions and the need to be ruthless when necessary. He also understood that the way forward, and the way to stamp his authority on the USSR, was to present a clean break from the Stalin era and introduce a series of reforms which became known in domestic and international circles as the 'thaw'. Domestically, this meant deconstructing the Stalinist apparatus of terror, which therefore required attacking the legacy of Stalin. It meant, in Khrushchev's opinion, a return to a Leninist Party approach to rule and an easing in the restrictions on Soviet life, particularly in cultural activities.

The motives behind this change of direction were not purely altruistic. Khrushchev, more than any of the Soviet leaders, was driven by his unpredictable and flamboyant personality, while reform was often a way to highlight personal rule and attack rivals. It is also simplistic to present the reforms as

1956 – February: 'Secret Speech' starts de-Stalinisation (25th)
March: Pro-Stalin riots in Georgia
June: Polish uprising gains concessions
November: USSR sends tanks into Hungary to crush uprising

1956 — 1957 — 1958

1957 – May: *Sovnarkhozy* set up
June: Failed coup of 'Anti-Party' Group
July: World Festival of Youth in Moscow
October: *Sputnik* launched
Zhukov forced to retire

1958 – March: Bulganin forced out as prime minister
June: Nagy, ex-Hungarian leader, executed
October: Pasternak's *Dr Zhivago* wins Nobel Prize
December: Pasternak forced to reject Nobel Prize
Shelepin head of new KGB

a clean break with the past. All the reforms, whatever their true cause, had limitations. The rule of Khrushchev is often presented as the communist regime entering its third (and final) phase. After the revolution of Lenin and the dictatorship of Stalin, Khrushchev plunged the USSR into a 25-year period of decreasing authority and self-belief, and therefore, despite the brief flowering of hope and enthusiasm, it marks the beginning of the end for the USSR.

WHAT WAS THE IMPETUS FOR KHRUSHCHEV TO TRY TO REFORM THE SOVIET SYSTEM?

The aims of Khrushchev: the struggle for succession 1953-56

'I have saved us all.'

These are the words apparently spoken by Beria, head of the secret police and deputy premier, when he boasted to the Presidium (as the Politburo was then known) of his murder of Stalin. This is according to Molotov's memoirs, in which Beria claims that Stalin was planning to purge all the main communist figures below him. There is no definitive proof of any murder, but the power vacuum left by Stalin's death unleashed a frantic series of plots and alliances over three years that not only saw Khrushchev as leader, but also a new direction for the USSR as all politicians involved tried to distance themselves from Stalin's excesses. Beria himself was not saved; though seen as most likely to replace Stalin at the moment of the latter's death, he was the first to be ousted, and the only one to be shot, as Khrushchev worked his way to the leadership.

As Stalin lay dying in March 1953, the leading figures distributed his powers among themselves.

- Beria became in charge of a new Ministry of the Interior (MVD) which included state security.
- Malenkov, who worked in close conjunction with Beria, became chairman of the council of ministers as well as holding the position of Party secretary. Many saw this dual role as potentially powerful.
- Voroshilov took the position of 'president' of the USSR, though this had more status than power.
- Molotov, Kaganovich, Bulganin and Beria were all deputy chairmen of the Council of Ministers.
- Khrushchev received no appointment, but he had considerable power within the Party structure and the Presidium, after his close connection to Stalin in his last years. Within two weeks, in an effort to weaken the Beria–Malenkov alliance, the position of general secretary was transferred to Khrushchev. The collective leadership that was emerging decided that having one man as chairman of the council as well as Party secretary was too similar to Stalin by putting too much power into a single person's control.

1959 - May: Third Writers' Congress speech encourages liberals

July: Kitchen debate with Nixon

1960 - May: Khrushchev walks out of Paris 'peace' Summit over U-2 spy plane

1961 - April: *Vostok 1* launched with Yuri Gagarin

1959 1960 1961

The bulk of power lay within the central ministries based in Moscow, while the Party's influence was secondary. Indeed, Stalin had let 13 years pass before calling a Party congress. The ministries were headed by the Council of Ministers (formerly *Sovnarkom*). In reality, the Presidium controlled both the state executive and the Party. All the leading figures were also members of the Presidium, with over half the Presidium also council ministers. One of the key conflicts to emerge in the period following Stalin's death was whether the Presidium would dominate through the ministries or through the Party.

It was Beria who made the first move. As head of the security forces he was most tightly connected to the violence and extreme brutality of the Stalin era, as well as being personally close to Stalin. In an effort to distance himself from the blood of Stalin's rule, Beria tried to implement a less repressive regime and ordered an amnesty for all prisoners serving fewer than five years (though this excluded political prisoners) and offered the West the opportunity to reunite East and West Germany, as well as ordering political reforms in East Germany, which triggered a series of major uprisings there.

The other leaders were fully aware that Beria had enough secret documents to implicate them in Stalin's crimes, and Khrushchev organised the collective response. Beria was arrested, put on trial on the trumped-up charge of being a British spy, found guilty (the verdict was announced before the end of the trial) and immediately shot. In the trial, Beria was blamed for all the mistakes and terror of the Stalin era. The security services were renamed the KGB and put under control of the Party, with Ivan Serov as chairman of the committee for state security.

EXTEND YOUR KNOWLEDGE

Beria: the monster within the monster

Not only was Beria in charge of the notorious security services and most guilty by association of its innumerable crimes, he was personally responsible for many himself. Rumours had always been whispered about Beria's appetite for sexually assaulting young girls. After his death, the bones of five girls were found buried in his garden. Declassified archives reveal that his bodyguards wrote about how girls were abducted, drugged and raped. If they resisted or threatened to talk, they were killed. He may have instigated a more relaxed attitude in his policy, but he would certainly have also killed his rivals.

When arrested at the Presidium meeting, he was confident that his alliance with Malenkov would save him. Only when Malenkov turned against him and guards, secreted in another room, burst in to hold him at gunpoint, did he realise the seriousness of his situation. Khrushchev said later that Beria was expecting the meeting to be his triumphant ascendancy to power, not the mechanism of his death. He was innocent of being a British spy, but guilty of much worse. After his execution, inmates in the gulags (labour camps) celebrated, while the remaining members of the Presidium breathed a genuine sigh of relief.

Malenkov, however, took up the demands for liberalisation. He admitted that atomic war would be catastrophic for the whole world, though he was forced to amend the statement to just the capitalist world. He called for more consumer goods to improve Russian civilians' standard of living, and hinted at a 'new course' in relations with the West, where both sides could peacefully co-exist. He also attacked Khrushchev's agricultural scheme to plough up the 'virgin lands' (see Chapter 2) using mainly volunteers from *Komsomol*, the young Communist Party.

Early in 1955, Khrushchev led the attack on Malenkov by urging a more hardline approach. By uniting the others around him, especially the Stalinist Molotov, he forced Malenkov to resign. He revealed Malenkov's involvement in the Leningrad Affair of the late 1940s, where Stalin had purged Party officials based in Leningrad (as Petrograd had been called since 1924), as he felt they threatened his Moscow powerbase. Over 2,000 public officials and their relatives had been removed, with many imprisoned and several executed, and Malenkov was incriminated in fabricating the evidence against them. However, he was allowed to become minister of power stations, rather than suffering the usual swift execution. This showed a clear shift in policy from the Stalin years, and marked the point where Khrushchev was recognised as the USSR's leading politician, though not yet absolute head of state.

At this point, Khrushchev adopted most of Malenkov's more liberal policies. Just like Stalin in the 1920s, he was ideologically fluid enough to use policies as weapons in a power struggle. He was quite prepared to join an alliance to attack policies in order to vanquish a foe, and then adopt those same policies to attack his former allies. Like all the contenders for power, Khrushchev had risen to prominence under Stalin, but he had perhaps learnt the **Machiavellian** lesson best of all. Therefore the first impetus to reform was to manoeuvre himself into a position where he could assume power.

KEY TERM

Machiavellian

A negative term used to characterise unscrupulous politicians, as described by the 16th-century Italian philosopher Machiavelli in his book, *The Prince*. The term has come to describe a leader who rules with an immoral sense of deceit, deviousness, ambition and brutality. In short, the ends justify the means – though this was not Machiavelli's true meaning at all.

SOURCE 1

Molotov (left), Khrushchev and Stalin on the rostrum of the Lenin Mausoleum in Moscow's Red Square, watching an athletics parade in 1936.

SOURCE 2

From *Khrushchev Remembers* (1970), written by Khrushchev in the years between his removal from power in 1964 and his death in 1971. Recorded versions were smuggled out to the West. Though he says little about the infighting in the period surrounding Stalin's death, he offers something of the atmosphere of the time. Beria is portrayed as the tyrant eager to take over and immediately doing deals with Malenkov.

Stalin was dead, and at the time his death seemed like a terrible tragedy; but I feared the worst was still to come. Each of us took Stalin's death in his own way. I took his death very hard. To be honest, I took it hard not so much because I was attached to Stalin – though I *was* attached to him... I was disturbed by the composition of the Presidium which Stalin left behind and particularly by the place Beria was fixing for himself. It all portended serious complications and some unpleasant surprises – I would even say catastrophic consequences... There was no power on earth that could hold him back now. Nothing could get in his way. Now he could do whatever he saw fit... I couldn't control myself. I started to weep, too, and I wept sincerely over Stalin's death. I wasn't just weeping for Stalin. I was terribly worried about the future of the Party and the future of the country. I already sensed that Beria would start bossing everyone around and that this could be the beginning of the end.

Other factors influenced the trend towards reform. The most unpredictable one was the personality of Khrushchev himself.

ACTIVITY
KNOWLEDGE CHECK

Khrushchev and Stalin

1. What do Sources 1 and 2 suggest about the relationship between Stalin and Khrushchev?
2. Why might you not trust the views expressed in Source 2?

Khrushchev's personality

'That little Pinya – that's me.'

Khrushchev was fond of comparing himself with the shoemaker Pinya in a short story by Vinnichenko. He would retell the tale that the US CIA used this character as the basis for a personality profile to inform President Kennedy about Khrushchev at the 1961 Vienna Summit. In short, while in prison the apparently useless Pinya is elected as a joke to organise a committee to distribute goods fairly. To everyone's surprise, he does a great job. Then, during an escape, the prisoners are afraid to go first as they fear they will be shot. Pinya volunteers. He was a humble, common man whose natural ability meant that he rose to the challenges of the office he was elected to. The CIA read the story as a sign of Khrushchev's awareness of his working-class origins, pride in his achievements and confident ability in his position of power.

Khrushchev's background does not suggest he was destined for leadership, especially compared with the educated and cultured Malenkov, who was seen by western observers as the most likely to seize power. However, Khrushchev's personality had helped him climb the career ladder during the 1920s and 1930s, and get into the position where 'little Pinya' could excel.

Born in 1894 into a peasant family, he first became a metalworker. His drive to succeed saw him become a miners' leader, helping to organise strikes before the outbreak of the First World War. In 1918, he joined the Bolshevik Party and became a leading member of the soviet after the revolution. What Khrushchev may have lacked in academic education and culture, he made up for with energy, passion and a folksy wit from his Ukrainian background that many people found hard to deal with. First impressions were often of a boorish man with peasant manners, but this meant, crucially, that Khrushchev was under-estimated by other Party members.

He rose through the ranks in Moscow by showing unquestioning loyalty to Stalin, and was fully immersed in the purges, which opened up his various promotions. Importantly, in the Second World War, unlike the other members of Stalin's inner circle, he was directly involved in the defence of Stalingrad. Not only was this a lifelong source of pride, it also earned the respect and loyalty of the army, which proved vital in his power struggles in the 1950s. After the war, the ageing Stalin brought him in to counter the emerging alliance of Beria and Malenkov, as the politicians started to take up their positions for the succession of power.

Khrushchev's personality, then, was not definitively inclined towards reform; it was inclined to drive him to do whatever was necessary in order to succeed, while his almost oafish appearance gave him the cover to do it. If engaging in reform was required, then that was what he would do, especially as he had an affinity with the Russian people. He enjoyed travelling around the country, meeting and joking with workers in the factories and the fields. This was not the case with more 'sophisticated' audiences. In May 1959, he improvised a speech to the Third Writers' Congress in front of Russia's cultural elite. It was a mumbled, random mess and he felt he had to ask for forgiveness for his crude delivery and homespun observations. The fact that the Party leader would ask for forgiveness is revealing, but he had none of this insecurity when dealing with the masses. This ability to connect persuasively with the people also proved important in obtaining their support, as well as revealing in direct personal experiences their desire for reform.

SOURCE

Sir William Hayter, British ambassador to the USSR in the 1950s, commenting on Khrushchev's personality. He acknowledges that he, like many, underestimated the rough-and-ready Khrushchev, and noticed that at a dinner in 1954 Khrushchev struggled to follow the conversation, needing everything explained simply and carefully. He later admitted that when Khrushchev applied his intelligence and considerable memory he could master any subject.

He spoke in short sentences, in an emphatic voice and with great conviction... grinning good-naturedly... [Khrushchev was] like a little bull who, if aimed in the right direction, would charge along and be certain to arrive with a crash at its objective, knocking down anything that was in his way... the typical peasant as he appears in the classical Russian novels of the nineteenth century, sly, shrewd, suspicious, cautious under the appearance of abandon, fundamentally contemptuous of the *barin*, the master... Khrushchev's shoulder retained its chip, even when he was head of one of the greatest powers in history.

ACTIVITY
KNOWLEDGE CHECK

Khrushchev's personality

1 Sir William Hayter is hardly complimentary about Khrushchev, but how can Source 3 be used as evidence of the advantages that Khrushchev may have had in a leadership struggle?

2 How could the traits shown in the source also favour Khrushchev in implementing a programme of reform?

Khrushchev's personality helped him climb to power, while his closer contact with the Russian people, as well as a desire to distance himself from Stalin, pushed him towards reform. However, his personality also had aspects that harmed his prospects and reduced the likelihood of any reforms working. When in full flow, his overbearing and uncouth mannerisms could simply be embarrassing. In 1959, he became caught up in a public argument with US Vice-President Nixon at a US trade exhibition near Moscow, over the number of gadgets in a US household. What became known as the 'kitchen debate' was shown on Soviet television, and many Russians were ashamed at Khrushchev's undiplomatic lack of manners and threatening slang. In 1960, he walked out of the Paris 'peace' Summit over a U-2 spy plane incident, acutely embarrassing the other members of the Soviet delegation. Later that year, he banged his shoe on the table to interrupt a speech by the British prime minister at the UN General Assembly. While Khrushchev saw this as highly amusing, leading members of the Presidium felt that his personality undermined both his reputation and any reforms.

SOURCE

Khrushchev visits the French village of Pleurs, during the Paris 'peace' Summit in 1960. He walked out of the summit, to the discomfiture of his fellow Russians. Here the larger-than-life Khrushchev uses an axe to split a tree trunk that is blocking his path. In 1969, he claimed that his actions at the summit marked the beginning of the problems that would eventually remove him in 1964, as he could no longer contain hardliners in the Soviet military.

In conclusion, Khrushchev's personality helped to place him in a position where he could take power, especially as his many rivals under-estimated him. Becoming leader was his ultimate aim, and a programme of reform would not only achieve that but would also help to remove rivals, especially by revealing their involvement in the murderous purges under Stalin. Khrushchev may have genuinely felt reforms were needed from his contacts with the regional peoples and officials of Russia, but he was equally prepared to denounce reform if this furthered his cause. In truth, he naturally favoured the status quo where the leaders told the others what to do, but the death of Stalin and the growth of more educated classes were starting to put strains on this system, which Khrushchev was able to pick up. He was just as steeped in the crimes of the 1930s, but these were conveniently ignored. When he did initiate reform, it was with the full zeal and passion of his dominant if unpolished personality, yet those traits also helped to derail his rule and perhaps meant his reforms lacked sufficient forethought and planning to make them successful, as his agricultural policies show.

Khrushchev and the Party

Khrushchev held the key Party position after wresting the post of general secretary from Malenkov a few weeks after Stalin's death. In the early 1920s, Stalin had used his position as general secretary to move loyal supporters into positions of power. Khrushchev did likewise. After Malenkov's dismissal, Khrushchev moved his ally, Bulganin, into the vacant position on the Council of Ministers, while the disgraced Malenkov quietly sought alliances with the more hardline Molotov and Kaganovich.

The leading politicians had formed two distinct camps: administrators, who happened to be Party members, who had enjoyed decades of influence and tended to favour Malenkov's approach, and Party members who dutifully administered the country and who tended to favour Khrushchev. Despite Bulganin's appointment, Khrushchev did not yet have the power to control the key positions in central government, so he focused on those within the Party. Here, he could use patronage to move former colleagues from his days in both the Ukraine and Moscow, or those who had lost out to Beria's or Malenkov's own intrigues, into positions such as regional Party secretaries or within the Party's machinery in Moscow. He gave them more power and removed police supervision of the posts. Any bright and ambitious young officials keen on a promotion over their superiors could align themselves with Khrushchev and wait for the call.

Here, he was applying the *nomenklatura* system used by Stalin. It was a list of available jobs and the available Party people to fill them. Khrushchev, as Party secretary, could make the appointments and thereby create a 'tail' of loyal subordinates. To counteract other leaders' 'tails' was a complicated game of opportunistic promotions, alliances and attacks, which needed both skill and luck to master. The luck was that Stalin had killed most of the truly clever politicians, but the skill was Khrushchev's reliance on the Party over the bureaucratic conservatism represented by Malenkov's faction. It is estimated that by the time of the Twentieth Congress in February 1956, Khrushchev had the direct loyalty of a third of the Congress. He mirrored these actions in the various communist republics that made up the USSR, by appointing his men to jobs such as top police officers and agricultural posts. This new development of the Party represented a clear break from the Stalin days, or perhaps a return to Lenin's days, and therefore naturally encouraged a more reforming attitude to go with it. In conjunction with Khrushchev's agricultural changes and ideas on foreign policy, it was a change in how politics should be done, with an emphasis on Party and mass participation, rather than the more closed bureaucratic circles of old. This linked with his personality and origins. It was Khrushchev who allowed people to buy a ticket to visit the previously forbidden Kremlin. Under Stalin, you could not even photograph it, but Khrushchev showed his common touch by allowing a New Year's ball and even a Christmas tree for the children in 1953.

Khrushchev's championing of the Party eventually culminated in the 'Anti-Party' Coup of 1957.

Pressure from the prison system

According to Beria's 1953 amnesty, only 221,435 of the 2,526,402 prisoners in the labour camps, or gulags, were too dangerous to the state to be released, and therefore a total of around a million people were freed, including all under 18, women with children under ten and pregnant women. Plots against Stalin, such as the Doctor's Plot, in which the Kremlin doctors were accused of poisoning Soviet leaders, were announced as having been fabricated and a general rehabilitation process began.

When Stalin died in March 1953, the response by the inmates in the camps was mixed. While some expressed hope that the terror was over, others felt shock and fear of the unknown and even grief for the fallen dictator. When Beria's death was announced in December that year, however, there was simply unrestrained joy from the camps. Since the end of the Second World War, as thousands of army officers, troops and civilians, who had been previously captured by the Germans, were transferred into the gulags as 'traitors to the USSR', trouble had regularly broken out, and Beria's death quickly encouraged more.

The most serious uprising was at Kengir camp in Kazakhstan, where 13,000 prisoners went on strike in the summer of 1954. The guards hesitated, uncertain from which direction the political wind was blowing. Excessive force could be seen as a sign of loyalty to the deceased Beria, while being unable to break the strike would be just as bad. This allowed the inmates to seize the camp and set up their own provisional government, headed mainly by former army officers. After 42 days, the state sent in tanks, killed 700 and regained control. However, the collective leadership had shown as clearly as possible the inadequacy of the prison and judicial system. The Central Committee set up an investigative commission under Pyotr Pospelov, a former editor of *Pravda*, briefed to make a full report on the repression of Party members from 1935 to 1940.

Meanwhile, work cautiously began on rehabilitating the innocent, some posthumously, with around 1,000 completed by the end of 1953, though these were chiefly the political elite and their relatives. They included the widow of Khrushchev's son, who had been accused of being a Swedish spy, as well as Molotov's wife, who had been accused of being a US and Israeli spy. Each individual case had to be reviewed by the Soviet Procuracy, a government department designed to supervise administrative legality, which slowed the process down. By 1955, some 250,000 appeals from political prisoners had been heard, but only four percent of prisoners were released. Between 1953 and 1960, some two million were released from the gulags, with another two million returned from exile in 'special settlements'. Some 750,000 former prisoners were rehabilitated, even though for the majority it was decades after their execution. The process was drawn out and arduous, and the authorities were obtuse in their dealings with people's lives. Rehabilitation brought no forgiveness or apology from the state, or even a sense that the victim was truly innocent. Information was blocked, or simply lost in the bureaucratic swamp.

The returning prisoners had two effects. Firstly, they created a significant class that was more ready to question the authorities openly. Secondly, they also highlighted an obvious question: how could the authorities hope to explain what had happened in the past with so many miscarriages of justice? Any criticism would need to avoid blaming the communist system, while at the same time concealing the personal involvement of all the Soviet leaders. Pospelov's report, delivered to the Presidium on 9 February 1956, provided the solution not only to this question, but also to that of how Khrushchev could cement his place as leader of the USSR: Khrushchev used the report to attack the legacy and stature of Stalin. By making such a definite break with Stalin, the period of reforms could begin, indeed had to begin, and help Khrushchev undermine his opponents, who tried to erode any reform.

SOURCE

Anna Akhmatova, one of the first great poets banned by Stalin, writing about the release of political prisoners in March 1956. Her husband was executed in 1921 and her son imprisoned in the gulag in 1935. Her poetry, despite official ridicule, was learnt by heart across Russia, though it was banned at the time of Stalin's death.

Now those who were arrested will return and two Russias will look each other in the eye: the one that sent people to the camps and the one that was sent away.

SOURCE

Khrushchev, according to his 1970 autobiography, *Khrushchev Remembers*, responding to the 1956 revelation in Pospelov's report that the persecution of political prisoners in the 1930s was based on fabricated evidence. This would become a key component for his 'Secret Speech'.

Comrades, what are we going to do about Comrade Pospelov's findings? What are we going to do about all those who were arrested and eliminated? The Congress is coming to a close, and we'll all disperse without having said a single word about the abuses committed under Stalin. We now know that the people who suffered during the repressions were innocent. We have indisputable proof that, far from being enemies of the people, they were honest men and women, devoted to the Party, devoted to the Revolution, devoted to the Leninist cause and to the building of Socialism and Communism in the Soviet Union. We can't keep people in exile or in the camps back any longer. We must figure out how to bring them back.

ACTIVITY
KNOWLEDGE CHECK

Pressure from the prison system

1 How do Sources 5 and 6 demonstrate the problems faced by Russia in 1956 as a result of the release of prisoners and the Pospelov report?

2 What possible solutions could there be for Khrushchev's rhetorical questions in Source 6?

A Level Exam-Style Question Section B

To what extent was the atmosphere for reform in 1956 the result of Khrushchev's personality? (20 marks)

Tip

Though the essay question is asking for a range of factors to explain a historical question, there is no single correct answer or 'universal key factor'. The skill in constructing a response is to evaluate the evidence for all the factors and attempt to link them together in a reasoned analysis. The exact degree of each factor's influence will also be partly governed by the individual writing the essay. Therefore do not get too focused on getting the answer 'right', but focus instead on how it is explained.

WHY DID KHRUSHCHEV INITIATE DE-STALINISATION THROUGH HIS 'SECRET SPEECH' IN 1956?

The Pospelov report shocked the Presidium, not just because of the scale of the arrests but because of the degree of fabrication of the evidence. However, the Presidium was split over the extent to which the report should be disclosed. Khrushchev wanted it read out in full to restore the people's faith in the Party, while Molotov and Kaganovich felt this might undermine the communist regime beyond repair. A compromise was reached whereby half the report would be revealed.

This was a real gamble by Khrushchev and the whole Presidium. It was not a great step from criticising Stalin to criticising the entire communist system. One problem was that Khrushchev had already given the opening report to the Twentieth Party Congress, before the Presidium had decided on its appropriate response to Pospelov's findings, and he had failed to indicate any concerns over the Stalin era. Therefore, it would look strange to deliver such an individual condemnation so suddenly. The solution was to give the speech to a closed session of the Central Committee and invited guests in what became known, quite inaccurately, as the 'Secret Speech'.

According to his memoirs, Khrushchev wished to end individuals' fear of repression and abuse by the Party, and thereby allow the Party to safely progress towards the true path of communism. However, the speech also presented a tactical opportunity to undermine his rivals: they would have to publicly back Khrushchev or be condemned with Stalin's legacy. Hence, it played a valuable role in gaining the support Khrushchev needed for his economic reforms. The speech would be a defence of the Party and, as the leading figure of the Party (the foundation of his influence), Khrushchev would deliver the four-hour, 20,000-word-long speech entitled 'The Speech on the Personality Cult and its Consequences'. It was an edited version of Pospelov's report, intercut with short passages by Khrushchev. Its sheer length could be seen as evidence that it had existed before the Congress began, and that therefore an under-pressure Khrushchev was acting to make the best of a bad situation and present himself as the only one brave enough to speak the truth, though an earlier speech at the Congress by Mikoyan, the minister of trade, did show a lack of respect to Stalin and mentioned names of purged Party members.

A Level Exam-Style Question Section A

Study Source 7 before you answer this question.

Assess the value of the source for revealing the motivations for Khrushchev delivering the 'Secret Speech' and the nature of the power struggle within the Communist Party of the USSR in 1956.

Explain your answer using the source, the information given about it and your own knowledge of the historical context. (20 marks)

Tip

This topic is set in the years 1956–61, but the question above requires some information from before 1956, particularly relating to the power struggle. However, any information from before 1956 must be made relevant to, and linked with, the events of 1956, in this case the 'Secret Speech'. Always write about the dates set in the question.

SOURCE

From *Khrushchev Remembers* (1970), in which Khrushchev recalls his difficulties in persuading the other leading Presidium members to agree to the speech. Khrushchev is tape-recording his memoirs once he has been removed from power and for publication in the West, not in the USSR where, by the time of his death in 1971, he was ignored by Soviet historians and politicians.

As soon as I finished speaking, everyone started attacking me,... [I said] 'Word will get out about what happened under Stalin, and then the finger will be pointed straight at us.'

Kaganovich chimed in, fiercely opposing me along the same lines. His position wasn't one of profound philosophical analysis of the Party issues involved. No, he was arguing against me out of selfish fear for his own hide. He was motivated entirely by his eagerness to escape any responsibility for what had happened..., Kaganovich wanted to make sure his own tracks were covered.

I answered these attacks as calmly and convincingly as I could... Sooner or later people will be coming out of the prisons and the camps, and they'll return to the cities. They'll tell their relatives, friends, comrades, and everyone back home what happened... I ask you to think about something else, comrades, we are conducting the first Congress after Stalin's death, and therefore we're obliged to make a clean breast to the delegates about the conduct of the Party leadership during the years in question... Therefore, comrades, I ask you to support me... to say that we didn't know anything would be a lie... and we must tell the Congress what we know.

Some knew what was happening and some even got their own noses dirty in the events we're speaking about. I'm prepared... to bear my share of the responsibility...

This time Molotov objected... Voroshilov protested vehemently that what I was proposing needn't be done... I decided to try the following device... May I remind you that every Presidium member has the right to speak at the Congress and to express his own point of view, even if it doesn't coincide with the line set by the General Report... If we are going to make a clean breast of the abuses committed by Stalin, then we must do so now, at the Twentieth Party Congress... Everyone finally agreed reluctantly that a speech should be given.

That left the question of who should actually get up and deliver the speech. They said I should make the speech... If Pospelov, another Central Committee Secretary, delivers the speech, it will make people wonder, 'Why didn't Khrushchev say anything about this business in his General Report?... If you don't give the speech it could contribute to the impression of dissension in the leadership.' This argument deserved consideration, and finally I gave in.

The speech given on the final day of the Congress, 25 February 1956, despite its length and revelations, was also very limited in its target. On Stalin, the speech was unrelenting.

- Stalin was guilty of a blatant abuse of his powers and a lust for personal power which betrayed the ideas of Leninism and the Party. Here, Khrushchev revealed the existence of the 1922–23 document known as 'Lenin's Testament' and its postscript, in which an ill Lenin roundly condemned Stalin and demanded that he be removed from any position of power for the good of the Party. In an effort to present a unified Party appearance after Lenin's death, the Testament had been suppressed.
- Stalin was personally responsible for the purges, with 70 percent of the Party Central Committee shot, mostly during their 1937–38 peak. Individual Party members were mentioned, with details of their tortures, forced confessions and fabricated evidence read out. Stalin's role in the 1934 murder of Party favourite Kirov was noted, as were the imagined 'Doctor's Plot' and 'Leningrad Affair'.
- Failures in foreign policy were highlighted, particularly the conflict with Yugoslavia and its leader Josip Broz Tito, who refused to acknowledge Stalin as his superior and therefore incurred Stalin's anger.
- Khrushchev was most emotional when attacking Stalin's record in the Second World War. He branded Stalin a coward who never visited the front line, and ridiculed him for using a globe rather than a map when planning military campaigns.
- The root of this abuse was Stalin's cult of personality, which evolved over many years. It was his obsession for eminence that had distorted and perverted communist values. Stalin had falsified Party history and his biography to encourage people to worship him. Khrushchev attacked the naming of institutions and places after Stalin.
- The speech was carefully constructed to cast suspicion on rivals like Molotov, Kaganovich and Malenkov, while diverting attention from his own past. For the leading Party members, he claimed that ignorance hid most of the crimes, and that the Presidium was too divided and had acted too late to resist.

The speech did not remain secret for long. Though the closed session was instructed to keep it secret, a transcript was sent to Party organisations to be read out to Communist Party members, while other copies were sent to communist leaders in the Eastern Bloc. From Poland, a copy was leaked to the USA, where it was published in June 1956, and subsequently copies of this version were smuggled back into the communist world. Though some countries, such as East Germany, had tried to suppress the speech, they could do little to stem its spread through the entire population. In the transcript that was published in the West, tumultuous prolonged applause was noted by the audience. However, the speech was in fact met by a deathly hush, as shock set in.

There were strict limits to the speech, even in its denunciation of Stalin. Its focus was from 1934 onwards, with no examination of Stalin's rivals in the 1920s struggle for power, such as Trotsky or Bukharin. The Communist Party was Stalin's victim, with no mention of the millions of others, the ordinary citizens, who suffered and died under his regime. The speech ended with a toast to Leninism and the Party.

SOURCE

Mikoyan, who had worked with Lenin, Stalin and Khrushchev and would go on to work with Brezhnev, was later asked whether the 'Secret Speech' could be applied beyond criticism of the show trials and to the trials before 1934 which dealt with Stalin's rivals. From A. Hochschild, *The Unquiet Ghost: Russians Remember Stalin* (1994).

No, they can't. If they were, it would be clear that the country was not being run by a legal government, but by a group of gangsters. Which, in point of fact, we were.

Even so, the reaction to the speech showed the divisions within the Party, split between Stalin's loyal supporters, who had risen in the purges, and those who secretly hated him. Whatever the individual's view on Stalin, the 25-year spell of Stalin's omniscience and omnipotence had been broken and all were left with a void that they were uncertain how to fill.

EXTRACT

From William Taubman's *Khrushchev: The Man and His Era*, published in 2003, in which he charts the reaction of Party members who were present at the speech. Taubman, a political scientist, won the Pulitzer Prize for biography with this influential book.

Vladimir Semichastny remembered it, the speech was at first met with 'a deathly silence; you could hear a bug fly by.'... Zakhar Glukhov .. felt 'anxious and joyous at the same time' and marvelled at how Khrushchev 'could have brought himself to say such things before such an audience.' Dimitri Goriunov, the chief editor of *Komsomolskaya pravda*, took five nitroglycerin pills for a weak heart. 'We didn't look at each other in the eye as we came down from the balcony,' recalled Aleksandr Yakovlev, then a minor functionary for the Central Committee Propaganda Department and later Gorbachev's partner in perestroika, 'whether from shame or shock or from the simple unexpectedness of it, I don't know.' As the delegates left the hall, all Yakovlev heard them muttering was *'Da-a, da-a, da-a,'* as if compressing all the intense, conflicting emotions they felt in the single, safe word, 'yes.'... 'We already knew a lot,' Chernoutsan [the Central Committee's cultural specialist] later wrote, 'but we were stunned by the way the truth caved in on us. But was it the whole truth? And how to distinguish the real social tragedy from the accusations that the speaker was angrily flinging this way and that.'

The more junior and mid-level state officials favoured the speech as they were too young to be held responsible. They formed a 1960s generation, known as *shestidesiatniki*, who felt that the return of the revolutionary Party could be begun again after the Stalinist interruption. They included the children of old Bolsheviks or the children – such as Mikhail Gorbachev – of those repressed in the 1930s. Gorbachev, as leader in the 1980s (see Chapter 7), organised a conference to remember the 'Secret Speech' and celebrate the gamble Khrushchev took. He saw himself and his reforming companions as 'the children of the Twentieth Congress'.

The more senior Party officials were less enthusiastic in their response. There were anecdotal reports of suicides and heart attacks, while two full members of the Presidium were added: Andrei Kirichenko and Mikhail Suslov, both loyal to Khrushchev. Fifty-four candidate members were added, the vast majority of whom were Khrushchev supporters, including Leonid Brezhnev, Marshal Georgy Zhukov and Dmitry Shepilov. By June 1956, Shepilov had replaced Molotov as foreign minister. Therefore, the speech can be seen to have strengthened Khrushchev's hold on power.

The confusion caused by the speech went far beyond the Party. In Stalin's homeland of Georgia, riots against the speech resulted in violent clashes, with the most serious causing dozens of casualties in Tbilisi during early March. On the other hand, many rejoiced at the speech and, as the leadership had feared, saw it as a call for further reforms.

SOURCE

Liudmilla Alexeyeva, a Moscow University student and later a well-known dissident, on the immediate impact of the speech. From L. Alexeyeva and P. Goldberg, *The Thaw Generation: Coming of Age in the Post-Stalin Era* (1990).

The congress put an end to our lonely questioning of the Soviet system. Young men and women began to lose their fear of sharing views, information, beliefs, questions. Every night we gathered in cramped apartments to recite poetry, read 'unofficial' prose and swap stories that, taken together, yielded a realistic picture of what was going on in our country.

These views were mainly from the intelligentsia, while the majority of the population had lived for too long in Stalin's shadow to openly question the system. However, the demands for civil rights prompted Khrushchev to send out a secret circular in June 1956 to regional Party executives, ordering the arrest of individuals who took their interpretation too far, while the Presidium wrote an article on the correct, or required, interpretation.

The effect of the speech on Eastern Europe was to encourage dissent against both the USSR and local communist leaders. Moscow had to order the Polish authorities to repress riots and demonstrations, though the Polish authorities did introduce some internal concessions. This was the spark for more radical concessions in Hungary. In October, Khrushchev sent in the tanks, which met with fierce resistance from the protesters.

When the Hungarian prime minister, Imre Nagy, took control, it looked as if the situation would follow the Polish model, but he then announced that Hungary would leave the **Warsaw Pact**. Khrushchev felt that this could quickly lead to the collapse of the Eastern Bloc, so in November the tanks rolled into Hungary once more and 20,000 civilians were killed. Nagy was taken to Moscow and executed in 1958 as a lesson for other Eastern Bloc leaders. Khrushchev's grieving over the bloodshed of Stalin's days did not extend to his own.

KEY TERM

Warsaw Pact
An organisation set up in 1955 as a response to NATO – the defensive organisation of the West created in 1949 whose membership was based on western nations around the Atlantic Ocean. The Pact was meant to be a defence alliance binding all the Eastern European communist states to the USSR. Its charter promised that internal affairs were independent, but it allowed Moscow to decide just what 'internal' meant.

Khrushchev's dire management of the Hungarian Uprising, despite registering little reaction in the average Soviet citizen, sharpened Presidium opposition against him. Hungary, now under the loyal leadership of Janos Kadar, needed funds for reconstruction, while de-Stalinisation had alienated both Albania and China. The uncertainty within the USSR saw many leading figures become increasingly uneasy over Khrushchev. This feeling increased as Khrushchev engaged in a flurry of trips and took apparent delight in appearing on the front page of the press, despite his 'aversion' to a cult of personality. The time was right for an overthrow.

ACTIVITY
KNOWLEDGE CHECK

Khrushchev's 'Secret Speech'

1 Do you agree with the view expressed in Source 8? Could Khrushchev have dated the abuses from 1924, or widened the scope to include non-Party members without destroying the communist regime completely?

2 How does Extract 1 demonstrate the psychological impact of the speech on the Central Committee?

3 Why would Khrushchev be worried by the views of Liudmilla Alexeyeva in Source 9? Is there any reason why this should not concern him so much?

The 'Anti-Party' Group, 1957

The trigger for the attempt to remove Khrushchev was the continuing battle over the Party and the administration. Khrushchev had been removing planning and financial responsibilities from the central government ministries throughout 1955 and 1956. Then, in May 1957, he created over a hundred councils of the national economy (*sovnarkhozy*) which eliminated the central ministries altogether. His rivals in the Presidium had to react if they wanted to keep their influence at government level. Molotov led the revolt and, with Malenkov, Voroshilov and

Kaganovich, he called a Presidium meeting for 18 June 1957. They would give Khrushchev a choice of either quietly becoming minister for agriculture or being arrested. Either way, Molotov would assume leadership. Khrushchev was accused of economic voluntarism, which was shorthand for implementing ill-conceived and hasty policies, but the main charge was diluting the authority of the Communist Party through his de-Stalinisation.

Only three full members of the Presidium supported Khrushchev: Mikoyan, Suslov and Kirichenko. Seven opposed him, with Bulganin the leading defector. Though Khrushchev had the support of the five candidate members, including Zhukov and Brezhnev, they could not actually vote. Sensing victory for what Khrushchev called the 'Anti-Party', Shepilov switched to Molotov's side. The Presidium demanded that Khrushchev stand down, but here the leader showed his toughness and ability to fight back.

Zhukov, the hero of the Second World War and now minister for defence, announced that the army would obey only him, and that he was loyal to Khrushchev. This gave Khrushchev the time to argue that only the Central Committee had the power to dismiss him. By the night of 19 June, Khrushchev's aides were drafting letters from Committee members demanding a plenum, or full meeting. Here he was restoring little-used powers to the Committee which previously had just rubber-stamped the Presidium's orders. The Party was imposing its domination over the administration.

Zhukov's military connections, with help from the KGB, organised planes to fly pro-Khrushchev members from all over the country. His patronage of regional Party executives was paying off. By 20 June, the 'Anti-Party' was in retreat and, on 22 June, the plenum met for a marathon six-day session.

Even from the start, the 'Anti-Party' had lost, and Zhukov was allowed to lead the counter-attack by accusing the conspirators of complicity in Stalin's crimes. The Presidium was enlarged to include Khrushchev's allies, including Zhukov and Brezhnev as full members, while the coup's leaders were removed from positions of power. They were not arrested or even expelled from the Party, but bureaucratically exiled in the remoter parts of Russia. Molotov was sent to Mongolia as Soviet ambassador, Malenkov was sent to manage a power station in Siberia, and Kaganovich was given a cement factory to run in Sverdlovsk. Others, like Bulganin and Voroshilov, were so weak that Khrushchev could afford to let them be for the moment.

SOURCE

After the 1957 plot failed, Kaganovich, fearing for his life, called Khrushchev to beg for mercy and not be dealt with in the 'Stalinist manner'. This was Khrushchev's gleefully delivered response.

Comrade Kaganovich, your words confirm once again what methods you wanted to use to attain your vile ends. You wanted the country to revert to the order that existed under the personality cult. You wanted to kill people. You measure others by your own yardstick. But you are mistaken. We apply Leninist principles with vigour and will continue to apply them. You will be given a job. You will be able to work and live in peace if you work honestly like all Soviet people.

Bulganin was forced to resign within a year, and Khrushchev took over his role. He was now first secretary of the Party and prime minister of the government, and controlled the Presidium. The Party dominated the government, and would continue to do so until 1989. For the time being, Khrushchev's position as supreme ruler was safe. Khrushchev was the chief personality and, to be sure of this, he quickly dismissed Zhukov, the man who had done most to save him. Zhukov was accused of the classic Bolshevik charge of 'Bonapartism', the desire to use the army to turn the revolution into a dictatorship as Napoleon had done in France. (This charge had also been aimed at Kerensky, Kornilov and Trotsky.) Zhukov had proved too independent by introducing army reforms without consulting the Party, and Khrushchev dismissed him, rewrote the history books to blame Zhukov for the failures of 1941, and gradually promoted officials he knew and trusted from his days in Stalingrad in the Second World War.

To his credit, Khrushchev never imposed a dictatorship on the USSR, despite fostering his own cult. He always relied on the Party apparatus to support his policies through the majority vote. Nor did he use the terror system that was Stalin's automatic reaction to opposition or dissent, real or imagined. The events of 1956 and 1957 showed Khrushchev to be a politician who was prepared to gamble and risk all. In many ways, it was a return to the Leninist principles of the Party ruling the state and, like Lenin, Khrushchev was practical in how this should be achieved. There are elements of self-deception and numerous examples of hypocrisy, but perhaps these were required to smash the brutal rule of Stalin and allow socialism to take a new path, or new course as Malenkov called it.

EXTRACT

From William Taubman's *Khrushchev: The Man and His Era* (2003). Taubman is retelling a story told by Fydor Burlatsky, a Party operative, who was present when Khrushchev was describing the occasion of his 'Secret Speech' to a group of foreign communist leaders in 1960.

As he spoke, Khrushchev waved a glass in the air, 'spilling brandy on the white tablecloth and frightening those next to him without being aware of it himself.' Only later 'did he carefully place the glass on the table, thus releasing his right hand which was absolutely essential to add conviction to his words.' Why had he given that speech at the Twentieth Congress? The answer required telling a story he read in school: 'There were these political prisoners in jail under tsarism – Socialist Revolutionaries, Mensheviks and Bolsheviks. Among them was a shoemaker named Pinya... And that's what I did in the Twentieth Congress,' Khrushchev continued. 'Since I was chosen to be First [Secretary], I had to – like the shoemaker Pinya. I was obliged to tell the truth about the past, whatever the risks to me.'

ACTIVITY
KNOWLEDGE CHECK

The 'Secret Speech', 1956, and the 'Anti-Party' Group, 1957

1. Using Source 10 and your own knowledge, why do you think Khrushchev allowed the members of the 'Anti-Party' to be punished with demotion and not arrest or worse?
2. Is Extract 2 a valid self-assessment by Khrushchev for the reasons for his 'Secret Speech'? What are the indications from the source and from your own knowledge that this might not be the case?

A Level Exam-Style Question
Section A

Study Source 11 before you answer this question.

Assess the value of this source for revealing the reasons behind the attempted coup against Khrushchev as well as the policies of Khrushchev's reform programme.

Explain your answer using the source, the information given about it and your own knowledge of the historical context. (20 marks)

Tip

Knowledge of the historical context should be used to both support and challenge the content gained from the source material. It is important to think about the context of the values and concerns of the society or group from which the source was drawn. What the source misses out, or merely hints at, can be as important in the answer as what the source clearly states.

SOURCE 11 On 4 July 1957, *Pravda*, the official newspaper of the Communist Party of the USSR, published the findings of the Central Committee Plenum that Khrushchev convened in order to give him their support after the attempted coup led by the so-called 'Anti-Party'.

The Central Committee plenum of 22-29 June 1957 considered the question of the anti-party group of Malenkov, Kaganovich and Molotov... With the aim of changing the party's political line this group sought through anti-party factional methods to replace the party's leading bodies elected by the CC plenum.

This was no accident.

During the past three to four years, when the party has resolutely set its course at overcoming the errors and shortcomings fostered by the cult of personality... when the party has made an enormous effort to correct past distortions of the Leninist nationality policy, the members of this anti-party group - discovered and fully exposed - kept up constant direct or indirect opposition to the course adopted by the Twentieth Congress of the CPSU. This group effectivity sought to reverse the Leninist course... They were against broadening the rights of the union republics in economic, cultural and legislative matters, and also opposed strengthening the role of local soviets in resolving these tasks... The anti-party group not only failed to understand, but even opposed, the Party's struggle against bureaucratism, designed to reduce the size of the inflated state apparatus...

This group sternly opposed and tried to undermine such important measures as the reorganisation of industrial management, the creation of economic councils [*sovnarkhozy*] and economic regions... On agricultural issues the members of this group failed to understand the need to increase material incentives for the collective farm peasantry to stimulate agricultural output. They opposed the abolition of the old bureaucratic system of planning in collective farms...

Comrades Malenkov, Kaganovich and Molotov stubbornly resisted those measures, which the Central Committee and our party pursued to overcome the consequences of the cult of personality, to eliminate the violations of revolutionary legality that had occurred and to create conditions that would preclude their recurrence...

The CC plenum resolves:

1 To condemn as incompatible with the Leninist principles of our party the factional activities of the anti-party group...

2 To expel Comrades Malenkov, Kaganovich and Molotov from membership of the Presidium of the Central Committee.

THINKING HISTORICALLY Interpretations (6a)

Ever-changing history

Our interpretations of the past change as we change. This may be because our social attitudes alter over time, perhaps a historian constructs a new theory or perhaps technology allows archaeologists to discover something new.

1 Work in pairs. Make a timeline that starts with 1956 and ends 50 years in the future. Construct reactions that illustrate the point when time changes history. In the 'future' box you can speculate how people might react to the event in 50 years' time. Below is an example that you can finish if you want to.

1956	1957	1970	1991	2066
Event: Khrushchev delivers the 'Secret Speech'	Hungarian citizen: 'This is a chance for freedom.' USA diplomat: 'This is a trick.' Chinese leader: 'A betrayal of Marxism.'	Russian leader: 'The speech and Khrushchev must be ignored.' Russian dissident: 'The speech changed nothing.'	Russian leader: 'The speech was a brave attempt and the right idea.' Western historian: 'The speech was the beginning of the end of the communist authority.'	?

2 Answer the following questions.

a) Identify three factors that have affected how Khrushchev's 'Secret Speech' is interpreted over time, or might affect it in the future.

b) If a historian wrote a book proposing a new interpretation of Khrushchev's thaw, how might other historians react? What would affect their reaction? How will the future change the past?

HOW DEEP WERE KHRUSHCHEV'S REFORMS TO THE ADMINISTRATION?

Nothing symbolises the Khrushchev years better than the Soviet achievements in the space race. In 1957, Russia launched the first satellite into space with *Sputnik*, resulting in a panicked terror in the USA when its radio signal was picked up soaring a few hundred miles overhead. On 12 April 1961, the *Vostok* spacecraft took Yuri Gagarin, the first human in space, around the globe. Russia was outdoing the USA. Gagarin toured the world, preaching the value of collective work as thousands of workers worked on the space programme. It seemed as if communism would be the ideology to explore and fill the universe, and Khrushchev loved every moment.

SOURCE 12

Khrushchev with his wife Nina Petrovna, and cosmonaut Yuri Gagarin and his wife Valentina, spending time together in a much-photographed visit to the Kremlin. Here they are reading media reports of the outstanding success of the *Vostok* mission. Gagarin was sent around the world, where he was greeted by hysterical crowds.

SOURCE 13

Khrushchev's unbridled pleasure at Soviet success in the space race. Here he is speaking at a gala reception for Yuri Gagarin in Moscow in April 1961. From *Pravda*, 15 April 1961.

> Arrogant commentators told us that Russians with their bast [birch bark] shoes and footcloths would never be a great power, but once-illiterate Russia has pioneered the path into space... That's what you've done, Yuri! Let everyone who has sharpened their claws against us know this! Let them know that Yurka was in space; that he saw everything; that he knows everything!

However, as the 1960s went on, Soviet success, with Valentina Tereshkova as the first woman in space and Alexei Leonov the first person to walk in space, was based on unrealistic expectations and stripped-down safety features. Sergei Korolyov, the mastermind behind rocket development, who had been violently purged in 1938, died in 1966. Russia's luck ran out. The next mission was forced to fly to coincide with May Day celebrations. The experienced pilot, Vladmir Komarov, knew the ship was not worthy: he plunged into the earth, his last words condemning those who killed him. A year later, his friend Gagarin, the most famous man on the planet, died in a plane collision. The early enthusiasm and promise had dissipated through Party interference, lack of planning and ignoring the advice of experts. Stunning, even pioneering, success at the start was followed by failure, disaster and policy collapse.

As with the space programme, Khrushchev's economic policies stagnated, his agricultural dreams withered and died in barren soils, even his foreign policy of peaceful co-existence was halted as crisis followed crisis, from the 1961 Berlin Wall to the 1962 Cuban Missile Crisis. His administration reforms suffered the same fate, with good ideas stifled by poor implementation and constant adjustment.

Decentralisation

Linked with the power struggle between Party and administration, Khrushchev embarked on a move to decentralise power and give more initiative to the people. This tended to go hand-in-hand with the policy of democratisation in which the traditional bureaucracy was weakened by transferring more responsibility to the people. Discussion about applying political decisions at a local, or grass-root, level was allowed, but the central Party would retain control over the political direction of the policies. The creation of *sovnarkhozy* can be seen as an example of this, but decentralisation took it further, though this gave rise to tensions as it contradicted the Party's dominance. The *sovnarkhozy* might have triggered the 'Anti-Party' Group, but the local party organisations that gained powers did not show much gratitude to Khrushchev. The scheme was full of inefficient and bureaucratic levels, and the *sovnarkhozy* lasted no longer than Khrushchev himself.

A further measure taken to promote decentralisation was to expand membership of the Party, which rose from seven million (3.6 percent of the population) in 1956 to 11 million (4.8 percent) by 1964. By expanding the base of the Party with working-class citizens, it could be said that power was drawn off the top level in Moscow. Non-Party members were invited to take supervisory roles and even attend the Party congress, while limits on terms of duty for Party officials were introduced. Plans were drafted to split the Party into urban and rural levels (these were enacted in 1962, but failed to work efficiently). Mass participation was favoured to generate popular enthusiasm for reform, especially as Stalinist terror and repression would not be used to coerce the masses. Street patrols were given the legal powers for their millions of local volunteers to combat individuals not sharing the new vision or doing their bit for Russia. Public courts with citizen jurors judged on minor cases. It was the same attempt to generate grass-root optimism that saw thousands volunteer to work on the 'virgin lands'.

However, it would be a severe exaggeration to declare that the decentralisation of power in Russia was complete under Khrushchev. The Presidium and Central Committee still ran the show, which included the administrative structure, army and state security. This can be most clearly seen in Khrushchev's removal from power in 1964, when a vote in the Presidium automatically transferred all authority to the new rulers. It is interesting to note that a similar move in 1991 failed completely, as by then the Party was virtually powerless.

KEY TERM

Socialist legality
This was a key principal of Khrushchev's government, in theory at least, that all government and Party organisations must act within the law.

The restructuring of the security apparatus

The whole system of state security went through considerable adjustments. The basis of the reforms was to create a sense of **socialist legality**, and thereby banish the terror, repression and arbitrary violence of the Stalin regime. Socialist legality particularly applied to the secret police, who had been carrying out arbitrary arrests. The release of prisoners and opening of the gulags was an impressive start, as was the lack of arrests and executions of political rivals, but Khrushchev had to ensure it could not happen again, and this meant restructuring much of the security system. This was arguably one of the most important breaks with the past, and the most completely achieved. They included the following.

- The security service was removed from the MVD and placed under the Committee of State Security, or KGB, while the MVD power to throw people into gulags without trial was abolished.
- The KGB was full of officers with direct connections to Stalin's rule, so in December 1958, Khrushchev appointed the energetic and ambitious Alekandr Shelepin as the new chief of the KGB. He had been the head of the *Komsomol*, and wasted no time replacing many officers with his *Komsomol* colleagues. This helped to bring the KGB under fuller Party control.

- The judicial system, under the Soviet Procuracy, was reformed to give it greater supervisory roles on the KGB. For the Procuracy to ignore malpractices and corruption in prisons was made a punishable offence. Jurists were given higher status.
- Trials of people accused of counter-revolutionary crimes, now rebranded as anti-state crimes, could no longer be held in secret, while the role of military courts was reduced to purely military and not political affairs. The emphasis shifted to finding guilt rather than proving innocence, and once innocence was established, it could be reviewed at any time.
- Labour camps were renamed 'labour colonies', though there was generally an improvement in conditions.
- Many of Stalin's laws were invalidated, while acts like abortion, absenteeism and leaving a job without permission were no longer criminal offences.
- However, in contrast to the spirit of progressive reform, the death penalty was considerably widened in scope to include repeated acts of bribe-taking. A special Presidium decree made some of the new sentences retroactive.

These reforms helped to remove the apparatus of terror and reduce the constant atmosphere of fear in Soviet citizens' lives, but there were limits. The street patrols used the 'Law against Parasites' to put citizens into internal exile for up to five years. This was aimed at people who were perceived as evading work. No trial was needed, only the agreement of the town soviet. In Moscow, 2,000 'parasites' were exiled in 1961, while 130,000 were identified in the whole of Russia, though many of the republics outside of Russia did not apply the law.

Though the KGB underwent restructuring, it retained its primary function as the secret police. One loophole around the blatant use of terror was to declare a person insane, the assumption being that only the mad would oppose a communist utopia. This became known as 'creeping schizophrenia' and as it was impossible to prove that you did not have it, the state could confine you to a mental hospital (*psykhushkas*), such as the Sernsky Institute in Moscow. These gained a reputation for the abuse of dissidents. In 1961, Khrushchev proudly declared that there were no more political prisoners in the USSR, but there were plenty of 'the sick'.

In conclusion, despite some retrograde steps, especially when crime levels rose, Khrushchev had installed a sense of socialist legality compared to the previous decades. Repression still existed, but the fact that people could complain about it suggested an honest move in the right direction. An individual could safely criticise the government, even if organised opposition, or even an organised audience, was still frowned upon. This blurred the boundaries of these concepts, which caused further tensions as Khrushchev tried to allow some degree of intellectual and cultural freedom while maintaining a one-party state.

New freedoms and old limitations: intellectual and cultural life

The period of change from Stalin through Khrushchev is usually described as a 'thaw'. The name comes from Ilya Ehrenburg's *The Thaw* (1954), in which a woman leaves her despotic husband during the spring thaw as new life emerges. The early days of Khrushchev's rule saw a flowering of literary expression as old artists were rehabilitated and their works published, and new artists found the courage and freedom to take on new themes. Viktor Nekrasov's *Home Town* (1954) portrayed servicemen returning from the Second World War disappointed with the land they find. Vladimir Dudintsev's *Not by Bread Alone* (1956) went further and told the story of a Soviet engineer whose creativity is strangled by state bureaucracy. This trend to allow criticism of certain aspects of Stalinist control was most famously tolerated by the 1962 publication in the journal *Novyi Mir* (*New World*) of Aleksandr Solzhenitsyn's *One Day in the Life of Ivan Denisovich*, which exposed the brutality of the gulags.

Although these novels queried life under Stalin, Boris Pasternak's novel *Dr Zhivago* was turned down by *Novyi Mir*, as it rejected the October Revolution itself. It was smuggled to the West and published in 1957, being awarded the Nobel Prize in 1958. At this moment, the full weight of the establishment descended on Pasternak, calling the novelist a 'pig who had fouled his own sty'. He was ridiculed in crude jokes, attacked as a Judas figure and made to reject the prize. He died within a year and the intelligentsia used his funeral to highlight the oppressive nature of the Khrushchev regime.

The irony is that Khrushchev was never consulted (at least in his memory of the circumstances) about the ban in which Russia's greatest novel was only available outside Russia. He later read Pasternak's epic and regretted the actions that took place.

The most radical and political of art forms in Russia, and one that carried real resonance with the masses, was poetry, and leading Russian poets such as Yevgeny Yevtushenko and Andrei Voznesensky began their careers at this point. Established poets such as Anna Akhmatova were rediscovered, but younger poets, particularly Yevtushenko, were received most enthusiastically. They were even allowed to visit the West for poetry readings.

SOURCE 14 From a 1956 poem 'All we who in his name...' by Pavel Antokolski. It was widely circulated among student groups in the late 1950s in the USSR.

He who has died we hate

Less than our silence

It would not take much for poetry, the conscience of the nation, to be considered a challenge to the state. In June 1958, a monument to Vladimir Mayakovsky was unveiled in Moscow. He was a leading poet of the 1920s and wrote many of the political slogans made famous by communist propaganda posters, but became disillusioned with Stalin and took his own life in 1930. Crowds gathered at the monument and spontaneous poetry readings began, becoming a regular occurrence at Mayakovsky Square, known as *Mayak* ('lighthouse'). In 1961, the authorities began to arrest participants for subversive activities. One person arrested was Vladmir Bukovsky, who lost his university place, but the event spurred him on to become a dissident.

Khrushchev was always uneasy in the presence of intellectuals, as his 1959 speech to the Third Writers' Congress showed. In 1957, at a spring writers' picnic at Semyonovskoye, he had berated liberal writers and the Pasternak episode left a sense of unease between the government and the intelligentsia. The conservative forces, which controlled the Writers' Union, played on Khrushchev's lack of understanding of modernist styles, while the liberals played on his anti-Stalin sensibilities. One example of this was the way the poet Tvardovsky managed to get part of his poem published after its anti-Stalin stance was banned by the censor. Tvardovsky, whom Khrushchev had actually fired as editor of *Novyi Mir* in 1954, gave the poem as a present on Khrushchev's birthday in April 1960. It was published within two weeks in *Pravda*.

Yet when Khrushchev attended a modern art installation at Manezh Gallery in Moscow in 1962 he castigated the artist, claiming that a donkey could paint a better picture using its tail as a brush. For the creative community, it paid to fit in with Khrushchev's tastes or, at the very least, to project the culture and spirit of Soviet society, as artists were informed in instructions given to them in 1957. To go against this 'spirit' would always cause the state security to interfere.

Alexander Ginzburg published an underground poetry magazine called *Syntaxis*. This was a Moscow-based publication illegally copied either by hand or carbon paper and distributed by personal contact. This type of distribution of illegal material became known as *samizdat*. Ginzburg was arrested in 1960, and was sent to labour colonies three times in the next decade. This trend is fairly typical of the Khrushchev period. Repression and censorship tended to harden the artistic community's attitude towards the state. In the 1960s, musicians like Yuliy Kim, artists like Erik Bulatov in the Sretensky Boulevard Group, even dancers like Rudolf Nureyev, who defected to the West in 1961 during a tour in Paris, all increased their political art.

One reason for the increase in art and creative material that questioned the state was the improved contacts with the West, particularly with western culture. Some citizens were allowed to travel abroad with the Bolshoi Ballet, Moscow State Circus or sports teams, where they had contact with western media. Khrushchev also expanded the USSR's travel organisation Intourist, which allowed foreigners to visit the USSR and, in theory, marvel at its achievements. This was the first opportunity for many Soviet citizens to see and meet westerners, though the tourists were restricted in the places they could visit.

SOURCE 15 The Sixth World Festival of Youth and Students in Moscow, 28 July 1957. US participants in Mayakovsky Square on their way to Lenin Stadium for the opening ceremonies of the festival, being mobbed by young Russian citizens.

In 1957, Moscow hosted the World Festival of Youth in which 34,000 delegates from 131 countries, including the USA, were invited to be dazzled by the achievements of the USSR. Instead, the Soviet youth fell for the teenage rock 'n' roll fashions of the West. Khrushchev's wish to show the world his new openness backfired as jazz and rock 'n' roll music began to be played on the radio. Some teenagers, usually children of the elite, dressed in rock 'n' roll style and became *stilyagi*; others favoured the US big band 'zoot suit' fashion and became *shtatniki*. Youth journals like *Yunost'* (*Youth*) and *Nash sovremennik* (*Our Contemporary*) were created and popular fiction such as detective novels and science fiction flourished. Films looked at traditional subjects such as the civil war with a new approach or explored new themes such as the examination of domestic life in *The House I Live In*.

Russians, particularly those close to Europe, could tune into *The Voice of America*, or Radio Free Europe. Young Russians built an image of the West through Hollywood movies such as *The Magnificent Seven*, *Some Like it Hot* and especially the *Tarzan* movies. The poet Joseph Brodsky discussed in his essay 'Spoils of War', half in jest and half seriously, how the Tarzan series did more to de-Stalinize Russia than all of Khrushchev's speeches. In a country where, by 1959, some 55 percent of the population was under 30, this would have a profound effect, as people felt closer to western culture from music, films and writers like Graham Greene and Ernest Hemingway, whose works were now available to buy and read. With only 10 percent over the age of 60, there were fewer and fewer people for whom the revolution was the key moment and meaning in their lives. A 1961 survey by the Institute of Public Opinion found the majority of Soviet youth disenchanted with the ideas of the 1917 revolution. Though the effect of this cultural transference from West to East is a shift that takes generations to evolve, the effects started in Khrushchev's thaw. Of course, the authorities reacted to this change, which helps to explain the paranoia of the 'Law against Parasites'.

Khrushchev's son later commented that Khrushchev held onto the traditional Bolshevik view that art and culture were weapons in the class war. This meant that any art not expressing the view of the state must be, by default, dangerous and therefore should be controlled. Too often, he would adhere to the view of the bureaucratic authorities without actually reading the suspected works themselves. While the function of powerful art is to question what it sees – not a comfortable concept in a one-party state – the fact is that many artists shared the same basic anti-Stalin stance as Khrushchev, but a lack of trust meant they were more often at odds than they were compatible. The fact that the older generation failed to understand the culture of the younger generation is not unique to Russia. Indeed, it is almost a universal human law. However, in the case of the closed society of Russia, culture did have a political aspect in beginning the process of showing young Russians that there was an alternative. Many in the government, quite accurately, saw this as a potentially harmful, but any action against it only served to encourage more.

ACTIVITY
KNOWLEDGE CHECK

Films and music

1. What evidence could be used to support Brodsky's views on the impact of the *Tarzan* series?
2. Using Source 15 and Brodsky's views, do you think the power of culture is equal to the power of political ideology? What are the links between the two?
3. Look up some of the Hollywood films or music mentioned in the text. How do they portray the West and why were they so appealing to young Russians?

Khrushchev and the Church

Khrushchev held traditional Bolshevik views on the Church and religious opinions. The Russian Orthodox Church had suffered as much persecution as anyone under Stalin in the 1930s, but had been allowed a respite during the Second World War in an effort to unite the population. After the war, although Stalin disliked the Church, it was largely left alone. Immediately following the 'Secret Speech', the Church felt greater confidence to practise openly. This would not last long.

The exact reason for Khrushchev's crackdown on the churches is unclear. It may have been simply that he wanted Russia to be a purely communist state, which meant that religion had to be removed. It could also be a deliberate part of de-Stalinisation, as Stalin had tolerated it in the 1940s, and a return to the days of Lenin, who actively and fanatically hated the Church. Whatever the exact reason, the restrictions on the Church began in the late 1950s and peaked in 1961 with a variety of measures.

- Anti-religious propaganda increased and atheism was embedded into the educational curriculum at all levels. For example, all higher-education institutions had a mandatory course on the scientific evidence for atheism. Children were banned from all services and parents were forbidden to teach them religion.
- Taxes on religious activities were increased, with extensive regulations placed on the services and on practices like the ringing of church bells.

- Churches, monasteries, convents and seminaries (training colleges for priests) were closed down. Orthodox parishes fell from 15,000 in 1951 to fewer than 8,000 by 1963. All seminaries were closed, and holy sites were shut, including the Monastery of the Caves in Kiev, which was the most sacred place in the Orthodox faith. Many church buildings were converted to secular use, such as museums or community centres which highlighted communist values. In this way, the restrictions on freedom also destroyed Russia's cultural heritage.
- Pilgrimages were banned, and vocal resistance from priests met with forced retirement, arrest and even the labour colonies. Monks from the Monastery of Pochaev Lavra faced being committed to the *psykhushkas* for being 'contagious'. By 1962, only 36 of the 146 monks in the monastery remained, though international pressure kept it open. Thirteen of the monks had even been conscripted into the military.
- Devout individuals could face the loss of their freedom, their careers or their children.
- Though the majority of actions were taken against the Russian Orthodox Church, all faiths were attacked, including Judaism and Islam. Jews were refused permission to emigrate to Israel. To a communist, all religions are relics of the past, despite the assertion from Andrei Shevchenko, his close aide, that Khrushchev himself still held some religious convictions.

The treatment of the Church seemed at odds with the rest of Khrushchev's policies during the early years of the thaw. Perhaps the lack of liberalisation for the Church, as well as in other areas such as ethnic minorities, shows that Khrushchev never had a clear programme for reforming the system, but only a desire to amend the aspects that he felt would distance him from Stalin, or secure and consolidate his power and help implement his own economic ideas. In other words, the thaw was more about Khrushchev than it was about the people of Russia.

A Level Exam-Style Question Section B

How extensive were Khrushchev's reforms to both administration and cultural policies in the years 1956–61? (20 marks)

Tip

To answer a question that asks you to judge how extensive a change was, do not just describe the changes. The issue of how far the policies actually changed must be addressed. To help you judge the extent of change, it would be useful to think about what Khrushchev hoped to achieve with the reforms.

Conclusion

Between 1956 and 1961, Khrushchev had gained enough influence and support to bring in his reforms and innovations. In 1961, with typical grandeur and self-deception, he announced that society was fully united and the state ruled for everyone. A pure communist state would be in place by 1980 and therefore a new 'Third Communist Programme' was heralded to guarantee that citizens of the USSR would have the highest standard of living in the world and that this generation (and all those after it) would live under a communist system.

Like much of Khrushchev's work, it was ambitious, brave and delivered with both passion and optimism. It was also hopelessly unrealistic. Within three years, the Presidium had built up enough opposition to remove Khrushchev and force him into retirement and internal exile. All his reforms, whether economic, social or administrative, had fizzled away and eventually sank in their own inertia. Good ideas failed through a lack of flexibility or poor application. People were asked to do things that simply could not be achieved, like growing crops in poor soil.

A good example would be the housing problem in Russia. The Third Communist Programme promised free rent and amenities for all. Since Stalin had neglected the desperate need for houses, Khrushchev announced a massive building plan. Apartment towers were built for 108 million people between 1956 and 1965. However, they were prefabricated multi-storey blocks, too rapidly constructed to meet safety requirements, and were quickly nicknamed *krushchoby* (Khrushchev's slums). They were meant to be a stop-gap lasting 20 years before new and better ones were built, but many were still inhabited over 50 years later. In Khrushchev's haste for success, the historic Arbat district of Moscow was torn down to make way for the tower blocks that line the street. They are referred to locally as 'Khrushchev's false teeth'.

Nevertheless, there is much to admire in Khrushchev, the man who rose from peasant origins through dogged determination and instinctive, rather than educated, skill to the position of supreme leader of one of the world's two superpowers.

Firstly, his 'Secret Speech' achieved what no one else had dared to do. It firmly marked Stalin and Stalin's methods as a mistake, a diversion, in the path to socialism. This alone would be a considerable triumph, but Khrushchev went further. His wresting of control in favour of the Party and the structure below it; his gradual if inconsistent thaw in the treatment of culture and artistic freedom; his refusal to rely on terror but instead to instil a sense of socialist legality into the system, meant that the USSR could not return to the Stalinist system and allow a new monolithic tyrant to return. Khrushchev tried to find solutions, often battling resistance within the Party and government elite. The impossible task was to change Russia without changing the system, to bring a more humane and efficient rule to a system that had demonstrated none of these traits so far in its existence. He had to motivate the masses by raising both living standards and optimism rather than by fear, but as his reforms and schemes derailed, the popular support did likewise. This left him open to a growing opposition within the Party elite who saw his reforms as a threat to their privileged position.

It is easy to see the larger-than-life, complicatedly flawed personality of Khrushchev as the beginning of the end of the communist regime, and there is much evidence of this. But it could equally be seen as the start of something new; a fresh approach, held back by his successors, but then continued by Gorbachev, who respected what Khrushchev had tried to do even if he was ultimately unsuccessful.

SOURCE

From *Pravda*, 16 October 1964, in which the Presidium give their reasons for the removal of Khrushchev. The fact that they felt they needed to indicates the significance of the changes that had occurred since 1953. 'Rule by fiat' means an order given by men in authority.

Subjectivism and drift in Communist construction, hare-brained scheming. Half-baked conclusions, hasty decisions and actions divorced from reality, bragging and bluster, a penchant for rule by fiat, and unwillingness to take into account what science and practical experience have already worked out.

SOURCE

Khrushchev talking to a friend on the night of his dismissal in 1964. From *Khrushchev: The Man and His Era*, by William Taubman (2003).

I am old and I am tired. Let them cope by themselves. I've done the main thing. Could anyone imagine telling Stalin that he wasn't wanted any more and telling him to retire? He would have annihilated them. Everything is different now. The fear has gone; we can talk as equals. That is my contribution.

ACTIVITY
KNOWLEDGE CHECK

Khrushchev

1. Make a list of the evidence that supports and challenges the view of Source 16, and then that which supports and challenges Source 17.
2. Which do you find the most convincing assessment of Khrushchev? Are there alternative views?
3. How accurate is it to say that Khrushchev was a courageous failure in the years 1956–61?

ACTIVITY
SUMMARY

Khrushchev and attempts to reform the Soviet system, 1956–61

1 Hedrick Smith spent three years touring Russia and reported back on what it was like in the mid-1970s under Brezhnev, who had helped to oust Khrushchev in 1964, and replaced him as leader. Smith offered a flavour of how Russia viewed the Khrushchev period. Many saw Khrushchev as an erratic buffoon whose policies failed. The leadership saw him as a scapegoat, whose de-Stalinisation made many look foolish for the sacrifices they had made in Stalin's name or, worse, feel guilty about their support for Stalin. An alternative view that Smith heard was that he was a genuine, if misguided, leader who rose from the bottom and passionately believed in what he was doing, unlike the dull, flat leaders of the 1970s.

Using evidence from this chapter, compile a list of evidence for each of the three views to deliver a speech in favour of their interpretation.

2 It is difficult, when evaluating the impact and significance of Khrushchev in the years 1956–61, to ignore the next three years where his policies failed and he was removed from power. What would be the possible differences in interpretation to judge Khrushchev in 1961 at the launch of the 'Third Party Programme' and then in 1964 after his internal exile?

3 Yevtushenko was the key poet in this era. In his 1962 poem 'The Heirs of Stalin', he wrote that while Stalin was physically dead, his spirit lived on, not just in the leaders who had partaken in the terror, but in every single Soviet citizen. Do you think that any attempt to break from Stalin was doomed to failure?

4 After the 'Secret Speech', Russia saw a flowering of culture which was subsequently reined in. Make a list of examples of 'politically dangerous' culture from other periods and nations. Does the culture reflect the political attitudes within a country, or does it help to change them?

5 How accurate is it to say the period 1956–61 was driven by a willingness to reform? What evidence could be used to support and challenge the view?

WIDER READING

Figes, O. *Revolutionary Russia 1891–1991*, Pelican (2014)

Khrushchev, N. *Khrushchev Remembers*, Little, Brown (1970)

McCauley, M. *The Khrushchev Era 1953–1964*, Longman (1995)

Pasternak, B. *Doctor Zhivago*, Vintage (1958)

Smith, H. *The Russians*, Sphere (1976)

Taubman, W. *Khrushchev: The Man and his Era*, Free Press (2003)

Gorbachev and the downfall of Soviet communism, 1985–91

KEY QUESTIONS

- What was the impetus to reform the USSR?
- How extensive was the impact of *glasnost* and *perestroika*?
- How did divisions within the reformist camp evolve into divisions within the USSR?

INTRODUCTION

'We cannot go on living like this.'

Addressing these words to his wife and close advisers, Mikhail Gorbachev made his intentions clear. Not only was change necessary in the USSR, but he was the one who would force it through.

The USSR faced a growing number of serious problems by the 1980s. A succession of elderly leaders intent on maintaining the status quo had left a society suffering from inertia and a stagnating economy. This could be seen in the failure to win the war in Afghanistan and the increasing Cold War tensions with the USA, both of which diverted funds that should have been spent on domestic problems.

The USSR's thirst for alcohol was harming its economy and its people, and its inefficient infrastructure and secretive media were demonstrated when the Chernobyl nuclear power station exploded in 1986. These problems helped to fuel a nationalism that was already growing in the Soviet republics. Many republics felt they would be better off without the dominance of the USSR and the Communist Party (CPSU). Like Khrushchev, Gorbachev was willing to try new ideas, as expressed in his desire for a more open society with *glasnost* (openness, see page 66), and a more creative and efficient economy through ***perestroika***.

Gorbachev has been misunderstood as the man who brought democracy to the USSR. In fact, he was a committed communist, who wished to maintain the Communist Party's control of a united USSR, but his reforms unleashed forces beyond his intentions. New leaders did not defer to the old system, **dissidents** demanded freedom, not just reform, and Gorbachev began to lose control.

As one side pushed for more, others pulled for less. A conservative backlash used Gorbachev's hesitation to try to force a return to the old days of dictatorship in an attempted *coup d'état* in 1991. Its failure sealed the fate of the Communist Party, Gorbachev and the USSR. The calls for reform had evolved into calls to dismantle the USSR and, by the end of 1991, this was complete.

KEY TERMS

Perestroika
A term meaning 'restructuring'. This was Gorbachev's parallel policy to *glasnost*, designed to reform the political and economic systems.

Dissident
An individual who publicly disagrees with the policies of the government. In the USSR, dissidents were frequently subjected to police harassment, internal exile and imprisonment.

1985 – March: Gorbachev becomes general secretary

Intensification of anti-alcohol campaign

1986 – *Glasnost* launched

April: Chernobyl nuclear disaster

December: Dissident Andrei Sakharov released from exile

1987 – *Perestroika* launched

October: Yeltsin attacks Gorbachev at closed Central Committee Plenum

1988 – June: Nineteenth Party Conference agrees multi-candidate elections

December: Basic Criminal Code frees more dissidents

Armenian earthquake kills 25,000

WHAT WAS THE IMPETUS TO REFORM THE USSR?

The Afghanistan War

Civil war throughout 1978 and 1979 in Afghanistan, located on the USSR's southern border, brought appeals by Afghan communists for military help from the USSR. For a while, Brezhnev rejected their pleas, as the ***détente*** in international relations maintained the peace, but in December 1979 the Politburo, influenced by military hardliners, ordered the Soviet army into Afghanistan. The hawks in the Politburo would not accept a gap in their buffer zone against the West, especially as the USA was funding Islamist opposition to the communist forces. The USSR was plunged into a ten-year war that drained its resources and soured its relations with the West. By the time Gorbachev came to power, his attempts to withdraw from the war heralded a 'new thinking' from the USSR, but also hardened military attitudes against his perceived weakness.

The war in Afghanistan was unwinnable. The rebels' mountain strongholds were impossible to conquer regardless of the number of troops, tanks and planes sent there, as wars both previously and since have proved. The war became the Soviet Union's 'Vietnam' in that, like the USA in the late 1960s, the USSR was involved in a hostile conflict in unfamiliar terrain against supposedly more 'primitive' military forces. In Vietnam, the Soviet-resourced Vietcong used guerrilla tactics in the jungle to wear down US forces. In Afghanistan, the US-funded **Mujahedeen** used guerrilla tactics in a war of attrition in the mountains. Both the USSR and the USA felt that a withdrawal would mean humiliation and therefore struggled to find an 'honourable' solution.

Gorbachev became leader in 1985. He rejected all of Brezhnev's policies, including those concerning Afghanistan, and in July 1986 announced the withdrawal of six army divisions within a year. In February 1988, he ordered the departure of all 115,000 troops, starting in May, with the last leaving in February 1989. The government announced that 13,310 Soviet troops had been killed and 35,478 wounded, but these figures did not include accidents and drug addiction, which was a big problem. Around 90,000 Mujahedeen and a million civilians died, with up to five million people displaced.

The Soviet death toll was not high enough to alter the political nature of the USSR, but the war influenced the atmosphere both in the USSR and internationally, increasing pressure for reform.

- The invasion had ended *détente* and US–Soviet relations entered a tense second Cold War period. The USA boycotted the Moscow Olympics in 1980, and the USSR did the same for the Los Angeles Games in 1984. President Reagan launched a new arms race and increased spending to seven percent of GDP. In an effort to maintain its position, the USSR had to spend 22–27 percent of GDP on the military, while the production of consumer goods froze. Reagan's plan was to force the USSR to spend itself into bankruptcy. Historically, this foreign impact on the Soviet economy can be over-exaggerated. Reagan's most ambitious and expensive programme was the Strategic Defence Initiative (SDI), commonly known as 'Star Wars', but there is evidence that the Soviet authorities were not concerned about it, as they were never convinced it would work. However, the escalation in Cold War tension did divert funds away from internal spending.

KEY TERMS

Détente
Improved relations during the Cold War between the USA and USSR, lasting throughout the 1970s. Both countries preferred to attempt to work together rather than raise tensions. The Soviet invasion of Afghanistan in 1979 and the election of the anti-communist Ronald Reagan as US president in 1980 ended *détente*.

Mujahedeen
Afghan guerrilla fighters against Soviet forces 1979–89. The term applies to Muslim fighters engaged in a *jihad* against the USSR, but has since been applied to other conflicts.

1989 | 1990 | 1991

1989 – November: Fall of Berlin Wall symbolises collapse of communist regimes in Eastern Europe

1990 – Gorbachev starts to appoint more conservative advisers

Economy spirals in sharp decline

March: Article 6 repealed, allowing new political parties

June: Yeltsin declares Russian sovereignty over USSR

Yeltsin resigns from Communist Party

October: 500 Days programme announced for market economy

1991 – June: Yeltsin elected president of Russian Republic

August: Attempted conservative coup

Communist Party banned in Russia

December: Dissolution of USSR

- The war was not cheap. While the USA funded the Mujahedeen by $1 billion a year, the USSR spent an estimated $8.2 billion a year on the war, using funds that were badly needed elsewhere.
- Once Gorbachev began the process of withdrawal, the nature of Soviet society began to be revealed. Information had been kept secret – even the news of the actual invasion was suppressed for three days – and as true casualty rates or the soldiers' experiences became known, people's mistrust of the state and official media increased. As Gorbachev lifted media restrictions with his *glasnost* policy, the torrent of corruption scandals, including the degree of drug addiction among the 550,000 Soviet troops who had served in Afghanistan, became known.
- The war encouraged political participation among the masses as protests started to grow. At first the protests were limited to underground papers like ***Ogonyok***, which catalogued the abuses, extortion, fraud and bribery perpetrated by senior officers during the war. Protests grew, often at soldiers' funerals, and though they were repressed, they increased in number and size throughout the 1980s. This was the first time the masses had opposed the authorities in open political action.
- Dissidents who opposed the war found their civil liberties restricted. The nuclear physicist and winner of the 1975 Nobel Peace Prize, Andrei Sakharov, was exiled to Gorky City, some 250 km east of Moscow and off-limits to foreign visitors. As a leading nuclear physicist, Sakharov had been granted more intellectual freedom than others, and he had written in various ***samizdat*** about scientific co-operation leading the way to world peace, with a freer USSR and a more socialist USA converging, but his open and persistent opposition to the war was not tolerated.
- One group that became particularly vocal and important later on were the veterans of the war, known as *afgantsy*. Some, traumatised by their experiences, turned to violence and crime, adding to the social problems that were gathering force in the USSR. Many became politically active in organising opposition to the war and the Soviet system. During the attempted *coup d'état* in 1991, a significant number of *afgantsy* were in the crowd defending the democratic parliament buildings.
- The failure to win the war did not go unnoticed by the republics that made up the USSR. Nationalists could see that the Russian heart of the empire could not control the situation of a 'primitive' satellite state. The war undermined the legitimacy of the USSR to rule an empire and further motivated nationalists to push for independence.

The war had helped to expose the decrepit system and the inner decay that the Soviet authorities had tried to gloss over. It helped to spur new forms of political participation and civil organisations.

KEY TERMS

Ogonyok
A magazine published in Russia and the USSR since 1899. During the *perestroika* years, under the editorship of Vitaly Korotich, it adopted a pro-capitalist position. By 1987, it had 1.5 million readers, growing to a peak of 4.6 million in 1990. Its circulation fell rapidly after the collapse of the USSR.

Samizdat
A grass-roots practice, starting in the 1960s, of self-publication to avoid official Soviet censorship. Documents and political leaflets, such as the 'Chronicle of Current Events', were reproduced and distributed, both often by hand. Writers faced harsh punishments, including imprisonment, if caught. The illegal self-publishing of unapproved music through tape recordings was known as *magnitizdat*.

SOURCE

1 The last Soviet troops leaving Afghanistan by crossing the border to the USSR along the 960 m bridge over the Amu Darya River near the town of Termez, Uzbekistan, on 6 February 1989.

It weakened the pillars of Soviet rule: the KGB, the military and the Communist Party all lost prestige and power because of the war. The KGB refused to follow orders from their chain of command during the 1991 *coup d'état*, while the tank commanders refused to crush the protesters. The Party appeared corrupt, opaque and out of touch with society. Gorbachev's plan to withdraw not only encouraged more protests and more revelations about the mishandling of the war, but also showed the media that liberalisation worked. It sent a signal to the people and the West that the USSR was changing, and Gorbachev and the Party would not be able to control the extent and pace of that change.

The withdrawal of Soviet forces focused the senior military's opposition to Gorbachev and his reforms, as they felt he had betrayed them. These were the reactionary forces who would attempt to impose their rule in the 1991 *coup d'état*.

SOURCE

The BBC correspondent Martin Sixsmith remembering his experiences with Soviet troops in February 1989, from his book *Russia: A 1,000-year Chronicle of the Wild West* (2012).

I have vivid memories of travelling on the last Soviet convoy to leave Afghanistan. The Mujahidin had celebrated victory by shelling the convoys that had gone before us, and the young conscripts were overcome with relief when we reached the Soviet frontier town of Termez. As the army commander Boris Gromov walked over the border to be the last man to leave Afghan territory, I asked one of his senior aides how it felt to be coming home. 'It is a humiliation.' I was told with a bitter grimace. 'The traitor Gorbachev has sold us out.' Like everyone, I had been aware of opposition to Gorbachev's reforms, but it was not until that moment that I realised the deep-seated, visceral contempt in which he was held by some sectors of the Soviet establishment.

ACTIVITY
KNOWLEDGE CHECK

Afghanistan

1 How could you question the typicality of the views expressed by Gromov's aide in Source 2 from looking at the provenance of the source?

2 The impact of the Soviet-Afghan War was complex. Make a list of the political, social and economic effects of the war for the USSR.

3 Was the Soviet withdrawal more of an impetus for reform in the USSR than the course of the war?

Economic stagnation

There is no doubt that the economy in 1985 had stagnated. Annual growth was less than one percent and the gap between living standards in the USSR and the West was widening. Oil prices had dropped by two-thirds from 1980 to 1985, which hurt Soviet exports. The communist regime had suffered periods of economic stagnation before. Indeed, the economy had been largely destroyed after the Civil War of 1919–21, but the Party had survived and even consolidated its hold on power. Yet under Gorbachev and *perestroika*, the economy spiralled into a decline that ushered in the end of communist rule.

In the early 1980s, it was more a matter of disappointment. The USSR had abundant oil, gold and other raw materials, but they were inaccessible, being located far in the East, when they were needed in the western USSR. Low birth rates, especially in the Russian Republic, meant that the working population had levelled. A lack of technology, inefficient workers, corrupt managers and uninspired political leadership created an economy that was mired in its own deficiencies. The USSR was a **command economy**, with uncoordinated decisions made at the top and passed down to the masses. Large-scale and inflexible projects had unforeseen consequences, such as irrigation schemes that drained the Aral Sea into a poisonous dustbowl. The result was a lumbering heavy industry and almost non-existent small-scale, consumer-driven industry. There was little incentive to work, and few luxuries to buy. Meanwhile, the imbalance increased in the 1980s as western capitalist economies picked up and the difference in living standards and industrial performance became clearer and wider.

KEY TERM

Command economy
A planned economic system in which targets, set by the state in the case of the USSR, are allocated resources to meet them. Such an economy typically involves a large central bureaucracy to manage it.

It is usually seen as a contrast to the market economy of many western states, where production is based largely on demand and the interests of private companies. It is possible to mix elements of the two.

An indication that the economy was failing was the authorities' attempts to disguise the truth. For years, false data had been used to inflate economic successes and meet the targets of the five-year plans. These economic plans were like steps giving a series of strict measures for agriculture and industry to be met (ideally before the end of the five-year period) and then the target was raised in the next plan. However, with the figures being manipulated, the previous step is inherently unstable and with each new plan, reality and fantasy moved further apart. In 1987, the Russian economists Khanin and Selyunin famously argued in the journal *Novy Mir* that Soviet income had not multiplied by 84.4 times between 1928 and 1985 as the official statistics claimed, but only by 6.6 times.

In 1961, at the launch of the Third Communist Programme, Khrushchev had declared that the USA would be overtaken, and a communist utopia would be constructed within 20 years. At the Twenty-Seventh Party Congress in 1986, it was admitted that this had not happened. Perhaps more important was Gorbachev's confession that the circumstances were not right for it ever to happen. The poor performance of the economy did not cause mass protests, it just inconvenienced people and they adapted. Many workers skipped work as it was the only time when the shops were open and they needed to queue. Though there was disillusionment with the regime, there was also a cynical acceptance that that was simply the way it was. Western culture might have been secretly passed from hand to hand, but few openly criticised the government and organised dissent. Private jokes revealed people's inner thoughts, but old habits, fear and deference kept protests to a minimum.

SOURCE

'Seven Wonders of Soviet Power', a popular joke printed in a Russian magazine during the 1970s. In eastern Europe it was shortened to 'We pretend to work and they pretend to pay us.'

1. There is no unemployment, but no one works.
2. No one works, but the plan is fulfilled.
3. The plan is fulfilled, but there is nothing in the shops.
4. There's nothing to buy, but there are queues everywhere.
5. There are queues everywhere, but we are on the threshold of plenty.
6. We are on the threshold of plenty, but everyone is dissatisfied.
7. Everyone is dissatisfied, but everyone votes 'yes'.

It was not the economy's effect on the masses that encouraged reform, but more the economy's effect on the leadership of the Party, particularly Gorbachev and other reformers. He felt that the promises of socialism had failed to deliver, and now he had the opportunity to do something about it, not unlike what Khrushchev had attempted after the 1956 'Secret Speech'. His failure in this dominated the political situation in the USSR for the next five years.

ACTIVITY
KNOWLEDGE CHECK

Economic stagnation

1 What does Source 3 suggest about the Soviet Union in the late 1970s and early 1980s? Think about what it says, but also what is implied by the source by looking at its nature.

2 The economy of the USSR had seen extensive periods of stagnation and crisis before without the need to radically reform it. Why do you think this period initiated the reforms?

Alcoholism and Chernobyl: a country in economic decline?

The decay of the Soviet economy can be reflected in the bottle: alcohol consumption in the USSR was among the world's highest. The drink of choice tended to be spirits such as vodka, rather than beer or wine, and the average Russian preferred to drink in bouts, which increased accidents. Vodka was one of the few products always available in the shops. A quarter of all alcohol was brewed illicitly in the form of *samogon*, a toxic spirit fermented from sugars and jams.

The USSR used sobering-up stations to ease the burden on the police. In 1979, an estimated 16–18 million drunks had used them, with 30 stations in Moscow alone. In 1982, *Pravda* blamed alcoholism for the fact that building sites were deserted on Mondays and Friday afternoons. Alcohol was seen as a primary reason for absenteeism, poor-quality products and work-related accidents. Numerous railway accidents were blamed on drunk drivers, but labour legislation meant that a person could not be removed if they smelled of alcohol, and a drunk driver must be given his job back after a fixed term.

In the early 1980s, Brezhnev, Andropov and Chernenko had all toughened the 'Law against Parasites', which focused more on people not working than on drunkenness. People were grabbed on the street, in shops, on trains and asked why they were not at work. A failure to give a convincing reason would end in arrest and a fine. Unsurprisingly, such heavy-handed tactics caused resentment. To Gorbachev, the rising rates of alcoholism, as well as mental illness, suicide and divorce, were all symptomatic of a failed economy leading to a failed society. The USSR Institute of Sociology estimated that, by 1985, alcohol was costing the economy 80 billion rubles per year.

If alcoholism revealed the deterioration of society, then the Chernobyl disaster proved how dangerous a poorly managed economy could be. On 26 April 1986, the fourth reactor of the Ukrainian nuclear power station of Chernobyl exploded, throwing high levels of radiation over a wide area. The disaster was caused partly by technological failure and partly by incompetence. The seriousness of the fire and contamination was concealed from the population. Indeed, it was workers at a Swedish nuclear plant over 1,000 miles away who first noticed the increase in radiation and brought it to the attention of the world, but Party officials quietly, yet quickly, removed their children from the area. As a panicking establishment muddled its response, fire-fighters and helicopter pilots sacrificed their lives to put out the fires. These people were known as 'liquidators', though not all were told how lethal the job was.

In the end, 500,000 workers constructed a giant sarcophagus over the reactor. An area with a radius of nearly 20 miles around the plant was declared a permanent exclusion zone, which would not be safe for human habitation for another 20,000 years. The death toll of 4,000, mainly from cancers caused by radiation, is hotly contested, with some figures predicting nearly a million premature deaths.

The USSR spent some $18 billion decontaminating the area, money it could ill afford. Even 20 years later, around six percent of the national budgets of Belarus (which suffered 60 percent of the fallout) and the Ukraine was spent on Chernobyl.

For Gorbachev, the disaster and its consequences were an example of the inadequacy of the Soviet system, and raised the need for *glasnost*. The chain of mismanagement, ignorance, malpractice and corruption could no longer be concealed and reform was absolutely required if the USSR was to survive. This reform would have to be directed from the top. Other disasters highlighted the combined effects of incompetence and secrecy.

In August 1986, the Soviet liner SS *Admiral Nakhimov* collided with a tanker in the Black Sea, resulting in hundreds of deaths, but the news was suppressed for days before leaking out. In 1989, the Ufa train disaster incinerated 575 people as two passenger trains ignited gas from a leaking pipeline. Even earthquakes (such as the December 1988 Armenian quake in which 25,000 died) did more damage because of negligent building practices.

If the USSR and the Communist Party took the credit for successes such as the space race, they could be blamed for these failures. This boosted anti-Russian feeling in the other Soviet republics.

EXTEND YOUR KNOWLEDGE

East and West working together

At a time of high Cold War tension, the Chernobyl disaster presented a rare opportunity for the two ideologically polarised sides to work together. Unfortunately, western and eastern scientists, keen to promote nuclear power, worked together to minimise the death toll from radiation exposure.

The number of potential deaths arising from the disaster is hotly debated. Arguments over radiation levels, and the exact cause of individuals' cancer, have made figures hard to calculate. There is also much debate about the influences of pro- and anti-atomic energy ideologies on these figures.

The World Health Organisation predicted 4,000 cancer deaths in surrounding countries, while the Union of Concerned Scientists put the figure from all contaminated areas at 27,000. A Greenpeace report put the figure for 1990-2004 at 10,000-200,000 deaths, though this was criticised for being influenced by an anti-nuclear energy agenda. Based on an analysis of medical records between 1984 and 2004, the New York Academy of Sciences published a report in 2009 predicting 985,000 premature deaths. This report claims that the International Atomic Energy Agency (IAEA) ignored reports from Eastern Europe, which generally have higher figures. The IAEA said the report was unscientific and exaggerated the figures.

Almost every aspect of the disaster, from causes to legacy, from the initial Soviet cover-up to the amount of clean-up required, has been argued over with additional and contrasting pressures from a myriad interest groups from all viewpoints. The situation is so complex and so loaded with far-reaching implications over who should pay for reconstruction, or the safety of the nuclear industry in general, that an objective view is extremely difficult to articulate. Whatever the exact details of the Chernobyl disaster, Ukrainian officials have estimated that an area some 20 miles in all directions from the reactor will not be safe for human habitation for 20,000 years, though the area was opened up for tourists in 2011.

SOURCE

Gorbachev writing in his 1995 *Memoirs* about the Chernobyl disaster, which became a financial disaster for the USSR as well as a human and ecological one.

[Chernobyl had] shed light on the many sicknesses of our system as a whole. Everything that has built up over the years had converged in this drama; the concealing or hushing up of accidents and other bad news, irresponsibility and carelessness, slipshod work and wholesale drunkenness.

SOURCE 5 Chernobyl nuclear power plant after the April 1986 explosion and fire. The remaining three reactors were still used to produce power after the disaster. After another fire in 1991 closed one reactor, the final two were closed in 1996 and 2000.

ACTIVITY
KNOWLEDGE CHECK

Chernobyl

1. Using Sources 4 and 5, as well as your own knowledge, explain how the Chernobyl disaster could help transform opinion in the USSR towards reform.
2. What weight would you give the Chernobyl disaster as an impetus for reform? Think carefully about the words you could use to assess its impact.

The rise of nationalism

One factor that has been somewhat overlooked by studies on the period is the rise of nationalism. Observers have tended to focus on leaders and to take a Russocentric view, and since there were few media centres beyond Moscow and Leningrad (St Petersburg), the growing nationalist and separatist feelings in the various republics across the USSR (Figure 7.1) have been overlooked.

Nationalism was a long-term pressure or a 'submerged' dilemma that had erupted at various points, both under the tsars and since the formation of the USSR in 1917. The republics, under Lenin, were meant to retain independence and the right to secede (withdraw), but they had been brought under direct Party control by force. This force increased as Stalin's purges and terror included deportations of entire ethnic groups, such as Germans and the Crimean Tatars, during the Second World War. In the 20th century, the USSR increased both in size and in the number of republics, for example the three Baltic states of Estonia, Latvia and Lithuania were annexed in 1940. From the 1930s, a programme similar to the tsarist policy of Russification (see page 89) had existed to promote Russian achievements and language. Large migrations of Russians into the republics helped to keep Russia dominant, so that many ethnic groups were almost a minority in their own republic, particularly in the Baltic states.

By 1985, many republics felt their identity was under pressure. Events like the Afghanistan War and the Chernobyl disaster only heightened their mistrust of Russia, especially in the Ukraine and Belarus, which were most affected by radiation fallout. In December 1986, riots occurred in Alma-Ata in the Republic of Kazakhstan, over the replacement of the first Party secretary by an ethnic Russian, while the Crimean Tatars protested in Moscow for the right to return to their homeland.

Though these problems were not created in the 1980s, the Soviet leaders had no plan to deal with any national question that arose, which tended to escalate the problem into a crisis. Conflict between ethnic groups within the republics increased as rivals fought for greater control. According to Vorotnikov, the chairman of the Presidium of the RSFSR (Russian Republic) Supreme Soviet, the extent of inter-ethnic ill-feeling had been under-estimated and therefore allowed to gather momentum. The Russian News Agency (TASS) reported that, between 1988 and 1991, some 1,200 civilians had been killed and 10,000 wounded in inter-ethnic conflicts. These occurred in almost every republic for a wide and complex variety of reasons. In Central Asia, conflicts tended to focus on the control of resources, whereas the persistent violence in Nagorno-Karabakh region was centred on ethnic clashes between the Armenian majority and the Azerbaijani authorities. The situation was made worse by an earthquake in December 1988, after which Moscow took direct control of the disputed region, encouraging further resentment. In the Baltic states, nationalist feeling grew to the extent that the Estonian Supreme Soviet passed a decree in 1988 stating that their own laws took precedence over Soviet laws. The Caucasus, Ukraine and Belarus republics had a long history of resentment against Russia, but the third republic, Georgia, almost moved towards independence after Russian troops killed 20 Georgians during a peaceful demonstration.

Nationalist sentiment grew, not just between Russia and the other Soviet republics, but also between different ethnic groups within a republic. Meanwhile, Moscow struggled to tackle the problem, as its power and authority ebbed away. Perhaps the best evidence for the importance of nationalism emerged in 1991, in the mass flight of the republics to leave the USSR and become independent. This could not have happened without strong nationalist sentiment brewing over a long period, even within Russia itself, as its president, Boris Yeltsin, wrestled for power with the Party leader, Gorbachev.

Figure 7.1 The republics of the USSR during the 1980s.

The significance of Gorbachev's personality and ideas

Another factor that has been debated is the significance of Gorbachev. All agree that he is important, but the argument focuses on his degree of competency. To many in the West, he is the great reformer, winner of the 1990 Nobel Peace Prize, responsible for the end of the Cold War and the architect behind the relatively bloodless dismantling of the USSR. He became almost a cult figure, comfortable with the western media as well as with western leaders. Margaret Thatcher, the British prime minister, announced in 1984 that he was a man with whom 'we can do business'. The veteran Brezhnevite foreign minister, Andrei Gromyko, praised Gorbachev's commitment to the Communist Party with the words, 'This man has a nice smile, but he has teeth of iron.'

In contrast, many within Russia have a different perception. As Gorbachev and his wife, Raisa, toured abroad, the Soviet public saw their world collapse and their economy diminish to the point of extinction. He was seen as a disastrous leader, who destroyed full employment and the peace between the republics, and lost the buffering security of the Eastern Bloc in an embarrassing climb-down to the USA. Gorbachev's significance does not necessarily depend on his results. His importance is that he was prepared to adopt new measures. He belonged to the 1960s generation, or *shestidesiatniki*, whose epiphany was not the 1917 Revolution but Khrushchev's 1956 'Secret Speech', which opened the possibility, even necessity, for change. The Afghan War, the failed economy and social discontent told him that new ideas were needed, though he wisely kept them quiet until he was firmly in power. The failure of some of his ideas, such as his attempt to retain the communist system while reforming the economy, detracts from his success, not from his importance.

During the early 1980s, the USSR had three leaders, all born before the 1917 Revolution and all devoted to maintaining the status quo. Brezhnev's replacement in 1982 was Yuri Andropov, a KGB man who wanted to beat the USSR into modernisation. He promoted Gorbachev, but kidney failure made him too ill to have much effect. His death after only 15 months saw the 73-year-old Konstantin Chernenko step up to the leadership. He represented a Brezhnev-like dedication to changing nothing. Within weeks of assuming power, he was diagnosed as terminally ill. His death in March 1985 made the Politburo see the need for a younger man and the 54-year-old Gorbachev was selected, marking the end of the **gerontocracy** and a shift towards reform. His early speeches mark him more as an orthodox Leninist than a radical social democrat.

Gorbachev had risen through the Party, after time spent as a model youth in the *Komsomol*, by doing all the right Party things and by being loyal, but began his leadership by focusing on the corruption and privilege within the Party and *nomenklatura* system (see pages 60 and 136).

Gorbachev was wary of the escalating nature of reform, and his ideas were more about ***uskorenie*** and *perestroika*, which both imply a more controlled approach. He correctly saw the failure of the economy as the prime reason for stagnation, but naively felt he was expert enough to solve it.

KEY TERMS

Gerontocracy
A form of oligarchical rule (rule by the few) in which the state is ruled by leaders who are significantly older than most of the adult population.

Uskorenie
Acceleration. Announced in April 1985, it was Gorbachev's first slogan and policy development based on accelerating the development of heavy industry by investment in science and technology. It caused further economic problems and by 1987 it was replaced by *perestroika*, which aimed at reforming the whole economy. It did, however, indicate Gorbachev's desire to attempt reforms.

SOURCE

Margaret Thatcher on Gorbachev after meeting him in London in 1984. His wife, Raisa, had gone shopping while the leaders conversed. From Thatcher's *The Downing Street Years* (1993).

Mr Gorbachev insisted on the superiority of the Soviet system... If I had paid attention only to the content of Mr Gorbachev's remarks, I would have to conclude that he was cast in the usual Communist mould. But his personality could not have been more different... He smiled, laughed, used his hands for emphasis, modulated his voice, followed an argument through and was a sharp debater... His line was no different from what I would have expected; his style was. I found myself liking him.

SOURCE

A cartoon by the Estonian-born Edmund Valtman, who emigrated to the USA in 1949 at the age of 35. This cartoon was published in the USA in 1977.

'DON'T LOOK NOW, BUT I'M AFRAID SOMEBODY IS FOLLOWING US'

Gorbachev's key ideas

Gorbachev's 'New Political Thinking' centred on the Soviet economy and formed the core of his policies. In international relations, this meant the rejection of the **Brezhnev Doctrine**, whereby the USSR directly interfered in the domestic and foreign relations of the Eastern Bloc crisis. This was seen in the suppression of the Prague Spring in 1968, and the threat of invading Poland in 1981 to ensure the removal of the Solidarity union movement. Gorbachev was sending a message to the Eastern Bloc nations that they were responsible for their own regimes. This would hopefully free up more funds for the economy. However, it also encouraged the people of Eastern Europe to press for more political civil rights and the lifting of travel restrictions, leading to the downfall of all Eastern Europe's communist regimes by the end of 1989, as the **Sinatra Doctrine** took hold. To the West, it meant a surprisingly rapid end to the Cold War, as Gorbachev refused to compete with the US arms race.

KEY TERMS

Brezhnev Doctrine
A justification of the USSR's 1968 invasion of Czechoslovakia, stipulating that it was a communist country's duty to defend any other communist country from turning capitalist. This allowed the military occupation of a country undergoing domestic protests and reforms, if Moscow deemed it necessary.

Sinatra Doctrine
A policy of Gorbachev's which replaced the Brezhnev Doctrine in 1989. Named after the Frank Sinatra song 'My Way', it was generally taken as Moscow allowing its allies to decide their own futures, without the threat of Soviet military intervention.

Funds were needed to apply the principles of *perestroika*, which, although not a new concept in the USSR, now took on a greater force. Similar to Lenin's NEP policies in 1921, it relied on the theory that western-style market forces could be combined with the planned economy to trigger economic growth (the target of the five-year plan 1985–91 was 25 percent) and a greater production of consumer goods. The creation of a 'socialist market economy' would allow the continuation of core matters such as areas to be invested in, but would allow market prices to govern day-to-day decisions. This took the form of *uskorenie,* accelerating the economy in 1985–86 by tightening discipline and raising production. The more radical *perestroika* reforms were introduced in 1987, when Gorbachev felt more secure in power.

To allow the economy to become more efficient and promote the discussion of good practice and ideas, Gorbachev realised there needed to be more openness in Soviet society. With regard to the Party, this meant **democratisation** in which genuine elections

KEY TERM

Democratisation
A policy announced in 1987 as part of Gorbachev's *perestroika* and *glasnost* reforms after the failure of *uskorenie*. Part of his attempt to rejuvenate the Communist Party with more dynamic members, it refers to the introduction of more democratic elements, such as multi-candidate (not multi-party) elections.

for Party officials would take place, while *nomenklatura* and unnecessary or undeserved privileges would be removed. This was his rather nostalgic attempt to return to Leninist principles that had been twisted by Stalin and fossilised by Brezhnev. The more revolutionary *glasnost* was introduced, bringing a greater transparency to society so that new and more efficient ideas could be shared without fear. However, the relaxing of censorship meant a loss of control over the mass media and the exposure of the USSR's deep-rooted problems.

Gorbachev hoped that the ideas born out of *glasnost* would facilitate the *perestroika* of the Soviet economy and lead to higher living standards based on communist principles, but its failure to materialise, combined with the people's right to express themselves through *glasnost*, spiralled events beyond his control. Gorbachev, with his naive belief that a change of attitude could fix an economy that had stagnated over decades, was the architect of both his own and the USSR's downfall.

SOURCE

Gorbachev's optimistic analysis of the need for *perestroika* is articulated in his 1987 book, *Perestroika: New Thinking for our Country and the World*. Here he is explaining how the policy can be seen as an umbrella cure for all the ills of society.

Perestroika is an urgent necessity arising from the profound processes of development in our socialist society... At some stage - this became particularly clear in the latter half of the seventies - something happened that was at first inexplicable. The country began to lose momentum. Economic failures became more frequent, difficulties began to accumulate and deteriorate, and unresolved problems began to multiply. Elements of what we call stagnation and other phenomena alien to socialism began to appear in the life of society. A kind of 'braking mechanism' affecting social and economic development formed... Declining rates of growth and economic stagnation were bound to affect other aspects of the life of Soviet society. Negative trends seriously affected the social sphere. This led to the appearance of the so-called 'residual principle' in accordance with which social and cultural programs received what remained in the budget after allocations to production... This unfortunately, is not all. A gradual erosion of the ideological and moral values of our people began... Propaganda of success - real or imagined - was gaining the upper hand. Eulogizing and servility were encouraged; the needs and opinions of the ordinary working people, of the public at large, were ignored. In the social sciences scholastic theorization was encouraged and developed, but creative thinking was driven out from the social sciences, and superfluous and voluntarist assessments and judgments were declared indisputable truths... The presentation of a 'problem-free' reality backfired; a breach had formed in word and deed, which bred public passivity and disbelief in the slogans being proclaimed... decay began in public morals; the great feeling of solidarity with each other that was forged during the heroic times of the Revolution, the first five-year plans, the Great Patriotic War and postwar rehabilitation was weakening... Party guidance was relaxed and initiative lost in some of the vital social processes... On the whole, society was becoming increasingly unmanageable... The need for change was brewing not only in the material sphere of life but also in public consciousness.

A Level Exam-Style Question Section A

Study Source 8 before you answer this question.

Assess the value of the source in revealing the problems the USSR faced in the 1980s and the need for Gorbachev's *perestroika* to solve them.

Explain your answer using the source, the information given about it and your own knowledge of the historical context. (20 marks)

Tip

Spend a good ten minutes reading the source carefully; highlight important phrases and short quotes (under five words). Do not be afraid to devote time to reading, reflecting and structuring an answer. Think, not just about who the speaker is, but who the intended audience would be. Think about the tone and language of the source and how they indicate its purpose.

ACTIVITY
KNOWLEDGE CHECK

Gorbachev

1. Compare Margaret Thatcher's view in Source 6 with Andrei Gromyko's more sinister view (page 159). Is it possible that both are correct? Explain your ideas using the sources and your own knowledge.
2. What does Source 7 imply about the importance of Gorbachev?
3. To what extent was Gorbachev the prime force behind the need for reform in the USSR in 1985–87?

HOW EXTENSIVE WAS THE IMPACT OF *GLASNOST* AND *PERESTROIKA*?

Perestroika was a considerable departure from the decades of the centrally planned economy, and Gorbachev realised he would need to shore up support in the higher echelons of the Party before it could be fully implemented. Hence, he first introduced measures to increase, or accelerate, production.

The anti-alcohol campaign

A good example of Gorbachev's initial *uskorenie* before *perestroika* is apparent in his anti-alcohol campaign. Here, he built on the anti-parasite work, especially of Andropov, but focused more sharply on alcohol. The decree announced in May 1985, known as the 'Dry Law', introduced greater fines for drunkenness at work as well as punishing those who resold alcohol and other consumer goods, in an effort to limit private trade. The goal was to lower production of vodka by ten percent by 1990, a target, typically for Soviet planning, that had already been achieved in 1986. The price of vodka was tripled, and restrictions on the time and place it could be sold were introduced. Vineyards and distilleries were closed and the minimum age for alcohol consumption was raised to 21. The intentions were sensible, but sugar and jam, the ingredients for the dangerous *samogon*, disappeared from shops overnight.

The police began breath-testing passengers on public transport and even guests at weddings or funerals. The 'drunk' were fined and lost any privileges, while reports were sent to their workplace. In short, the campaign followed the familiar path of overreaction and state interference in people's lives.

The fall in vodka sales deprived the state of taxes, resulting in a 17 percent loss of revenue in 1985, which meant fewer funds for consumer goods. Criminals circumnavigated the ban by selling alcohol on the black market. Meanwhile, the authoritarian nature of the decree and people's difficulty in obtaining drink, if only to temporarily unwind from reality, surely increased resentment at a time when the state needed people's support. The campaign demonstrates the ill-conceived nature and lack of foresight in such an ambitious, or unrealistic, crusade when a campaign to promote moderate drinking might have had a far greater impact. The anti-alcohol campaign was finally abandoned by Gorbachev, or 'Comrade Orange Juice' as he was known, in 1990. In July 1990, *Pravda* claimed that the root of all the subsequent economic problems was the budget shortfall of 10 billion rubles in 1985 because of the anti-alcohol campaign. While the USSR went on to experience many economic crises between 1985 and 1990, this poor start meant that the economy could never progress.

The treatment of dissidents and voices of discontent

While economic reforms had a staggered start, *glasnost* was implemented and spread more quickly. Gorbachev saw *glasnost* as a political policy and a key component in generating the creativity needed to modernise the market economy. It was also a useful tool to bypass Party opposition by appealing directly to the people. After the suppression of information on the Chernobyl disaster, Gorbachev commented, 'We need *glasnost* like we need air.' His early actions signalled his new approach.

In May 1985, Gorbachev took the unusual step of speaking without notes on Soviet television. Then he gave an interview to the US *Time* magazine and a live broadcast to a French journalist in which he was asked about Soviet treatment of dissidents. This resulted in Anatoly Shcharansky, a Jewish 'refusenik' (someone who was refused permission to emigrate to Israel) being exchanged in February 1986 for an East European secret agent. In December 1986, Gorbachev personally phoned the most renowned Soviet dissident, Andrei Sakharov, who had been in exile for six years with his wife, the poet Yelena Bonner. Sakharov was allowed to return to Moscow. He immediately recommenced his political activities and proved to be a considerable thorn in Gorbachev's side. His release showed others in the USSR that *glasnost* was a genuine policy and not merely rhetoric.

Perhaps to distance Gorbachev's rule from the past, or because the past is a safer target for criticism, the media, embracing the spirit of *glasnost*, began a re-analysis of the past by uncovering the truth of the regime's crimes, particularly under Stalin. This was directly encouraged by Gorbachev in his November 1987 speech to celebrate the 70th anniversary of the October Revolution. However, with each new revelation of past terror and torture, it seemed that the present was under scrutiny. During 1988, all Stalin's rivals from the 1920s, such as Bukharin, Zinoviev and Rykov, were rehabilitated, as was Marshal Tukhachevsky, who had been executed in the purge of the military in the 1930s. In 1989, the USSR finally admitted its role in the murder of 15,000 Polish officers at Katyn during the Nazi–Soviet Pact, while mass graves became a common discovery in the Slavic republics, fuelling nationalist sentiment there. With the perpetrators long dead, the shocked public searched for someone to blame. It was a logical path from blaming Stalin, to blaming Lenin, to blaming the communist system itself. Fiction provided a space to explore these issues. George Orwell's attacks on communism, *Animal Farm* and *1984*, were both published, as was Rybakov's novel *Children of the Arbat*, set in Stalin's heyday. The journal *Novyi Mir* rejuvenated itself and once more became an intellectual force with the publication of Solzhenitsyn's *Gulag Archipelago*. The weekly paper *Argumenty i Fakty* (*Arguments and Facts*) stopped producing state propaganda and started revealing the reality of Soviet life. Its circulation rose from two million in 1986 to 33 million by 1990.

Television played a significant role in a more liberal climate. As with the relaxation of censorship laws under Alexander II, writers and now broadcasters strained to test the boundaries. The British prime minister, Margaret Thatcher, appeared live on Soviet television in 1987, outwitting the Soviet journalists in a debate over nuclear weapons. What is important is not just that Thatcher clearly out-argued the aggressive questioning, but that the Soviet authorities allowed a 45-minute uncensored interview with an ideological enemy to be broadcast. Even the battered Soviet journalists were secretly in awe, while Thatcher's arguments were a rare and new contrast to the official Soviet line.

Home-produced shows like *Vzglyad* (*View*) and *600 Seconds* produced outspoken commentaries on current affairs. By 1988, Soviet school history textbooks were destroyed (causing exams to be cancelled) and plays, journals and films questioned the achievements of the past and, by implication, the system of the present. Even *Pravda* and the monthly Party journal, *Kommunist*, appointed a new, more *glasnost*- and Gorbachev-friendly editor. The result was that *glasnost* politicised citizens, with 60,000 'informal' groups and clubs formed by March 1991. These groups took to the streets and demanded further reforms.

The December 1988 Basic Criminal Code ended deportations, restricted prison sentences and capital punishment, and released many more dissidents, who naturally joined the chorus of discord. Andrei Sakharov was prominent among them and, in October 1988, he was re-elected to the Soviet Academy of Sciences, providing a wider platform for his criticism. The new frankness about the past, the questioning of Soviet ideology and the release of dissidents raised fears that *glasnost* was going too far, and a backlash manifested itself within the Party. Gorbachev believed that Party bureaucracy, or *apparat*, was deliberately blocking reforms at local level and that individuals in the Party leadership were intent on hampering reform. He wanted to reduce the inefficiency of the economy, but the people required to implement these reforms were those whose privileged positions were at risk. Gorbachev felt he had to openly discuss this dilemma, encouraging workers to go above any Party official who obstructed his initiatives. Gorbachev told his adviser, Anatoly Chernyaev, in 1989, that his reforms had to continually inspire further reforms, and that any deviation or conservative reaction would lead to his removal from power. He had to spend the first years of his rule gathering reformers to his cause.

SOURCE 9 **Soviet academician, Andrei Sakharov, being interviewed by the press on his arrival in Moscow at the Yaroslavl railway terminal on 23 December 1986 after six years of internal exile.**

SOURCE

French historian and political thinker Alexis de Tocqueville writing in *The Old Regime and the Revolution* (1856). He offers an insight into the difficulties that a more open society can cause for an authoritarian government.

The most dangerous moment for a bad government is when it begins to reform... Patiently endured so long as it seemed beyond redress, a grievance comes to appear intolerable once the possibility of removing it crosses men's minds.

ACTIVITY
KNOWLEDGE CHECK

Dissidents and reform

1 How does Source 9 illustrate the inherent dangers of *glasnost* in the USSR?

2 Using your own knowledge, give evidence of the situation in the USSR to support de Tocqueville's maxim in Source 10.

3 Gorbachev instinctively felt that the reforms should always drive forward. Is this an accurate assessment of the situation in 1989? Could the reforms be halted, or even reversed?

Gathering support: Gorbachev's new appointments

The process of moving his supporters and sympathisers into Party and government positions began as soon as Gorbachev was appointed to power. The remnants of Brezhnev's regime were retired or sidelined. Eduard Shevardnadze replaced Gromyko as foreign minister, despite a complete lack of experience. He was an old friend of Gorbachev, and his most like-minded adviser, and had founded a public-opinion forum in Georgia which pre-dated *perestroika*. Alexander Yakovlev, former ambassador to Canada and a pro-westerniser, was brought in as adviser for ideology and culture as well as foreign relations. He was the most pro-active in promoting *glasnost*. To head the Moscow Party and sit on the Politburo, Boris Yeltsin was appointed; he had worked with Gorbachev, not always smoothly, since the 1970s. Yeltsin crusaded against corruption and privilege, though he made many enemies.

In the secretariat of the Party's Central Committee, nine of the 12 members were appointed by Gorbachev between 1985 and 1986. While the 1986 27th Party Congress was still largely traditional in its outlook – often against the wishes of local members – only 59 percent were re-elected, while in the 1981 Congress, 90 percent had been re-elected. Therefore, though support was not total, Gorbachev was able to get his key advisers into positions of power and the mood of the Party was with him.

Not all senior politicians supported him, however. Under Andropov, Yegor Ligachev was made second secretary of the Communist Party, the second most senior post in the USSR. Despite his openness with foreign journalists, he came to represent the Party's reactionary faction. The 1986 Central Committee Plenum (a meeting that all members were expected to attend) was delayed because of arguments over the course of action and when, it finally met in January, Ligachev and Gorbachev argued through speeches about the need for reform. However, the tide for the moment was with Gorbachev, and *perestroika* began to gather pace. The Chernobyl disaster helped him to harness popular anger to dismiss opposition, as did the curious incident of Mathias Rust.

In May 1987, an 18-year-old German, Mathias Rust, with only a few hours' flying experience, flew a light aircraft from Helsinki, Finland and landed it in central Moscow. Soviet aircraft tracked him, but were not ordered to shoot him down, and his plane was mistaken for a friendly aircraft as it neared Moscow. A source of mirth in the West, it was acutely embarrassing for the Soviet military to have allowed an unchallenged landing in their capital city. The landing, caught on video by a British tourist, ruined the military's reputation with the Russian people. Gorbachev used the incident to purge hardline military leaders such as the minister for defence, the heads of the Soviet Air Defence and border troops. By 1990, he had replaced over 100 senior military officers with new ones who were more open to reform.

In his speech to the February 1988 Central Committee Plenum, Gorbachev presented his vision of a renewed socialism. The economy was yet to collapse; *perestroika* seemed to be working, especially as *glasnost* was yet to focus on the present. Gorbachev was at his peak and everything was possible.

Perestroika in action: economic changes and administrative battles

With support in place, Gorbachev could speed up *perestroika* with two major economic reforms.

- The 1987 Law on State Enterprise allowed a limited amount of free enterprise with the goal of raising efficiency. Factory managers gained more powers in decision-making, prices and quotas, but central planning remained, as did the refusal to let profit dictate the direction of production.
- The 1988 Law on Co-operatives lifted restrictions on small private businesses, mainly in the service industries, though various restrictions remained on size and workforce. The new co-operatives – all employees had to be co-owners – were also taxed. The socialist-sounding label 'co-operative' helped Gorbachev steer the measure into law.

Meanwhile, several administrative reforms were introduced to shift power from the Party to the soviets.

- More finances were allocated to the soviets, while the electoral term of soviet deputies was increased to five years from two, giving them the resources and security to perform their duties.
- In September 1988, attempts were made to streamline the Party and the state. The number of departments in the Communist Party Central Committee was reduced from 20 to six broad commissions. While some were merged, others were abolished altogether and their functions handed to the state. The change ended the power of the bureaucracy to monitor and control the political processes within the country, and this removed another hurdle to *perestroika*.
- At the state level, ministries were conglomerated into giant organisations to simplify planning. For example, five previous ministries now made up the Ministry for Agriculture.

The results were inconsistent, and successes were largely based on trial and error, but the entrepreneurial spirit sprang into action as restaurants, small shops and kiosks opened up, especially as vodka was again legal. Despite the tinkering in the administrative apparatus, the economy did not lurch forward but moved sluggishly on, with no rise in living standards. Panic buying of goods led to food rationing, with 26 out of 55 USSR regions rationing meat in 1988. The economy began to sink into debt, made worse by inflation (ten percent by 1989), falling oil prices and strikes. In 1987, industrial production fell by seven percent, while the government had promised welfare to anyone adversely affected by *perestroika*, which took more money from the budget.

While the solution would seem to be a total deconstruction of the central-planning Soviet economy, even these NEP-style reforms, a mere shadow of capitalism, provoked severe opposition among hardliners. Ligachev spoke out against the Law on Co-operatives for undermining the Party, and backed Nina Andreeva, a Leningrad chemistry teacher, who published a letter in March 1988 expressing discontent against the changes (see Source 11). It quickly became the manifesto against *perestroika*.

SOURCE

From *I Cannot Waive Principles* by Nina Andreeva, published in *Sovetskaia Rossiia* (a Russian political newspaper), 13 March 1988. Andreeva was a chemist and lecturer at Leningrad's Lensovet Technology Institute, and therefore in contact with many young students. Though this long letter at nearly 4,500 words is from her point of view, there was evidence that Yegor Ligachev, a leading opponent of the reforms, had a hand in it. Released while Gorbachev was in Yugoslavia, it began a conservative backlash against the reforms of the late 1980s.

I decided to write this letter after lengthy deliberation. Students nowadays... are gradually becoming charged with the energy of revolutionary changes. Naturally, discussions develop about the ways of restructuring and its economic and ideological aspects. *Glasnost*, openness,... often result in the raising of problems that are, to a greater or lesser extent, 'prompted' either by Western radio voices or by those of our compatriots who are shaky in their conceptions of the essence of socialism. And what a variety of topics that are being discussed! A multiparty system, freedom of religious propaganda, emigration to live abroad, the right to broad discussion of sexual problems in the press, the need to decentralize the leadership of culture, abolition of compulsory military service. There are particularly numerous arguments among students about the country's past... Take, for example, the question of Joseph Stalin's place in our country's history. The whole obsession with critical attacks is linked with his name...

A Level Exam-Style Question Section A

Study Source 11 before you answer this question.

Assess the value of the source for revealing the reasons for the opposition to Gorbachev's reforms as well as the results he was trying to achieve.

Explain your answer using the source, the information given about it and your own knowledge of the historical context. (20 marks)

Tip

When evaluating a source, try to take into account the weight the evidence will bear as part of coming to a judgement. Examine the source carefully to determine the degree of certainty with which aspects of it can be used as the basis for claims. Think about whether the source is assertive or emotive in its reasoning, or whether its claims are supported and logical.

The industrialization, collectivization, and cultural revolution which brought our country to the ranks of the great world powers are being forcibly squeezed into the 'personality cult' formula. All of this is being questioned. Matters have gone so far that persistent demands for 'repentance' are being made of 'Stalinists' (and this category can be taken to include anyone you like)...

I support the party's call to uphold the honour and dignity of the trailblazers of socialism... When it comes to the class struggle in the countryside, for example, excessive emphasis is often placed on the 'rural' commissars who 'shot middle income peasants in the back.'... But in the mainstream of our life are commissars who were shot at, commissars who had stars carved on their backs or who were burned alive. The price the 'attacking class' had to pay consisted not only of the lives of commissars, Chekists, rural Bolsheviks, members of the committees of poor peasantry, or the 'Twenty Thousand' but also those of the first tractor drivers, rural correspondents, girl teachers, rural Komsomol members and the lives of tens of thousands of other unknown fighters for socialism...

This is what we stand for now, and this is what we will continue to stand for. Principles were not given to us as a gift, we have fought for them at crucial turning points in the fatherland's history.

Andreeva's letter articulated the nostalgic longing for security that many wanted, particularly with the failure of the economic reforms, which seemed to serve the rich and the criminal rather than the masses. It took three weeks for an official response to appear in *Pravda*. To Gorbachev, the letter represented a threat that the opposition was gaining support in the Politburo. As First Secretary, he was appointed by the Politburo and, like Khrushchev, he could be removed by them. Therefore, he embarked on a series of radical measures to widen his support base and separate the Party from the state. Ligachev was demoted to secretary of agriculture, but continued to criticise the reforms whenever he could.

The system of government was a complicated blur of administrative, bureaucratic and Party organisations (see Figure 7.2), with many politicians and officials holding similar level positions on both, and the *nomenklatura* system favouring the Party and the loyal. After tense discussions and false starts, it was announced at the lively Nineteenth Party Conference in June 1988 (the first conference since 1941) that a new government body would be created: the Congress of People's Deputies. This body of 2,250 seats would meet twice a year and elect from within its own membership a Supreme Soviet consisting of 542 members, as well as a president. The Supreme Soviet would act as a national parliament. The key aspect is that around two-thirds of the seats on the Congress were contested by election, and the Supreme Soviet debated policy and did not just rubber-stamp it as before. The president assumed many of the powers previously held by the first secretary. Many thought this would mean little, as they expected Gorbachev to be both first secretary and president, which he rather hypocritically was in October 1988. The resolution 'On the Democratisation of Soviet Society and the Reform of the Political System' was passed with some clever political trickery and manipulation by Gorbachev, as he slipped it on to the agenda at the very end of the last day. However, as with all his reforms, the outcome did not meet his expectations.

The structure of the new elections allowed for a range of candidates, but only from the Communist Party, and a third of the seats were reserved for Party organisations. This was socialist pluralism, rather than a genuine democratic multi-party pluralism. However, over 80 percent of the population voted. The first session of the Congress in May 1989 was watched on television by an estimated 100 million people. They heard Gorbachev ask for suggestions to slash the 1989 military spending of 77.3 billion rubles and the 40 billion rubles spent on the country's administrative apparatus.

The Congress symbolised the new opportunities to criticise openly, whether for or against reform, whether supporting Gorbachev or opposing him. Gorbachev listened impatiently to speeches against him, but he endured them. It was a taste of democracy that the citizens of the USSR savoured. Similar structures were created in the republics to mirror the Congress, and many republics elected separatist candidates, such as in Latvia, where the Popular Front won 25 out of 29 seats.

Gorbachev's aim was to strengthen the Communist Party by showing that it was accountable. In contrast, the elections had sprouted resistance to the Party and highlighted the hardening divisions within it. It was the moment when Gorbachev lost control over the nature and pace of reforms.

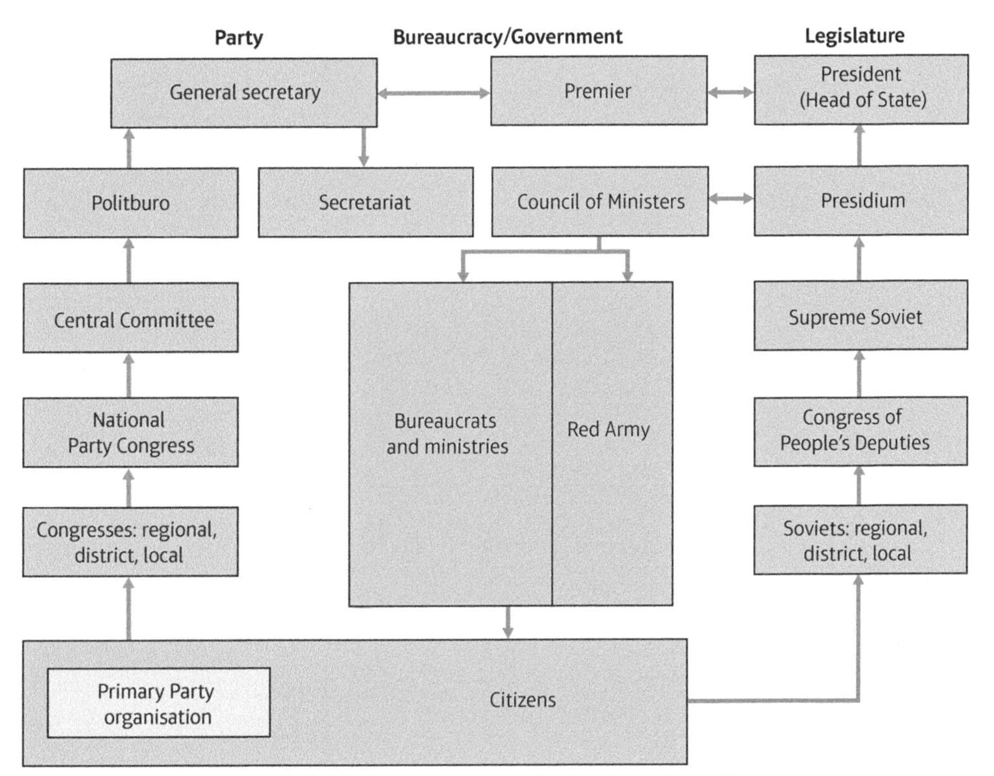

Figure 7.2 The structure of the Soviet government that had developed by 1985.

SOURCE 12 A joke circulating around Minsk in 1986.

Gorbachev, Reagan (US president) and Mitterrand (French president) meet and start discussing their problems. Mitterrand says he has nine mistresses and one is cheating him. He can't work out which one. Reagan says that this is a minor problem compared to his. He has 50 bodyguards and one is a KGB agent but he can't discover who he is. Gorbachev waves all this aside and complains that his problem is much more serious. He has 100 ministers in his government and one of them is implementing *perestroika* but he doesn't know which one.

ACTIVITY
KNOWLEDGE CHECK

Perestroika

1. How does Source 12 indicate the basic problems in implementing reform within the USSR?
2. To what extent do you think that by beginning the reform process Gorbachev was creating future problems, both for himself and for the USSR as a whole?

A Level Exam-Style Question Section B

'*Glasnost* had more effect on the USSR than *perestroika* between 1985 and 1988.'

How far do you agree with this statement? (20 marks)

Tip

There are many ways to structure an answer to open questions like this. Think about the possible criteria. Is the effect positive or negative? Is the effect more pronounced politically, socially or economically? Is the combined impact greater than the sum of the individual parts? Your response needs careful reflection and structuring to present a clear and readable answer.

HOW DID DIVISIONS WITHIN THE REFORMIST CAMP EVOLVE INTO DIVISIONS WITHIN THE USSR?

Though 87 percent of the elected deputies of the new Congress of People's Deputies were communists, they quickly split into two factions. The *Soyuz* (Union) faction wanted to halt reform and preserve the status quo. The Inter-Regional Group consisted of around 400 deputies who wanted to increase the pace of reform. These included Andrei Sakharov, who demanded the end of **Article 6 of the Soviet Constitution**. Gorbachev was caught in the middle. He refused to repeal Article 6, but was beginning to see that restructuring would not go far enough. His speeches were laced with calls for checks and balances, and separation of powers.

KEY TERM

Article 6 of the Soviet Constitution
The article that, since the 1930s, had given the Communist Party a monopoly of power within the USSR and to both direct and control the apparatus of government. The campaign to repeal it helped greatly to focus opposition to the Communist Party from all over the USSR. Sakharov's death finally persuaded Gorbachev to amend the Article in March 1990 to allow other political parties.

The split in Congress was mirrored in society as a whole. The many groups that were set up included *Pamyatnik* (Memorial), which campaigned for monuments to mark Stalin's crimes, while *Pamyat* (Memory) wanted to promote Russian nationalism and had a strong anti-Semitic element. The Democratic Union was set up in May 1988, though its leader was arrested 17 times, with each arrest followed by a hunger strike until she was released.

Gorbachev leaned towards the reformers, yet his relationship with many of the reforms was stormy. Sakharov bombarded him with demands for democracy, producing a petition with 60,000 signatures live on television during the December 1989 Congress of People's Deputies. Gorbachev suffered the indignity of a slow handclap, but the Congress conservative majority defeated the repeal of Article 6. To Sakharov, the architect of *perestroika* was becoming its enemy. While composing a speech against Gorbachev two days later, Sakharov died of a heart attack. His funeral, attended by 80,000 mourners, turned into a political rally, with a copy of his call for democracy and a eulogy from the poet Yevgeni Yevtushenko placed on his coffin. Gorbachev once more shifted towards reform.

The growing rivalry with Yeltsin

Gorbachev's difficulties with Sakharov were nothing compared to his problems with Yeltsin. Although Yeltsin had been brought in to shore up support for Gorbachev, they fell out as early as October 1987, when Yeltsin accused Gorbachev of moving towards a cult of personality. Gorbachev counter-accused Yeltsin of 'political adventurism' in questioning the Party's sincerity for reform. Yeltsin resigned from the Politburo and was demoted to a junior post. The rivalry was personal as well as ideological.

While Yeltsin seemed destined to remain in the background, he used the time to forge links with other reformers, like the Church, strikers and other demonstrators, to solidify his Moscow powerbase. The opportunity for a political comeback came with the first elections to the Congress of People's Deputies in May 1989. Despite a vicious campaign to discredit him, Yeltsin was voted in for Moscow with five million votes, some 89 percent of the total, and joined Sakharov and other former dissidents like Roy Medvedev, as the leading lights in the Inter-Regional Group. There, they attacked all aspects of the communist system, from the KGB to Gorbachev himself.

Sakharov's funeral focused support for a repeal of Article 6. In February 1990, over 250,000 people demonstrated at the Kremlin, carrying placards that read '73 years on the road to nowhere'. In March, Gorbachev ended communist dominance by allowing a multi-party state with a US-style president. Gorbachev was immediately appointed president, but conceded that the term of office would be decided by a general election. Many reformers noted that the man who had brought in a multi-party system and elections had never been popularly elected. This left him open to criticism and political attack, while a successful election would give him the legitimacy he craved. At the May Day parade, Yeltsin's supporters gatecrashed the march past the nation's leaders. As they chanted anti-Party slogans and called for freedom and democracy, Gorbachev stormed back into the Kremlin in disgust.

Gorbachev was pushed to a more conservative stance as he tried to keep a divided Party together. He bullied through the appointments of more reactionary Party politicians such as Marshal Dmitry Yazov, who was appointed defence minister, and Valentin Pavlov as prime minister. Old supporters like Alexander Yakovlev warned him of the dangers of trusting such hardline men, and pleaded with him to split the Party, something he had been asking since 1985. Yakovlev hoped that dividing the Party would create one 'wing' or movement that was focused on reforms, while having two parties, even if one was traditionalist, would start the process of a more plural political system. Gorbachev hesitated over this step as he feared it might lead to a struggle over which 'party' controlled the armed forces.

As Gorbachev toyed with traditionalist views, Yeltsin moved to become the leader of the Russian Republic, as many of the republics set up their own Congresses. In the uncertainty of this new political system, the power relationship between the USSR and the individual republics was untested. As leader of the Russian Republic, by far the largest republic, Yeltsin represented a challenge to the USSR. It was a situation similar to the dual power of the Provisional Government in 1917. Yeltsin was using his reputation as an anti-establishment figure to set up his own party, the Democratic Russia Movement, and in June 1990 he declared Russian sovereignty. This was more a symbolic gesture than a transference of power, but he followed it up at the July Twenty-Eighth Communist Party Congress by publicly resigning from the Party, to whistles and shouts of 'shame' from Party members.

SOURCE

Boris Yeltsin talking about his aims in a 1989 interview with Martin Sixsmith. It shows how reformers felt they needed to use coded language , even when thousands demonstrated in the streets for reform. Gorbachev had compared Yeltsin and the Inter-Regional Group to gangsters.

Some people say I am not trying to improve the system, but to abolish it. Well, I cannot confirm that. But I can say that I am in favour of a whole series of things that are - in all senses of the word - revolutionary... Multiparty democracy shouldn't be a taboo; the people must be allowed to talk about it; then we can draw the necessary conclusions...

SOURCE

Gorbachev in a televised address on 2 July 1990 after the end of Article 6.

In place of the Stalinist model of socialism, we are coming to a citizens' society of free people. The political system is being transformed radically, genuine democracy with free elections, the existence of many parties and human rights is becoming established and real people's power is being revived.

ACTIVITY
KNOWLEDGE CHECK

Rivalry with Yeltsin

1 What do you think Yeltsin really means in his interview in Source 13? Why does he have to be so careful in his approach? Think about the nature of the source in your answer.

2 How does Source 14 articulate the change in Gorbachev's ideas between 1985 and 1990? How genuine do you think his motive was in repealing Article 6?

3 Is there any way that Yeltsin and Gorbachev could work together? Is their rivalry based on ideological differences, or is it more about who has personal power?

The conservatives' attempted *coup d'état*

Conservatism or reform? The growing pressures on Gorbachev

As Communist Party power unravelled from the top, the Union of the Republics was shattered by forces from below. Much of Yeltsin's support was founded on the idea of democratic independent republics, and this issue was accelerated by the events of late 1989. Within a few weeks Eastern Europe had rid itself of communist rule. Without military support from Moscow, the regimes were unable to hold back the popular democratic movements. Solidarity ousted the communist government in Poland. Hungary followed soon after, and the opening of their borders to the West led to the tearing down of the Berlin Wall and the end of communist control in East Germany. Czechoslovakia's peaceful Velvet Revolution saw the dissident playwright Václav Havel become president before the New Year.

Naturally these events encouraged nationalists within the 15 republics of the USSR and the Baltic states. Georgians and Armenians were quick to call for independence, while large ethnic sections of the Ukraine and Moldavia organised campaigns. In 1990, nationalists won elections for their republics' parliaments in all the Baltic states. Their cause was helped by the USSR's violent repression of the independence movement. In April 1989, 19 demonstrators were killed by Soviet police in Tbilisi, Georgia, and 17 were killed in Lithuania and Latvia in January 1991, both incidents leaving hundreds injured. The repression, headed by the KGB and the military, aimed to provoke nationalist violence to justify a state of emergency in a last-ditch attempt to save the USSR. The idea was seemingly supported by Gorbachev, determined to hold the Party together, as he appointed more hardliners to powerful positions: Boris Pugo as minister of the interior and Gennady Yanaev as Soviet vice-president. Nevertheless, republics raced to declare that their laws took precedence over USSR law.

Gorbachev's wavering from reform to reaction can be explained by his desire to achieve two incompatible results. He wanted to introduce elements of democracy and hence leant towards reform, but he also wanted to preserve the USSR and the united Party, which meant concessions to the hardliners. By 1990, this was impossible, as could be seen in August 1990 when, despite their mutual loathing, Yeltsin and Gorbachev assembled experts to resurrect the economy. They planned to move it to an open market with a '500 Days Programme'. Both approved the plan, but when the Party faithful condemned it as a capitulation to capitalism, Gorbachev changed his mind.

In November 1990, defence minister, Yazov, increased the military's power to defend themselves against separatist demonstrations. The KGB warned of Cold War plots by foreign agents to poison communism, which could only be met by a crackdown on civil liberties. The liberal Yakovlev warned of a military takeover and revealed army pamphlets that called for a Hitler rather than Gorbachev as dictator. Shevardnadze went as far as resigning in December 1990; he did not blame his friend Gorbachev directly, but implied that the hardliners needed to be stopped. Within a month, special USSR forces captured media stations in Riga and Vilnius, the Latvian and Lithuanian capitals; thirteen civilians were killed. As Gorbachev returned from yet another foreign visit, this time with the Nobel Peace Prize in his hand, and to the charge of 'murderer' by Yeltsin, he ordered the troops to pull out, but did not remove the hardline leaders from power. This left them free to plot more deeply.

SOURCE 15 The liberal commentator and filmmaker, Alès Adamovich, speaking to Congress after the resignation of Eduard Shevardnadze from Gorbachev's advisers in December 1990.

By losing such allies as Shevardnadze, you are losing your own strength, your prestige. If this process goes on, the president will soon be surrounded by colonels and generals. They will surround the president, making him a hostage. Gorbachev is the only leader in soviet history who has not stained his hands with blood, and we would like to remember him for that. But a moment will come when they instigate a bloodbath, and later they will wipe their bloodstained hands against your suit, and you will be to blame for everything.

The attempted *coup d'état*

In a referendum on whether to keep the USSR together, six republics refused to vote, though 76 percent of the other nine voted to maintain the Union, which showed grass-roots support. With Yeltsin, they drafted the 'April 9+1' Treaty (nine republics plus Russia), in which many powers were transferred from the Soviet president to the republics. Yeltsin was now the most powerful person in Russia, having been elected to the new post of Russian president with 57 percent of the vote. By August, the Treaty had created the Union of Soviet Sovereign (not Socialist) Republics, though the Ukraine had pulled out. It would be the end of the USSR. So, with Gorbachev on holiday in the Crimea, and due to fly back on 20 August to ratify the treaty, the conservatives saw their moment to act.

Gorbachev was placed under house arrest, while in Moscow the *coup d'état*'s leaders (Yanaev, Pugo, Pavlov, Yazov and Karuchkov, the head of the KGB) declared themselves a State Committee of the State of Emergency which would last for at least six months. They appeared on television to announce Yanaev, his hand visibly shaking, as the new president. Tanks were ordered into Moscow to enforce order, but here the *coup d'état* began to weaken.

Yeltsin, who was not arrested, led demonstrators to the Russian parliament to protest against the measures. The tank commanders were half-hearted in their support for the *coup d'état*, with the Tamanskaya Division switching allegiance and allowing Yeltsin to address the crowd on one of their tanks. The defection of the tanks was a crippling psychological blow to the *coup d'état*, as it was broadcast to Russia and the world. Yeltsin's charismatic performance galvanised the opposition to the campaign, while Yevtushenko hastily wrote a poem which called on the spirit of Sakharov to preserve freedom. One KGB unit refused to attack the Russian parliament and the conspirators lacked the ruthlessness, or support, to violently suppress the demonstrators, despite three young men being crushed by the tanks. On the fourth day of the *coup d'état*, some of the leaders flew to the Crimea to plead with Gorbachev. Yeltsin sent a plane with armed troops to arrest them for treason.

The failed *coup d'état* destroyed any reputation the Communist Party had. On 23 August, Yeltsin suspended the Communist Party in Russia, and statues of former politicians were pulled down in Moscow. To many, Yeltsin was the hero, while Gorbachev had been betrayed by the men he had appointed, then rescued by his rival. Gorbachev returned to Moscow looking dishevelled and exhausted. He credited the *coup d'état*'s failure as a victory for *perestroika* and was reluctant to thank Yeltsin. In their statements and appeal to the public, the leaders of the coup had recognised the unease and harsh economic conditions created by *perestroika*, but failed to appreciate how much attitudes towards the Communist Party had changed.

SOURCE 16 Some points from Resolution No. 1 of the USSR State Committee for the State of Emergency, 20 August 1991. This 16-point programme of new laws contained some populist measures to gain support, but was chiefly an attempt to ensure Communist Party control.

1 All bodies of power and administration of the USSR, the Union and the autonomous republics, territories, provinces, cities, districts, settlements and villages are to ensure unswerving observance of the conditions applying in a state of emergency in accordance with the USSR law...

3 Laws and decisions of bodies of power and administration that are at variance with the USSR Constitution and USSR laws are henceforth to be considered invalid.

4 Activity by political parties, public organisations and mass movements that impedes the normalisation of the situation is to be suspended...

7... The holding of rallies, street processions and demonstrations, as well as strikes, is not permitted...

8 Control is to be established over the news media, with the implementation of this control assigned to a specially created agency under the USSR State Committee for the State of Emergency.

SOURCE 17 A pro-democracy supporter fighting a Soviet soldier on top of a tank in front of the Russian Federation building during the August *coup d'état*. Thousands of protesters in Moscow, Leningrad and other cities answered Yeltsin's call to man barricades against tanks and troops. On 21 August, the tanks were withdrawn, signalling that the coup had failed.

ACTIVITY
KNOWLEDGE CHECK

The attempted *coup d'état*

1 How do Sources 16 and 17 show how the *coup d'état*'s leaders had misjudged the mood of the country and the changes in society over the *perestroika* years?

2 What changes would the *coup d'état*'s leaders have had to introduce to improve its chances of success? You can use your own knowledge in your answer.

The downfall of Communist Party rule

Even as the depths of Communist Party support for the *coup d'état* were revealed, Gorbachev still argued in favour of Party rule. With most of the leaders of the coup in jail, though Pugo had shot his wife and himself in fear of repercussions, Gorbachev insisted that most Communist Party members were democrats. Yeltsin, riding high on world adulation, caught Gorbachev in a trap when he invited him to the Russian Parliament, where Yeltsin humiliated him on television by showing him proof of the scale of Party support for the coup. In front of a crumpling Gorbachev, Yeltsin banned the Communist Party in the Russian Republic, setting the precedent for the other republics to follow. At the funeral for the three civilians killed by tanks, Yeltsin, who pleaded for forgiveness for allowing them to die, was elevated to hero. On 24 August, Gorbachev resigned as the Party's general secretary, as the Russian Parliament started to seize the Party's considerable assets.

SOURCE 18 Yeltsin and Gorbachev at the Russian Parliament, 23 August 1991. Yeltsin is angrily gesturing to Gorbachev to read the minutes of a cabinet meeting of the first day of the *coup d'état*. It showed that all its supporters had been Gorbachev's appointees. To tumultuous applause, Yeltsin then banned the Communist Party from the Russian Republic.

SOURCE 19 From the editorial of *Pravda*, 22 August 1991. Two days earlier it had carried Resolution No. 1 imposing the State of Emergency.

In recent days, a group of men attempted to carry out an illegal, anti-constitutional *coup d'état* in our country. Like other newspapers, *Pravda* showed a lack of objectivity in its reports. We admit frankly that a long history of relying on orders from above about what we print is behind the reasons for this. Much of the blame for the lack of integrity shown by this newspaper lies with the senior editorial team. In the coming days, the editorial team will be replaced.

All 15 republics declared that they would leave the USSR. Though Gorbachev had resigned, he still had a few months to form economic links with the republics and set up a new Union Treaty. However, on 1 December, the Ukraine voted to secede, which ended any hope for Gorbachev. The Ukrainian president and Yeltsin formed the Commonwealth of Independent States (CIS), without consulting Gorbachev, and invited the other republics to join. On 25 December, Gorbachev announced the dissolution of the USSR, and at midnight on 31 December, in the Kremlin, the hammer and sickle flag was lowered, to be replaced by the Russian flag. Yeltsin was already in Gorbachev's office.

A Level Exam-Style Question Section B

To what extent was the downfall of communism in the USSR 1985–91 due to Gorbachev's political naivety? (20 marks)

Tip

Focus on the question. This question is not just asking how far Gorbachev was responsible for the event in question, but whether his 'naivety' was the root of it.

Conclusion

While the attempted coup and its aftermath had resulted in casualties, the collapse of the USSR at the end of 1991 happened quickly and with no bloodshed. While there might have been passive support at large by the population for a federal state, it was the individual leaders of the republics, particularly Yeltsin, who ended any chance of compromise. Likewise, the reforms that began the process stemmed from Gorbachev, not from the will of the people but, once the people's voice was finally released, it proved impossible for a single man to control. Gorbachev, a committed communist, fought to save the Communist Party and the USSR, but ended up as their destroyer.

For the masses, facing economic ruin and mounting social problems, the pattern would not follow that of Eastern Europe. There, the old guard had been largely removed from office, but under Yeltsin there was little democratisation of political power or economic wealth – 1991 was the downfall of communism, rather than a year of revolution or lasting change.

THINKING HISTORICALLY Cause and consequence (7a & b)

Questions and answers

The questions that interest us define the history that is written, but these change with time and place. Different historians give different answers to the same questions, depending on their perspectives, methods of interpretation and evidence. The three historians below had different areas of interest.

Thomas Carlyle	Karl Marx	Thucydides
19th-century political historian. Interested in the idea that great men shape history.	19th-century economic and political historian. Interested in the role of the working classes and their contribution to historical change.	5th-century BC historian. Interested in the imperialistic nature of a state in aggressively maintaining an empire. Studied relationships between powerful states (realpolitik).

These are some key events in the downfall of communism 1985–91:

Appointment of Gorbachev as first secretary	Withdrawal from Soviet-Afghan war	Chernobyl nuclear disaster
Release of Sakharov from internal exile	Introduction of *perestroika* and *glasnost* reforms	Collapse of Soviet economy after 1988
People power removes communist regimes from Eastern Europe 1989	Failed *coup d'état*, August 1991	Yeltsin bans Communist Party from Russia

Work in groups of between three and six.

1 Which of these events would have most interested each of the three historians named above? Why?

2 Take one historian each and devise a question that would interest them about each of the events.

3 Discuss each event in turn. Present the questions that have been devised for each historian and offer some ideas about how they might have answered them.

4 For each event, decide as a group which question is the most interesting and worthwhile of the three.

Answer the following questions in pairs.

5 What approach might each historian take in writing about the political rivalry between Gorbachev and Yeltsin?

6 In what ways would Carlyle and Marx differ in their explanations of the significance of the failed *coup d'état* in 1991? What would be the focus of their arguments?

Answer the following questions individually.

7 These three historians might produce very different accounts and explanations of the same piece of history. Whose account would you prefer to read first? Explain your answer.

8 Do the differences in these accounts mean that one is more valid than the others?

a) Explain why different historical explanations are written by different historians.

b) Explain why different explanations of the same event can be equally valid.

ACTIVITY
SUMMARY

Gorbachev and the downfall of Soviet communism, 1985-91

1 List the positive and negative outcomes of *perestroika* and *glasnost*.

2 Would *perestroika* have had more success without *glasnost*? Could one exist without the other?

3 Write short biographies of leading characters in the narrative: Gorbachev, Yeltsin, Sakharov, Yanaev.

4 Though the downfall of communism was within the USSR, how important were external events, such as the end of the Cold War or the collapse of communist regimes in Eastern Europe at the end of 1989, in the timing and direction of events?

5 Discuss the role of the media, both domestic and foreign, in the period. Were they a force for change? Did they reflect public concern or create opposition?

6 In groups, gather evidence to put together the case for each of the following factors in explaining the downfall of communism in the USSR:

- the influence of individual leaders, especially Gorbachev
- the impact of the Cold War and of Afghanistan
- the economy and *perestroika*
- people power and *glasnost*
- growing nationalism
- the ending of the gerontocracy
- inadequacies of the Communist Party itself.

Make links and form a clear, reasoned judgement to explain why communism ended during the period.

WIDER READING

Figes, O. *Revolutionary Russia 1891-1991*, Pelican (2014)

Gorbachev, M. *Memoirs*, Doubleday (1995)

Marples, D.R. *The Collapse of the Soviet Union 1985-1991*, Pearson (2004)

Plokhy, S. *The Last Empire: The Final Days of the Soviet Union*, Oneworld (2014)

Sakwa, R. *The Rise and Fall of the Soviet Union 1917-1991*, Routledge (1999)

Sixsmith, M. *Russia: A 1,000-year Chronicle of the Wild West*, BBC (2012)

Preparing for your A Level Paper 3 exam

Advance planning

Draw up a timetable for your revision and try to keep to it. Spend longer on topics that you have found difficult, and revise them several times. Aim to be confident about all aspects of your Paper 3 work, because this will ensure that you have a choice of questions in Sections B and C.

Paper 3 overview

Paper 3	Time: 2 hours 15 minutes	
Section A	Answer 1 compulsory question for the option studied, assessing source analysis and evaluation skills.	20 marks
Section B	Answer 1 question from a choice of 2 on an aspect in depth for the option studied.	20 marks
Section C	Answer 1 question from a choice of 2 on an aspect in breadth for the option studied.	20 marks
	Total marks =	60 marks

Section A questions

There is no choice of question in Section A. You will be referred to a source about 350 words long, printed in a Sources Booklet. The source will be a primary source or one that is contemporary to the period you have studied, and will relate to one of the key topics in the Aspect of Depth. You will be expected to analyse and evaluate the source in its historical context. The question will ask you to assess the value of the source for revealing something specific about the period, and will expect you to explain your answer, using the source, the information given about its origin and your own knowledge about the historical context.

Section B questions

You will have a choice of one from two questions in Section B. They will aim to assess your understanding of one or more of the key topics in the Aspect of Depth you have studied. Questions may relate to a single, momentous year, but will normally cover longer periods. You will be required to write an essay evaluating an aspect of the period. You may be asked about change and continuity, similarity and difference, consequences, significance or causation, or you may be given a quotation and asked to explain how far you agree with it. All questions will require you to reach a substantiated judgement.

Section C questions

You will have a choice of one from two questions in Section C. Questions will relate to the themes of the Aspects of Breadth you have studied, and will aim to assess your understanding of change over time. They will cover a period of not less than 100 years and will relate to the factors that brought about change, or the extent of change over the period, or patterns of change as demonstrated by turning points.

Use of time

- Do not write solidly for 45 minutes on each question. For Section B and C answers, you should spend a few minutes working out what the question is asking you to do, and drawing up a plan of your answer. This is especially important for Section C answers, which cover an extended period of time.
- For Section A, it is essential that you have a clear understanding of the content of the source and its historical context. Pay particular attention to the provenance: was the author in a position to know what he or she was writing about? Read it carefully and underline important points. You might decide to spend up to ten minutes reading the source and drawing up your plan, and 35 minutes writing your answer.

Preparing for your A Level exams

Paper 3: A Level sample answer with comments

Section A

These questions require you to analyse and evaluate the source with respect to its historical context.

For these questions, remember to:

- look at the evidence given in the source and consider how the source could be used in differing ways to provide historical understanding
- use your knowledge of the historical context to discuss any limitations the source may have
- use your historical understanding to evaluate the source, considering how much weight you would give to its argument
- come to a judgement on the overall value of the source in respect to the question.

Study Source 6 (Chapter 4, page 94) before you answer this question.

Assess the value of the source for revealing reasons of discontent and methods of revolt in Russia during the years 1904 and 1905.

Explain your answer, using the source, the information given about its origin and your own knowledge about the historical context. (20 marks)

Average student answer

The extract from the Workers' Petition, dated 9 January 1905, gives a valuable insight into some of the reasons for discontent such as the demand for a Constituent Assembly. It also states some of the methods the masses will use, such as a strike and demonstrations, but then implies they are willing to go further and sacrifice themselves. The value is somewhat limited because it was written by Father Gapon, who was actually working as an agent for the ochrana, the tsar's secret police, and it only talks about the attitudes of the people in St Petersburg, the capital of Russia. Therefore the value of the source is limited.

Although the introduction is aware of the dual focus of the question and gives an example of each, it is a weak introduction as it does not develop its argument. Gapon is labelled as an agent, but the effect of this on the weight of the source is not explored. The judgement is simply expressed.

The Petition was meant to be handed to the tsar at the Winter Palace in St Petersburg, but Tsar Nicholas was not present and his troops opened fire on the demonstrators, killing around 200 of them in an event that became known as Bloody Sunday. This was seen to trigger a series of violent uprisings and protests across the Russian Empire that took a year to bring under control and nearly cost the tsar his rule.

Though the student's own knowledge is accurate, it is not relevant in this form to the focus of the question, which requires more of an examination of what led to the petition, rather than its consequences. The knowledge could be used if tied more directly to the source, but there is no attempt to integrate the source and the historical context.

The source gives a number of reasons to explain the discontent of the people. It explains that they felt little more than 'slaves' and this had been the case for a long time as 'patiently we endured this'. Though there were no actual slaves in Russia at this time, it is referring to the fact that they had no political power at all and no right to freedom of press, assembly and speech as they were 'devoid... of speaking, thinking and meeting'. Therefore, the protestors wanted a 'Constituent Assembly' or elected *duma* which they could all vote for in 'universal suffrage'. This is true as tsarist Russia was an autocracy and Nicholas had no intention of allowing any form of elected body. Pressure for these political reforms had been growing in the

This paragraph is better. The student quotes from the source to illustrate causes of discontent and tries to support the view with their own knowledge. They also use their own knowledge to indicate areas of discontent not mentioned in the source. Their own knowledge could be more detailed and a judgement could be given at the end of the paragraph.

previous years as groups called for the four-tailed formula of universal, direct, equal and secret suffrage. They feel the Russian Empire is now 'too vast' to be run by an imperial bureaucracy but that 'the people should assist'. Indeed, the Russian Empire was very large and many of the extremes of the empire such as Finland did not want to be ruled by the tsar. The petition was written in January 1905, just as news of disastrous defeats in the Russo–Japanese War was becoming known. The war was another cause of discontent, not directly specified in the source, but the defeats directly inspired the St Petersburg strike, that Father Gapon then took over to plan his demonstration at the Winter Palace.

The source also highlights some of the methods of revolt in the period. It says that they have 'left work' and 'shall not resume it'. This refers to the St Petersburg workers who went on strike in January 1905. The source indicates that they are loyal to the tsar himself as it is personally addressed to the tsar and they address him in deferential terms such as 'O Tsar' and 'O Emperor'. It also implies that they feel they should protest through the Church as they link their demands to 'God's commandments'. This is not surprising as Father Gapon was a priest and the protestors carried religious icons while chanting prayers and slogans of loyalty to the tsar. Finally, the source indicates that if their demands are not met they will be forced to die for the cause as they go 'to the tomb'. This implies that the methods could escalate into more violence. Therefore the source is valuable for showing the time when peaceful methods were perhaps on the verge of becoming violent.

This paragraph is good at selecting relevant information from the text, but the extent of own knowledge is limited, especially in challenging the inferences and examining the wider reasons, such as violent methods used by more revolutionary groups.

However, the value of the source is limited as the author was Father Gapon, who also worked as an agent for the ochrana secret police and informed on more radical elements within his protest group. This means he would be careful not to promote disloyalty to the tsar, and it might even have been drafted by the authorities. Indeed, Gapon was later murdered by the opposition to the tsar, who found out his connections to the police. The source also completely focuses on the activities of the opposition in the capital St Petersburg and therefore does not necessarily take into consideration the views of the rural population who hungered for ownership of the land or the cancellation of the redemption payments.

Here the answer addresses considerations around the nature and purpose of the source. However, it is simplistic in its assertions and loses focus when writing about Gapon's murder. Some good points are made, but the evaluation is somewhat 'added on' to the essay. There is a missed opportunity to describe other protest groups. Information on the increasing violence could be brought in here.

In conclusion, the source offers a snapshot of discontent in the capital, particularly the harsh political restrictions for the masses. It also shows that demonstrations, petitions and strikes were the most common methods of protest and that the protesters remained loyal to the idea of the tsar. In short, they wanted a constitutional monarch. Though the source is useful, if focused on St Petersburg, the fact that it was written by the agent Father Gapon must limit its value, as it is not necessarily the opinion of all the protesters.

The conclusion does address the dual focus of the question and the provenance of the source enough to make a judgement based on valid criteria. However, it is a series of statements rather than an argument that justifies its conclusion. There is little indication of the weight of the evidence that the source provides.

Verdict

This is an average answer because:

- it shows an understanding of the source material and identifies the key issues, but they could be explained more clearly
- it shows own knowledge of the context, but this could be developed to both support and challenge the points
- it has some evaluation of the source, but it is limited in its analytical depth
- the final judgement could be more developed to make it substantial.

Use the feedback on this answer to rewrite it, making as many improvements as you can.

Paper 3: A Level sample answer with comments

Section A

These questions require you to analyse and evaluate the source with respect to its historical context.

For these questions, remember to:

- look at the evidence given in the source and consider how the source could be used in differing ways to provide historical understanding
- use your knowledge of the historical context to discuss any limitations the source may have
- use your historical understanding to evaluate the source, considering how much weight you would give to its argument
- come to a judgement on the overall value of the source in respect to the question.

Study Source 6 (Chapter 4, page 94) before you answer this question.

Assess the value of the source for revealing reasons of discontent and methods of revolt in Russia during the years 1904 and 1905.

Explain your answer, using the source, the information given about its origin and your own knowledge about the historical context. (20 marks)

Strong student answer

The source was written by Father Gapon, the head of the Assembly of Russian Factory and Mill Workers of St Petersburg, as part of the petition to give to Tsar Nicholas II at the Winter Palace on 9 January 1905. It was in the demonstration to present the petition that the massacre known as Bloody Sunday occurred and triggered a year of spontaneous and violent results across the Russian Empire. Therefore, the document offers a condensed summary of the discontent of the St Petersburg population and indicates their desired methods of revolt, though this became more violent after Bloody Sunday.

A focused opening that briefly comments on the two aspects of the question: discontent and methods. The source is placed in precise context of the period by linking it to the economic and military context of the time.

The document mentions many grievances that had been building up in the previous years. Father Gapon used the strike at the Putilov Iron Works in early January, which had spread to 150,000 workers, as the opportunity to present his demands. The strike had come about partly in response to the humiliating surrender of Port Arthur by Russia to the Japanese, as well as a reaction to the harsh economic realities of urban life. Indeed, other parts of the petition called for an end to the war, as well as improvements in working conditions such as an eight-hour working day. Though the contents of the petition were soon overshadowed by the reaction to Bloody Sunday, it provides a detailed account of the key areas of discontent of the day.

Gapon writes that the fundamental cause of unrest was the lack of a 'Constituent Assembly', or an elected duma, which he equates with basic human rights that Russians 'of all classes' should enjoy. He complains correctly that these have been denied for some time and the mounting pressure for them has been ignored. Though they have 'patiently… endured this', he feels the time is now due. Here, Gapon is referring to the four-tail formula of universal, direct, equal and secret suffrage that groups like the Union of Liberation had been openly campaigning for since the start of the military defeats in 1904. However, Gapon is at pains to stress the protesters' loyalty to the tsar, with deferential references such as 'O Emperor' throughout the text. Indeed, the demonstrators marching towards the Winter Palace carried religious icons, and shouted slogans of loyalty to the tsar, their 'Little Father'. This attitude was not, however, shared by all protesters at that time. Anger at the Russification policy of the tsar had triggered significant unrest in Finland, and even collaboration between Polish rebels such as Józef Pilsudski and the Japanese. The petition's respect for the authorities could also be explained by the fact that Father

This paragraph tackles the key issue of discontent described in the source. The issues it raises are then both supported and challenged by extensive knowledge of the historical period. The provenance of the source is integrated into this and fully evaluated with a clear judgement of its influence.

Gapon was also a police informer. Indeed, many in Gapon's Assembly originated from the St Petersburg Union set up by the police and ochrana to infiltrate and supervise radicals. However, Gapon's role of an informer can be exaggerated, as this was not uncommon at the time and should not detract from his genuine desire to reform Russia.

The source also highlights some of the methods prevalent at the time. The petition itself is a proclamation of a strike as the workers 'have left work' until their demands are met. This was common in Russia at the time, with 176 strikes a year between 1895 and 1905, with a strike in Vladikavkaz including 225,000 workers in 1902. The petition itself was, according to the source, to be delivered by a mass demonstration of 'three hundred thousand', while this might be a large embellishment of the actual figures (which vary from officially 3,000 to perhaps as many as 50,000), it still shows a wide support base. In its desire to be seen as loyal, there is no suggestion of revolutionary methods. This, however, was not the case for all opponent groups. The Social Revolutionaries had formed in 1902 and used assassination to put their message across, including the murder of Plehve, the interior minister, in 1904. Though the petition stresses non-violence, it does suggest in two separate places a willingness to 'die here on this square' as they prefer death to 'the prolongation of our unendurable tortures'. The change in tone in these parts, despite the overblown language, does hint at a possible escalation of violence if the situation were to remain unchanged. This proved to be an accurate prediction, as within hours 200 civilians were shot. It was partly a reaction to this tragic bloodshed that the methods rapidly increased in scale and violence, with general strikes, independent republics, mutinies, revolutionary soviets and thousands of peasant uprisings directed at local landowners. The source, which helped to create these, certainly did not intend any of them.

Here the key issue of methods is addressed. Again, historical understanding is used to develop and challenge the points raised. The tone of the source is explored to tease out inferences, while a limit to its weight as evidence is explored by historical knowledge of its aftermath.

In conclusion, the source offers a snapshot of St Petersburg at the start of 1905, which became known as the year of revolution. Being the start, it demands reform rather than revolt in its sycophantic pleading for a constitutional monarch. It tells of a fundamentally loyal working population willing to sacrifice themselves for democracy rather than the imposition of any one ideological view as 'let all be free to elect whom they will'. It threatens strikes and sacrifice rather than violence, and this does limit its weight as evidence as Russia, beyond the imperial capital city, was becoming more radical. The fact that its author was later murdered as an agent of the secret police shows just how brutal the methods of revolt would become in the aftermath of Bloody Sunday.

A balanced conclusion that explains the source's significance in showing the discontent and methods of revolt and puts the source clearly in position in the historical context.

Verdict

This is a strong answer because:

- it identifies and illustrates the key points in the source
- it deploys some effective own knowledge to develop points and provide context
- it reaches a clear and substantiated conclusion.

Paper 3: A Level sample answer with comments

Section B

These questions require you to show your understanding of the period in depth. They will ask you about a quite specific period and require you to make a substantiated judgement about a specific aspect you have studied.

For these questions, remember to:

- organise your essay and communicate it in a manner that is clear and comprehensible
- use historical knowledge to analyse and evaluate the key aspect of the question
- make a balanced argument that weighs up differing opinions
- make a substantiated overall judgement on the question.

To what extent was Gorbachev the prime force behind the need for reform within the USSR in 1985–87? (20 marks)

Average student answer

Gorbachev became leader of the USSR in 1985 and by 1987 many reforms had been put in place. Gorbachev was key in introducing these reforms, such as glasnost and perestroika. The USSR was facing many problems in the early 1980s, such as a stagnating economy and defeat in the Afghan war, and Gorbachev was the only leading politician with the vision and personality to implement changes even if they ran contrary to communist ideology.

This is a weak introduction. Though it shows an understanding of the focus of the question, it does not explore the central issues very far. It gives a straightforward assertion on Gorbachev, while other potential factors, such as the economy and the Afghan War, are merely implied.

It would be better to define clearly the range of factors that created the impetus for reform, and state the degree to which Gorbachev was the prime force.

At 54, Gorbachev was much younger than the previous Soviet leaders such as Brezhnev, Andropov and Chernenko. This meant that he was of a generation that was influenced by Khrushchev's 1956 'Secret Speech' which set out to reform aspects of Stalinism. Therefore, when Gorbachev became leader he was more open to new ideas. Many leaders in the West could see that Gorbachev was different. Even before he was leader, Margaret Thatcher, the British prime minister, remarked that he was a man with whom 'we can do business', which suggests his different approach. One of the biggest problems that Gorbachev had to face in 1985 was the failing Soviet economy. This had been stagnating for years and the workers had few incentives to improve efficiency, which lagged many years behind the industry of the West. Gorbachev's new idea was called uskorenie, or acceleration, which focused on investing in both science and technology in order to improve the performance of heavy industry. This was not particularly successful and by 1987 it was replaced by Gorbachev with perestroika, or restructuring, which aimed at a wider restructuring of the soviet command economy.

This paragraph contains some precise detail, though it lacks some specific terms such as 'gerontocracy', that could be applied. It does make the link between the need for reform and the economy, but tends to describe the problems and Gorbachev's reforms. The paragraph does not always support its statement with the depth of evidence, such as on the extent to which the economy was failing.

The focus of the essay is on the need for reforms rather than whether the reforms were successful, and there is no attempt to give a judgement on the economy's impact on the need for reform.

Another significant problem that pushed Gorbachev into introducing reform was the war against Afghanistan. This war had been going on since 1979, when Brezhnev ordered Soviet troops to invade in order to defend Soviet interests against the Mujahedeen. In total, some 550,000 troops were sent to Afghanistan and there were some 50,000 Soviet casualties. It is estimated that the USSR spent $8.2 billion every year on the war. The war had other effects as well. It caused international relations to sour between the USSR and the West and thereby increased tension in the Cold War. The war also sparked protests within the USSR, as families of killed soldiers demonstrated at their funerals, and individual dissidents, such as the scientist Andrei Sakharov, actively protested against the war. Thus the impact of the war made Gorbachev realise that it had to be ended and he started to withdraw troops in 1986, and had ordered a full removal by early 1988. This can be seen as part of Gorbachev's New Political Thinking in which foreign policy was reformed to allow satellite states to be in full control of their own destiny. However, this would have a devastating long-term effect on the USSR, as the Eastern Bloc countries chose to get rid of their communist governments. Still, the Afghan War helped to promote the circumstances for reform.

In 1985, there was also the Chernobyl nuclear disaster in which a nuclear reactor exploded and spread radioactive material over a wide area. This caused extensive economic and environmental damage. The government had to spend at least $18 billion cleaning the infected land and there is a permanent exclusion zone around the site. Information about the explosion and subsequent fire was suppressed from the Soviet population as a whole, causing much fear and resentment, especially in the republics of Ukraine and Belarus, which were most harmed by the disaster. This made Gorbachev comprehend the failures of the Soviet system and the need for reform. He introduced glasnost, or openness, which aimed to provide more transparency to allow more discussion of political and social affairs within the USSR. This included discussion about the failing economy and Afghan War, which caused even more pressure for Gorbachev to reform them.

These two paragraphs introduce other factors to explain the impetus to reform, though they are not explicitly analysed in their own right, but merely as reasons for Gorbachev to act. There is some well-selected detail, but it is mainly descriptive rather than helping to explain the factor in relation to the question. The answer does start to widen the discussion of the Afghan conflict beyond the war itself, by addressing its impact on domestic protest. However, the final link between it and Gorbachev's reform is simply expressed, and it loses focus by introducing the long-term effects of reform and thereby straying outside the time period specified in the question.

There is a good link between *glasnost* resulting from Chernobyl and increasing resentment of the Afghan War, but this link could be explored in significantly more depth. The final judgement on the impact of each factor is underdeveloped.

In conclusion, Gorbachev was the prime mover behind the need for reform in the years 1985–87. He was young enough and open enough in his approach to politics to comprehend that change was needed if the USSR was going to survive. In 1985, there were a number of serious problems that the Soviet system could not cope with as it was inflexible. The economy was failing; the war against Afghanistan was draining resources and the goodwill of the population, and the Chernobyl disaster highlighted how the system was not working. Gorbachev could see this and, therefore, he felt he had to adapt the system mainly through glasnost and perestroika.

The concluding paragraph makes a relevant judgement, but is simplistic in its reasoning. There are no links between the possible factors, which are merely listed as being present at the time.

It would better to show how each 'serious problem' combined and influenced the others, and especially Gorbachev, to increase the pressure for reform.

Verdict

This is an average answer because:

- it does not explicitly explore or evaluate other factors beyond the stated factor
- it has limited use of precise evidence and terminology
- it slips into passages of description rather than explanation.

Use the feedback on this answer to rewrite it, making as many improvements as you can.

Paper 3: A Level sample answer with comments

Section B

These questions require you to show your understanding of the period in depth. They will ask you about a quite specific period and require you to make a substantiated judgement about a specific aspect you have studied. For these questions, remember to:

- organise your essay and communicate it in a manner that is clear and comprehensible
- use historical knowledge to analyse and evaluate the key aspect of the question
- make a balanced argument that weighs up differing opinions.
- make a substantiated overall judgement on the question.

To what extent was Gorbachev the prime force behind the need for reform within the USSR in 1985–87? (20 marks)

Strong student answer

When Mikhail Gorbachev admitted that, 'we cannot go on living like this', he was acknowledging that he would implement reforms to ensure the USSR's survival. However, this was not an ideological attack on communism. Indeed, Gorbachev was determined to maintain the Communist Party's central control of the USSR. There were other forces that were applying pressure on the system. The economy was in decline, which in turn exacerbated social problems and turned incidents into disasters as the system failed to cope, as at Chernobyl. The increase in discontent also fuelled nationalist sentiment within the republics, who in turn called for reform. Gorbachev was fundamental in turning the need for reform into actual reform, and was able to articulate them into viable policies for reform, even if not always successfully.

This is a strong introduction because it provides a clear focus on the question. It clearly acknowledges other factors and the links between them, while giving an argument on the extent that Gorbachev was the prime mover.

The USSR often suffered extreme economic and social problems. However, the limited reforms to tackle these did little to address reform of the Soviet system. What made the situation unique in 1985 was the promotion of Gorbachev as leader. Breaking the tradition of the gerontocracy, the 54-year-old leader's formative political experience was Khrushchev's 1956 de-Stalinisation 'Secret Speech'. This showed Gorbachev that a degree of change was possible and that a reactionary approach would achieve little. He recognised that the problems faced by the USSR required new ideas beginning with the failure of the Soviet offensive in Afghanistan since 1979. The Afghan War was costing the USSR an estimated $8.2 billion a year, but it had wider implications beyond economics which increased demands for reform. Protests started to appear at the funerals of some of the 13,000 Soviet soldiers killed in the conflict, while veterans, known as 'Afgantsy', also participated in opposition to the war and the government itself. The war provided a focal point for general opposition to the state, such as the dissident scientist Andrei Sakharov who was internally exiled for his protests. It was Gorbachev, against the advice of the military, who began the withdrawal of Soviet troops in July 1986, and ordered a full withdrawal in February 1988. The war had also caused tension with the USA in the Cold War, which had increased military spending to between 22 and 27 percent of the USSR's GDP each year. This was money that Gorbachev would have preferred to spend elsewhere, so he introduced his New Political Thinking to allow more autonomy in the Eastern Bloc and thereby diffuse the tension between East and West. Indeed, in 1984 he had visited western Europe and was found by Margaret Thatcher, the British prime minster, to be a man she could do business with. Therefore, the open wound of the Afghan War provided an impetus for reform, but it required a politician brave enough to start the process of ending it.

These paragraphs quickly explain the stated factor and then link it to another factor to show a deeper understanding of the context. Precise detail is used to support the explanations. The influence of the war on Gorbachev's reforms is explicitly stated and a judgement on the extent of the factor in answering the question ends the paragraph.

The war added to the drain on the USSR's resources, but the economy was already in long-term decline. While the economy had always suffered from a lack of technology or workforce incentives, the gap with the market economies of the West was growing wider. Workers themselves had often joked that 'we pretend to work, and they pretend to pay us'. Gorbachev initially introduced the concept of uskorenie, or acceleration, to promote extra investment in the traditional heavy industries, but the scale of the problem pushed for wider solutions and by 1987 Gorbachev adopted the policy of perestroika, or restructuring, to remodel the Soviet economy to create higher standards of living for the population. Indeed, as the economy stalled further, social problems like alcoholism and drug abuse, prevalent among the 550,000 Afghan War veterans, became more severe. Previous leaders had attempted to address specific problems, such as Andropov's anti-alcohol campaign. However, to Gorbachev, alcoholism, as well as mental illness, suicide and divorce, were all symptomatic of a failed economy leading to a failed society.

Nowhere was this lesson clearer than in the aftermath of the Chernobyl nuclear disaster of April 1986. The cost of cleaning up the radioactive material was at least $18 billion, but the disaster showed the combined effects of out-of-date technology and incompetence. The subsequent cover-up, which endangered the public while Party officials moved their families out of the danger zone, proved to Gorbachev the inadequate nature of the Soviet system and raised the need for greater transparency. This became Gorbachev's policy of glasnost, or openness, which would allow greater discussion of social and political issues as well as democratisation to rejuvenate the Party membership.

These sections continue the explanation. The emphasis is on the need to reform, rather than the impact of the reforms. Again the factors are linked back to the stated factor to show the relationship between key features of the period.

These particular reforms acted as a catalyst for further pressure by encouraging public demands for reforms that quickly gathered momentum. Magazines such as *Ogonyok* revealed the abuses that occurred in the Afghan War, the falsification and manipulation of economic data to exaggerate economic successes was revealed in 1987 by Khanin and Selyunin in the journal 'Novy mir'. As the extent of the deadly environmental damage of Chernobyl was published, it all combined to create an impetus for reform both within Russia and increasingly in the republics of the USSR. From Central Asia, where there were riots against Russian political appointments in 1986, to the Ukraine and Belarus, where mistrust of Russia grew after the radioactive dust had settled, to the Baltic states keen to stress their independence, nationalist sentiments were another factor that strove for reform. This, however, was the one that Gorbachev would try to hold back, for it was the one he could not allow without dismantling the USSR itself.

Here the analysis is taken further to show how Gorbachev's reforms actually increased the impetus for further reform as well as introducing a final factor, whose limited impact in the time period specified in the question is clearly articulated.

In conclusion, Gorbachev can be seen as the individual most important to the process of reform in the years 1985–87 because he had the temperament and the political clout to introduce reform. However, as the prime mover, he was a pragmatic politician working within the special circumstances of the time. It was the failed economy, damaged further by an unsuccessful war, environmental disasters and social problems, that necessitated change. Perhaps it was the image of the ruined fourth reactor at Chernobyl billowing its deadly smoke that exposed the USSR, not just to radiation, but to the whole decrepit system. Whoever was in charge would feel the same pressure for reform, but because Gorbachev was leader, measures were actually introduced to begin the process. Indeed, it quickly became the very measures themselves, in particular glasnost that accelerated the calls for further reform that would by 1988 start to overtake the abilities of the communist state and Gorbachev to control them.

The concluding paragraph makes a relevant and reasoned judgement. It addresses the key concept 'prime mover' and explores it in relation to other factors. Using a strong image, or a key quote, helps to focus the key point in the mind of the reader. The relative significance of the stated factor is evaluated in the substantiating overall judgement.

Verdict

This is a strong answer because:

- it considers the precise focus
- it gives a reasoned and evaluative judgement on the stated factor and its relationship with the other factors
- it displays high-level thinking skills
- each point has precise examples to support the explanation and analysis fully
- the quality of written communication, logical coherence and conceptual understanding are all excellent.

Paper 3: A Level sample answer with comments

Section C

These questions require you to show your understanding of a subject over a considerable period of time. They will ask you to assess a long-term historical topic and its development over a period of at least 100 years, and they require you to make a substantiated judgement in relation to the question.

For these questions, remember to:

- organise your essay and communicate it in a manner that is clear and comprehensible
- use historical knowledge to analyse and evaluate the key aspect of the question covering the entire period
- make a balanced argument that weighs up differing opinions
- make a substantiated overall judgement on the question.

To what extent did agriculture successfully meet the demands of the population in Russia in the years 1861–1991? (20 marks)

Average student answer

For much of the period between 1861 and 1991, agriculture failed to feed the population. During imperial times, before 1917, it was the cities which tended to go hungry first, while under communist rule it was the countryside, as the government insisted the workers were fed first. However, famine was common in both periods. Even when there was enough food, the variety on offer was always limited.

This introduction does give an answer and indicates that it will cover the whole period. However, there is no argument to develop the basic and broad idea. It is a series of assertions with nothing to thread it together.

For the second half of the 19th century, a basic lack of technology and modernisation restricted the capacity to produce consistent harvests. The mir controlled the farming techniques, which had changed little since the medieval period. The subsistence strip-farming failed to cope with the population growth, especially as the strips were continually being redistributed to partition out land. The fact that 750,000 peasants had avoided the redemption taxes by taking 'beggar holdings' also meant that many went hungry. The cities were largely provided for by the estates of the nobility. However, famine was never more than a few seasons' bad weather away. The famine of 1891 killed over 500,000 and regular shortages were seen as just part of life, meaning little action was taken to prevent them.

By the 20th century, a concentrated push for migration to Siberia to open new lands meant that the new lands rather than improved farming produced crops and meat for the rest of the Empire. It was this, as well as fine weather, that mainly kept the population fed. This was to change sharply in the years of the First World War when the chaos of war saw grain production fall from 90 million tons to 64 million tons, and the cities empty as their population fled to the countryside to search for food. The lack of food helped to trigger both the February and October Revolutions of 1917 which saw the Bolshevik communists take over.

There is plenty of precise knowledge and the information is both accurate and relevant. However, it is descriptive in approach and, therefore, limited in its analysis.

It was at this point that the pattern of agriculture changed. The communist government believed that the workers should be fed first, before the peasants. At first, this was partly for practical reasons, so the Bolsheviks could guarantee that the workers produced weapons for the civil war, 1918–21, but later it was the ideological foundation of the rapid industrialisation, when peasants were forced into collectivisation throughout the 1930s. The peasants' grain would be taken for workers' food and foreign exports to raise investment. On both occasions, the result was massive famine in the countryside and the death of millions. Under Stalin, feeding the peasant population was simply not a concern, and starvation was even used as a method of terror and control. It was only in the late 1930s that technology, particularly tractors, was provided in enough quantity to raise levels of grain production, even if other crops were ignored. The only variety in the Russian diet was from the produce of the small private plots that were reluctantly allowed to each peasant household. These provided most of the fruit, meat, dairy produce, vegetables and honey for the population and, therefore, they were the chief reason why Russia managed to avoid further famine, with the exception of 1946 after the devastation of the Second World War.

Even though Russia was relatively self-sufficient by 1953, the system was under strain. When Khrushchev pushed agriculture further with unrealistic targets in order to compete with the USA, the system broke. Farm yields remained low and production only increased because of the increase in sown area because of the Virgin Lands Scheme. When this and other schemes, such as maize mania, inevitably failed, the result was increasing food shortages. This resulted in unrest and violence, such as Novocherkassk in 1962 in which 16 people were killed and seven later sentenced to death. Still there were bread queues and the threat of rationing, forcing Khrushchev to import grain from the West. Though this managed to feed the people, it set a precedent that became an annual purchase under Brezhnev in the 1970s and 1980s. As Russia became more exposed to life in the West, the Russian population could see how the restrictions on their diet, based on bread and potatoes, compared with the variety of the Western nations' diet. Grain for bread was given priority and needed vast subsidies to keep it cheap to buy, at almost $33 billion a year. This focus meant nearly everything else was in short supply. As before, it was the private plots, whose produce was often sold at roadside markets, which provided any sort of variety in the diet beyond the staples.

This continues to be a chronological narrative of the time frame, which is easy to fall into when covering a long period. The considerable own knowledge could be better applied if it was organised around thematic factors that explained agriculture's impact on feeding the population.

In conclusion, in Imperial Russia, the backwardness of agriculture as well as the traditional nature of the village mir, meant agriculture struggled to feed the cities and often slipped into famine if the climate proved unfavourable to farming. The government of the period did little to rectify this. During the communist period under both Lenin and Stalin, the government chose to feed the workers and ignore the plight of the peasants. Agriculture in the USSR found it difficult to recover from this, and Khrushchev and later Brezhnev only found a genuine solution by importing grain. Therefore agriculture often struggled to meet the demands of the whole population and never managed to provide a varied diet for the people.

Here, there are hints of analysis with the factors or a lack of technology and the role of the government, but the conclusion largely repeats the content that has been expressed in the body of the answer. It lacks a persuasive argument.

Verdict

This is an average answer because:

- there is some attempt to address the topic in general, but there is insufficient analysis regarding the specific question
- there is good deployment of own knowledge, but it is descriptive and recounts a narrative about the time period
- there is a judgement, but it is not substantiated.

Use the feedback on this essay to rewrite it, making as many improvements as you can.

Paper 3: A Level sample answer with comments

Section C

These questions require you to show your understanding of a subject over a considerable period of time. They will ask you to assess a long-term historical topic and its development over a period of at least 100 years, and they require you to make a substantiated judgement in relation to the question. For these questions, remember to:

- organise your essay and communicate it in a manner that is clear and comprehensible
- use historical knowledge to analyse and evaluate the key aspect of the question covering the entire period
- make a balanced argument that weighs up differing opinions
- make a substantiated overall judgement on the question.

To what extent did agriculture successfully meet the demands of the population in Russia in the years 1861–1991? (20 marks)

Strong student answer

Russian agriculture failed more than it was successful in meeting the demands of the Russian people. This was fundamentally due, first, to a lack of modernisation which resulted in inefficient yields and, secondly, to the attitudes of the various governments towards feeding the population. While some governments were merely indifferent towards the hungry, others actively saw it as either a price they were willing to be paid or a tool of control and coercion. Though different social groups suffered at different times, the rule was that supply was often limited, while variety was almost non-existent. It was only the peasants' attitude to grow what they could that provided any respite.

This is a focused introduction, which identifies the key issue and offers factors to explain it. It is also aware that there are subtleties within the scope of the question.

Agriculture struggled because it lacked the technology for efficient production. During the imperial period after 1861, the village commune or mir controlled the subsistence strip-farming and stubbornly resisted new innovations. Food for the cities, and for export, was mostly grown on the estates of the nobility. However, population growth placed strains on the mir as peasants' holdings were repartitioned, meaning that farms not self-sufficient rose from around a quarter in 1861 to a half by 1900. Over 750,000 peasants had avoided redemption payments by taking a smaller allocation after their emancipation. These 'beggar holdings' never provided enough food. Agriculture was only able to keep up with population growth (155 million by 1913) by expanding the total sown area rather than the efficiency of the yields. This can be seen in the large migrations to Siberia in the 1890s and 1900s, which provided half of the meat for the major cities. In the 1950s, Khrushchev's Virgin Lands Scheme saw relentless farming drain the soil of its nutrients and harvests declined. Attempts to improve the structure of farms, such as Stolypin's creation of kulaks, had little success and any progress quickly reversed in the First World War as people sought the security of the traditional mir.

The increase in farmed land was needed as technology was not delivered. In 1914, European Russia possessed only 166 tractors compared with 14,000 in the USA. The drive for collectivisation in 1928 was built on the promise of mechanisation, but the Motor Tractor Stations remained empty. For most of the 1930s, the grain was forced from starving peasants rather than grown in abundance, and there were never enough machines in the Soviet period, either in quantity or quality. The inefficient collective fields compared poorly to peasants' small private plots, where yields were 8–12 times higher. This might be partly due to the incentive of profit for the peasant, but it meant that the private plots would play a vital role in providing variety in people's diets from 1932 to 1991, becoming the chief source of meat, vegetables, fruits, dairy products and honey.

Here the question is answered thematically rather than chronologically. The factor of the extent of mechanisation is explained and supported with extensive knowledge. The whole period specified in the question is covered.

Just as important as the lack of technology was the attitude of the government towards feeding the population. While yields were low, the government could actively make it worse. For the tsars, agriculture was more about social control than food production. It was a way to reinforce loyalty and a source of revenue in exporting grain, with Russia becoming the largest grain exporter by 1913. Shortages and famine were seen as part of the rhythm of life and, therefore, little action was taken to prevent them. If the imperial government was indifferent, the communist leaders saw the peasants as a tool to exploit. Under War Communism (1918–21) and then collectivisation (from 1928), they plundered supplies to feed the workers. To Lenin, it was needed to win the Civil War. To Stalin, it was an ideological war to crush the peasantry. While the cities tended to go hungry under the tsar, under the communist regime the peasants were sacrificed.

The government attitudes can best be demonstrated in regard to their response to famine. All governments had a poor record of aid during periods of famine, usually triggered by poor climate. In 1891, as 500,000 died, Minister Vyshnegradsky continued to export grain. News of the famine was censored, delaying any relief. Eventually only voluntary relief was permitted. In 1921, Lenin created a 'food army' of 76,000 to steal the peasants' food. As the people died, and cannibalism became common, Lenin denied the famine's existence and criticised state charity organisations for being sentimental. In the end, it was left to private charities to help, including the American Relief Administration, which fed 10 million people. By the 1932 famine, Stalin refused any aid whatsoever as more than 10 million peasants were 'liquidated' so that their grain could be fed to the workers or exported for foreign capital.

These paragraphs explain a second factor to give weight to the argument. Considerable knowledge of the period provides a close comparison of the different governments' response to an issue. This allows a deeper analysis.

It was only by the 1960s, when poor harvests threatened both more famine and political unrest, that Khrushchev's solution finally involved actually feeding the population as, to his embarrassment, he authorised grain imports from the West in 1962. The continued inefficiency of farming meant that these imports would become an annual event in the Brezhnev years from 1972 onwards, with $35 billion worth of food purchased in 1981–85.

Even sympathetic policies hindered the variety of people's diet. The communist emphasis on cheap bread (the price of which did not rise from 1955 to 1980) meant huge subsidies were needed to cover the cost ($33 billion in 1981), while other crops were ignored and nearly always defitsitnyl, or 'in short supply'. A potential rise in food prices could trigger uprisings as at Novocherkassk in 1962, while bread queues were a focal point of resentment in the 1917 revolutions and in the 1991 collapse of the USSR. It was the private plots that delivered any sort of variety, but even the later communist leaders introduced regular policies attacking them, such as higher taxes and Khrushchev's removal of livestock.

This paragraph looks more deeply at issues within the question, such as the variety of diet, while making links with the factors explained earlier.

In conclusion, both the lack of technology and the attitudes of the government meant food supply was always inconsistent, resulting in regular shortages, rationing and famine. The variety beyond bread and potatoes did improve slightly over time, but it never matched the West, with Moscow restaurants in the 1970s organising 'meatless days'. However, whatever the period, the favoured elite always gained access to food. The aristocracy enjoyed splendour under the tsar, but starved under the communists, who favoured the workers above all. Throughout the last two decades of the USSR, as the queues stretched outside empty shops, Party officials had privileged and secret access to uninterrupted supplies. It was because the peasants themselves were never trusted to manage their farms that agriculture was marked by incompetence and neglect, hence its inability to meet the demands of the population.

The conclusion draws the factors together and sums up the overall argument. It uses the 'privileged' elite of each period to show the thematic link across the whole time period. There is a clear and reasoned judgement on the question.

Verdict

This is a strong answer because:

- it identifies a range of thematic factors in its argument
- the analysis is well supported with sufficient knowledge
- it provides a confident and persuasive judgement on the question.

Index

advokatura **72**
afgantsy 154
Afghanistan war 152–5
agricultural methods 23, 24, 41, 44, 45
agricultural regions 39
agricultural schemes 50–1
agricultural subsidies 60
agricultural systems 40, 42
agrotowns **26**, 29, 33, 47
Akhmatova, Anna 137, 146
alcoholism 152, 156–7
Alexander II, tsar (the Liberator) 12–13, 64, 65
assassination attempts 78, 80, 84
serfdom abolition 13, 14, 15, 18
Alexander III, tsar 69, 72, 73
Alexandrovich, Grand Duke Sergei 95
Alexei, Prince 112
American Relief Administration 58
amnesty 99, 136, 137
Andreeva, Nina 165–6
Andropov, Yuri 157, 159, 164
anti-alcohol campaign 161–2
'Anti-Party' group 141, 142
anti-Semitism 87, 100, 127
Antonov, Alexander 21
April 9+1' Treaty 170
April Theses 116, 117
Aral Sea 156
aristocracy, decadence of 113
arms race 153, 160
army actions 57, 97
arson attacks 97, 104
Article 6, Soviet Constitution **167**, 168
artistic community 147
autocracy **12**, 95

'bagging' and bagmen 57
Baibakov, Nikolai 61
Baltic states 158, 169
Bar Councils 72
Basic Criminal Code 163
Battle of Alma 66
Battle of Mukden 89
Battle of the Yellow Sea/Ship 88
Battle of Tsushima 89, 90, 91
Battle of Yalu River 88, 89
'beggar holdings' 14, 56
Belarus 158
Beria 131, 132, 133, 137
Bezdna 14, 78
Black Hundreds 100, **104**
black market 57, 61, 162
Bloody Sunday 86, 92–6
Bolshevik government 121, 123–4, 126
Bolsheviks **19**, 20, 21, 108, 116, 120
bread, cheap 60
Brest-Litovsk Peace Treaty 20, 22
Brezhnev Doctrine **160**
Brezhnev, Leonid Ilich 33, 34, 48, 51, 151, 157
bribes 71
Brusilov, General 112, 119, 120
'Brusilov Offensive' 109–10
Bukharin 23, 24, 126
Bulygin's Rescript **96**, 98
burzhui 124, 127

cancers from radiation 157
cannibalism 58
cartoons 70, 113, 160
Caucasus, The 94, 158
censorship 81
charities 56, 58
Cheka **21**, 23, 44, 125
Chernenko, Konstantin 157, 159
Chernobyl 152, 157, 158
Chernyaev, Anatoly 163
child mortality 15
cholera 56
Civil War **20–1**, 57, 108, 123, 127
Cold War 121, 153, 157, 159, 160
collective farms 21, 26, 27, 53, 46, 47
collectivisation, mass 26–7, 29
command economy **155**
Committee of State Security (KGB) 132, 144, 145, 155, 169
Commonwealth of Independent States (CIS) 171
Communist Party downfall 171
concentration camps 23
Conference of Soviets 115
Congress of People's Deputies 166, 167–8
Congress of Soviets 117, 121, 124
Conquest, Robert 30, 45
conscription 19, 21, 68, 70, 127
consolidated farms 16, 17, 18
Constituent Assembly 20, 124
constitution of 1906 101, 102, 105
Constitutional Democratic Party (Kadets) 98, 101, 115, 124
constitutional monarchy 89, 93, 99, 102, 106
Contemporary, The 81, 82
corporal punishments 71
corruption 71, 154
Cossacks 43, 97, 100
Council of People's Commissars (*Sovnarkom*) 124
coup d'état 121, 152, 155, 170, 171
courts, new 71–2, 73
'creeping schizophrenia' 145
Crimean War **12**, 66, 68
Criminal Code, Article 107 26
crops 41, 44, 46, 57
cultural life 145–8
Cultural Revolution 24
culture, western 147, 148
Czechoslovakia 127, 160, 169

dairy farming 18, 34
debt arrears, peasants 15
Decembrist uprising 71
decentralisation of power 144
defitsitnyl **60**
dekulakisation **29**
Democratic Movement 168
democratic plans 91
Democratic Union 168
democratisation 144, **160**
demonstrations 59, 88
de-Stalinisation 130, 137, 140, 141, 145, 149
détente 61, **153**
dissidents **152**, 154, 162, 163
'Dizzy with success' 28–9
'Doctors' Plot' 139
Dr Zhivago 146
drought 32, 49, 55
'Dry Law' 161
dual power 114, 117
duma **16**, **77**, 91, 101, 102, 108
Durnovo, Pyotr 103–4, 109
dustbowls 49, 156
Dzerzhinsky, Felix 21, 125

East/West co-operation 157
East Germany 169
Eastern Front 110
economic figures 1971–90 155
economic stagnation 155–6, 161
economists 156
economy, more open 170
Edict of Emancipation 13, 14, 41
electrification 24
emancipation of serfs 13, 14, 15, 18, 64, 65
estates, nobility 43, 44
Estonia 158
ethnic group deportations 48, 158
exam preparation 175–87
exile 23, 72, 94, 116

factory and mill workers 26, 92
family farms 52
famine 21, 32, 55, 56, 58
in 1932 29, 30, 32, 59
'famine bread' 56
farms, consolidated 16, 17, 18
February Revolution 19, 57, 113–14
Festival of Youth 147–8
Figes, Orlando 15, 18, 40, 99, 121, 127
films 46, 93, 97, 121, 148
Finland 89, 94, 101
First World War 18–19, 57, 109–10, 117, 119–20, 128
impact of 111–12
Five-Year Plans 26, 29, 51, 160
'Food Army' 58
food as a weapon 62–3
food consumption 60
food queues 57, 61, 111
food, self-sufficiency 59
food shortages 29, 61, 89, 111
'four-tail formula' 89, 98
Franco–Prussian War **68**
freedom of speech 72
freedom of the press 124
Fundamental Laws **101**, 102

Gagarin, Yuri 143
Gapon, Father 92–3, 94
General Strike 98, 99, 101, 103
Georgia 94, 158
German attempt on Petrograd 126
gerontocracy **160**
Ginzburg, Alexander 147
glasnost **66**, 152, 161, 163
Golovnin 78, 79, 80
Gorbachev, Mikhail 35, 51, 52, 152, 159–61, 170
new appointments 164
rivalry with Yeltsin 168–9, 171
Gorky, Maxim 58
Gosagroprom 52
Gosplan **61**
Government Messenger 72, 73
government reform 74
government structure in 1985 167
grain 34, 38, 49, 55, 61, 89
grain exports 29, 43, 56, 58
grain imports 49, 60, 61
grain production 17, 23, 29, 49, 57, 58
Greens 21, 23, 127
Gregorian calendar 5
Gromov, Boris 155
Gromyko, Andrei 159, 164
Grossman, Vasily 27
gulags 27, 132, 136, 137, 144, 145
gymnasiums 69, 79, 80

haemophilia 112
Harvest of Sorrow, The 30, 45
health care 75
holodomor 30, 59
Hosking, Geoffrey 100
housing problem 150
Hungary 140, 169

identity cards 78
Imperial Decree 96
imperial guards, slaughter of 110
inflation 111, 120, 165
Instructor Group (IG) 33
internal passports 35
Inter-Regional Group 167, 168
Intourist 147

Ishutin Society 80
Izvestiia 98

Japan conceding land to 91
Jews 61, 73, 87, 100, 149, 162
jokes 156, 167
judicial system 71, 145
Julian calendar 5
July Days coup 118, 119, 120
juries, use of 71, 72
justices of the peace 71, 72, 73
justice system, two–tier 73

Kadets 98, 101, 115, 124
Kaganovich, Lazar 30, 138, 141
Kaplan, Fanny 127, 128
Kazakhstan 49, 158
Kerensky, Alexander 72, 95, 118–22
KGB 132, 144, 145, 155, 169
Khrushchev, Nikita Sergeyevich 32–3, 34, 130, 134–6
  and agriculture 34, 47–9, 50–1, 59
  autobiography 48, 133, 137, 138
  and the Church 149
  plot to remove 140–1, 142
  reforms 143–4
  removal from power 49, 51, 144, 149, 150
  'Secret Speech' 33, 137, 138–9, 140, 141
  speeches 48, 50, 143
Khrushchev, Sergei 60
'Khrushchev's false teeth' 150
Khvostov, Alexei 112
kolkhozy **21**, 26, 30, 32, 33, 34
Komsomol **24**, 25, 27, 48, 144
Kornilov Affair 120
Kronstadt Mutiny **21**, 118
Kropotkin, Prince 14, 56
kulaks **17**, 20–1, 23, 54, 58, 102

labour camps (gulags) 27, 132, 136, 137, 144, 145
labour unions 92
Land Bank 15, 16, **42**, 43, 44
Land Captains 15, 16, 73
Land Decree 19, 20, 21
land reforms 15, 52, 102, 119
Latvia 94, 158
'Law against Parasites' 145, 148, 157
Law of Seventh-Eights 29
Law on Co-operatives 165
Law on Land Reform 52
Law on Peasant Farms 52
Law on State Enterprise 165
leaders in exile 116
legal reform 71–3
Lenin, Vladimir Ilich 19, 72, 103, 108, 116–17, 124
  decision to murder the tsar 127
  hold on power 123
  personality 119, 128
  speeches 58, 116
Leningrad 108
Leningrad Affair 132, 139
'Lenin's Testament' 139
Ligachev, Yegor 164, 165, 166
literacy 15, 24, 83
Lithuania 158

loan to Russia 101
Lvov, Prince 112, 113, 118

Machiavellian **132**
Machine Tractor Station (MTS) 32, 33, 45
magnitizdat 154
'maize mania' 49–50
Malenkov 47–8, 132, 134, 136, 140–1
maps 11, 39, 126, 159
market economy 52, 156
market forces 160
Markovo Republic **97**
Mayakovsky, Vladimir 146
Medvedev, Roy 168
Mensheviks **94**, 115
migration to cities 15
migration to Siberia 17, 18, 42
military reform 68, 69
Milyukov, Pavel 98, 111, 113
Milyutin, Dmitry 67, 68, 69, 81
Ministry of Agriculture 42
Ministry of Internal Affairs 81
mirs **13**, 14, 17, 19, 20, 23, 32
Model Collective Farm Charter 30, 32
Molotov 48, 133, 140–1
Moscow 78, 103, 126, 164
Moscow Uprising 1905 **103**
MTS 32, 33, 45, 50
Mujahedeen **153**, 154, 155
Mukden defeat 96
Municipal Regulations Act 76
mutinies 90, 97, 104, 118

Nabokov, Vladimir Dmitrievich 119
Nagorno-Karabakh 158
NATO 140
Naval Review magazine 66
navy 109
Nazi–Soviet Pact 162
nedefsitnyl **60**
Nekrasov, Nikolay 81
nepmen 25
New Economic Policy (NEP) 22, 23, 24, 25, 59
'New Political Thinking' 160
new press, impact 82–3
Nicholas I, tsar 12, 66, 78
Nicholas II, tsar (the bloody) 86, 90–1, 96, 101, 106, 114
nihilists 81, 82
Nikolaevich, Grand Duke Konstantin 66–7, 78
Nikolaevich, Grand Duke Nicholas 95, 99
Nobel Prize 146, 154, 159, 170
nomenklatura system **60**, 136, 161
Notes from the Fatherland 81
novels 78, 81, 145–6, 148, 162

obshchestvennost **76**, 77, 83, 84
ochrana 66, **92**, 104
October Manifesto 91, 99, 100, 101, 102, 103
October Revolution 19, 121
Octobrist **101**, 102
Ogonyok **magazine** **154**
OGPU 26, 27

oil and gas 61
Olympics 153
orphans 31, 58
Orthodox Church 27, 56, 149
Orwell, George 162
Ottoman Empire 12
over-population 15

paintings 13, 75, 100
Pamyat and Pamyatnik 168
Pasternak, Boris 146
Pavlov, Valentin 168
Peasant Land Bank 15, 16, **42**
Peasant Union 98
peasants 11, 15, 21, 23, 33, 35
  crushing 26, 53, 58
  deference to tsar 105–6
  resistance 12, 27, 40, 41
People's Cause, The 84
People's Will 13, 15, 84
perestroika 52, **152**, 160, 161, 165–6
periodicals 81–2
Peter and Paul fortress 78, 120
Peter the Great 67
petitions to tsar 94, 96
Petrograd (St Petersburg) 57, **108**, 126
Petrograd coup 118
Petrograd Soviet 19, 108, 113–15
Petrov, Anton 14, 78
Pinya 134, 141
Plehve 86, 87, 92
Pobedonostsev, Konstantin 84, 95
poems 90, 113, 146, 147, 170
poets 80, 137, 146, 168, 170
pogroms 100
Poland 61, 89, 94, 127, 169
  rebellion 68, 70, 79, 140
'police socialism' 92
Politburo **22**, 25
political prisoners, release 136, 137, 144
political thinkers 82–3
Pomgol 58
population growth 15, 17, 42, 55, 57
Port Arthur 88, 91
Pospelov, Pyotr, report 137, 138
posters 28, 48, 65
Potemkin (battleship) **90**, 97, **121**
poverty 14, 52
Prague Spring 160
Pravda 28–9, 33, **117**, 118, 142
Presidium 33
Presnia 103
press regulations 81
Primary Party Organisation (PPO) 33
private farms 52
private plots 32, 34, 35, 51, 59
privatisation, move towards 52
proletariat **38**
propaganda films 46
propaganda posters 28, 48
Provisional Government **19**, 20, 114, 115, 117–20
Prussian army 68
Pushkin 12
Putilov Iron Works 88, 93, 111

queuing 57, 61, 111, 156
quotas, grain 26, 31

Radio Free Europe 148
Radzinsky, Edvard 95
railways, expansion 43
Rasputin 109, 110, 112–13
rationing, food 165
raznochintsy **76**
Red Army **21**, 126–7
Red Guards 120, 123
redemption payments 16, 99
redemption tax **13**, 14–15
Reds 21
republics 152, 154, 158, 159
  independence 168, 170, 171
  nationalism 158, 169
Resettlement Administration 42
Revolution of 1905 86
rural to urban economy 26
Russian Messenger 82
Russian Word, The 81
Russification **89**
Russo–Japanese War 87–91
Rust, Mathias 164

Sakharov, Andrei 154, 162, 163, 167, 168
samizdat 147, **154**
samogon 156, 161
satellite launch 143
Schmidt, Commander Pyotr 97
schools 75, 79
'scissor crisis' 22
Second World War 31, 32, 59
Secret Committee on Peasant Affairs 13
secret police 21, 26–7, 66, 79, 92–3, 104, 125
'Secret Speech' 33, 137, 138–9, 140, 141
security services 132
serf emancipation 13, 14, 15, 18, 64, 65
Sevastopol 66, 97, 104
Shelepin, Alekandr 144
shestidesiatniki 140, 159
Shevardnadze, Eduard 51, 164, 170
Siberia 15, 17, 18, 42, 56, 71
Sinatra Doctrine **160**
Sixsmith, Martin 155, 169
slavophiles 66, 67
slogans 116, 124
smychka 23, 32
Social Revolutionary (SR) Party **19**, 20, 92, 98, 101, 115
socialist legality **144**
'socialist market economy' 160
socialist pluralism 166–7
soil deterioration 49, 50
Solidarity 160, 169
Solzhenitsyn, Aleksandr 145, 162
Soviet Constitution 167
soviets, creation 99
sovkhozy **21**, 26, 33, 34
Sovnarkom 124
Soyuz faction 167
space race 143
Sputnik 143
St Petersburg 14, 79, 108

St Petersburg Soviet **98**, 99, 100, 103
Stalin, Joseph 25, 26, 28–9, 116, 118, 130
  and agriculture 33, 45, 46–7
  collectivisation 29, 32
  cult of personality 139
  rehabilitation of rivals 162
  responsibility for purges 139
  rule of, attack by Krushchev 33
starvation 29, 30, 32, 56, 57, 58
State Agroindustrial Committee **52**
state farms 49
state secrecy 154, 157
state security reforms 144–5
Statute on Socialist Land Organisation 21
steppes 43, 44, 48
Stolypin, Pyotr 16–17, 18, 86, 101, 105
Stolypin's necktie **105**
Strategic Defence Initiative (SDI) 153
strikes 61, 88, 92, 93, 94, 124
strip farming 12, 40, 41
student unrest 78, 79, 80, 94
Stürmer 110, 111
Tambov 21, 23
targets 26, 27, 59, 156
Tauride Palace 114, 118
taxes 32, 34
television 162–3
Thatcher, Margaret 160, 162
'thaw', the 130, 145, 149
'Third Communist programme' 149, 150, 156
'third element' 76
Third Section **66**
Tolstoi, Count Dmitry 69, 80, 84
Tolstoy, Leo 56, 82
TOV co-operatives 23, 26
'tractorisation' **45**
tractors 26, 30, 31, 46
Trans-Siberian Railway 42–3, 56
Travopolye system 46, 50
Treaty of Brest-Litovsk 125, 126
Treaty of Paris 66
Treaty of Portsmouth 89, 91
Trepov, Dmitry 73, 95, 100, 103
trials, secret, end of 145
Trotsky, Leon 20, 25, 86, 108, 117, 121, 127
memoirs 98, 99
Trubetskoy, Prince Sergei 91
tsarina, power of 112, 114
Turgenev, Ivan 81, 82
'Twenty-five Thousanders' 27, 33

Ukraine 30, 32, 50, 158, 171
Union of Liberation 89
Union of Towns 112
'Union of Unions' 98
Union of Zemstva 112
United Nobility 101, 112
universities 78, 79, 80, 94
urbanisation 26
uskorenie **160**, 161
US-Soviet trade agreements 60–61
USSR 152, 159, 169, 170, 171

Valentinov, Nikolai 119
Velvet Revolution 169
villages 23, 40, 41, 52
Virgin Lands Scheme 48–9, **132**
vodka 111, 156, 165
***volost* courts** **72**, 74, 76
Voroshilov 131, 138, 140–1
Vostok mission 143

War Communism **21**, 22, 57
war loans 111
Warsaw Pact **140**
West, contact with 147–8, 157
Whites 21, 127
Winter Palace demonstrations 88, 92, 93, 94, 100
Witte, Count Sergei 87, 91, 93, 99, 100, 101, 105
writers 78, 81, 146, 148

Yakovlev, Alexander 164, 168, 170
Yazov, Marshal Dmitry 168, 170
Yeltsin, Boris 159, 164, 168–9, 170, 171
Yevtushenko, Yevgeni 168, 170
Young Russia 78–9, 84
Yugoslavia, conflict with 139
Yusupov, Prince 112

Zaichnevsky, Peter 79
Zasulich, Vera 73
Zemgor 112
zemstva **56**, 64, 74, 75–6, 79
Zinoviev 22, 117, 118

Acknowledgements

The authors and publisher would like to thank the following individuals and organisations for permission to reproduce photographs and text in this book.

(Key: b-bottom; c-centre; l-left; r-right; t-top)

akg-images Ltd: 13, 24, 75, 106, 113, Erich Lessing 136, NordicPhotos 110, Pictures From History 28, Universal Images Group/Sovfoto 147; **Alamy Images:** Everett Collection Historical 118, ITAR-TASS Photo Agency 133, 143, 154, National Geographic Creative 6; **Bridgeman Art Library Ltd:** State Russian Museum, St. Petersburg, Russia 100; **Getty Images:** Dima Tanin/AFP 171l, Fine Art Images/Heritage Images 48, 65, 82, Hulton Archive 104, PIKO/AFP 171r, Print Collector 40, Slava Katamidze Collection 17, Sovfoto/UIG 50, SVF2 163, The Cartoon Collector/Print Collector 70, Ullstein Bild 46, Universal History Archive 58, 88, Valentin Obodzinsky/MCT/MCT 158; **Library of Congress, Prints & Photographs Division:** Edmund Valtman/LC-DIG-ppmsc-07959 160; **Rex Shutterstock:** Sovfoto/Universal Images Group/Rex/Shutterstock 9; **TopFoto:** Fine Art Images/ Heritage Images 31t, Topham Picturepoint 31b

Cover image: Bridgeman Art Library Ltd: Private Collection/RIA Novosti

All other images © Pearson Education

Figures
Figures 2.2 and 2.3, 2.6 from *Tsarist Russia 1801–1917* Causeway Press (John Hite, 1989) pp.23, 82 and 81, reproduced with permission from Pearson Education Ltd. Figure 2.5 from *Years of Russia and the USSR, 1851–1991* Hodder & Stoughton (David Evans and Jane Jenkins, 2001) p.279, tab. 52 and 53, reproduced by permission of Hodder Education; Figure 2.7 from *The Rise and Fall of the Soviet Economy* Longman (Philip Hanson 2001), p.116, reproduced with permission of Taylor & Francis Books UK.

Tables
Table p.23 from *An Economic History of the USSR* Penguin (Alec Nove, 1969) (Allen Lane The Penguin Press, 1969, Third edition, 1992) Copyright © Alec Nove, 1969, 1972, 1976, 1982, 1989, 1992; Table p.155 from *The Rise and Fall of the Soviet Union 1917–1991* Routledge (Richard Sakwa, 1999) p.426, Copyright © 1999 Routledge, reproduced with permission of Taylor & Francis Books UK.

Text
Source 3 p.14 from *Russia and the USSR, 1855–1991* Routledge (Stephen Lee, 2006) p.184, reproduced with permission from Taylor & Francis Books UK; 3 short extracts on pp.14 and 18 and extracts on pp.15, 18, 40, Source 10 p.58, Source 12 p.58, p.95, Source 8 p.96, p.103, short quotes on pp.95 and 98, p109, Source 5 p.113, Extract 2 p.121, Extract 4 p.122, short quote p.126, Extract 6 p.127 from *A People's Tragedy* Pimlico (Orlando Figes, 1996) pp.89, 230, 95–97, p.240, pp.91–92, p.618, p.781, p.181, pp.177–78, p.199, p.187, p.250, pp.283–84, p.478, pp.337–38, p.544, reproduced with permission from Random House Group Limited; Extract p.20 from *A History of Modern Russia* Penguin (Robert Service, 1997) pp.73 and 86 (Allen Lane, 1997, Penguin Books, 1998, 2003, 2009). Copyright © Robert Service, 1997, 2003, 2009; Quote p.25 'to root out...', Extract p.156 from *Revolutionary Russia 1891–1991: A Pelican Introduction*, Pelican (Orlando Figes, 2014) p.203, p.379 Copyright © Orlando Figes, 2014; Quote p.25 'we must make...' from *Stalinist Russia*, Heinemann (Steve Phillips, 2000) p.20, reproduced with permission from Pearson Education Ltd; Extract p.27 from *Forever Flowering*, Andre Deutsch (Vasily Grossman, translated by Thomas P. Whitney, 1973) p.142, reproduced with permission from Carlton Books Ltd; Extracts pp.29, 33, 117 and quote p.108, from Marxists Internet Archives; Source 4 p.48, p.134, Source 5 p.137, Extract 1 p.139, Extract 2 p.141, p.143, 2 extracts p.150 from *Khrushchev: The Man and His Era*, Free Press (William Taubman, 2003) p.262, p.XVIII, p.XVIII, pp.273–74, p.274, p.492, p.620, p.620 Copyright © 2003 by William Taubman. Used by permission of W.W. Norton & Company, Inc.; Extract p.150 from *Khrushchev The Man and his Era*, Free Press (William Taubman 2003) p.13, Copyright © 2003 by William Taubman. Used by permission of W. W. Norton & Company, Inc.; Extracts pp.50, 89, Source 4 p.90, Source 9 p.96, Source 7 and Source 8 p.116, short quotes pp.117, 120 and 131, p.140, Source 2 p.155, Source 13

p.169, p.171 from *Russia, A 1,000-Year Chronicle of the Wild East*, published by Woodlands Books (Martin Sixsmith, 2012) p.418, p.164, p.165, p.170, p.192, p.196, p.196, p.413, p.452, p.462, p.492, reproduced with permission from Random House Group Ltd; Extract 3 p.54 from *Stalin's Russia*, Bloomsbury (Chris Ward and Claire Knight, 1993) © Chris Ward and Claire Knight 1993, Bloomsbury Academic, an imprint of Bloomsbury Publishing Plc; Extract 4 p.54 from *A History of Twentieth-Century Russia*, Penguin (Robert Service, 1997) p.172, Copyright © Robert Service, 1997; Extract 5 p.54 from *Communist Russia under Lenin and Stalin* Hodder and Stoughton (Chris Corin and Terry Fiehn, 2002) p.172, Reproduced by permission of Hodder Education; Extract p.60 from *Nikita Khrushchev and the Creation of a Superpower*, Penn State University Press (Sergei Khrushchev, 2001); Extract 6 p.62 from *Ancient Greece: Using Evidence*, Cambridge University Press (Pamela Bradley, 1988) Copyright © Cambridge University Press 1988; Extract 7 p.62 from *The Spartans: An Epic History*, Macmillan (Paul Cartledge, 2003) p.75, reproduced with permission of Pan Macmillan via PLSClear; Extract 1 p.67 from *Russia and the Russians: A History*, Harvard University Press (Geoffrey Hosking, 2001) p.277, Cambridge, Mass.: The Belknap Press of Harvard University Press, Copyright © 2001 by Geoffrey Hosking; Extracts pp.70, 100 from *Russia: People and Empire 1552–1917*, Fontana Press (Geoffrey Hosking, 1997) p.195, pp.412–13, Reprinted by permission of HarperCollins Publishers Ltd © 1997 Geoffrey Hosking; Extract p.73 from *Lectures on European History 1789–1914: Men, Machines and Freedom*, Wiley-Blackwell (J. McManners and J. M. Thomson, 1966) p.337, reproduced with permission of Blackwell in the format Book via Copyright Clearance Center; Extract p.77 and Extract 3 p.85 from *Alexander II and Modernization of Russia*, English Universities Press (W. E. Mosse, 1958) pp.112–13 and p.31; Extract p.79 from *Alexander II, The Last Great Tsar*, Free Press (Edvard Radzinsky, 2005) pp.138–39, Copyright © 2005 by Edvard Radzinsky, used with permission. All rights reserved. English Translation copyright © 2005 by Simon & Schuster, Inc.; Extracts p.80, Source 5 p.90, p.120, Source 14 p.125, p.146 from *Endurance and Endeavour: Russian History 1812–2002*, Oxford University Press (J. N. Westwood, 2002) p.93, pp.154–55, p.225, p.250, p.420, By permission of Oxford University Press; Source 12 p.85 from *Russia under the Old Regime* Penguin (Richard Pipes, 1997) p.266, Copyright © Richard Pipes 1974, 1995, used by permission of The Wylie Agency (UK) Ltd; Extract p.102 from *Imperial Russia: A Source Book, 1700–1917*, Dryden Press (B. Dmytryshyn (ed.), 1974) source 49; Extracts pp.115, 142, 170 from *The Rise and Fall of the Soviet Union 1917–1991*, Routledge (Richard Sakwa, 1999) p.33, pp.325–26, pp.476–78 Copyright © 1999 Routledge, reproduced with permission of Taylor & Francis Books UK; Source 11 p.119 from *Encounters with Lenin*, Oxford University Press (N. Valentinov, trans. P. Rosta and B. Pearce, 1968) pp.149–50, by permission of Oxford University Press; Source 12 p.119 from *The Memoirs of Vladimir D. Nabokov: V.D. Nabokov and the Provisional Government, 1917*, Yale University Press (ed. V.D. Medlin and S.L. Parsons, 1976) p.83, reproduced with permission from Yale University Press; Source 13 p.121 from *The October Revolution*, Lawrence & Wishart (J. Stalin, 1936), reproduced with permission; Extract 3 p.122 from *Lenin*, Macmillan (Robert Service, 2000) p.277, reproduced with permission of Pan Macmillan via PLSclear; Extract 5 p.125 from *Russia: The Tsarist and Soviet Legacy* Routledge (Edward Acton, 1995) p.177, reproduced with permission from Taylor & Francis Books UK; Source 15 p.127 from *A History of Soviet Russia: The Bolshevik Revolution 1917–1923*, Macmillan (E.H. Carr, 1950) p.175, reproduced with permission of Palgrave Macmillan; Extract p.128 from *Lenin: Life and Legacy*, HarperCollins (Dmitri Volkogonov, 1994), Reprinted by permission of HarperCollins Publishers Ltd © Dmitri Volkognov 1994; Source 5 p.48, p.133, Source 6 p.137, p.138 from *Khrushchev Remembers*, Little, Brown and Co. (N. Khruschev, with notes by Edward Crankshaw, 1970) pp.322–23, p.347, pp.347–50, reproduced with permission from Carlton Books Ltd; Source 8 p.139 from *The Unquiet Ghost: Russians Remember Stalin*, Houghton Mifflin Harcourt (A. Hochschild, 2002) Copyright © 1994 by Adam Hochschild. Reprinted by permission of Georges Borchardt, Inc., on behalf of the author; Extract p.140 from *The Thaw Generation: Coming of Age in the Post-Stalin Era*, University of Pittsburg Press (L. Alexeyeva and P. Goldberg, 1990) p.354, reprinted by the permission of HSG Agency as agents for the author. Copyright ©1990 by Alexeyeva, Ludmilla and Paul Goldberg; Extract p.160 from *The Downing Street Years*, Harper Collins (M. Thatcher, 1993) pp.460–61, Reprinted by permission of HarperCollins Publishers Ltd © Copyright Lady Thatcher. Further texts available at margaretthatcher.org, the official website of the Margaret Thatcher Foundation; Extract pp.165–66 from *Gorbachev and Glasnost*, edited by Isaac J. Tarasulo Copyright © 1989. Used by permission of Rowman & Littlefield Publishing Group. All rights reserved; Extract p.161 from *Perestroika: New Thinking for our Country and the World*, HarperCollins (M. Gorbachev, 1987), used with permission; Source 15 p.169 from BBC Written Archives Centre, Summaries of World Broadcasts, Soviet Union, SU/0807, 04/07/1990, C1/1-C1/18 at p.C1/1.